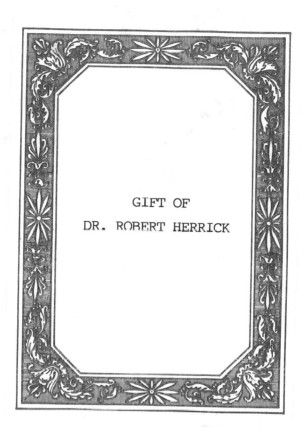

THE SOCIOLOGY OF THE BAY COLONY

THE SOCIOLOGY OF THE BAY COLONY

By MORRIS TALPALAR, LL.B.

Philosophical Library
New York

Library of Congress Catalog Card No. 75-27960
SBN 8022-2176-9

Manufactured in the United States of America

This study of the sociology of the Bay colony stops with about the year 1700. The infirmities of age require its premature publication. I'm convinced that my work as it now stands is a contribution in this field: it is said that there is a mystery in creation; a thorough study of the colony in its earlier decades establishes its foundation, without a knowledge of which later events cannot be properly understood. The effort to do the eighteenth century will be diligently pursued, and I'm in hopes that I may be destined to have sufficient time and virility to finish it.

The Author

TABLE OF CONTENTS
PROLEGOMENA

PROLEGOMENON A— SOCIOLOGY
    DISCIPLINE   3
    ETHICS   4
    SOCIAL DYNAMICS   5
    SOCIAL HISTORY   7
    GOVERNMENT   10
PROLEGOMENON B— THE HERITAGE OF EUROPE
    HEBRAISM   14
    HELLENISM   23
    ARISTOCRACY   28
    THE RENAISSANCE   32

BOOK ONE
THE BACKGROUND IN ENGLAND

INTRODUCTION   43

CHAPTER ONE — FEUDALISM: LAND   44
CHAPTER TWO — TUDOR PURITANISM:
    TRADE & THE REFORMATION   52
CHAPTER THREE — RELIGION: ANGLICANISM;
    EPISCOPACY & REFORM   76
    ANGLICANISM: EPISCOPACY   77
CHAPTER FOUR — EPISCOPACY vs REFORM   113
    POLITICAL ASPECTS   113
    DOCTRINAL ASPECTS: RENAISSANCE vs
    REFORMATION   120
    CALVINISM   127
    WYCLIFFISM   131
CHAPTER FIVE — SOCIAL CHANGES IN
    STUART ENGLAND   140
    FEUDALISM vs CAPITALISM   140
    STUART CAPITALISM: THE STRUGGLE
    WITHIN TRADE   156

BOOK TWO
THE MASSACHUSETTS BAY COLONY
1620-1690: THE BIBLICAL COMMONWEALTH

CHAPTER ONE   —   LAUNCHING   169
INTRODUCTION: 169
   METHODOLOGY   169
   EURO-CENTRICISM   170
   THE PROJECTION OF THE BRITISH EMPIRE   176
   THE PURITANS   178
   THE PROJECTION OF NEW ENGLAND   182
   PRIMEVAL AMERICA   202
CHAPTER TWO   —   FOUNDING   215
   ECONOMY   215
   GOVERNMENT   232
   RELIGION   241
   MORALS   275
CHAPTER THREE   —   ESTABLISHMENT   286
   ECONOMY   286
   GOVERNMENT   304
   ETHICS   317
   TRADE & ETHICS   323
CHAPTER FOUR   —   THE ABORIGINALS   334
CHAPTER FIVE   —   WITCHCRAFT   352
CHAPTER SIX   —   RELATIONS WITH LONDON   360
CHAPTER SEVEN   —   THE BIBLICAL COMMON-
   WEALTH: SUMMATION   380

REFERENCES   388

INDEX   393

PROLEGOMENA

PROLEGOMENON A—SOCIOLOGY DISCIPLINE

Man is a social animal—a being who lives in togetherness. Animal being is sometimes gregarious—herd, flock, school. There are qualitative differences between sociality and gregariousness; the former is based on contact, association and interaction, while the latter is confined simply to contact and association. Man has always regarded separation from his fellows—imprisonment, solitary confinement, as punishment—as "quarantine", "the horrors of isolation"; he came into existence to live as well as to live with his fellow man—there is no salvation for man apart from society. A social organism is greater than any of its members, and its claims are more important than those of any individual comprising it. According to Macaulay:

"in proportion as men know more, and think more, they look
less at individuals and more at classes";

from which they eventually move on to society. The social organization of man expresses itself in a variety of forms. The establishment of a settlement of people, of men and women, is per se the founding of a social organism—a particular way of life. It is said that creativity is at bottom a mystery: this makes the subject of origins—the coming into being, a most exacting study; the creative work is never really a finished product—there is no end to simplifying. There is the "science of society", which is called "sociology". Sociology is here posited as a necessary and pertinent study, and is understood in an historical sense— not in a statistical sense; it is defined as simply a description of the institutions and the values of a people in a particular time and place; and the emphasis is on the life, rather than on the mechanism, of social

3

organization. Sociology can reduce a subject to its logical components, where emotions disappear; it can discover the fertile inter-relations of institutional and ideational forces. It is competently held that "sociology is a term we have to live with", and whether it is a science depends on the strictness of one's definition of science.

ETHICS

Man as a social animal implies ethics: man is per se both a social and an ethical being, as he cannot be the one without at the same time being the other—they are mutually inclusive; thus ethics is universal, it is inherent in man at all stages of his development, it gives meaning to man's history, and it is part of his subjective being—he is ethical, usually unconsciously. Man's ethical birthright may be divine—given unto him by God, or it may simply be in his "nature" to be that way; the thinker "Goethe pits natural law against moral law as vital and equal forces", and man is a natural being as well as a social and ethical being. This subjective condition takes objective expression as a Code of Ethics—a system of do's and don'ts—whose content and form vary with time and place, and are subject to alteration and even to change. And man's ethical compulsives—his morals, values, ideals—are essentially a matter of feeling, rather than of logic. The philosopher Descartes said that knowledge is based on contrast—as good and evil; a good definition of genius may be—consciousness of the all-pervasive, which tends to elude mental grasp, to obliterate awareness; "the most obvious facts are the most easily forgotten". The genius of the prophet of religion lies in the fact that he discerned—that he became aware of, this phase of man's subjective life and rendered it objective; the prophet did not create the principle of ethics in man.

There is the patent co-existence of good and evil in the world: good and evil are regarded as antipodal—mutually exclusive; yet total absence of the one is total absence of the other—they both exist or neither exists. There is a universal and eternal struggle going on between light and darkness—between Church and Anti-Christ, and the life of man is confined to within the gray areas between the two extremes. It has been held that evil is the positive condition, and that good is negative as it is simply the absence of evil; yet man as a social being renders categorical the fact that good is fundamental, because if it were the other way society

4

would be impossible. Life is always greater than its evils; the attempt to kill the human in man is unavailing—beneath the crazy violence a residue of humanity always inevitably comes to view. The forces operating towards uniting men, the interests which they have in common and which bind them together, are always far more powerful—more important and numerous, than those which drive them apart; society cannot be created out of anti-social instincts—hate, fear, suspicion, jealousy. The disparities between men—racial, lingual, caste, religious, economic— throughout history, were great; yet the underlying cohesive tendencies in sociality—the tendencies towards togetherness, were never to be denied. William Shakespeare in his play "Julius Caesar" says "the evil men do lives after them, the good is oft' interred with their bones": man generally tends implicitly to take for granted, unconsciously to expect—the good, in his fellows; he is very much conscious of evil, and he is much more voluble in blame than in praise.

SOCIAL DYNAMICS

Man, who throughout pre-technology was physically and mentally confined to his own planet, is always interested to understand the world he lives in. Aristotle saw change in the world but no change of the world: the conditions of climate remain the same, the nature of human beings— of men and women, remains the same; the underlying principles of social phenomena—the coherence of politics, religion, economy, is eternal. However, there are variants of the eternal propositions, their expression does take different form, but their content goes on forever —and the more things change the more they remain the same. And the purpose is to get at the underlying principles in which a way of life is rooted—at the permanency amidst the change. The part of man which distinguishes him qualitatively from the brute creation lies in his attempts to order his own nature and the environment; he has not only bred most wildness out of his domestic animals—he has domesticated and conditioned himself readily to complex institutional forms of order he once did not possess. This introduced the principle of social dynamics—of revolution, in the life of man: it is pertinent to change the world, not merely to interpret it; the social world is man-made, and it is therefore man-changeable—there is the creative solution; the outward change in institutions and values takes

5

place. Thus there is the principle of social process, which moves steadily onward—although not in a straight line; there is a surface fluctuation—an occasional swing backward, but the underlying trend is onward. Social revolution is evolvement, not substitution; it is never a sudden—an abrupt, incursion; the process of togetherness evolves from what has gone before, and no society jumps into new discovery without resting in and starting from previous efforts of mankind. The annals of man establish that the direction of social change is not from primitive simplicity to modern complexity, but from instinctive and highly complex confusion to reasoned order. Thus in his attempts to understand the world man found that he had to rely chiefly on rationalism; few people, however, were ever persuaded by the appeal to reason—the wars of history establish that it is too much always to expect rational accommodation from human beings; but he never gave up the hope that reasoning could settle everything—for "to despair of reason is to despair of man", and this caused him to postulate the rational man in history.

"Social development is wiser than the wisest man", "everybody knows better than anybody", "men's control over the forces which shape their destinies is limited indeed". Social phenomena constitute a mosaic: any one strand in so complex a picture can be a study in itself; and concentration in the field of sociology comprehends the sum totality of life—the rich tapestry of time and place, the bewildering diversity and fullness of human experience. Sociology—the being of man, how humans live and work and die within the iron conditions of their society—is *weltanschauung* or world view; it is not philosophy—a system of logically consistent thought; life—especially some aspects of it, certainly religion—is full of emotion, of inconsistency, and even of contradiction. Yet chaos conceals order; there is an underlying unity in multiplicity and diversity—*e pluribus unum.* "The common chords of living sound across the ages"; from the flux of Time may be cut out an arbitrary period—a segment in social history, exhibiting the diversity of human behavior that makes up the texture of daily life—for study, for analysis and synthesis. There can be an attempt to bring the incongruities of things into harmony, as in a work of art;

> "the study of history resembles the art of mosaic; from an infinite number of pieces can be constructed an infinite variety of patterns";

6

it is stressed that in times of crisis what masses of people believe to be true is more crucial than the truth of events, and "man's ideas of truth are more potent forces in history than the actual truth"; all of which renders a complete restoration of past reality historically impossible. Yet this does not preclude an attempt at a reasonably consistent presentation of it.

The past is fixed; a study of the root causes in social phenomena requires constant probing, and the principles underlying the continuity between changing states of culture must be perpetually sought. In the attempt to reclaim the past the student can discover what lies beneath the surface only by making an abstract from the primary sources; there must be a thread-by-thread unraveling of the tangled skeins; and this enables depths and reaches to become available that were hitherto unexplored. The scholar's patience, precision, attention to detail, his helpless sincerity in the search for the truth, can bring out the order that is implicit in chaos; there is the logic of events—they can be woven into a pattern; the attempt to compose the varieties of this field into a rational harmony is a profound, complex undertaking, which necessarily transcends the limits of the locale of its consideration; and the student learns as he goes along—he grows with his subject.

SOCIAL HISTORY

The development of science and technology as social forces, and their application to man's production of the goods of life, eliminated the economy of scarcity and introduced the economy of abundance; and this necessitated a complete re-ordering of social relations, in terms of institutions and values. The present study is confined to the world of pre-technology—to the economy of natural scarcity, with everything that it implied; and there must be an attempt to recreate the past. The preparation of the student for an understanding of primary data is in itself a study: the person of today must avoid the tendencies to "projection", to interpreting history backwards by reading his own mind into the heads of his subjects; he cannot thus appreciate the writings inherited from a vanished way of life.

Land, trade, labor are universal; they are present in all forms of economy. These activities could each be a means of livelihood, and could each also be the foundation of a given sociology—respectively feudalism, capitalism, socialism; thus they are to be understood in terms of values or quality, not in terms of wealth or quantity. What differentiated one sociology from another as within the economy of scarcity were the inter-relations of men—the values, the laws—as concerning land, trade, labor. These different forms of economic activity as means of livelihood have always co-existed within civilization, but only one of them in a given time and place could take over society and constitute itself the foundation of the way of life.

Yet the land—the earth, that is the beginning and the end of us all—has primacy: "I take joy in life on earth"—man knows no treasure, no benefactor, to match the fecund earth; the fact of our human "earthness"—that man is,

> "earth of the earth, his body earth, his hair a wild shrub
> growing out of the land"—

is patent. Man was tirelessly in search for a green patch of grass and of life-sustaining waterholes: all green shall perish, yet there is the detectable freshness of rebirth—of the ever-beckoning green, of life and growth;

> "you could cover the whole world with asphalt but sooner or
> later green grass would break through";

the roots of the growing tree—"these stubborn shoots"—are not to be denied; they can crack man's artifacts—even the concrete, that stand in their way; and life is always renewing itself—meaningless perhaps, but indestructibly fertile. Nature is universal and eternal—the foundation under any condition; nature is primary as against art—it can get along without art, but this is not true the other way; to the man of feudalism the earth was the ultimate source of the goods of life—it is all-absorbent as everything in nature comes from, and ultimately goes back into, the earth; trade, artifact, their products, and the way of life that develops around them, can be eliminated—but the earth can never be eliminated;

> "No one can own or sell the Earth, our Mother".;
> "The mountains and forests were here long before we were.
> They don't need us. And we can't improve them";

8

and in the early days of industrialism man regarded artifact as incidental in comparison with nature.

Land in nature is wilderness, a medium of ranging; land in sociology is arable. Man is a land animal; as such he is a phenomenon in nature—he has a basic economic need. Man on land as a phenomenon in sociology is human; he has *rights* in land—and his striving is for more than basic economic need. Land was immemorially the direct means of livelihood—and it was also the foundation of a way of life. The agrarian society, the rule of land—feudalism, was civilization's first social expression; it was evidently inherent in man's emergence from primitivism, as it was universal before communications; it is civilized man's social order of longest duration; and it laid the foundations in institutions and values from which succeeding social systems benefited. The social organism was always established on the vertical principle, and it was based on the great law of subordination: where the differences between men were qualitative—caste, blood, or aristocracy and commonalty—the distinctions were hierarchical; and where the differences were quantitative, or in terms of money—the distinctions were conical. This caused man always to accept the principle of government, as he was more afraid of anarchy than of dictatorship; he regarded the state as a necessary evil. The structural order of society under feudalism was hierarchical: in this life—in the realm, in the church; and also in the hereafter—in heaven; and there was a hierarchical relation between the cultivator, proprietor and sovereign, with a view to the sharing of the produce of the land. There were differences in detail in varying times and places, but the underlying principle was the same. Thus the feudal economy was based on agriculture, whose expansion was extensive—and its productivity was limited by the tillable land available within the realm.

The trader was universal as within civilization, and he existed in all of the pre-Christian Mediterranean city states—Judaea, Greece, Rome. These cultural entities had little, if any, contacts with one another; this gave each of them certain incidental peculiarities, which were acquired also by the trader portion of the population, yet fundamentally the trader was the same everywhere.

GOVERNMENT

The institution of "government" has always existed among civilized people, and it was always based on ethics—it was identified with a particular doctrine that was thought of as in conformity with justice. The principles of freedom and discipline, each looked at in absolute terms—as abstraction, are mutually exclusive, they are antipathetic; each exists at the expense of the other. Yet man is convinced that the good life must include both order and freedom: man does not live in a vacuum—freedom cannot deal with the detached individual in isolation, but only with man as in relation to a community; history teaches that authority may end in tyranny, and liberty in license and chaos; and he finds himself confronted by a contradiction—he has the feeling that freedom is incompatible with, and at the same time inseparable from, security. As a social being he *ipso facto* accepts the principle of organization—which is per se vertical and implies leadership, and hence obedience; his practical experience in life teaches that liberty and efficiency are both present in a relative association, which renders them complementary; each acts as a check on the other—and there is a fluctuation in their reciprocal domination, depending upon conditions. There is the libertarian, to whom freedom is man's supreme value—transcending also life: he knows that freedom can lead to evil, yet he thinks the risk well worth taking—"injurious is the gift that takes away freedom"; and there is a general preference for liberty in spite of its penalties—"better self-government than good government". And man has the problem of maintaining order while preserving freedom.

The world has never had a basic monolithic sociology; mankind has always had varying kinds of social organization operating in co-existence—tribalism, feudalism, capitalism, socialism, with each a self-contained entity in terms of its own institutions and values. This gave rise in various times and places to ideological wrangles concerning the retention or the change of the basic social *status quo*; it was not easy to attain an understanding of a complex process of many strands, involving misconceptions by each side of the other's intentions. Each was anxious for peaceful rational persuasion, yet each wanted the distracting influences composed only on his own terms; this introduced the theory of creative violence—the vindication of the truth cannot always be achieved

10

without making some disturbance; and it sometimes brought on civil or national ideological war. It is declared that,

> "The greatest source of tyranny is the conviction that there is a single way of determining truth, and that it should be interpreted by a single disciplined organization";

the claim of infallibility is the foundation of intolerance and persecution. The dictator must always operate within the limitations of his doctrinal system—he is a prisoner of his own tenets. The objects of despotism change but its spirit remains eternal, and it is not unusual for events to transpose a repressed minority into a persecuting majority. He who imposes truth on others is no longer concerned really with the truth, but with the imposition. There is the extremist conviction against toleration —truth is absolute, and dissent is worthy only of extirpation; and persecutors are certain that dissidents will submit if they are treated with sufficient harshness. The cause of division in the community is not the toleration of errors and differences but the attempt to compel everyone to think alike; yet the difficulties of compulsion are greater than the difficulties of toleration; persecution can be a weapon more dangerous to its users than to their victims; and the cruelty of execution is as evil as the crime which it punishes.

Nonetheless, the foundation of a given social order, from which flow its institutions and its values, is arbitrary—the principle of First Cause is inescapable, and it must also be fundamentally monolithic; a basic premise is taken for granted, which may not be impugned; and logic may be used in its attempted justification—which renders rationalism incidental to authoritarianism. Political freedom exists only as within the limitations of the mental atmosphere that rises from a given social foundation; the right openly to criticize the basic *status quo*—to bring the foundation into question, cannot be made in terms of itself; it can therefore be made only in terms of the ways and the values of a different social foundation. The person who is born and brought up within a given social milieu lives his life subjectively in terms of its ways; the basic *status quo* is *weltanschauung*, which runs far deeper than logical conviction or political doctrine—one feels it, lives it. With the introduction of a new, or in the attempt to preserve a fading, social foundation there is an

11

absence of ideological or mental control over the masses, and physical controls—dictatorship, have to be substituted. The experience of man establishes that a dictator is valuable in a crisis—he is "a necessary evil"; there is the use of power to meet the responsibilities of power; the policy of physical force is substituted for logical persuasion; yet this is a sure sign of weakness, as mental control is always infinitely more powerful. With the passing of the generations the objective social foundation slowly becomes part of the subjective life of the people— tradition, custom—and physical controls concomitantly evaporate. According to R. H. Tawney—

"Once the world had been settled to their liking, the bourgeoisie persuaded themselves that they were the convinced enemies of violence and the devotees of the principle of order."

With the trader ethics and values constituting the way of life of his society, the Puritan had a sense of freedom as within it—he was living "in the best of all possible worlds".

The essence of one's ideological being is sacred: the social foundation has been often declared ordained of God, and any imputation cast upon it was denounced as heresy; there is a hyper-sensitivity concerning it— man is rendered uncomfortable when the ways he lives by are brought into question, and a purported rationally objective analysis of it is intolerable. Man has always longed for an underlying condition of law and order; he has a suspicion and fear of basic change—an instinctive compulsion to resist social upheaval. Construction must be planned, and it is painstaking—while destruction is indifferent; "Rome wasn't built in a day", but it took no more than a day to burn it down. Interference with tradition is disruptive of the routine habits of life, the foundation is pulled from under one's feet, and it endangers the peace; there is a drop in morals, and a breakdown of law and order, and there are tendencies to treachery and terror; people are displaced as though by magic, alienated, plundered, exiled; times are transformed, and there is an anarchy of values as they fall into new perspectives. And the organized movement which constitutes itself a challenge to the basic societal order appears like a conspiracy against the state, and it does not have normal political freedom.

12

The expression of the principle of sociology in terms of institutions and values took different forms throughout pre-technology, although they were all based on the economy of natural scarcity. In the era before automotive power the fundamental source of energy for laboring was life—chiefly human; the social organisms were based on the Aristotelian doctrine that "some men are born to be masters, while others are born to serve"; and their thinking was in terms of "those who by nature command, and those who by nature obey". The common man was the unit of economy—he had to labor; and paternalism, the binding relation of a man of property as "master" with the impoverished as labor, was inescapable. The Hellenes taught that masters,

> "are not the object of law; for they are themselves a law: and it would be ridiculous in any one to endeavour to include them in the penalties of the law".

It is historically true that a social category of man known as "aristocracy" succeeded in establishing itself as outside of and above social institutionalism: the patricians always everywhere transcended government, law, the penal code; but they remained perforce securely under the restraints of values—of *weltanschauung*; they were men of honor—at all times in "honor bound".

The social system known as "socialism" is based on technology, which results in the economy of abundance; since the machine of steel and oil has replaced the machine of bone and flesh, aristocracy's transcendance of government may attain universal application—it may bring about the disappearance of the principle of government over men.

PROLEGOMENON B—THE HERITAGE OF EUROPE
HEBRAISM

Man's life is not to be understood only in terms of his daily practical knowledge of it; it is also a mystery, evoking his wonder no less than his fortitude. Man somehow has never been able to find full satisfaction as within his world: he found himself "wandering forlorn and distraught in a universe of which he was not competent to grasp the plan"; he has been engaged in an eternal effort to fathom the mystery of his being—"know thyself", "where do we come from, where do we go to, why are we here", "I—why"?; to seek this answer is a characteristic of human being as distinct from animal being; and experience has left him with the feeling that this effort transcends his ability. Man begins with the consciousness that he is a purposeful being, and he is convinced that the noblest purpose of his life is the attempt to understand it—"we are born to inquire after truth". This interest is stimulated by his uniqueness in knowing that he must die; he is conscious of his own transience as he marches from nowhere to the grave, and the prospect of death as eternal extinction is unacceptable. Man is awed by the miracle of life: he has an interest in its beginnings; he has a gnawing hunger for knowledge, a human need to find meaning in life; and he is animated by a perennial, eternal attempt to throw a bridge between himself and the ultimate secret of things. He cannot explain the origins of the world, of life, of himself according to natural law, through his own intelligence; he finds himself in a condition where is he groping for a door in a blank wall—"the naked human intellect arrayed against cosmic forces hidden from man since the beginning of time"; and he therefore traces it all to an act of special creation by a Supreme Being or supernatural Intelligence—man found God in the commonplace. And there is a tragic discrepancy between God's creation, and His particular creature who has the urge to un-

14

derstand it. Thus man has a need to believe in the mysterious; his vanity stimulates his temptation to suppose that he is somehow in on the secrets of the cosmos.

Religion and ethics are necessarily universally applicable, as they are matters of daily life—while philosophy and law are specialized studies. And there took place an adaptation of Eastern religion and philosophy in the unenlightened West: the great religions of the Occidental peoples had originated in the Orient; the Europeans were never creative in this respect, they had no spiritual symbols of their own with which to oppose those brought in from Asia, and all they could do was to receive, with a view to reciprocal adjustment, the alien religious influences. This resulted in the Hebraic ideological domination of Occidental civilization: the concept of Messianic redemption was introduced into Europe by the Jews; the collection of their ancient writings—the Old and the New Testaments, called the "Bible"—was accepted as the revealed Word of God; it became the foundation of the Christian religion, from which the highest values of the Western culture derive—and it is thus the most influential single book in the history of man; and the Jews have been involved in the life of other nations to a greater extent than any other people on earth.

The roots of civilization lie deep in the ages gone by, and some of man's worthiest achievements date from the remote past—are ageless. The Mediterranean world introduced the age of reading and reasoning: its civilization had moved north into trans-Alpine Europe—Judaea for religion and ethics, Hellas for rationalism and philosophy, Rome for law; the mind of the West is,

"an amalgam produced by the interaction of Greek and Hebrew and Roman cultural strands. For it is from their interaction, rather than from the disparate strands of isolation, that the civilization of Europe derives".

The profound thinker has the ability to speak "out of time and place": through the Renaissance and the Reformation the voice of the past appealed to an alien people and age; mysteriously that Other Time penetrated the West, and it left its mark with cultural influences that are at once derivative and superlative—to the poet Shelley the ancient thinkers were "the sons of light". It seems that the most lasting influences in

15

history are non-tangible, and Judaea and Greece have each always been to mankind a time of life, a state of mind—rather than a geographical entity. Yet wisdom is not per se a matter of time; there are differences in the various areas of the world concerning the length of time in the existence of civilization, of rational development—but in view of the immensity, the profundity, the complexity, of the ultimate problems of life man feels called upon to grapple with, these differences can be only quantitative.[a] The development of science and technology on a social scale where they are remaking the world, the life of man—may, in the course of the generations, supplant the Mediterranean values, the traditional seminal cultures of Occidental civilization, with a universal such culture—Anglo-Saxon Scientism.

As civilization spread throughout the continent tribalism evaporated, and communications improved. European quality through conquest and travel mingled and interbred, while the commonalty of each nation remained fundamentally aboriginal. Sixteenth-century Europeans were living in the era of pre-science, when the nascent knowledge of mankind—the wisdom of antiquity, was still the foundation of life. It was before the days of the theory of progress, and of the concept of evolution—of qualitative evolvement, when improvement in the life of man was per se out of this world. The Aristarchus heliocentric doctrine had not yet penetrated to them; they did not think in terms of infinity—of time and space, and they did not seem to be conscious of the fact that the earth is simply a rock whirling in space. They thought in terms of geo and of anthropo, centricism—the earth as the center of the universe, and man as the central purpose of creation; and they expected answers to the problems of life and death along the lines of absolute certainty. And theirs was the economy of natural scarcity, when the sharing of the goods of life was within ethical teaching—"Give us this day our daily bread". They had a religion, the principle that there is an Intelligence in the universe—which was known as "Christianity": they thought of the world as a supernatural order—there was an adumbration of a natural order of life, but it was rejected as "paganism"; in their cosmology the world was a cozy corner—"the ends, the four corners, the pillars, of the earth"; and the apex of their ambition and achievement was limited to within their own planet.

Their religion consisted of three basic propositions: Scripture; "theol-

16

ogy'' or sacred doctrine; and ecclesiastical organization—which took the form of "church", "clergy", "laity".

It was part of the Christians' subjective being that there is a God—a beneficent Intelligence in the universe who created everything. They accepted the Athanasian creed: the numeral three seems to have had a mystic connotation in their religion; it postulated the triune Godhead—the Father, the Son and the Holy Ghost. They held to the Hebraic idea that divinity periodically assumes human guise, and they regarded as sacred truth the principle of the Messiah—a divinely-created Being sent by God to deliver mankind from evil—who in their case was Jesus Christ of Nazareth. The Messiah is a Person upon whom are reflected the attributes of God: the doings and sayings of divinity while in the flesh are in the nature of Holy Revelation to mankind; Revelation is wisdom transcending simple human truth; it is qualitatively superior—it is divine cognition concerning the mystery of a Reality beyond reality. God had revealed Himself, His wisdom, His divine plan, to man for his guidance in life, forever; man's knowledge of the world, of life, of himself, was confined within the principle of *final* revelation, *veritas eternitatis*—which is infallible; the Word of the Revelator is committed to writing, for preservation and transmittal to posterity into eternity; and this collection of sacred writings, which was Hebraic—was regarded as Holy Writ, and was identified as the "Bible". Thus were the Christians convinced of a qualitative difference between the writings they had inherited from the past; they regarded the Hebraic writings as divinely inspired, while all the others were merely human—the Greek and Roman writings on religion were classified as "mythology".

God had created the world, and He created man—whom He put on earth. God is involved in, He is not separate from, the world—He takes an interest in man's doings on earth; there is supernatural intervention in the affairs of man, and history is understood as the interaction of the divine and the human. Part of holy revelation to man about himself is that he has an immortal soul. Christianity recognized that there is in human nature an innate tendency towards evil, which it called "original sin"; man, by Adam's and by his own acts of disobedience to divine commandment, alienated the love of his Creator, which put the welfare of his soul into jeopardy. Thus man is born into a condition of original sin, and he lives his life in sin;

"I was shapen in iniquity, and in sin did my mother conceive me"[1];

he is utterly corrupted by his very nature—inherently evil, not merely prone to evil; and it was hardly possible that man could ever be good per se; all of which condemned him to mortality.

Religion is the attempt to manage the world by love rather than by force—the concept of sin in and of itself suggests that of mercy. Man's alienation from God could be terminated by God by His Own willingness to do so, and by His redeeming act of Self-sacrifice incarnate through "His only begotten Son"—Jesus Christ; with the coming of the Messiah—of the Savior and His Scriptural message—the secret of the ages was revealed unto man; and Holy Writ was the foundation of the Christian's belief—his faith, and as such his most precious possession. The Bible was regarded as representing the principle of *final* revelation, but as within itself it seems to suggest the principle of *progressive* revelation; there is a postulation of the remorseless retribution of the Jehovah of the Old Testament who ruled by Law, which was succeeded by the abounding love of the Heavenly Father of the New Testament who ruled by Grace; the Bible constituted in essence the eternal verities, which rendered it infallible—yet eternity was not synonymous with statics. And religion is a way of reconciling the goals of life with the problems of mortality: death, in a Christian universe, is illusory; man has immortality in another life—in heaven, where he lives in eternal bliss; or in hell, where he is in a condition of eternal torture. The devotee's first concern was, "what must I do to save my soul"?, and God gave man the opportunity to do so and win eternal life in bliss by dedicating himself to faith and works. Thus is man confronted with his triune epic—his creation, fall and redemption- "For as in Adam all die, even so in Christ shall all be made alive".[2] And the church, as well as the faith, was potent in man's hope of achieving salvation, for if one did not go to church he did not go to heaven—in a sacred place men get a feeling of worth. Religious commandments are independent of human authority, and they are the ultimate norms of man's conduct, in his private life and in public affairs.

The devotees of Jesus—the Christians, felt themselves divinely instructed to have a definite expression: this was to take the form of the Church, as ideology and as edifice; there was the "Church" as social

18

institution—whose local unit was the "church", which comprised a building and its grounds; the church was dedicated to worship, and to the teaching and propagation of the faith. With the split in Christianity between the Western and Eastern Churches, the former continued to be identified as the Roman Catholic Church—and was regarded as constituting the religion of western Europe. The Savior had founded "His Organization"—the one and only Church—into eternity, which represented and taught His divine revelation to man; and one day of the week—Sunday, was set aside as the Lord's Day, a day of worship, prayer and contemplation in church. Thus the Christian Church and its Holy Writ are divinely ordained; the church edifice and its grounds are consecrated; Christ is truth, and there is only one understanding of Christ—that taught by the Holy Roman Catholic Apostolic Church of God. The clergy was a body of men professionally trained and ordained by the Church for the service of God; it was organized on a hierarchical order; its members were the official authority of, they constituted—the Church. The laity comprised the vast mass of the people who were devotees of the religion, and who were shepherded by the clergy.

The Roman Catholic Church, being alone endowed by God as His Church on earth, had the power to transmit its divine integrity and beneficence to mankind. The Faith taught that the principle of quality is applicable to every phase of human life—spiritual and temporal. The Christian was conscious of qualitative difference, as between—God and man, the souls in heaven, the ancient Hebraic writings and all other writings, the varying ranks within the clergy, and as between clergy and laity. The man who was ordained by the Church as priest became thereby per se endowed with certain divine attributes and powers. The Church emphasized the principle of the indispensable intermediary—the priest, only through whom the beneficence of God can flow to the worshiper; he was qualitatively different from the layman—the individual soul is not potent in its own right, and as in relation to God it can be only a passive participant. In the traditional faith several factors had spiritual content and potency: the Scriptures—and the theology which is derived therefrom; the Church—its discipline, consecration, sacraments; prelacy—from which are derived the principle of ecclesiastical hierarchy, of the Vatican, and of the Church Fathers, whose teachings became holy doctrine. The Christians introduced into Europe the principle of "sacred theology"—the inquiry into, and the understanding of, the su-

19

pernatural aspects of life—on man's relation to the whole drama of creation. The Scriptural writings seemed to necessitate an interpretation of their meaning, and the Church accepted the principle of the integrity of explication by ecclesiastical divine endowment. The Roman confession held that the way to the truth about revelation is through a congress of Christian learning; Scripture—and theology, its interpretation and understanding by the hallowed Fathers, are of equal sacredness and authority, and are equally immune to alteration and excision. The Christian theology regarded Divine Revelation as the highest form of knowledge that man can possibly attain: the foundation of man's life was the teaching of God—His Word, Holy Writ and His Work, Nature; yet it is through His Word—not through His Work, that we gain a knowledge of God. Christianity taught that the acceptance of the Scriptures, and of their hallowed understanding, are synonymous; the principle of clerical divine quality enabled the unity of Scripture and Theology as a monolithic entity—the devotee implicitly accepts both as One.

The varying ranks within the hierarchy of priesthood ascended to the Bishop of Rome, who was by divine right Pope, the earthly head of the Church of God enthroned in the Vatican—he was the Vicar of Christ, and there was emphasis on the spiritual essence of the Papacy. The authority of the teaching Church is the devotee's first guide to knowledge of religion; he learned everything about the faith, and what was expected from him, through the priest; and doctrinal insubordination—opposition to the teachings of Mother Church, is heresy. The infallibility of the Bible renders Rome the final Word concerning interpretation; the acceptance and the understanding of God's Word are identical; there is an underlying harmony in the authority of the Scriptures and in the teachings of the Church; and salvation comes from a combination of faith and works, and acceptance of the ultimate authority of the Church. Clericalism was a law unto itself; it was exempt from the common law, as it was confined to the jurisdiction of the canon law. The church services were conducted in Latin, which gave them an aura of mystery and awe—and this rendered the atmosphere unintelligible to the worshipers. Thus the Roman Catholic clergyman was a priest, whose power was hierarchical—and it was triune: jurisdictional—legislative, judicial, disciplinary; magisterial—decisive in explaining sacred truth; ministerial—potent in transmitting divine beneficence through the sacraments. Roman Catholicism was Christianity of the Sacraments: its rituals of confession and absolution were strictly dependent upon a constantly-stoked consciousness of sin; and holy ceremony—the administering of the sacraments, centered on the altar. Thus the clerical power over the laity was complete: the Bible was sacred, and was contemplated with awe; the commoners' access to it was never expressly forbidden, but they were thought unfit to meddle with sacred theology—with priestly, and with royal, affairs. Yet the Church was the one avenue of commonalty advancement;

"humble birth did not debar a man from attaining the highest positions in the church";

and although many of its priests stemmed from the depths they did achieve the spiritual qualitative superiority. Man is prone to sin: the faith was committed to confession—to the relation of priest and penitent, the erasure of self before God through the Church for absolution; after which the suppliant emerged with a clear conscience.

The religion of Rome has been described as "the most compelling influence that has ever risen among men": the Church had her beginnings in the Mediterranean area, and spread northwards; and her millennial history is coincident with the rise of civilization in Europe. Medieval man adhered to the doctrine of dual authority, the spiritual Vatican and the temporal Monarchy, which rule the world—"render unto Caesar that which is Caesar's, render unto God that which is God's"; and this definitely dissociated man from the concept of the emperor-god. In addition, the Papacy in itself was both spiritual and temporal. Yet the mind of the epoch was fundamentally monist: the medieval ideal was one empire within one religion—the principle of universalism prevailed; the Church was the basic social institution; the spiritual—theological, preceded and was superior to the temporal—political; Boniface VIII declared in 1302 that obedience to the Pope is altogether necessary to salvation, and the Vicar of Christ claimed also to be "King of kings"; the Church and the State, the mitre and the crown, were respectively the sun and the moon of the medieval world. Her theology was the foundation for the perfect society, St. Augustine's City of God; feudalism was the way of life, and its institutions and values were universally subjectively accepted; the Roman theology was not just another subject of study—rather was it the vessel within which life was contained, and from

21

within which everything flowed, including all specialized forms of learning. Everyone was sincerely convinced that it is easy for all men of good will to know right from wrong in religious belief, and that one couldn't in all good faith commit a doctrinal error; any deviation from sacred theology—which could be disruptive of the foundation of life, was "heresy"; heresy was regarded as a false and noxious doctrine, a sin that is the outcome and manifestation of other vices—the heretic put his own view before God's view. Traditional Europe accepted implicitly the proposition of "life for life in the present, and soul for soul in the next, world"—to thrust away a soul from God is a greater injury than to deprive a man of bodily life. With a given theology as the foundation of life any other theology necessarily appeared as a state within a state—which was heresy, a sin and a crime, unpardonable per se; the enemies of the faith are the enemies of man; and the heretic could be condemned to ex-communication—he had committed the deed which forever put him beyond communion with mankind. The truth alone had rights—freedom of conscience for both tradition and dissent was inconceivable, and there could be no religious toleration; there was apprehension about popular interest in Holy Writ, as it could lead to schism, and maybe even to heresy; the Church was the traditional arbiter of uniformity and supremacy, and it emphasized her role as defender of orthodoxy and extirpator of heresy.

And she was the intransigent stronghold of tradition as she encouraged monasticism—the ideal of virtue realized in a life lived wholly for virtue's sake. Respect for control of the natural urges is induced by religion: the essence of monasticism was enclosure as man lived enveloped in a cowl, and he took the vows of asceticism—poverty, celibacy, obedience; and it was also a birth control measure—the normal increase in population exceeded that in economy, which could result in a devastating rate of maternal, and especially of infant, mortality—and many people never became parents. Thus feudalism constituted two distinct worlds, the inner and the outer; those who were unsuited to be chivalrous knights became penitent monks; the monastery afforded the extravert—warrior, trader, actor—who was sick, crippled, disillusioned, an opportunity for concentration on the inner life through contemplation and prayer. There was also an acceptance of external acts of contrition, of shortcuts to God's favor—veneration of patron saints, belief in the power of relics, burning candles before statues, pilgrimages

22

to shrines, alms-giving, indulgences; and there developed the cult of rival images, as one was held more potent than another. During the centuries of her dominion the Roman Catholic Church stood as a fortress of Christian morals in a world where death from plague, war, famine, fire, and from public execution for crime, witchcraft, treason, heresy— was ever a dread reality; she punished the heretic but indulged the sinner; she was essentially a force for solace, and for peace—she had introduced the principle of sanctuary and was regarded as neutral ground, and she served as a meeting place where enemies could confer, and arbitrators could decide a land quarrel.

HELLENISM

The Greeks had a talent for recognizing the eternal in the ordinary: they created Hellenism, the classical mind; it has been said that Socrates brought philosophy down from heaven to inhabit among men. The Hellenes were stimulated by an interest in the world around them: they introduced the principle of mental order—of systematic thinking; they thought in terms of the universe—not of the multiverse, not of the chaoverse. And they were dedicated to the principles of rationalism, the confidence in the ability of man to achieve an understanding of the world through thinking; of humanism, the exaltation of man; of naturalism— the appreciation of, and the curiosity about, nature. They exalted the human body: they cultivated, and they were proud of, their athletes and warriors; and they were esthetes—they emphasized the theatre and sculpture. Yet Aristotle speaks for them when he says that "the mind is a more valuable part of man than the body"; the body disappears, the mind can survive—memory can outlast steel, for "the pen is mightier than the sword"; and civilization has always regarded mental endeavor superior to physical—the body should be subject to the mind. They had attained independence of mind: there was never an organized priesthood in Hellas to intimidate open inquiry; and they were in large measure free from the writings and the authority of religion. And they introduced the principles of logical classification, and of logical consistency: they applied these principles in the field of sociological study, which adumbrated the scientific division into social institutions; while those alien to Hellenism thought of the world of man as a compound, and did not appreciate

23

consistent thinking as a value. The Greeks thought of nature in terms of rationalism: they did not understand nature as consisting of a company of evil spirits; and they saw life as a blessing to be enjoyed, not as a curse to be endured. They thought of the sun as fact: it exists—it has objective reality, and it is known to be the source of life; and they were convinced that sun worship is a sensible religion. The supernatural is the natural not yet understood, and they thought that the discovery of the laws of nature is what constitutes man's knowledge of the world. And they were concentrated on an attempt to understand the good, which is ethical—the beautiful, physical—and the true, metaphysical. It was a uniquely seminal era—"the magnetism of Athens".

Man has a number of cognitive faculties, or ways of knowing— intuition, authority, rationalism, empiricism. Man's effort to fathom the mystery of his being in terms simply of the intuition and the authority of religion did not bring him full satisfaction; and he developed a feeling of frustration, which left him mentally agitated. He therefore used his power to reason with which to set goals for himself; he found rationalism as a way of knowing *ab initio* indefeasible, as the attempt to disparage it has to be made in terms of itself; he was convinced that reason is the foundation of intellect, and he relied on it to explain the ultimate problems of life. Man thinks from the known to the unknown; the way of thought, the character of wisdom—is therefore deductive, and as such inherently rational; the philosopher abhors a contradiction—he is over-mastered by an anxious consistency; the contemplation of the eternal truths of intuition must be in terms of methodical, systematic thinking— which is the foundation for the mental qualities of orderliness and originality. This rational dedication requires an intensity of mental concentration that only a rare few throughout all time have shown themselves capable of—an intensity that renders one oblivious to the world around him, and is in the nature of a coma; it is man's ultimate effort in the achievement of creativity and profundity, and it presupposes a spiritual and intellectual development and insight that can come only from a lifetime of learning and contemplation.

This caused mankind to become conscious of its potency to produce the "priest" type of person:[b] to the priest the purpose of life is to learn its meaning; he leads the contemplative life—he thinks deeply and moves slowly; he cannot find full satisfaction from anything in this world, he is not concerned with the transitory—yet the eternal is not synonymous

24

with the static. The ultimate problems of life are a challenge to man's understanding: the priest readily accepts the challenge; he is happiest when he comes to grips with the seemingly insoluble problems, when he extends himself beyond man's normal capacity, when he is in a state of mental torture; he reaches for the very bottom of things, which causes him—like the eel, to slip away into muddy abstraction. His disinterested dedication to the ideal of learning in the abstract, education as a value simply for its own sake, renders him indifferent to the ordinary ambitions of man—property, power, prestige, pleasure, even provision—which means the life of sackcloth and ashes; the life of celibacy and poverty which, in freeing man from worldly care facilitates such endeavor, is something the priest yearns for and regards as an achievement—it is not an act of self-sacrifice, and has no necessary relation to a vow. It may be that the quarry is all the time in the pursuer, and the insatiable quest for satisfaction is inherent in the endeavor—the results cannot be appreciated quantitatively. What matters to the priest type is the elite of mind—not of blood, wealth, place, saintliness; a sense of cultural affinity is fundamental—it erases all possible differences between men. There is the paradox of man as both created and creative: Aristotle describes the culturally creative person as "a god amongst men"; he is a strange being—a stranger in the world; creativity flourishes regardless of the environment, for it achieves expression under the most sordid conditions—genius will out. The creative work is unique, and can only be imitated: it is universal and eternal, it blends with all time and space, which renders it latent and thus unassailable; and it has freedom—always, everywhere.

The concern with origins is man's most exacting sentient effort; man always everywhere has been groping for an answer to the ultimate questions about the world he comes into, and about himself. Intuition as a sentient quality is confined to alleged individual inner experience—feeling, vision, dream: the dissemination of its teaching is predicated upon mass faith in the inspiration, sincerity, intelligence of the seer, which establishes him as authority; thus religion is based on faith—on intuition or inner feeling, and on authority or external command. Yet Christianity came to accept the conclusion that man's ultimate questions are subjects not only of intuition and authority, but that they can also be treated of, and determined by, rationalism; and the Church always had a belief in the power of the pre-Christian "heathen" Greek and Roman thinkers to provide learning and to teach the ways of wisdom. The combination of man's cognitive faculties of intuition and reason creates the intellect: theology and philosophy are both based on the intellect; in theology intuition is more important than reason, while in philosophy it is the other way. Religion antedates philosophy—intuition came before reason; yet, which is qualitatively primary—the heart or the head? The differences between the theologian in the divinities, and the philosopher in the humanities, are important—but their similarities are fundamental. Man from the beginning has attempted to explain the mystery of his being in terms of religion; with the development of civilization he retained religion, and he re-inforced it with the answers of philosophy. There are the fundamental postulates of religion—God, immortality, free will, teleology—which are universal and eternal; and there are the particulars, the theology, of religion—Hebraism, Buddha, Shinto, Islam—which are limited in time and space, and are subject to alteration and even to change. Man was convinced that a good case can be made in reason for the eternal verities of faith: he attempted to grapple with the fundamental postulates (settled questions) in religion, which are the fundamental problems (open questions) in philosophy; and with the proposition that *ethics*, and the principle of *quality*, have a relation per se with the idea of a universal Intelligence.

Man's mind is—he thinks with, his wisdom emanates from—his brain, his heart, his blood: he tries to translate his emotion—his feeling, into rational terms; yet he experiences something that he *feels* but cannot communicate. Man's attempt to grapple with the ultimate problems of life is to besiege—to invade, the fort of the mind; he is in the field of his most exacting thinking power, which is necessarily in the province of the priest. It may have a two-fold expression: as in relation to the universal principles of religion it is essentially in the realm of philosophy; and as concerning the doctrines of *a* religion—the particular interpretation and understanding of the universals, it is essentially in the realm of theology. Mental power, depth—genius, is priestly; Plato and Christ had advanced to a nobility of abstract thought—to metaphysics or disembodied intellect, that is attained only by the great minds given to religious contemplation—they are both the priest. There is the obvious fact of the ruins of time, yet it was thought that hidden within the transient is the permanent: they were convinced that there is the noumenon, an underlying rule of order behind the multiplicity of phenomena in the world—the Logos,

26

whether in terms of Hebraic sacred theology, or of Hellenic rational philosophy, or of both; they thought in terms of an ultimate, universal, unifying element, the Idea or Form from which flow many particulars— the unity that is implicit in diversity. Is this unity Mind, is it Intelligent? Only God can make a flower, a tree: it appears that the making of a flower was the work of the ages; and a man is much more complex than a tree. Is God immanent, or transcendent—or both? A monastic revival, with monks vowed for life to poverty, chastity, obedience, meant a resuscitation of learning—an emphasis on the cultural values;[c] and this led to "scholasticism", a state of mind within the rarefied, the empyreal atmosphere or the area of pure light. Mental conception is per se limitation: in the absence of the Cartesian law of contrast there is no awareness—gloom and glare are equally blinding; where there are no distinct boundaries there is a tendency to wander, to stray, and maybe even to lose one's way. And it establishes the legitimacy of the atmosphere of scholasticism as man's fundamental dedication.

Language is the basic instrument of human thought. The Grecian language and literature were regarded as the origin, and the source, of all humanist conceptions. The philosophy of Hellenism became the handmaiden of theology, and there was an attempt to establish the truth of revelation in terms of reason—which could be both abstract or pure, and also practical. The ways of knowing traditionally identified with religion were always present and primary, yet in proportion as the Church had to go deeper into rationalism in the formulation of its beliefs the Greek philosophical terminology, which was the only vehicle then available for precise thought, had to become increasingly an essential part of Christianity. Thus Rome continued Hebraism as a living effective force; but Hellenism—rationalism and philosophy as removed from everyday life, was interred for over a millennium in the studies of the scholastics—they were the custodians of the classics, which they carefully preserved as precious for mankind. Moreover, it is said that the teachings of St. Paul in the New Testament are to quite an extent Greek: Christian ethics incorporated much of the ancient current popular thinking, especially the principles of stoicism; and in this way the Church participated in the perpetuation and propagation of Hellenism. The languages of antiquity—Hebrew, Greek, Latin—were considered the foundation of all cultural endeavor and creativity: it was declared before printing, when every writing was a manuscript, that all serious thought—the ideas of

27

theologians and philosophers—could find no expression in the language of the common folk; there was a contempt for the vernacular—for the "mother tongue", which was looked down on as jargon, as cheap and boorish; and it was generally accepted that Latin is the language of the divinities, as well as of the humanities—of intellect, profundity, sensitivity, refinement.

ARISTOCRACY

Feudalism was based on the conviction that there are qualitative differences between human beings: a small minority of men are superior, while the great majority are inferior; the superior—the quality persons, are based on blood, which is an immutable condition: the social order rests on the great law of subordination, and it must be modeled upon an externally fixed hierarchy—with aristocracy, those born into station, being in domination of the lower order of people, the commonalty. Theirs were the values of mature, highly cultivated men:

> "The existence of aristocracy in all times and climes is historically justified, since it was the creator, the patron, and the custodian of culture; intellect was always everywhere venerated—the ancient patriciate tolerated even the cultured slave on a social level; and it preserved and handed down to posterity everything that is associated with the good, the beautiful and the true.";

society was to be ruled by an intellectual elite, who had a supremacy of learning, virtue, power, and whose state approximated a "republic of the professors".

Monarchy epitomized the rule of land, which was entirely for the benefit of quality. And the Hellenic heritage was a powerful influence in forming the mind of the European aristocracy;

> "A great literature which comes to us in translation and across an undeniable culture gap must always be something rich and strange".

There was strong attachment to tradition, to the family and its station—

and to the landed estate upon which everything rested. They had the feudal castle—complete with family ghost—which symbolized all they represented, and was protective as fort. And it was esthetic as architecture: the crusaders had brought home with them some ideas from Islam; and the castle—"that poem in glass and stone", was a thing of beauty, and of power.

They lived in medieval isolation: the life of the elite was set in nature—they knew nothing else; they believed in the redemptive powers of the agrarian way of life; they were in love with the pastoral tone of their surroundings, which they identified with peace of mind; they deified the earth, forests, waters, hills, skies; they were enveloped in the sensuous beauty of their landscape—and they melted into, and blended with, their surroundings; the man and everything living grew out of the earth—like the tree; the horseman was an ensemble, a fusion of man and horse as a single being;[d] and they were like the ancient Greek Antaeus, whose strength was identified with the Sacred Earth—"the giants grew strong again by touching the earth". Land is conducive to the life of the mind, as cultural creativity is always generated.[e] Their exaltation and emulation of the Mediterranean values latinized their native tongues, which raised them to the status of classical languages, and the confinement of serious thought to pure Latin was receding. They engaged in "honorable", in non-economic, pursuits—political, military, ecclesiastical, athletic; they made history. This created an atmosphere for the appreciation of learning, which was thought of as the heart of life and was identified with quality; cultural values received top consideration, for the man of classical creativity was a star in the heavens. The mentally complex was traditionally identified with the elite, as it was considered beyond mass grasp, and there was no concern with popular education; aristocracy always had state power—cultural activity was never in any political involvement, and it always had freedom. And they were esthetes: esthetics was the supreme value as they were sharply alert to the natural beauties within which their life was set—the ornamental was preferred to the useful; and they were ornate—at times even magnificent, in expensive attire and cortege. They were humanists—persons who lived the life of the mind, and who put cultural values before ethical values: the primary index to the apex of civilization was the sacredness in which the work of art was held—destroying works of art was the fatal crime, deadlier than destroying human life, and they were more likely to weep at a torn manuscript than at a severed head; yet they never eschewed humanitarianism—their Christianity did render them capable of condescending philanthropy.

And the individual life span was short: there were no mechanical means for the perpetuation of the past,[f] and it was readily buried; and most of the breathing, living actors of the time were no more than silhouettes. From about the fifteenth century men began to show a self-consciousness in relation to the future: the care and wealth that were lavished on the tombs of the time suggest a secular bias; and there was an increasing emphasis on the preservation of the identity, of the biographical materials, of the great—through portrait painting and printing. There was a developing appreciation of objects that endure; and there was better protection of landmarks, which were made fire-proof through the use of steel and brick;

> "they indulge in pleasures as if they were to die tomorrow, while they build as if they were to live forever".

Aristocracy throughout the ages was founded on landed wealth; yet it also engaged in and profited from trade, although it never let capital become the *end in itself*. The patricians concentrated on the cultivation of the earth, rather than on the fabrication of the artisan—and theirs was always the economy of maximum land and minimum trade; engagement in pursuits leading to a separation from the landed way of life was *contra naturam*—it was interment. According to Aristotle;

> "where the citizens are men of intrinsic goodness, none of them should be permitted to exercise any mechanic employment or follow merchandise, as being ignoble and destructive to virtue; neither should they be husbandmen, that they may be at leisure to improve in virtue and perform the duty they owe to the state".
> "It is also necessary that the landed property should belong to these men . . . the citizens should be rich . . . no mechanic ought to be admitted to the rights of a citizen".
> "work is to be esteemed mean . . . all those arts which tend to deform the body are called mean, and all those employments

which are exercised for gain; for they take off from the freedom of the mind and render it sordid''.

The pursuit of gain as an end in itself was thought immoral and reprehensible: the trader, with his ways and his values—his capital foundation, intensive economy, development of towns, pursuit of riches, greed for gold, resort to usury, practice of thrift—is as old as history; in the Athens of Socrates it was held that ''both money and self are what all men love'', and it was said of the trader, ''He does not possess wealth—it possesses him''.

And the Old Testament of the Bible says;

> ''In thee have they taken gifts to shed blood; thou hast taken usury and increase, and thou hast greedily gained of thy neighbours by extortion, and hast forgotten me, saith the Lord God.''
> ''Behold, therefore, I have smitten mine hand at thy dishonest gain which thou hast made, and at thy blood which hath been in the midst of thee.''[3]

The ancients thought of the traders as ''levying their interest till it exceeds by many times the parent sum''; interest on money to the feudal mind was ''usury'' per se; and they declared that ''usury is most reasonably detested'', and that money should not be allowed to breed. Plato says, ''he gets the money, but on condition of enslaving the best part of himself to the vilest''; and Aristotle says, ''the major part of mankind are rather desirous of riches than of honour''—these desiderata evidently being regarded as in conflict; the patricians were not economy conscious, and there was never a scramble for wealth. In their eyes the qualities of strength, skill, courage were identified with fighting—not with laboring, which gave the former a precedence in prestige. Fighting presupposed thorough training in the use of weapons, and in stoicism: it gave one a feeling of manliness, of competition—and was often associated with the man on horseback, who had a sense of domination, freedom, speed; he had a weapon, which gave him a sense of power; he could travel, often to distant places—and to conquer, to subjugate. They were convinced that ''it is courage which makes one lovely . . . for courage is commanding

31

and invincible''; and the warrior was also an athlete. And they taught that the man who is cowardly in war is to be "degraded to a craftsman or a farmer"; there was a qualitative difference between the individual exploit of prowess, and mass routine drudgery; fighting was associated with romance, which inspired song—while laboring was prosaic, monotonously repetitive; wars often took on the characteristics of the gymnastic bout, they were won by individual combat—by the grimness, skill, bravery, of the champion fighter—rather than by economic power or laboring; and in pre-firepower dexterity in the use of instruments for fighting in war was much more difficult to achieve than in those for laboring in peace. Their values were identified with quality—not with quantity; they did not think primarily in terms of amount—acreage, labor, money. They were convinced that money can never have anything but quantitative value—it buys only mediocrity; it is confined to the market-place, which was never a school of social ethics—of economic and political responsibility; the nobleman—the "man of honor", who found himself within it would soon be devoured; and the mart—with its people, values, ways—was unknown to the patricians. They were convinced that men engrossed in the pursuit of money are unfit to rule a state: the tendency to insouciance was a mark of the well-bred, while thrift characterized the vulgar; the mart—trade as a livelihood—was wide open and free for all, but the trader under feudalism was not allowed to make his way the foundation of the social organization; and he remained fundamentally an individual—an alien in a world ruled by the ways of an aristocracy of blood and land.

THE RENAISSANCE

It seems to be a law of nature for everything in life to go through the inevitable cycle of birth, growth, decline, death. It is historically established that days of sterility often follow times of greatness; Hellenism for some generations had been developing inner tendencies to decline which in time culminated in decadence, there seemed to be a move towards reversion to barbarism, and Hebraism stepped in to fill the vacuum. Moreover, civilization and Christianity are concurrent in transmontane Europe: there is a chasm between civilized and primitive which is very wide and very deep; it took centuries for this area to bridge the chasm—to clear itself completely of its aboriginal heritage; and this was the foundation of what is known in the history of Europe as the "Dark Ages". During this era there was an identification of education—of knowledge and wisdom, with religion; the Roman Catholic Church built the great Cathedrals of Europe, stone testaments to an age of faith and mental creativity; she founded Universities throughout the continent— the great institutions of learning, as theological seminaries and centers of religion, which were to teach divine truth to Christian people and guard them from error; and the essence of medieval philosophy lies in its theological conclusions. The life of reason—the rational ideal, was fed down the centuries by the magic spring of Grecian thought and culture, and it underlay western European civilization. The soul of Roman Christianity inspired the cultural values: throughout the medieval era that distant and glorious world, Hellenic-Roman—the times that were preeminent for literature and art, which are known as "the classical ages" had shone with romantic splendor; the scholastics were,

"the people who have kept the fund of knowledge, without which each new generation would have had to re-invent the world";

none of the Hellenic traditions ever died out—they spanned the centuries intact; and the Church's tendencies to mental creativity slowly—yet inexorably, spread throughout the trans-Alpine continent. And during the fifteenth century there began to develop from within the Christian world in Europe—from within the Roman Catholic Church, a movement known as "the Renaissance—which was a revival of classical culture, that brought about a flowering of the genius of mankind";

"the medieval Church spiritually fructified the cultural milieu in which the Renaissance appeared".[4]

There followed the Renaissance emphasis on the rationalism of philosophy, or the attempt to reduce complicated thought to simple logical expression—and on the empiricism of science; and there was a feeling of confidence in the ability of the *mind* of man—in his perceptive and thinking qualities—to achieve an understanding of the world. The modernates predicated their ways of apprehending phenomena on man's rational and empirical faculties, and they brought about the beginnings of natural science as a social force. The cognitive faculties, the ways of knowing—of authority, and of "feeling" in terms of intuition, emotion, sensation—can all be treated, analyzed, understood by the way of rationalism, but not vice versa; and from the empiricism of science— experience, experiment—general principles are deduced; evaluation and deduction can be achieved only in terms of rationalism, which gives it a priority in cognitive endeavor. The intuition and authority of religion, and the empiricism of science, cannot dispense with reason; and even the attempt to depreciate rationalism has to be made in terms of itself. It is rationalism that holds together a doctrine with all of its complications, and constitutes the foundation of examination, criticism, explanation: with the advance of knowledge reason was exalted at the expense of the emotions, and man was regarded as truly man in proportion as he is mind rather than feeling; the system of belief that is untenable in reason and experience is per se false; rationalism abhors inconsistency and con- tradiction—and logical consistency in thinking became a primary value, as it was regarded as the true index in the attempt to understand the world.

The Revival of Learning had its essential origins in "Italy, that paradise of culture", and "cultivated Italians (were) the finest intellec- tual product of the Renaissance". She set out to recover the past, to act in emulation of it, and to bring about a meeting of the modern with the ancient mind; she was the impetus to the classical revival, and she became the Occidental center of cultural endeavor and creativity. "In all branches of activity Europe became a province of Italian civilization": its painting, music, architecture, sculpture, poetry, were venerated as "the soul of art"; members of the upper classes throughout the continent made the "journey into Italy to drink of the heady fountains of human- ism"; and the royal court of each country was its cultural center. European aristocrats were proud to become "Italianated"—to become the custodians of the classics, of the best in the past; they took fondly to anything Latin, which was the key to all the professions; and patronage of scholars was a characteristic of quality.

Hellenism—which inspired the Renaissance, had hitherto been con- trolled by and subordinated to the purposes of, Christianity; it became self-assertive, surged forth in its own behalf, achieved independence and set itself in opposition to its former custodian. The Renaissance brought a resuscitation of the non-Hebraic writings of the pre-Christian era—an

34

emphasis on the mind and work of ancient Hellas and Rome; it was dedicated to the principles of rationalism, humanism, naturalism— which were spreading to north of the Alps; and it was an attempt to substitute Hellenism for Hebraism as the dominant ideological influence in the Occident. Moreover, man has never been able to understand why—if God is good, evil exists in the world; and he concluded that prayer is not efficacious in eliminating evil, and that he must therefore help himself—which results in an emphasis on science; and it was thought that natural phenomena must be explained in terms other than as acts of God. This introduced the golden Age of Reason: Europeans preferred to rule themselves through the sovereign powers of reason; and this development was moving towards the rise of the post-biblical era. Cultural freedom, the fascination of pure study, the right of access to the humanities—the classics, and philosophy, science; the right freely to drink at the fountain of human goodness, beauty, wisdom—became a supreme value in the life of western man. And all this gave its greatest impetus to the development of science.

Thus the Renaissance insisted on the primacy of rationalism, and anything that offends it is per se worthless: it accepted as within the tenets of philosophy the fundamental postulates of religion—God, immortality, free will, teleology; and it held that the principles of *ethics* and of *quality* have an inherent relation to the idea of a universal Intelligence. The atmosphere of the Renaissance was never conducive to mechanical materialism; the Revival of Learning was identified with the principle of Deism—religion without revelation; the spirit of Godliness in a man, not his adherence to a particular doctrine of communion, is all that really matters; the timeless values of religion, the integrity of the eternal verities—*veritas æternitatis,* are invincible; the thinker can see more— there *is* more, of Intelligence in a flower than in all of man's masterpieces of creativity. The attempt to make a case in philosophy for the concept of the ultimate as Mind is world-wide and eternal—it was never confined to religion; a better case can be made in rationalism for the universe as mental, than for the conclusion that it is mechanical.

It was concluded that there is truth in the world outside of religion; there took place a move from the biblical to the classical, from the divinities to the humanities—''the proper study of mankind is man''; and this found its ultimate expression in the idealization of the natural man in

35

"humanism, with its renewal of interest in the classics, and in man as man rather than in man as an object of salvation".

As interest in the study of nature encouraged a revolt against scholasticism there developed a tendency towards a natural order of life, and people became confident that religion could be established on a system of natural philosophy—on Pantheism; there was a move towards the revival of paganism, of nature worship, and the attitude of the Deist became, "I believe in the comely proportions of Dame Nature, of this most beautiful theatre—the created world". The house of worship began to appear like a flight—like a separation of God, from nature: the attempt to discover truth was thus taken out of the atmosphere of supernaturalism, and brought into the open—into the world of nature; heaven became only sky, and explanations of phenomena ceased to be attributed to spectral powers as they began to be brought nearer to earth.

Primitive man understood everything in the world in terms of anthropomorphism. The Renaissance, as philosophy and science— found biblicism antedeluvian, the doctrine of divine revelation untenable, and the concept of God as Jehovah repugnant. The tendency to the rampant skepticism of the time is exemplified by the statement attributed to Pope Leo X (1513-1521), "What profit has not that fable of Christ brought us!"[5]; and the Papacy of the High Renaissance has been described as "secularized". There began an attempt to create a rational and scientific, in place of the theological, foundation for the explanation of the origin and development of the world, of life, of man—and for the ethical and moral code; and Deism regarded the prophets of the bible, and the Savior of Christianity, as human—as great religious thinkers, but not as divinely inspired. Supernaturalism was thought of as inimical to cultural freedom, and the Revival of Learning developed as an endeavor against the authoritarian church. It was a reaction against the doctrine of divinely revealed eternal truth upon which the wisdom of man was based: it was held that man's worship of God is not tantamount to self-effacement; that an understanding of the universe is a subject of continuing development; and that it is within the competence of man to achieve this understanding through his own investigation with the scientific methods of observation and experimentation. It was thought that philosophy is an indispensable element of man as human—that the mind is ill-trained that has not come under the Greek discipline, for

36

enlightenment begins when one learns to doubt; life without thought and discussion—separation from the world of the mind, is characteristic of man as beast. There followed the exhumation, appreciation, and emulation of the classics of antiquity—which restored confidence in man's own mental faculties; the responsibility for fathoming and explaining the world was thus thrown upon man, who was ready to follow wherever his own thinking would lead him; the reliance on rationalism emphasized the contemplative, speculative life—which brought a revival of learning, and a stimulus to liberty; and the great thinkers of antiquity began to displace the saints of religion as the inspiration of men. The resurrection of the classics—the eternal monuments to the mental power of universal man, emancipated human intelligence; learning was no longer confined to the recluse, as it became a part of life; it made this life—the only life man actually knows, worth living for its own sake; and there was exultation in the rediscovery of the value of nature and of man.

The Renaissance, the pattern of thought known as the Enlightenment—"a magnificent flowering of art and learning"—had a profound reciprocal influence on the Roman Catholic Church; St. Thomas Aquinas pointed out that of all the living creatures in the world it is given to man alone to contemplate the truth as an end in itself. In Judaism God is an abstraction—pure Idea. In Christianity God is symbolic in form, and He may have material manifestation—which led to an identification of divinity with objects apprehended by the senses, with images; this dedicated the Church to art as an essential part of religion, and she was the world's foremost patron of the arts; and the Sistine Chapel in Rome is an eternal monument to the mental creativity of man. The Hellenes built for the ages, and they left monuments in stone; the concept of Moses is Hebraic, and it is Roman Catholicism that gave it physical expression—Michel Angelo's statue of Moses was inspired and patronized by the Church.

Hellenism inspired the Renaissance, which emanated chiefly from aristocracy, and was dedicated to cultural creativity. Hebraism inspired the Reformation, which emanated chiefly from the commonalty, and was dedicated to popular education. Hellenism was rational, and Hebraism was authoritarian; they represented opposing forces—science and mysticism. The Greeks had the principles of heliocentricism, of the engine, of man as animal, although their science never developed as a social force; and they introduced the principle of logical classification of the

37

subjects of their interest. The Jews were mystical, nebulous, compounded in their view of life; to Hebraism everything in the world was contained in God, and the man of exceptional quality—the leader, the teacher, was per se divinely inspired. The Christian teaching—"'render unto Caesar that which is Caesar's, render unto God that which is God's"—seems Greek, as it implies a qualitative difference between state and church; it recognizes the existence of, and attributes integrity to, the secular world as separate and different from the divine world.

The Roman Catholic Church was based on Scripture, which was Hebraic; and it was based on Theology, which was developed through use of the rationalism of the Greeks. The dawn of the Renaissance was marked by a general interest, inspired and supported from within the Church, to try to achieve an underlying harmony between the revelation of Hebraism and the philosophy of Hellenism—to bring together the sacred and the secular in a fundamentally consistent monolithic system of thought. The rationalism of philosophy and the empiricism of science were the cognitive faculties considered most conducive towards merging, or at least linking, the two seminal streams. By the thirteenth century—the time of St. Thomas Aquinas, rationalism was a thoroughly developed way of knowing, while empiricism was only in its introductory phases. Thomism is the endeavor to establish the truth of Christianity, to arrive at an understanding and justification of scriptural revelation, in terms of rationalism and empiricism—in addition to intuition and authority. This endeavor failed—there are St. Thomas's oft-repeated words, "All that I have written seems like straw." Scripture could not survive rational analysis, and revelation had therefore to be embodied in faith—"even though it does not comport with reason, believe it; accept it on faith". The empirical scientific mind emphasized evidence as the index to truth; the belief that the bible is divinely inspired was universally accepted on authority, as it was wholly without evidence; conviction on authority—without understanding, or blind faith—was the only alternative to rationalism in determining the mass mind; this rendered authority offensive to rationalism as it is belief without thinking; and since it is easier to believe than to think, such encouragement tended to deaden the mass mentality. The Church had to give up in its efforts to achieve harmony, and Occidental life and thought throughout the two millennia of Christianity were characterized by the underlying irreconcilable dualism of Hebraism and Hellenism. Thus the intuition of the

38

Jews and the reason of the Greeks could not live together, yet neither could they live separately; can the head and the heart, the truth of the mind and the truth of the emotions, exist apart?—and it became a question of emphasis, rather than of fusion or of exclusiveness. There was an essential need for authority in religion: all Christians were agreed on the primary integrity of revelation—I AM THAT I AM; it was superior to reason, the emphasis on which varied with time; revelation as on a plane with rationalism, and certainly as subordinate, is no longer divine; and the Church developed an hostility, especially towards science, that did not stop at intolerance.

NOTES

aThe mental power of Baruch Spinoza the Jew, and the mental power of Immanuel Kant the German, are qualitatively on a par.
bNot necessarily the ecclesiast—institution, vow, vestments.
cNot on popular education.
dWhen primitives first saw the mounted European they thought they were beholding a single living being.
eTrade is fabricated; there is a poetry, color, romance, in the man on the horse, that is absent in the man on the motorcycle.
fPublishing, photography, tape recording.
gThe Arian doctrine stemming from the Council of Nicaea in 325—that Jesus Christ partakes only of human attributes, found expression throughout the succeeding centuries as Socinianism, Deism, Unitarianism.

BOOK ONE—THE BACKGROUND IN ENGLAND

INTRODUCTION

The background in England is treated here only to the extent that it casts light on the central theme of this work, the sociology of the Bay colony.

The movement of continentals—Latins, Nordics—through invasion, conquest, emigration, into England resulted in the ethnical compounding especially of her upper classes; and her commonalty, the grass roots—is her purest racial stock. England had her French sociological influences: the Normans towards feudalism, which introduced chivalry; and the Huguenots towards capitalism. The developments leading to the establishment of Anglo-America took place during the sixteenth and seventeenth centuries—during the Tudor-Stuart regimen. England in these times is a study fundamentally in sociology—the struggle between land and trade to rule the realm:

"The things themselves are simple enough; it is the relations they set up in society, the social and legal arrangements, that are so various and complex";

history alone cannot explain what happened. The social commotions found their expression in the doctrine and structure of state and church, and a study in the sociology of the times must take into consideration the ethical aspects of economy and theology. Religion was fundamental in these social struggles, and it took the following expression— Christianity: Romanism vs Anglicanism; Anglicanism—Episcopacy vs Reformation; Reformation—Wycliffism vs Calvinism; Wycliffism— sectarianism; Calvinism—Presbyterianism vs Puritanism. England's Church disputations are studied here only in their sociological implications. New England is the creation of the English Reformation, and the definitive understanding of the latter is the foundation for such an understanding of the former.

43

CHAPTER ONE—FEUDALISM: LAND

Civilization in England had started with the manorial system; the manor was a little world in itself—a unit of hierarchical social organization, with a "lord" at the top. The manor was subject to the "feud"—to military assault by enemies from without; and as within each estate there was a castle, which was located on a strategic spot and organized as a fortress. Feudalism was basically a monolithic sociology—everyone within it was a fully civilized being; power was overwhelmingly concentrated on, and was entirely in the hands of, the agrarian economy. The castle was the home of the lord, as well as his administrative center; and it was the foundation of the safety of, and of the law and order within, the manorial estate. At the base of the manor's social structure were the tenants, who were its most numerous inhabitants; in the course of the centuries they had built up certain relations to the land that became identified as rights—in tradition, custom, law, "the contrary to which the memory of man runneth not"—and for which the head of the unit had to have respect; yet he was overlord of a mass of rent and tax paying people, and he had an attitude of paternalism towards them—the "commonalty". An area within the manor was also set aside for the location of the indispensable craftsmen—blacksmith, carpenter, tanner, weaver, butcher, baker; this area was the nucleus for the development of a town. All the inhabitants of the manorial estate were within the concern of the Church: men develop a sense of worth in an atmosphere of sacredness, and they had complete equality in the eyes of God; they were entitled to the full benefits of religion, which included respect for the integrity of the family; the manner of the lordly towards the lowly of the land could not be capricious, and there was no auction block and no trafficking in human flesh. Yet the castle was an island of affluence in an ocean of human misery; the lord was absolute master—the tenants had to pay him rent in perpetuity, and although they worked the agricultural lands on various conditions of subordination they were essentially in a status of serfdom. The great majority of the people—the commonalty, didn't count: the texture of their life was determined much more by the traditions and customs of the social order—of the lord's manor, than by government—legislative enactment, judicial decision; they had no legal being in the community, no representation in government in their own right, none of the civil liberties—franchise, trial by jury, habeas corpus; and they were without property, clerical, educational rights. There was little they could do about their condition; yet they felt that their salvation could come only from within, and the stern castle was preferable to their only alternative—the forbidding forests. In this social microcosm there occurred the multiplicity of problems arising from the complexities of human relationships. Problems of economic, class and sex relations, law enforcement, religion and morality; ethical standards or concepts of good and bad, right and wrong, success and failure, reward and punishment—were all there. The thinking patrician was in a position to contemplate, and to try to deal with, the problems arising in his tiny social world.

The great manors dominated the societal order, and each of them was in the nature of a petty principality; and the average native was a countryman. It was the world of the idle rich, the feudal barons, the absentee landlords, whose wide acres and princely estates were founded upon mass degradation. The communications were primitive, and the realm was in a condition of political decentralization; a neighboring manor was like a foreign country, an adjacent shire was remote, and a few weeks of bad weather isolated whole communities. The lords of the manors were in constant jealousy of one another: their way had a tradition of palace intrigue, as reflected in the plays of William Shakespeare; the story of the spite and vendetta of inter- and intra-family conspiracy, duplicity, venality, becomes dreary. A study of medieval England is a step back into a wild heroic past: the horse was the unit of personalty, and wealth was tallied in mounts; training for the feudal gentleman was in excellence, which centered on chivalry, on the Sir Galahad image, the man of action on horseback—"a horse, a horse, my kingdom for a horse"—the dashing, intrepid, hot blade cavalier; and what emerges is a portrait of a pre-rational society—elemental, reckless, violent. They felt close to, and thought wholly in terms of, the misty

45

past—the future was a blank. *Feuda*lism's noblest occupation was fighting; and there was the glamorization of war for its own sake, as chivalry prized military glory above the pursuits of peace. The values of the age regarded physical courage as the test of being—and they engaged in the exaltation of heroes, whose deeds were sung in poetry; and everyone was brought up in the assumption that true greatness comes from success in battle. Thus life and feud were inseparable; war was a normal condition—a way of life, and the country was in a continual state of strife; and peace was a truce between wars. Yet it was in the days before total war: there was a relative ineffectiveness of medieval weaponry, and the brutality of the warfare of feudal knights tended to be tempered by the play and excitement of the tournament; inter-manorial strife was per se secondary to the menace of a foreign invasion; and the castle was always the unit of the defense of the realm—the combination of castles was of vital importance in confronting an alien enemy. Gradually a few of the lords became much more powerful than the rest, until one dominated them all, and he achieved a qualitative distinction—he became identified as "king"; and monarchy introduced the principle of political centralization, as all of the inhabitants of the realm were under the king as "subjects".

England's sociology—feudalism, was a hierarchy; it rested on the holy trinity of monarchy, church and aristocracy—no country without a king, no church without a bishop, no land without a lord—which established a union of state, church and economy (realty property). The population was divided into two castes, aristocracy and commonalty; power descended from majesty to aristocracy, which in turn ruled the commonalty—and there were gradations within each caste, with varying degrees of dependence on the one next above. The aristocrats were divided into lords spiritual and temporal, or respectively first and second "estate"; the commons, which were based on capital or trade were, regardless of wealth, identified as the "third estate". The differences between the estates—cleric, lord, commoner—were qualitative; while the differences within the third estate—which could be great, were quantitative. There was universal acceptance of the principle of monarchy, and of the throne as hereditary: the Crown was a social institution; the king was a person, the symbol of the state—he was at the apex of the social system; and who was the legitimate heir sometimes met with the

46

almost hopeless problem of untying the genealogical knot. The monarchy was deiform: the king was ensconced in the necessary mystic and moral authority of the central executive; he owed his majesty to "the grace of God", and he ruled by divine right; he was the state—the one fixed star in a madly revolving universe; there was a condition of king worship, and resistance to "his majesty" could be held deicide; and solemnity and heroism, as well as magnificence—esthetics, pomp, pageantry—symbolized royalty. The patricians' household, and their appearance, were in imitation of monarchy; and the age expected the blooded to be as fierce as lions and as gaudy as peacocks. The aristocrats sometimes succeeded in elevating a weakling to the Crown whom they could dominate, and then the king was more peacock than lion as he lived for appearance only. It was a world of fealty, chivalry, honor; chivalry—loyalty and service to God, king, lord, woman—prevailed; and the masses learned by seeing, rather than by understanding. Subjects often judged their king by the order he brought, and they basked in the reflected glory of the royal sun; they felt elated when their sovereign was thought great, and was universally feared, as this gave them a sense of power. The power of England's monarchy—sanctioned by divine right, was absolute in principle: yet in practice London supremacy was modified by the medieval communications, and by the inefficiency, and the venality, of many royal officials—there was "much theft and little thrift"; this precluded effective central control, and the king did not interfere in the affairs of the realm's governmental unit—the shire; the federalism of England's political organization—the autonomy of the shires, effectively modified regal absolutism; primary responsibility was at the local level, the lord continued to be complete master of his manorial estate, and he was a local potentate as his fealty to the king was practically nominal.

The "whole, splendid, bustling world of sixteenth-century England" was a simple artisan society, little removed from the ways of the ancient Mediterranean civilizations: under her sociology—the institutions and the values of feudalism—land was always more important than capital, and the urban interests were caught up within, and dominated by, the rural power structure. Land had contempt for trade and labor, and the caste divisions were based on a distinction between activities that were

47

considered honorable or debasing: the market place with its people, values, ways; the pursuits identified with daily livelihood—industry, trade, work; this was always looked down upon by blood—the men of the mart were commonalty.

The medieval sociology was based on land: it was hierarchical—their world attached primary importance to place, prestige, priority; one caste did not know how the other caste lived. It was organized on the principle of infeudation—primogeniture, entail, mastery, tenancy, quit-rent payment. The land occupant was "seised" of land—he "held" his land by "grace" of a superior or overlord. There was "quality of title", which denoted both rights in land and social station; the landholder— from tenant, through freeholder, to quality—had to pay the one next above him a "quit-rent"; this was an acknowledgment that he held the land by inferior title, or by grace; thus the quit-rent was simply the due of an inferior to a superior;

> "The quit-rents were not regarded as a fiscal measure, or a tax; they were a recognition of the king's ultimate sovereignty, in whom the title of all lands was vested."

Land was limited; the soil in England had been immemorially worked. The union of property with state and church was maintained by the institutions of primogeniture and entail; under primogeniture the family's entire real property was automatically inherited only by the eldest son, and entail precluded its alienation and encumbrance; the operation of these feudal traditions created and perpetuated the aristocracy by freezing a landed estate with one family indefinitely, for without them estates could be broken up by descending divided and be liable to continual change of hands. The physical transfer of personalty— alienation of livestock, furnishings—is simple: realty—lands, tenements, hereditaments—is immovable, and it is the foundation of life, which gave it its social meaning; and the fee simple independent title— the alienation of "reality", was beyond the comprehension of the feudal mind. And rights to realty were always "subject to"—they were never clear-cut, independent. Feudalism followed a normal routine activity, which was identified with stability, security, serenity; and there was a condition of social stratification—the painted society upon a painted world. Their political and economic values were Hellenic;

48

"That the gifts of fortune, both personal and external, are an essential condition of excellence, is an axiom of the point of view of the Greeks. But . . . we never find them misled into the conception that such gifts are an end in themselves, apart from the personal qualities they are meant to support or adorn".

Thus land was the great source of power and prestige in feudal England: lordship was a way of life, not an economic condition—economy was taken for granted; the great proprietorships combined the title to land and the powers of government in a few hands; it was part of their subjective being that "those who own the country ought to govern it"—they ruled the realm; and they constituted a traditional aristocracy—the best, who were entitled to prerogative.

Their society being based on "birth" vertical fluidity among the classes was precluded: with their property and social position assured by the state there was no need for individual initiative and efficiency; the manors were thus largely haphazardly directed, and with the constant price fluctuation and the absence of definite money standards and of specie most of the proprietors were hazy on what they owned and owed. Land ruled over finance, and entail precluded speculation and turnover. Commerce was outside their milieu, they were characterized by the traditional "scorn of trade", and capitalistic promotion was an alien activity: they were without the profit motive, there was no concern with investment, and they had no brokerage—and no money lending with all of its implications; "business"—economic endeavor with its subordination of everything else to work, was no part of their way; they did not have the ledger—the dichotomous type of mind, and did not think in terms of "assets and liabilities"; rationalization, the intent to get the most for the least, was alien to the patrician mind—and they could never see the importance of exact calculation, were indifferent to precision concerning estate boundaries, and were unfamiliar with bookkeeping and accounting. They eschewed the state of mind which could not see life beyond profits; there was no "strife between wealth and virtue"—they were never blinded to human values by the dividend mania; and they regarded the exploitation of people by one another—the mind to use, as petty and anti-social. Their relations were always social, never economic; they did not live off one another, were not out to "make

49

money", had nothing to sell, never thought in terms of "driving a bargain", did not view their fellows as customers, and there was never a cash nexus in personal relations. The tendency to cupidity was nonexistent; the habits of thrift and close-fistedness were unknown; they never produced a miser, and they created the tradition of quality hospitality. The absence of money values had its influence on the mind —and they seem like Homer's Odysseus, who was "bitten to the quick" when he was accused of being,

> "such an one as comes and goes in a benched ship, a master of sailors that are merchantmen, one with a memory for his freight, or that hath the charge of a cargo homeward bound, and of greedily gotten gains."

Thus were the patricians innocent of the mysteries of high finance: their way of life precluded them from appreciating the importance of, and developing an interest in, the subject; and when they found themselves confronted with it they tended to derangement.

The heritage of European elite created an atmosphere for the rapid spread of the Renaissance: England's aristocrats were true to form—their traditional ideal of culture had its origins in Hellenism; and this profoundly influenced life at the apex, as well as in the Church. They were a leisure class: they were very careful of their economic base, but they never gave their lives to the pursuit of gain; they regarded the concentration of one's life on economy—labor, trade, investment—as incompatible with excellence, with intellect and virtue; for cultural creativity grows—it flowers from the earth, not from trade, it is always generated, never fabricated—"the stark poetry of the soil". Cultural endeavor received top appreciation, and everything was subordinated to the values of creativity: they were fully aware of the difference between creativity as value and as achievement; they were convinced that the classical work is really the center of the universe, and its attainment is the beginning of life—and aristocracy is the medium through which its light flows and finds expression. Their exaltation and emulation of the Mediterranean culture latinized English, which raised it to the status of a classical language; and the Revival of Learning in England attained eminence in literature and in philosophy. And the traditional religion was losing

50

prestige with the cultural elite, as its doctrines could hardly compete with the charm of reviving pagan thought.

The English patricians were in a voluptuous, passionate love affair with nature—with the earth and the sea and the sky around them. They were inspired by "that ancient intoxication—pride in blood": they believed in qualitative, in caste or in blood, distinctions between men— nobility and commonalty, priest and laity; as society tapered towards the top quantity became transmuted into quality; and they were characterized by a keen caste-consciousness—they took it for granted that they would always be the favored families, and the world would forever be theirs; the proprietor was a "lord", which status most nearly approximated heaven on earth; the lord never had the common touch, and he was much more than exalted—he was deified.

CHAPTER TWO—TUDOR PURITANISM: TRADE & THE REFORMATION

Feudalism in civilization was universal, and it seemed eternal. Man's hopes were identified with an afterlife: under the medieval economic scarcity conduct in this world could be only for the sake of the life to come; the emphasis on other-worldliness predicated the achievement of heavenly bliss upon self-denial in this life; the human appetites had to be subdued—there had to be the mortification of the flesh; and the traditional faith gloried in the apostolic asceticism of the disciples. The celibate clergy discouraged increase in population, and they never worked; their faith was identified with help for the poor, yet the Church was more the recipient than the dispenser of alms; they renounced the world, and many of them took the vows of poverty—"having nothing, they would gain everything"—which was identified with holiness. Economy was a matter of incidental routine: there was an attitude of insouciance towards money—it was always the servant, never the master, of man; mendicancy was an accepted way of life, and the commonalty under feudalism was traditionally settled to a condition of material minimum and spiritual maximum;

> "the church stood behind the established order and taught the villagers to be satisfied with the state to which God had called them".

Economy had been originally a struggle between man and nature, with men in basic cooperation; as man was moving towards an understanding and control of nature he was enabled to produce more of the goods of life than was required for his own individual survival, and the accumulated surplus became identified as "capital"; thus capital is concentrated labor of brain and brawn—labor is the parent of capital. This brought a development from the simple economy of the earth to the inclusion of the artificial; men began to produce wealth through "manufacture"— "artifacts", on a social scale, from which the "trader" had his origin; and trade—as an *end in itself*—was always identified with the commonalty. Land is limited in nature, and it is inherently static in economy; its expansion is extensive, and a maximum area is required for a minimum yield. Manufacture introduced a new principle—it is intensively expansive, it gets the most from the least, and its potential is illimitable. Thus artifact held forth a promise to the entire population: a condition was developing from which the common man was acquiring hitherto unprecedented economic opportunities; a brighter future was opening up for him than he had ever had in the past, and this introduced an age of hope for the members of the "vast submerged". "The People" were beginning to become economy minded: they began to think in terms of machines, skills, resources, enterprises; there was introduced the principle of the "economic man"—worker, trader, speculator; this meant commonalty liberation as its members also attained the possibility of improving their lot in life; and it brought a universal money-consciousness. The commonalty's economic appetite was whetted, and with the consistent increase in capital a general mass energy was released towards its individual accumulation; the ambition for power through economic aggrandizement—the pursuit of gain, the striving for wealth, the acquisition of the goods of life—was ceasing to be an isolated hope, and was becoming a mass mania; the idea of profit in economy as the fundamental value, the elemental urge, the all-absorbing purpose—in life, was moving towards pervasion of the realm; and this resulted in classifications known as "rich" man and "poor" man. The commonalty's aggressiveness and ambition were confined within the mart, which became the field of their keenest competition; and they concentrated all their time, mind, effort on the processing—producing, repairing, selling, shipping—of things of economic value. Thus in the time of the initial accumulation of capital, as man began to produce more of the goods of life, the field of economy was transformed from one of cooperative normal routine—the labor for mere existence, to a scramble for individual acquisition of the surplus or the accumulation of a private-property estate;

"the character of the struggle for existence changed in some degree from a struggle of the group against a non-human environment to a struggle against a human environment";

and there took place a change basically from struggle in nature to struggle in society. Nature is extensive and limited while art is intensive and unlimited, and man went from the economy of productive scarcity to that of productive reserve—he began to accumulate capital. The change from scarcity to reserve introduced a qualitative departure or new principle in the history of man.

The commonalty, which was identified with trade, was—regardless of the economic condition of its members, classed as the "third estate"; this made up the masses, among whom there were many differences— banker, master, craftsman, apprentice, laborer, beggar. Thus the great majority of the vast submerged of the kingdom, who went to make up the proletariat—constituted the base of the social cone. It is at the local level that the everlastingly human is found; and contact with the roots of life brought out the ordinary folk, "the pooralty of the realm". They concentrated their time on the commonplaces of existence, on the vital activities, which are the foundation of life—laboring, begetting, praying, fighting; and indigenous and indigent were synonymous—the men of the soil were per se identified with poverty. They were traditionally illiterate, superstitious, besotted, mentally confined to their locale, and they had little sense of time and place and of events.

Tudor Albion introduced the period of greatest religious dynamism in the history of the realm: it was the time that saw the traditional faith displaced by Anglicanism; as well as the beginnings of the commonalty move towards self-assertiveness—resulting in the succession of "Lollardy" by the "Reformation", which gave way to "Puritanism", that in time became identified as "Protestantism". The Reformation was a European movement; its English expression at first followed in the teachings of John Wycliffe, which took the form of Lollardy. With the enunciation in 1534 of England as a non-papal state Reform became legal; Lollardy as a ready existent movement immediately became identified with it, and Wycliffism took a leap forward as many latent sympathizers emerged in its support; and it was beginning to become a potent force in English life. There were, however, many Roman and Episcopal communicants who went over to the Reformation, but who

54

stopped short of Lollardy. England's Tudor queens were contemporaries of John Calvin: the Marian interlude drove many new Churchmen and Lollards to the continent, where they came under the influence of Calvinism; the accession of Elizabeth was followed by the return of the *emigres*, the majority of whom arrived as "English Genevans"; and Calvinism as a native expression began to emerge in discernible proportion from around 1565. Moreover, from 1534 there had begun a steady flow of French Huguenots to England, where it is said they brought the textile industry—and Calvinism; and there was a sudden flow of such immigration from St. Bartholomew's Eve in 1572, during the reign of Elizabeth. The exiles intended to become English, and it seems that most of them settled in East Anglia just east of London, which was the country's most populated shire, and the chief site of textile manufacture; and there was a close connection in England between Calvinism and the cloth trade. Up to the emergence of Calvinism the Reformation was synonymous with Wycliffism, which continued predominant throughout the century; and the two doctrines eventually came under the name of "Puritanism".[a] During the Tudor Reformation Puritanism was understood as a general term that included many conflicting doctrinal groups, yet it tended to certain tenets—as in contrast with Episcopacy—concerning Scripture, doctrine, church, clergy, laity. Episcopacy and "Tudor Puritanism" developed tendencies to grouping together in what came to be thought of as the Anglican Church. The emergence of "Anglicanism" found Episcopacy with its doctrines in complete organizational control, which it consistently maintained.

By the beginning of the sixteenth century the "little Isle" had not suffered an alien invasion for about half a millennium, and a practical condition of basic peace had prevailed; household manufacture was the pioneer—the backbone of industrial economy, and the productive pursuits "in the fat years of peace" had a chance fully to develop; England was always regarded by foreign visitors as economically self-sufficient, and London was reputed to be the richest city in Christendom. The medieval merchants huddled under the walls of a castle, the smithies on the lord's estate, did not see themselves as the potential architects of a society built around their own functions. Yet from during the fourteenth century the towns of the realm were rapidly becoming important: manufacture—the intensive production of the goods of life—enabled the

55

accumulation of great wealth in small areas, which promoted the town; this gave rise to the *burgher-citizen* "entrepreneur"—one who undertakes to start and conduct an economic enterprise, assuming full control and risk; and there took place a separation of home and business, as man went from domestic industry to the factory system. The bourgeoisie became interested in the use of science in the doing of the world's work: the well-informed layman, who was achieving a commercial counting-house education, was beginning to increase; there followed a rapid rise in the production of personal property, to the extent that it was becoming more important than real property; personalty is movable, which renders wealth fluid; this tended towards its diffusion among the masses, and there took place an increase in the distribution of wealth. The great towns governed themselves under a charter from the king; a few of the burghers had been knighted for loyalty and for bravery in war, yet "a tradesman hated the gentry"[1]; the towns regarded the surrounding countryside as inimical, and each of them enclosed itself in a wall, which had a gate that could be raised and lowered; yet they were consistently growing from forts or places of security to centers of population and trade; and they were firmly in the control of an oligarchy of capital. A money economy—which was fundamentally a phenomenon of trade, was noticeably modifying the feudal and manorial manner of life; the striving for money began to be considered the only worthwhile commonalty pursuit; and the consistent increase in the quantity of cash was steadily eating into feudal institutions and values, and chivalric ideals tended to become obsolete in the commercial environment. With time the capital elements used their economic power to achieve political potency, which took expression in England's Parliament as the House of Commons.

"The Tudor monarchs emphasized their power by ascending into a cloud of awe"; they had a genius for creating a modern institution with a medieval form, and they knew also how to be human. During the rule of the House of Tudor (1485-1603) England began to depart from the slowly moving world of agriculture, and to experience a social dynamism: there was a sudden increase in upward social mobility, and the introduction of important economic changes; there were rapid ebbs and flows in population—estimated at about three million—which were brought on by steps against celibacy, and by plagues, increased high seas activities, civil and foreign wars; and a move set in for the founding of overseas settlements. From King Henry VIII capital began to influence, and to move towards taking over, the social organism of the country; this tendency reached its apex under the last monarch of the Tudor Family— Elizabeth First, when there took place a definite emergence of capital accumulation and power as the bourgeoisie were developing industry, with its economic activity and expansion; and there followed a coincidental development of the mart to national proportions, together with the centralization of the state. In "Elizabethan England, that Age of towering imagination and high bold enterprise", there occurred the beginnings of basic social change: the increasing differentiation of an advancing society brought greater complexity; men were becoming sociology conscious—they were thinking in terms of a "new Society", a different way of life; the realm was swirling with, and men began to realize the explosive force of, new ideas; her people were conscious of—they were puzzled by, social problems; social dislocation brings social speculation, and from the Tudors England picked up where the Hellenes left off—she was rich with theories of the model society. During this Age there is the beginning of an awakening to the potency of the masses—"the People": with the rise of industry and the increase in wealth the vast submerged became restive as they began to feel that they count; they couldn't find satisfaction with their place in the world; they were convinced that they could not achieve improvement as within the *status quo*, and this induced them to support revolutionary movements intending to introduce changes in the pattern of social organization. The most remarkable attribute of the Age was the passion to learn new facts and methods; men for the first time were looking more to the future than to the past; there were new economic trends in production and distribution; there was a thirst for material information, as differentiated from cultural endeavor—an emphasis on practice rather than on theory; the life of action stood before the life of contemplation—of the mind, and before even the life of the soul; and they were ready to change, to experiment in anything—in what they made, ate, wore, wrote, read.

The secession from Rome and the dissolution of the monasteries had set the third estate an example of authority revolt against tradition. Puritanism was not confined to theology: it had social content—it was the religion, and also the way of life, of the masses; its protest came from below, from trade; it was brought into being, and was subsidized, by the class of entrepreneur and of the urban working population—the voiceless vastness that made up "the People", who were common folk. The commonalty as such never had an organization; it achieved an awakening through religion, and the church was the first form of its organized expression; the submerged masses struck out for themselves, and they developed vocal religious leaders—men of the Scriptures who stemmed from their own world, and with whom they were at home. The Roman theology, continued by Episcopacy, could no longer constitute the foundation of the religion, and of the way of life, especially of the town folk. The rising industrialism had brought an increase in the production, and in the distribution, of wealth; the commonalty, who didn't count under feudalism, regarded this new development as especially their opportunity, and it gave them an unprecedented sense of potency; and there began a move towards social revolution—towards the displacement of land as the foundation of the way of life. The third estate—capital, wanted to make itself the foundation of the social structure of England. As the trader way was slowly yet inexorably penetrating to the heart of the realm; as the ancient natural economy based upon land—the manor, was being supplanted by a new economy based upon artifacts—the city, industry, trade; as the feudal ties were being replaced by the cash nexus—the men of capital were concomitantly developing towards crystallization into an organized movement having sociological implications, in state (politics), church (religion), economy (property); and they became identified as Puritans. The ways and interests of capital in society are as old as civilization; Puritanism was the social expression of the third estate—it gave rise to the *rule* of capital, to the capitalistic sociology, with its own institutions and values. Trade was traditionally a means of livelihood; the Puritans were the first to see it fundamentally as also a way of life—

"the capitalistic order was a creative development of Calvinistic principles in the world of business".[2]

The development of the Reformation in England was patent proof of the rise of the commonalty. Puritanism was a theology of social change: as a sociology it had its theoretical background—its system of logically consistent thought, but it was not a philosophy; rather was it a *weltanschauung*—a world view, as it developed the values, motives, interests of the trader into a doctrine; it was a conception of spiritual life

58

and moral conduct; and the Puritans were the pioneers in the development and rise of capitalism as a social system.

It was in the days when the processes and products of science were first beginning to take on social proportion, and were becoming the world's most powerful force for social change. It was held that if man was to get the most out of the knowledge—out of the proficiency he had achieved, he would have to formulate a new way of life; the ways and the ambitions of the trader world could not be projected into the feudal landed world; and a new sociology, capitalism—of which trade would constitute the foundation, would have to be introduced. Capital had the temerity to propose the unprecedented—that there is no final type of sociology in civilization, as it is subject to various forms of such organization, and a new society could be introduced in the realm; yet the time was not without its prophets of doom, and many thought that the end of feudalism is the end of civilization—they stand and fall together. The proponents of change had acquired the values of practical efficiency; they felt that capitalism was the Logic of the Age, and that obtuseness to this stimulus could bring on mass hysteria leading to mental derangement, and ultimately even to insanity. Thus capital became a challenge to the power of land—to agrarianism, which brought a confrontation between them; their differences were qualitative and fundamental.

The trader originally engaged in his activities on the feudal lord's sufferance—on his *grace*; with the passing of the generations he began to exercise his way by *right*—of custom, which in time was strengthened also by law; and right was steadily encroaching on grace—on the paternalism, of *noblesse oblige*. Puritanism was an urban phenomenon, whose strength came from the industrious kind of people; and its devotees intended to impose the ethos of a town civilization on the entire population—to substitute urban for rural rule. The new problems could not be resolved with the old methods, and the Tudor realm was undergoing a creeping capitalism; society was being remolded by the efforts of a traditionally subordinate class—the men of money; and two distinct ways of life were in conflict as the country was moving out of medieval agrarianism and into modern industrialism. Trade in England was entirely native. The men of capital were importantly instrumental in helping to expropriate the Church: they were convinced that medieval agrarianism is inimical to the best interests of commerce; that the economic progress of the country was retarded because so much of the land was in static hands, which deprived it of its full productive potential; and that the confiscated land could be sold to private purchasers, whose concentration on this world would tend to the exploitation of the soil with a view to greater productivity and profit. The introduction of new methods in industrial production, and a consistent increase in the amount of the goods of life and in their general distribution—brought many new and complex problems, and forced drastic social changes; and trade was slowly but surely moving towards taking over the state, which would bring it opportunities it otherwise couldn't have.

When man began to manufacture surplus wealth—which introduced the beginnings of capital accumulation, a condition had been reached in which the principle of the intensive development of economy had taken root; industry was getting a maximum yield from a minimum area—and the ability to get more from less was constantly increasing. Tudor Puritanism was generative, and amorphous; it began to make itself felt on a social scale in the early years of Elizabeth, when the Englishman was beginning to engage in a struggle for profit, for the economy of wealth and power—rather than simply for survival. The kind of rules a faith enjoins is subordinate to the type of character it esteems and cultivates— "the Puritan's antipathy to the feudal way of life"; it is declared that,

"whereas the Catholic Church had taught that the person who devoted his life to money making was risking damnation, the newly rich of the 16th century came nearer to believing that prosperity was a sign of God's blessing, and that poverty was sinful".

The traders had the conviction that man has the right, and he should have also the power, to alter nature for his own benefit; renunciation of the world was never a part of their doctrine; and they developed the self-confidence to face up to reality—to the problems of life in experience. The faithful wanted utmost efficiency—the full use of the natural and human resources of the country, which they were convinced was being neglected; and they revolted against the confinement of man's basic economy to land. Their doctrine was an attempt to create the social—the institutional, and the ideological (spiritual, moral, legal)—sanctions,for the way and the rule of capital, and for the elimination of the "taint of trade"; in their scheme of things feudal relationships were being sup-

60

planted by the cash nexus, and the yellow of gold was catching up with the blue of blood.

The trader economy was based on the third estate, on the people: the entire population could participate in the life of the country; everyone was becoming property conscious, and the conviction was developing that ordinary people are also meant to be rich—they too have a stake in their country's fortunes. The mart as a mass phenomenon was a fluid quantity in ceaseless process; it was introducing the principle of economic dynamism, and stratification was regarded as stagnation. There took place an introduction of the principle of "success", which was concentrated in economy; and the *right* of the commoner to the accumulation of a private property estate or quantitative accretion, was clearly asserted. This gave the commonalty the opportunity to attain substance in the mart, they came within the atmosphere of property consciousness and rivalry, and a free-for-all condition was introduced; and the field of folk economy was transformed from one of cooperative normal routine—the labor for mere existence, to a scramble for individual acquisition of wealth.

The immemorial economic scarcity, and the suffering of the masses, had endowed the goods of life with an abnormal preciousness, and had developed in the people the inherent characteristics of selfishness and greed; their mad scramble for pelf, and the heritage of the medieval feud, brought a cut-throat competition in the trader world; and this resulted in an emphasis on material values that soon pervaded the entire social organism. The mart, which was based on the unlimited lust for wealth—money as the supreme end in itself, with its denizens and its ways, achieved free rein as it took over, and it organized and controlled, the body social; and the trader type of mind, with its ends and means, was setting its own stamp on every aspect of English society, which was making it one vast market place. This raised the mart to a position of social power and decisiveness: the heroic age of capitalism had arrived—economy was moving towards full freedom, and it was taking free rein; and trade as the foundation of life created the capitalistic sociology. Economy was the source of commonalty, of "the People's" potency; the trader's economic and political power rested on and flowed from the mart; capital ceased to be the servant as it acquired mastery, the balance of power became economic, and finance and commerce became the forces that kept society in motion. The alliance of Puritanism with the

61

masses and the principle of private property, brought capitalism—which proved invincible; capitalism was the opportunity of the common man to attain mastery in economy.

The Reformation introduced the principle of popular education. The commonalty was broadening politically from localism to the inclusion of all of the realm's inhabitants: English was acquiring the integrity of a national language; the economic upsurge—manufactures, merchandising, banking, commerce—introduced efficiency and thrift as primary values, and brought ledger responsibilities necessitating literacy in the use of the alphabet and of numerals; and printing began to be introduced into the country on a social scale. They were animated fundamentally by the universal characteristics of the trader; the Reformers' underlying motivation was in sociology, and economic activity was an ethical matter and was within the purview also of religion. Thus initiative in economy constituted the beginnings of commonalty self-expression: it created a development towards mass literacy, which began to give them a sense of accomplishment, of manliness; they began to develop, under the cover of religion, the feeling that they count; there was nothing in life to which they could not aspire, be admitted, and become an integral part of; the spiritual—the sacred, became a subjective part of the life of everyone, and each felt himself within religion, a personal participant in it, dependent upon it, and entitled to its blessings; they suddenly became flushed with a sense of power as they realized that they could be introduced even to the mysteries of sacredness—they could rival any man, including the theologian, in the knowledge, interpretation and understanding, of Holy Writ.

From time immemorial the masses had followed implicitly the spiritual and temporal authority: trade introduced a basic change in the sociological foundation; the commonalty went from nature to artifact—from land to capital, from rural origins to urban surroundings; and the Reform church, whose exponents generally stemmed from the depths, was the center around which a community developed. Urbanization—the separation of man from nature, is among the most fundamental events in all of man's history; it constituted virtually the creation of another self, of a *new* human being. This began to give the masses an unprecedented view of life, with its wants and ambitions; they were becoming proponents of a new economy, which they attempted to justify in terms of Christianity; and they were dedicated to the Biblical *Common*wealth—to

62

religion as the foundation of sociology, of life. They were becoming accustomed to a way of organizing religious life that made it adaptable to strange conditions at home—town life, factories, peaceful pursuits; as well as to life in remote continents, in primitive frontiers and forests. Thus was established the worthiness of the mass man, around whom the world gyrates—it created "the People" mystique; for the first time in history he felt himself elevated as he was drawn into the vortex of human ambitions—into the social whirlpool of the Age.

The scramble of the immemorially deprived to build a private property estate was something new; the attempt to achieve this from nothing pre-supposed the accumulation of sufficient capital for a start in an economic enterprise, and this required the concentration of the sum totality of one's being; there were no precedents to go by, and the new status of commonalty introduced new ethical standards. The Calvinistic teaching—the ambition in economy as the supreme motive—brought a planned regulation of one's life, a constant self-control, a check on the temptations of the flesh;[b] and Puritanism was identified with an austerity that shunned luxury as squanderous, as irrational use of God's gift to man—property. Wealth to the trader was a symbol of power and prestige rather than of prosperity, for he believed in maximum income and minimum expenditure—there was never a proportionate relation between them; and a policy of thrift—even of miserliness, was necessary for indigent accumulation of sufficient capital for entrepreneur investment. The Puritan mind was horrified by waste, of anything—money, goods, time, labor; idleness was a sin, and leisure was per se indolence— "you smell as if you never sweated in your life"; and trade was convinced that no man need be poor if he would only work, and that poverty is God's punishment for improvidence. And the importance of industry and labor to society came to be accepted: the mind of Englishmen was beginning to shift from winning the battle to winning the war, which was being identified with the staying power resulting from economic superiority; and it was realized that there is a qualitative difference between working in peace and fighting in war, as the first was becoming increasingly constructive, and the second increasingly destructive—the peaceful pursuits were becoming much more productive of the goods of life.

It was in the days of pre-technology, during the economy of natural scarcity.[c] Social economic endeavor was identified with competitive individual enterprise and ingenuity.[d] Private property was thought of as an extension of the person: bourgeois industry was carried on within, and primarily for, the subsistence of the household; domestic and social economy blended to constitute one's private property estate, and consumption followed hard on production. Medieval society was a federation of communities—town guilds, villages, monasteries; feudal community ownership was beginning to be replaced by individual ownership, and a development took place from a hierarchy of communities to an agglomeration of equal competing individuals. Social property was a logical development from personal property, and there was no clear-cut distinction between them; with time there followed a spacial separation of places of work from those of residence; and a move was setting in from the monastery to the factory. And people unconsciously took it for granted that the principle of private ownership in the personal property of the household economy may be extended to include the socially necessary economic complex, that the corporate business enterprise may be understood as within the meaning of one's personal private property estate. There was an emphasis on the material values: the value of a desideratum was determined by its availability; the acquisition of the objects of private property became the supreme ambition; wealth—the goods of life, was at a premium, and its possession was the primary mark of success; and personal independence was identified with domination in business enterprise.

Man's supreme value is never quantitatively final—no one ever has "enough" of what he gives his life to—his grasp always exceeds his reach; the greed for gold, the mania for money, has always been an uncontrollable impulse, and is as old as civilization. There were a few supermen of capital always everywhere during pre-technology—in the economy of scarcity: they were mostly natives of the particular country, while a few were foreign; they stood beyond good and evil, and theirs was a worldlier-than-thou philosophy of life. Their purpose was ruthless acquisition—of gold, the precious, life-giving metal, of money for its own sake—through cold-blooded, calculated rationalization; they were heartless—without a sense of sin, were bound to no ethical norms, considered the ethical appeal naïve, had no place for the human element. But their way was alien to the world they lived in—they were only individuals; they existed on sufferance within a traditionally established social milieu that was based on land, the agrarian way of life—feudalism. From the time of King Croesus there have been few viruses as virulent as gold fever; and to the manorial mind usury—the way of the money-lender, appeared as "the pound of flesh". The usurers did *take* "the pound of flesh", but they also *paid* with it: they were isolated, and were regarded as an essentially strange, hostile element; they were separated from the mainstream of life, as they were ethically quarantined—detested, shunned, and at times subjected even to physical assault; and their tendencies to unrestricted adventurism were effectively controlled.

In England the third estate—capital, wanted to make itself the foundation of the country's social structure: under the Tudors the trader had gained political power and, for the first time anywhere in history, he was moving from an isolated condition towards the taking over of the entire social organism—towards achieving the mastery of a potent realm; he had a positive practical program—the capitalistic sociology, with its own institutions and values, its own ways and its own ethical maxims for the conduct of life—with which he could supplant tradition.[e] There was a fundamental difference between the trader under feudalism, and under his own sociology; between his attitude as an individual capitalist existing by grace in an alien social milieu, and his expression of a self-assertive attitude—by right, which stemmed from the ethics of a way of life existing in his own kind of world, where he had a sense of belonging and felt at home. There was a vast increase in the opportunities for the satisfaction of the acquisitive instincts in economy under capitalism, and more people could acquire more of the goods of life than ever before.

In times of basic social change a departure from traditional ways takes place, and there is a transitional period from old to new values; nobody is certain whether given patterns of conduct are right, and for many people the ethical changes appear like deterioration—a drop in morals; the dissolution of the monasteries took the principle of sanctuary with it, and material quantitative values began to replace the spiritual qualitative values; and the introduction in England of the cash nexus—the substitution of economic for feudal ties, created a state of bewilderment and confusion. An unprecedented mammonism gripped the Tudor realm, and this reached its apex in the Elizabethan Age—whose real god was gold. There were the evils of the cash nexus, which were especially accentuated in its beginnings: money became the foundation of power,

65

prestige, euphoria; the love of money expressed itself as the master, rather than as the servant, of man; and a condition of economic competition resulted, which developed as a form of social strife. The mind of the entrepreneur was solely on profit; human values became universally economic, as living rights were subordinated to property rights; the cash nexus was often disguised with spiritual pride—God appeared as tradesman; and men were power hungry rather than constructive. The person caught up in the realities of the money power and the market—with the resultant state of mind, could not be much concerned about the welfare of others: the evil in man, especially the tendency to greed, was emphasized; there was an introduction of the proposition that "time is money"; the attitude of cold, calculated exploitation—the mind to use, to get the most for the least, top production at bottom cost—became a general social condition; this brought an attitude of rationalization towards everything, including human beings—"they make tallow out of cattle, and money out of men"; and there arose references to "blood money". The market was a place where people were permitted to deceive one another: the sophisticated were taking advantage of the insouciant; the exploitation of one's fellows, mart-craft-sharpness, cheating, gouging, was regarded as a mark of mental superiority; individual aggrandizement in economy took the place of social responsibility, and even professional service did not exist for its own sake as it became incidental to lucre.

They moved from the physical brutality of the warrior to the conniving selfishness of the trader; and the callousness of the Age was transferred from the feuding battlefield in the countryside to the market-place in the town—the mart was an arena of amoral competition. Wealth and virtue were regarded as antipathetic: men tried to reap where they had not sown—to move from poverty to riches was per se to travel the road of iniquity; the trader, like the warrior, could not always practice restraint—the ways of the mart were separate from and beyond ethical consideration. The poet Goethe said;

"The man of action is always ruthless; no one has a conscience but an observer."

It is declared that,

"Elizabethan times disclose a moral decay in all classes which can hardly be paralleled in English history".[3]

And the Age was tolerant of frailties;

"A man esteemed worthy in Tudor times could . . . rob his neighbours by legal chicanery, take bribes in the performance of public duties, fawn and flatter with complete insincerity, burn his fellows for rejecting a creed, or hang them for necessity of state. Such things the Age allowed . . ."[4]

Public office per se included many rights and privileges, and was regarded as a form of property subject to purchase and sale; there was uncertainty concerning the ethics of office-holding, which created problems of pluralism—the owning of several places simultaneously, and of the exercise of non-resident or absentee official power.

Puritans were showing a greater sophistication in business undertakings than their fellow countrymen, and a few were growing rich beyond even the dreams of avarice. The opulence of Elizabethan men of capital was reflected in the constant activity and bustle in economy—the 'buzz and hum', the noise, color, clamor, of daily city life, especially in the seaports: the naïvete of the countryman was being replaced by the cunning of the townsman—"our cities are monuments to greed", and theirs was the wisdom born of the streets; the appetite of man in the economy of scarcity—before the machine displaced him as the unit of laboring and fighting—was insatiable; and 'the earthly first mover—money, money, money'!—cold, hard "coin of the realm"—became the most potent single element of power, on the accumulation of which people concentrated their lives. The trader existed for his business, rather than the other way; his business was the *raison d'etre*, the sustenance—of his family, for which he was ready "to work his fingers to the bone"; it was more important to him than his own blood and limb, and even than his life.

During pre-technology man lived either in the "country" or in the "town": these places were thought of as in contrast, rather than as complementary; there were sharp differences in the psychology of those who lived from land, and of those who lived from trade; the one was characterized by a naturalness, naïveté, insouciance—while the other

67

had developed a sophistication or world wisdom; and the man of the soil was land bound—he was rooted, while the town dweller was free to migrate, to be itinerant. The discovery of the turnip as a cheap winter feed for sheep enabled their large scale breeding; there was a developing export market for wool and its products; and this brought the enclosure laws—the turning of arable into pasture, which drove labor from the countryside into the towns—the existence of which provided an outlet, and enabled the mass separation from nature. The move towards urbanization created a tendency to the commercialization of agriculture: the raising of produce simply for local subsistence was expanded to include its sale in the town markets—farming for profit; wool was taken from the sheep's back, processed into cloth and packed into the merchant's warehouse—and these steps brought industrial employment, which tended to offset the hardships resulting from the separation from the soil; and England's economy was concentrated on agriculture in the countryside and weaving in the towns. Thus England was the pioneer in the mass movement from the country to the town; the enclosure laws had social revolutionary significance—they constituted the aggression of trade against traditional land.

It is said that man has accomplished far more that is good and great with the profit motive than without it, yet in basic social change the evil is more immediate and visible than the good: the man of nature regarded the man of artifact as denatured—as condemned to dysfunction, or to a condition of mental and physical deformity; the conventional values of feudalism continued to dominate the social atmosphere—the men and the ways of the land were regarded as respectable, and those of the mart as reprehensible. Tradition saw the bourgeoisie as the emergence of an alien interest, which applied sordid means to the pursuit of anti-social ends: land thought that the rise of the trader had introduced an unsavory chapter in the history of man; the relations of men were in terms of the cash nexus, and were comparable to those of "wolves snarling over carrion"; men began to inquire into the principles by which human society is distinguished from a pack of wolves; life was confined to the mart, and the martman was regarded as a covetous, petty-minded person of cheap extraction who could not see life beyond his stall; the concentration on profit was narrowing and ignoble, as it excluded principle, idealism, honor—and it was held that the mart displaced spiritual and cultural values for material ones; and "trader" and "pedlar" were terms of

68

opprobrium. The pursuit of profit was always cynically regarded even by the denizens of the mart, when they used phrases like "filthy rich", "mean end". The insouciant, carefree mind of land was replaced by the trader's ledger, or budget type of mind—assets and liabilities; and the landed feudal qualitative caste society where men held by grace, was being transformed by revolutionary capital into the quantitative class society where men own by right. The development of the capital economy resulted in a society with bourgeois characteristics—such as graduated income and wealth, and the rise of new classes with conflicting economic interests; and class relations were moving towards fluidity.

In pre-technology—especially under feudalism, and also throughout the better part of capitalism—man was the most efficient source of labor power, which made it predominantly human; the social conditions rendered labor essentially coerced, and it was inherently discontented. The proletarian activity of the time took three forms: "husbandry", endeavor in relation to the living thing—animal and plant, to help it be fruitful and multiply; "labor", simple physical economic effort in daily routine; and "work", artisanship, which tends to creativity—workmanship is instinctive, and is more or less present in all men.

The sociology of medieval feudalism was inherently static—everything was rooted: there was no place within it for the free landless individual; and the status in relation to the land, of labor especially, had to be stratified. The existence of a class of people whose status is temporary and changing was feared for its socially disturbing implications. In the agrarian economy brute labor can be very profitable: the skilled worker is a small minority, and efficiency is not a primary value; there is a relative absence of a sense of time, the worker goes about his tasks with a certain amount of leisure, there is no strict separation between work and play, and no limit is necessary on the daily hours of work. Thus everyone was leisurely: there was an atmosphere of insouciance—of economic indifference; labor tended to a lackadaisical attitude; they had many holidays, and men worked no more than they had to as they led a hand to mouth existence; and they tended to idleness, and to frolicsome boisterousness.

Under feudalism a line could be drawn between mastery and labor, while under capitalism the one shaded into the other. The new order was faced with problems of labor discipline; the poor in the towns found themselves separated from the land, and they were forced to work through fear of starvation. The attempt to pull the masses out of the apathy of tradition had to be based on divine stimulus; religion had to be the purpose, and the goods of life the reward, behind the drive to elicit mass economic ambition and energy. Their comatose tendencies were eliminated by rationalization, which eventually brought a sense of responsibility; and there began the development of labor regularity or routine habits of work. Under the use economy efficiency and skill became primary values: wage labor takes the place of serf labor because manufacture requires forethought and care, which cannot be exercised without a promise of reward and presupposes worker training; and the worker must concentrate mentally in making an article, and he is handling high-priced and dangerous tools. And the commonalty folk were developing skills through the specialization of occupation, the division of labor—whose performance at times required strength, and even courage—and was beginning to be regarded as "working"; the move from laboring to working was a move from mindless drudgery towards creativity, and the workingman began to be identified with individuality and ability—some craftsmen were better than others; and there was always a shortage of specialized workers, so that colonial ventures had to import foreign skills. Under the new way work and play were strictly separated; there could be an introduction of speed-up, which tends to feverishness; and the daily hours of work had to be limited because the absence of relaxation induces fatigue. And the vast submerged began gradually to rise out of their condition of servility; the individual was developing the right and the freedom to bargain and to contract for, to sell, his labor power—he was moving towards achieving mastery of his person. The free hired status, working for wages in cash rather than in kind—was the height of labor ambition; and the skilled worker was beginning to acquire social value and human rights as his indispensability and difficulty to replace eventually enabled him to wrest concessions from the world he lived in.

When a social revolution brings an abrupt change from one way of life to another, a transitional period is inevitable: the worst features such upheavals always entail—the destruction of the old, accepted ways of doing things before the establishment of the new, with their brutal dislocation and moral deterioration—had to be borne by those at the bottom of the social edifice; they were the victims of the economic

70

advance that was making the fortunes of their betters. The societal foundation went from theology to economy, from the temple to the mart: the shift from land to trade, from feudalism to capitalism—disrupted the paternalism, the sense of social responsibility inherent in baron and bishop, and substituted the emphasis on the self-reliance of Puritanism. There had taken place a transition from the patriarchal unit of communal production to the capitalistic enterprise in the town, which created an antithesis between the individual and the community. This brought a move from spiritual to material values: with the church lands falling into lay hands the paternalistic attitude of traditional religion towards husbandry disappeared; and the atmosphere of sacredness was removed from everyday life, as it became confined simply to the church. There followed a tendency towards the rationalization of labor; the elimination of dedicated celibacy increased the population; and some commodities were cheaper as imports than as home manufacture; all of which resulted in increased unemployment and destitution. The countrymen were very much out of place and unhappy in town life, to which they had to adjust themselves; the security of the masses was immemorially based on complete subordination, and there was an initial fear of responsibility among them due to their poverty-ridden tradition, with its debilitating effects—their lack of capital, education, self-confidence. The mass shift of people from the land to the town brought on by enclosure instantly deranged the traditional means of coping with pauperism. The towns could not immediately absorb the sudden influx of migrants, who could not easily adjust their lives from a natural setting to the artifacts of the town. Man was immemorially planted in the soil; separation from the soil was humanity uprooted, and the masses without leaders were without value; all of which gave rise to the derelict—the people without a community, the social outcasts, the "masterless men". The parish—the local community, broke down as a unit of social security; there could be no substitute for traditional welfare until the new problem crystallized to the extent that it could be recognized and properly dealt with; and this gave rise on a mass scale to anti-social conduct—to crime, vice, vagrancy, beggary; and economic destitution claimed far more fatalities than executions. The responsibility for the relief of pauperism was thus transferred from the medieval local welfare parish to the Tudor welfare state, and it was declared that "Villeinage ceases but the Poor Laws begin". And the entrepreneur values had not yet fully pen-

71

etrated the masses; there was a tendency to indictment of feudal attitudes in terms of capital ways; and what appeared to the Puritans as organized parasitism existed at both ends of the social edifice—indolent favorites at the top, and charity paupers at the bottom.

The decline of feudalism and the rise of the cities tended to the tapering of paternalism: displaced labor followed from its serf status in the countryside to the hired system in the town; Puritanism's emphasis on the dignity of labor encouraged individual tendencies to self-reliance—to sobriety, orderliness, diligence, thrift, even to ingenuity. A reformation also was going on in land: the change from the manorial to the capital domination was a development which introduced a qualitative departure—new principles, in sociality; it was a move from caste blood family relations, to economic relations or the cash nexus; a new world was being born from the womb of the old. There was a tendency to the commercialization of agriculture, and the raising of produce was expanded to include its sale in the town markets—farming for profit. The feudal and the capital laboring economic routine in the land during pre-technology was basically the same. But the mental attitudes were wholly different: under the capital way the denizens of the land were developing "rights" in relation thereto leading towards the fee simple title in individual tract-owning; and the values—their hopes and ambitions, were towards the achievement of independence and self-assertiveness. And a condition had developed that actually emboldened some men to act as individuals—to go off on their own; but most of them still needed a master to give them orders and relieve them of initiative and responsibility.

During the days of the baronial feuds a general condition of economic insouciance, and of lawlessness, had prevailed throughout the realm among all classes, and nobody was secure in his property; in addition, trade had always been an object of landed contempt, and respect for trader property was not easily come by. With the achievement of intensive expansion and the developing ability to produce wealth through working the necessity for extensive expansion through fighting, retaliatory spoliation—the right to private warfare of feudal knights—disappeared. The Battle of Crecy marked the end of the knight in armor: the castle was the nucleus of the medieval social organization; the appearance of artillery firepower, which resulted from the development of manufactures, neutralized the castle. The realm was moving from a

72

condition of feuding disruption and poverty to "the fat years of peace"—to a state of basic harmony, which brought prosperity; the more general distribution of property tended towards the establishment of a condition of social stability; and the men of the land were becoming aware of the challenge of capital, which gave them a community of interest. Hunting and fighting for economic aggression were beginning to be denounced as predatory—men were using force to reap where they had not sown. The principle of arbitration was eliminating the decision by arms, which tended to undermine the cult of heroes. With the rise of urban economic power and the consequent rural recession there was a move from the last castles to the first factories; the rule of law and order came to be preferred, as the arena of conflict—the feud, was transferred from the battlefield to the court room, from military generals to civil lawyers; and the habit of litigation succeeded the brutality of physical imposition. Thus under feudalism the tendency to acquisitiveness was confined to a few at the top for additional realty, while under capitalism it was open to all the people—the many were in a competition for money. Private warfare was outlawed, but the lords continued feuding until the social conditions resulting in such activity were substantially eliminated. And domestic peace descended upon England as there took place a definitive cessation of conflict within land, and the country ceased to be feud ridden; from the sixteenth century housing began to be thought of more in terms of comfort than of defense; and energies were henceforth to be expended in working in peace.

Trade was becoming empowered, and it could stop at nothing in order to achieve respect for its place in the world. The Puritans, especially the *parvenu* among them, developed a mystical reverence for the rights of private property, which brought a sharp consciousness of the distinction between the community—and private ownership. They became the pioneers in the new rational analysis of the laws of wealth—the trader worship of mammon, thinking confined to money, the ledger, the budget; they understood state and church as protecting property rights before living rights; and the principle of divine right was transferred from royalty to property. That the rich have a right to rule the poor was a law of nature, and of God; and the idolatry of, and the idealization as a virtue of the habit of mean subservience to, wealth and social position—became the accepted standard of conduct.

73

The increase in the production of wealth under capitalism could have resulted either in its equal distribution among the people, which would have brought a condition of mass sufficiency—or, in the concentration of wealth in the hands of a few for crystallization into capital for expansion investment. The latter condition—productive abundance and distributive scarcity—fundamentally prevailed; wealth distribution was far from proportionate, and a condition of mass poverty continued to exist as the great majority of the people remained on a minimum subsistence level; all of which tended to the perpetuation of the class or vertical form of social organization.

Yet a goodly number of commonalty did rise economically more or less—a few even skyrocketed, which created a class of *nouveaux riches*; and the new way was feeding more people better. Money became the measure of all things, which empowered the banker: capital has its ethical implications; the difference between "interest" and "usury" in mathematics is quantitative; in morals it is qualitative. Land is definitely limited in area and in its number of owners, and it is inherently static; the application of interest here can be exacting, or per se usury. Artifact is intensively expansive and dynamic, its potential is illimitable, and it can be within the ambition of the entire population; thus interest here is generally applicable, and it can always be proportionate to the increase in productivity; and Calvinism thought it legitimate for people to invest their money at fair and equitable interest. The love of money as applied to land was the root of all evil, yet as applied to manufacture it was the source of wealth, of social prosperity. And there were differences in economy between personal enterprise and corporate investment: during the initial Puritan way the source of income in industrial endeavor was chiefly from personal enterprise and work, rather than from corporate forms of organization or impersonal capital investment; and the attitude of paternalism—of personal contact and understanding, did generally prevail in owner and labor relations. And as capitalism tended towards depreciation of qualitative, and towards rise in quantitative, differences between men—the glaring economic disparities rendered them objectively conscious of what appeared as inequitable distribution, which encouraged the development of social thought and thinkers—inequity began to be regarded as iniquity. Capitalists contributed towards the sharing of wealth or economic justice through social philanthropy—

74

"beggars . . . gave the person of means opportunity for good works through giving alms".

And the development of anti-social conduct on a mass scale did force a measure of increase in distribution.

NOTES

aThe Reformation was a much greater influence in Anglo-America than in England.

bPuritan abstinence is not to be confounded with the asceticism of traditional monastery other-worldliness—the hermit, the recluse. The monk of religion never had gold; the trader of the mart had gold, but he didn't want to part with it; both existed in economic austerity, but for wholly different reasons.

cBefore the planned curtailment of production and the destruction of existing wealth, so as to create an artificial scarcity in order to continue the values of the past.

dMuch that is now mechanical was then human; development in economy towards intricate socially organized cooperative experimentation confined to scientifically trained personnel, and requiring time, effort, expense—was in the future.

eYet it was not until England's Glorious Revolution of 1689 that capital succeeded in definitively winning a powerful state, and introducing fully its own way; and money as a remorseless monomania acquired social proportions.

75

CHAPTER THREE—RELIGION: ANGLICANISM; EPIS-COPACY & REFORM

The Bible was written and compiled in a time and place before the introduction of the principle of rational thinking—systematic classification, analysis and synthesis—and logical consistency was not a value. The Old Testament is a history[a] of the ancient Jews; each of its books is a conglomerate presentation of the life of the time—how people labored, loved, prayed, fought. The dissolution of the Roman Empire eliminated the Caesar principle—the monolithic State, and a multiplicity of petty principalities took its place; and as the State ceased to be a decisive force in Europe it was supplanted by the Church, and the princelings ruled by the grace of God—through permission, express or implied, of the Papacy.

Pre-Renaissance Europe was a solidly frozen theocracy; she was under the rule of the clergy, the theologians of an ecclesiastical organization—the Roman Catholic Church, which had been so endowed by God. Religion was the containing vessel of her sociology—feudalism, which was a Christian civilization whose ideological atmosphere was spiritual, not secular; everything in the life of man was within the Bible, within the covenant with God; and the medieval social organism was an institutional compound. The direction and guidance which religion gives society and the individual under theocracy are complete: it conditioned its people so that they had a subjective attitude towards their social organism, and they lived their lives normally in terms thereof; and they could not form a concept of difference between Church and State, nor of the co-existence of several religious denominations within the same community. The feudal society was to comprise a monolithic body of believers—there was no place for "heretics". The jurisdictional monism enhanced the disciplinary elements of the divine state, which insured the effectual operation of the Will of God in the life of the people.

With time there became noticeable the beginnings of a popular consciousness—an adumbration, of interests in sociality that were different and separate from the Church; men were developing an awareness of society as divisible into institutions—state, economy, family, school, defense; and the social institution State was becoming self-assertive towards the Church. Yet the Will of God continued as law eternal and immutable; all the inhabitants—authority ecclesiastical and civil, ultimately derive their rights and powers from, and are responsible to, God.

ANGLICANISM: EPISCOPACY

The Occidental peoples north of the Alps never knew civilization without Christianity; the native of western Europe implicitly accepted certain tenets as basic in his religion; there was only one understanding of the Christian Godhead—that taught by the Roman Catholic Church. This religion had established and maintained for well over a millennium a theological and institutional uniformity throughout England, a realm that was organized in all other respects on the principle of local autonomy. Feudalism was the immemorial way of life: the Church was centralized—she was a practical monolith, the Mother of social institutions; and government, economy, school, defense, were decentralized. The Papal supremacy was firmly entrenched; religion—"the age-old implicit faith", was more powerful than nationality, the English were primarily conscious of themselves as Christian, and as Catholic they were under foreign domination. However, a new world had been opened up by learning, science, discovery: the Renaissance had created a tendency to skepticism throughout the cultural centers of the western world concerning the sacred theology of Christianity; there developed a good deal of cynicism in powerful places within the Roman Church—a tendency to regard its fundamental teachings as myth. This caused concern among the devout, who felt that the revival of learning had led many of the faithful away from Christ.

John Wycliffe, who lived in the fourteenth century—"professor at Oxford . . . the greatest scholar of the age"—was the ideological forerunner of a movement that spread throughout Europe, and became known as the ''Reformation''; it is declared that,

''in England with Wycliffe the Reformation had begun and spread thence to all the world'';[5]

Wycliffe became the articulate head of a definitive revolt against the Papacy; and he gave rise to a movement in his country identified as ''Lollardy''. With the spread of the Reformation the doctrine of Erastianism, the principle of the domination of the Church by the State—including even in ecclesiastical affairs, began to grip the mind of many people. And from the early days of this movement there began a series of Statutes of Premunire, which tended to make it a crime for an Englishman to acknowledge any foreign authority whatever as higher than that of the Crown. This involved questions such as: may the civil power invade the ecclesiastical sanctuary for the apprehension of escaped criminals? can the Pope order the imprisonment of Englishmen in their own homeland? should money leave the country for the Papacy? The economic restiveness of the commonalty was having serious effects on their religious thinking; with the passing of the generations the ideological heirs of Wycliffe—the Lollards, were beginning to make themselves felt; they were developing a strong, determined following especially in the towns; some of the masters of industry had acquired sufficient economic power to enable their achievement of municipal control, and even of membership in the House of Commons; and many of them and their apprentices were fanatically pre-disposed to anything anti-Papal.[b] And whatever the Crown's relations with the Papacy at the end of the fifteenth century may have been, a profound change in the ecclesiastical *status quo* in England was inevitable.[c] From around the beginning of the next century a trend was rapidly developing towards the displacement of theology by economy as the foundation of the realm's sociology. The mass mind was definitely moving in a new—in an untried, direction.

The dawn of the sixteenth century found England in a condition of confrontation between two sociological extremes, both of which operated within religion—the Church representing the interests of land, against the Lollard movement representing the interests of capital. The doctrines of John Wycliffe seemed to the ancient faith to be both heresy

78

and anarchy; they appeared as anti-Christ, or the denial of the Christian faith; and they implied the complete subversion of the social structure—in fact, of the world as it had been known in England throughout her civilization. During the century and a half of Lollardy its adherents were outlawed, and they led an underground existence. As the hostile ideologies were approaching a showdown (which was taking place on the continent) the king Henry VIII took steps to avoid civil war: he moved towards compromise by repudiating Rome in 1534, which brought into being the "Church of England"; and this stimulated a reciprocal move from the Lollards when they identified themselves with the new Church. And during the ferment anent the Reformation religion ceased to be the societal containing vessel, as it was supplanted by economy. The principle of church and state as *compound* was succeeded by the principle of state and church as *union*, temporal power belongs only to laymen, spiritual power only to clergy—the theologian is to make, the Crown is to enforce, Church law; and in the event of an impasse the supremacy of the State in ecclesiastical affairs prevails.

Henry VIII—"a despot who had no superior on earth"—is among the most capable crowned heads in the history of the world. He was a man of superb executive ability: he was an ultra realist—he saw through the mists of political intrigue to the great issues that governed the fate of nations; and he had a thorough knowledge of the condition of his country, and of the mind of his countrymen. His statesmanship was to avoid extremes by holding the balance; and his was a minimum of pressure and a maximum of tact—he donned the lion's skin, or the fox's, with invincible elan. Henry VIII had been born, baptized and brought up a Roman Catholic; he was the Defender of the Faith—he was loyal to Rome. However, the Union of the Roses in 1485 had signaled the development of trade to the extent that it was beginning to become a factor in English economy and government; the people of the industrial towns had risen to their greatest economic and political power—a few had achieved the status of "merchant princes"; and this brought an opposition to ecclesiastical supra-nationalism that became irresistible. Institutions based on archaic ideas share the fate of all organic things which are kept too long; they reflect past reality, are overtaken by events, and become essentially fossilized; and excesses are inevitable whenever customs survive beyond the age for which they were designed, and are

79

forced into activity long after the time has passed for which they were suited.

King Henry VIII introduced a new principle: before 1534 England was a theocracy, a sociological compound; with the separation from Rome there was introduced the principle of the union—as differentiated from the fusion, of state and church—each became an institutional identity in its own right, and they came together for their mutual benefit. The king continued to rule directly by the grace of God—the potency of the state superseded that of the church, and the crown dominated the mitre. The state could regulate the church if it brought forth inimical tenets, but the church alone was concerned with problems of heresy; religion prosecuted the heretic, while government punished him.

The king accepted and continued the traditional faith—Christianity, and the inherited basic principles identified with it—theology, Church, clergy, laity; yet he was astute enough to sense the potency of the new development while it was still amorphous; he evidently felt that he must guide social change or be its victim; several entire jurisdictions on the continent had been taken over by the Reformation, and he knew that an attempt to stand in its way at home would commit the realm. The king therefore tried to forestall the trend to religious anarchy coming from below by taking over its leadership; since he couldn't drive the mass mind he decided to lead it; a few of the top *nouveau riche* were admitted into the aristocracy, and preferred to positions of national political power; the "base-born" Thomas Cromwell was the first man of capital in the history of England to reach the top, in 1533—to be suffered in the shadow of royalty; and sociological changes were,

> "no matter of disputed religious dogma, but facts altogether independent of the truth about trans-substantiation or the divine origin of the primacy of the Roman See";

and the rank and file of the embattled economic commoners were happy to have royal support. All of which culminated in 1534 in Parliament's ready enactment, in cooperation with the king, of what is the most fundamental *coup d'etat* in history—the Act of Royal Supremacy, which severed all relations of the country's spiritualty from Rome. The Pope was denounced as "anti-Christ": the political aspects of the faith—

traditionally regarded as of divine inspiration, were alleged "human invention"; the Roman supremacy was declared "a monstrous usurpation"; and all Papal authority in England was repudiated as it was endowed in the king.

> "Parliament had acknowledged that Henry VIII, King of England was—without any qualification at all—immediately under Christ Supreme Head on earth of the English Church; it had also recognized in him the sole authority to appoint bishops, to control all ecclesiastical legislation, all religious order, all marriages".
> "The act of parliament of 1534 made the king pope in England".[6]

Thus Henry VIII forged and maintained a unity of purpose; he organized the state, reduced the feudal nobility to order, rallied the gentry and the bourgeoisie about the Crown, attached the Church to the monarchy, asserted English independence. His attitude toward religion seemed to be that of the freethinker Pope Leo X, who in 1521 conferred on Henry the title of "Defender of the Faith"; and Socinus and Servetus, also contemporaries of England's greatest monarch, were making an impression in Europe with their deistic teachings. The king and his court, the lords both spiritual and temporal—were evidently carried away by the emphasis on rationalism and the spirit of paganism of the Renaissance; and in addition to alterations in Church organization, the king made modifications, changes, and even some erasures, in theology—by *edict*. The English Lutheran Dr. Barnes, whom Henry burned at the stake, had told Martin Luther, "My king does not care about religion".[7] All classes in England at the time had their differences with Rome: the principle of Erastianism became the cornerstone of Tudor policy; the Crown, and eventually Parliament, required all Englishmen to belong to and support the Established Church; the Elizabethan Bishop Aylmer declared, "God is English";[8] spiritual integrity in its own right seemed non-existent, and sacred theology was tampered with as it became subject to political expediency.

> "In the reign of King Henry VIII almost the whole kingdom,

81

bishops, prelates, and learned men innumerable, renounced the faith and the authority of the Pope at a single word from the tyrant'';[9]

and they took with them the country's predominantly illiterate commonalty masses. The king was supported by England's leading universities; as statesman he responded to ''the pull of the future'', and Henry VIII was the pioneer in the introduction of the post-biblical age. Churchmen in this era were the normal advisers of monarchs: to do this successfully they had to be thoroughly versed in the ways of the world;[d] and they were generally not above ''the pious fraud''—the higher clergy of nascent Anglicanism were primarily statesmen rather than spiritual leaders.

Royal Supremacy was postulated as a purely political matter—it was not a subject in sacred theology: in substituting the crown for the mitre Henry had the self-assurance to defy the Holy See; he renounced the principle that the Pope is by divine right the earthly head of the Church of God—which had constituted the foundation of Christianity for a millennium and a half. Nascent Anglicanism—the Church of England, denounced some features of the traditional worship as superstition and idolatry; many of the Roman practices regarded as sacred are not ordained in Scripture; and it held that the pure teachings of Christianity are contaminated, often even clouded, by banal conceptions. Moreover, it was alleged that the Roman Church services were conducted in Latin, which gave them an aura of mystery and awe—and this rendered the church atmosphere unintelligible to the worshipers, and kept them in the status of passive participants; there was an illiterate identification of divinity with objects apprehended by the senses—with images; there was the tendency to worship the Pope and the Church, rather than to worship God and Christ; and it denounced all external acts of contrition as entirely futile and without spiritual significance, maintaining that they really obscure the fundamental precepts of Christianity. In addition, the Royal Supremacy asserted its right to detect and denounce alleged theological doctrine as heresy—which did not exclude the Pope and his works; and to inflict the capital penalty on offenders. Economic improvement had introduced a feeling of confidence as it tended to ease shortage: the need for population control declined; and in view of the flagrant abuse of celibacy there was an elimination of the doctrine of the ''sins of the flesh'', and Anglicanism did not require such vows from its clergy. And

82

it abolished confinement to Latin in the church services as it introduced the Book of Common Prayer, which is "common" in the sense that it is in the mother tongue—in the vernacular, and everyone understands what is transpiring.

The principle of the English church preceded that of the English nation. With the Tudor secession from Rome the religion of governed nativity emerged as a princely, no longer as a priestly, affair—it seemed that a caesaro-papistical potentate had been created; deification of the monarchy gave the sovereign the right to determine the religion of his subjects, and all alike were required to worship God according to the dictates of the state. All Papal pronouncements were to be ignored, whether political—anathema, ex-communication; or theological—doctrinal interpretation, ministerial sacrament. And no one was allowed to exercise any ecclesiastical office outside of the new regimen with all of its implications. The monarch as both king and pope put state and church under one head: yet the immemorial feudal hierarchical structure precluded an equality in the status of the two institutions; the tendency had been consistently towards Erastianism—the political domination of the ecclesiastical, towards putting the potency of the state before that of the church, and the crown dominated the mitre. Thus there was the elimination of the Pope, but not of popery; his majesty had priestly, and seemingly even divine, attributes—to be king of the English was to possess a supernatural power that God gave to no one else; and to deny the principle of Royal Supremacy in matters ecclesiastical was to court charges of treason. With the Crown as the supreme arbiter—the last word, in the realm of all spiritual as well as of temporal causes, the clergy was taken from under the rule of the canon law and rendered subject to the common law and to lay jurisdiction.

The Reformation shattered the religious doctrinal and institutional unity of the realm; but the temper of the Age still wanted truth in terms of absolute certainty, and the English continued implicitly to expect a unity and order in their country, all of which they associated with religion. The inherited Roman Church theology and structure were largely maintained, and they constituted a pattern for the foundation of the Church of England; yet although the new religion's emergence from tradition lent it a measure of cognition, Christianity in England was for all practical purposes in an amorphous condition—it was ideologically little better than one vast cloud formation; and the vicissitudes of its formative period, especially the Marian interlude, kept it sufficiently nebulous for all those with an anti-Papal bias to identify themselves with it. Thus in the earlier years of separation a tendency to derangement in the uniformity of the past was inevitable, which brought confusion and uncertainty; more than a generation was required for the Church of England to achieve especially doctrinal crystallization—a clear, distinct identity as such; it did not really do so until towards the end of the Tudor era, and in the meantime it could be no practical substitute for the old faith.

The ideological shapeless mass that constituted Christianity in sixteenth-century England was, very slowly over the decades, beginning to tend towards an organizational congealment sufficient for the discernment of "Episcopacy", whose supporters came chiefly from the landed and ecclesiastical hierarchy, and who were anxious to preserve most of the past; and of the "Reformation", whose protagonists came from the third estate—from "the People", or the trader and labor elements in the realm. Yet although Christianity had its vicissitudes of doctrinal and institutional expression from 1534, its answers to the problems of life and death were areas of basic agreement among all its adherents. They believed that there is a God, a beneficent Intelligence in the universe—Whom they regarded as transcendent, rather than as immanent; God is not a Being Who can be set over against other beings, but Being itself; and they understood Him in terms of the Holy Christian Trinity—Father, Son and Holy Ghost. God created the world, and He created man—whom He put on earth; God alone is free, subject to no law; He is involved in, He is not detached from, the world—He takes an interest in man's doings on earth; there is divine intervention in the affairs of man—"the life of God is the soul of man"; God is the fountain of all truth, and in His light alone can man fully understand himself and the possibilities of his existence.

Episcopacy inherited the Christian religion: it intended to continue to hold fast to the immemorial tradition of Throne and Altar—to the union of State and Church, and to conduct itself in terms of the divine revelation of the Hebraic Scriptures as interpreted and understood by the Roman theology; and the clergyman continued as priest, having qualitative superiority to the laity. And after the Church of England's separation from the Papacy, she began to modify the traditional theology by her acceptance of the doctrines of Arminianism. Yet the emphasis of Christianity on philosophy had been going on for some decades before the

84

break with Rome, and Episcopacy inherited the atmosphere of the Renaissance from Mother Church. Hellenism is dedicated to the principles of rationalism—the confidence in the ability of man to achieve an understanding of the world through thinking; of humanism—the exaltation of man; and of naturalism—the appreciation of, and the curiosity about, nature; and the Greeks were concentrated on an attempt to understand the good, which is ethical—the beautiful, physical—and the true, metaphysical. Episcopacy, which was in consistent control of the new Church, accepted the Hellenic classical discipline, and with the expulsion of the Jesuits from the country the patronage of the Renaissance received an even greater emphasis; and Anglicanism was confronted by the age-old problem of Thomism—the achievement of an underlying harmony between Hebraism and Hellenism.

The attempt of Episcopacy to grapple with the relation of theology and philosophy—of faith and reason, confirmed the experiences of its predecessor; it was confronted by the inability to unite the sacred and the secular in a tenable belief. The truth in religion must be in essence monotheistic—God; divisions, each of which is subject to sub-divisions, may follow. There can be no dualism—nothing is ever on a par with God: it cannot be concluded that what is true in the one may be false in the other; and the New Church did not follow in the traditional teaching of faith as belief despite reason.

Revelation was melting away before the application of rationalism. The ecclesiastical hierarchy—the lords spiritual, seemed concentrated on the interests of the mind, rather than on the interests of the soul; they approached the bible with the mind of reason studying the pages of history, rather than with the mind of faith absorbing the pages of revelation; and before science became a social force the Episcopal clergymen were the most rational, the most educated and cultured, class in England. Thus there took place a transition from scriptural authority to rational inquiry: soon revelation—in the light of logic, history, experience—began to lose its attributes of sacredness; the new Churchmen differentiated the idea of a cosmic Intelligence from the biblical Jehovah; they couldn't understand that there is a qualitative difference as between the various writings of antiquity—that the Hebraic writings are divine and sacred, and there was a developing tendency to class them together with the ancient Hellenic religious writings as mythology. They began to distinguish cultural values from theological values, which introduced the

85

principle of learning as secular; religion was ceasing to be the foundation, as it was dwindling into a phase, of life; and theology was emerging from the basic overall study to which all other studies are subordinate, and was becoming just another subject. Henry and Elizabeth appear to have been freethinkers, as they did not hesitate to subordinate religious doctrine to political necessity; and the Bishops of the Church were more secular than spiritual figures. And Episcopacy was the pioneer in the introduction of the post-biblical age—it was the chief secular impulse in English society. The bible was far from the prelates' most precious possession: the divinity of its Savior tended to be tempered; they seemed to regard the external and practical manifestations of religion as subject to change; their association with it became simply institutional or a matter of belonging, rather than ideological or a matter of believing; and this cost the Church prestige and tended to spiritual attenuation. Episcopal control constituted the crystallization and perpetuation of the full Renaissance influence on Christianity: biblical ideas were grafted upon humanist doctrines; there was a seeming indifference to the theological implications of scripture and its revelation, as worship was reduced to an arid formalism; a development took place from theology towards philosophy—towards the proposition that abstract or speculative reasoning is superior to intuition in understanding the world; Episcopacy's supreme value shifted from biblical insight to cultural creativity, and it looked up to the person so gifted as "a god amongst men"; it became the most rational-minded single denomination in Christianity, and farthest removed from the original inspiration—Hebraism; its tendencies were to avoid *ex cathedra* commitments on scriptural problems, as its spokesmen had recourse to "with our feet firmly planted in mid-air", which could occur often enough to create the impression of deism.

It became a question of emphasis: unlike its mentor the new Church put philosophy before theology; it was the only denomination within Christianity that was essentially other than biblical; it was a product of the Renaissance—Greek instead of Hebraic. It may be regarded as "Christ-haunted", rather than as strictly Christian; and Episcopacy has been described as an expression of "religionless Christianity"—"it is arguable that the Church of England is not Christian at all".

The Church of England symbolized social stability, was primarily an instrument for the perpetuation of the *status quo*, and represented the religion of the "gentleman". It continued the principle of the hierarchical social organism, with its emphasis on caste-consciousness; and there were qualitative differences among men—as between blood and commonalty, between clergy and laity, and as within blood and within clergy; and there was a refusal to eliminate non-Hebraic influences in Episcopacy. It emphasized ritual and art, not theology: its preachments were devoid of basic spiritual doctrine and of ethical content—and salvation was by faith, not works; and church services were in adoration of the Lord or pure prayer meetings. Art was identified with religion: there were numerous manifestations of art in the High Church edifice, furnishings and services;

"Charles I was the greatest patron of the arts in the history of England, and his court attracted artists from all over Europe".[10]

Religion as an emotional experience and moral guide characterized the lower classes, and quality therefore identified it with baseness and held aloof. And absence of Establishment theological positivism—doubt on specifics, encouraged the dogmatism of the Reformation.

The separation from the apron strings of the ancient mother, Rome—the assertion of secular independence, the supremacy of the state over the church— had its inevitable economic implications. A great part of the land in the realm was in the hands of the Church; expansion under the rule of land was fundamentally quantitative and extensive—improvement was at a snail's pace. The secular world had developed towards the industrial way, whose expansion was primarily qualitative and intensive; life outside the monastic walls had grown rich in opportunities for living; the parish priests, the clergy closest to the mass man, were often engrossed in, and influenced by, everyday life; the world was invading the religious establishments set apart from it; and a tendency was developing within the Church to exchange the monastic routine existence for the vigorous give-and-take of secular life. The Papacy had moved into a condition of worldliness: religion was being permeated by a mundane atmosphere; a gap was beginning to yawn between the image, and the fact, of the Church; people were becoming conscious of the Church as spiritual, and as worldly; a generation of men was rising who were being increasingly dominated by fact rather than by tradition—they were working for the worldly, rather than for the heavenly, weal; religion forbade usury and adultery, yet they were firmly entrenched in society; and it was coming into question whether people were to be guided fundamentally by the canons of the Church or by the ways of the world. Was it to be a holier-than-thou, or a worldlier-than-thou, attitude? were these attitudes really antithetical? The reform of the Church was the motive at first: soon there developed a fierce anti-clericalism—a resentment especially against a property-holding clergy; from the Tudors no money could leave the realm for foreign parts without official permission, and they considerably curtailed the clerical exactions of which lay folk were complaining; in addition, it was often felt that a successful move towards change was dependent upon confiscation of ecclesiastical property; and the immemorial Church was emasculated also of economic power—England's State abolished the monasteries and expropriated the Church of its realty property, which was sold to private purchasers.

Yet although there had been tendencies in this direction for two centuries the reality of the change revealed a good deal of loyalty to the traditional faith: it seems that most of the clergy, especially of the lower strata, were motivated by fear of the king rather than by conviction; and the withdrawal from the Roman obedience was an external acquiescence instead of a change of heart. The clergy instinctively recoiled from Caesar's invasion of a world that is not Caesar's; they denied utterly that temporal government could possess any authority to treat of or to define whatever concerns the faith, the sacraments and ecclesiastical discipline, for this—

"has hitherto belonged, and ought to belong, to the pastors of the church alone, whom the Holy Ghost has placed in the Church of God for this purpose, and not to laymen".

Priestliness cannot be taken lightly—its realm must be respected: the truth of religious tenet exists only in its own right, as an end in itself—it can never serve any other end; sacred theology, a product of man's most exacting mental effort—where do we come from, where do we go to, why are we here?—must rest squarely and solely upon truth, upon the external verities—*veritas eternitatis*; the admittance of any other consideration is per se vitiative of sanctity. Revelation—together with its interpertation and understanding, is eternal; responsibility in this ultimate endeavor presupposes a spiritual development and insight that can come only from the inspiration of life with God—of a lifetime of learning and contemplation; heresy is a mystery, whose presence the theologian alone is qualified to recognize. And all this cannot be outside the confines of canon law. On Elizabeth's accession Parliament granted her supreme authority in matters of religion; and the Royal Supremacy in Anglicanism, in its church structure and sacred theology, was to be in the hands of a queen—a woman was pope. Royalty can make satisfactory secular laws, but it can never have a genuine religious attitude: it may have a say on church organization, but it can have no say concerning sanctified doctrine; the superficiality of laity enactment in religion is patent; how can there be a legislative, statutory uniformity in theology?—the Faith cannot be dependent upon an Act of Parliament, for what one king established by statute his successor can repeal. And there was fear of the re-introduction of the ancient principle of the emperor-god, which Christianity had always renounced.

With the enunciation of the principle of Royal Supremacy and the elimination of the Papacy from England, the Crown acquired the right to make changes in basic theological doctrine—by decree. Under Episcopacy impetus stemmed from above; authority descended the gamut of hierarchical structure, from king and archbishop through the bishops to the parish churches. Henry wanted to retain stability: structure is the essence of the Church—a church is not a Church without a form of organization in which the clergy, especially the prelacy, has a status and authority not shared by the laity; agreement upon a common creed embodied in a united comprehensive Church was essential to an ordered and stable national existence; the realm was to continue as a religious monolith; freedom of dissent in religion appeared at the time as a state within a state, which was anathema—the king was not concerned about the liberty of the individual; rather was he anxious to secure uniformity within the Church, and conformity to the new order from all the clergy as well as from the masses. Yet the departure from Rome introduced a void in religion, which caused the Church to drift and resulted in mass confusion; there was loss of organization and stability as Protestantism split into hostile factions and brought religious anarchy; no one was sure of the degree of change—whether it was complete or merely superficial; and the doctrine and the discipline of the Establishment in its transition days were amorphous and negative. With time it was realized that a basic change in tenet—the elaboration of a new body of theological teaching, is a problem of great complexity; the achievement of a positive doctrinal pattern by the Church of England had to be a matter of development over several generations; and it could bring on a Church schism, which may be accompanied by serious social dislocations. The Tudors therefore never made any changes in non-political sacred doctrine: the old Church structure was maintained largely intact and used for the new religion; and they had no intention to disengage their minds from the principles of ecclesiastical authority, and of classical tradition—the immemorial sacredness of Throne and Altar would remain. The Anglicans continued the doctrine of only one interpretation of Scripture—the acceptance, and the understanding, of God's Word are identical; Catholicism was divine truth, universal and eternal—and they retained and preserved the Roman theology;

> "Henry, while changing many things in the church, would not allow any deviation in essentials from the religion of Catholic Europe".

Outwardly times changed but the underlying conditions continued; there were variations of form and expression, but not of substance; there were changes of emphasis on phases of doctrine, but there was no change of doctrine. The Anglican church edifice and its grounds were consecrated, and holy ceremony—the administering of the sacraments, centered on the altar.

Thus there resulted what appeared like "the old-new Church"; and the break was entirely political—it was not fundamentally institutional or theological. Queen Elizabeth followed a period of erratic monarchal succession; from the absolutism of Henry, to the impotence of Edward, to the femininity and Romanism of Mary. The first Statute of Uniformity was not achieved until 1549, two years after Henry's demise—but it was erased during the Marian interlude. From Elizabeth religion had again to begin at the beginning, and the Settlement of 1559 was accepted as the final arrangement of England's Christianity. The priestly power was continued as essentially hierarchical—espiscopal, prelatical—and also as triune: jurisdictional—legislative, judicial, disciplinary; magisterial—decisive in interpreting sacred truth; ministerial—potent in transmitting divine beneficence through the sacraments. Thus the principle of qualitative difference between clergy and laity—of the indispensable intermediary, the priest, only through whom the beneficence of God can flow to the worshiper—was retained. Yet it took the national Church more than a half century— well into the Elizabethan Age, to clarify all of its provisions in terms of practical understanding and application—to crystallize as "Anglicanism".

The Tudor changes in the Church of England were initiated from above—by quality, in order to counter the Reformation, which came from below—from commonalty. Henry VIII's fundamental motivation was ultra-practical: he was "the man who had never in his life been crossed"—because he knew where, when and how, to give; hitherto the anti-papal attitude had been always confined to bottom elements; by yielding to the new what he felt he absolutely had to Henry won trader support—which enabled him to give his own direction to, and to put his own limits on, the movement; and he thus managed to retain most of the old.e He knew that the separation from Rome would set the masses an example of authority revolt against tradition. There followed a union of Church and nation: the Church *in* England was supplanted by the Church *of* England—by Anglicanism as the national religion, which became the Establishment; the supra-national principle in church and faith was supplanted by the native expression; the Pope ceased to be considered the Vicar of Christ as he became simply the Bishop of Rome; the national Church became isolated from western Christendom on the continent; Latin was eliminated as church services were being conducted in the mother tongue; and the introduction in England of the principle that the secular authorities are the final arbiters of theological disputes subserved the Church; all of which increased the power of the Crown as it introduced the principle of the State Church. Henry Eighth's differences with Rome were political; the Church of England was, and continued throughout to be, fundamentally a quarrel within Catholicism—it created the English Catholic Church, whose controlling power from inception was consistently Episcopalian. Anglicanism was not a move back to primitive Scripture; it is not to be identified with the Reformation. Thus the breach with Rome was far from total; and despite their cleavage they always had an underlying affinity as against the Reformation, and the differences between the old and the new Christianity were qualitative.

The foundation of the Roman Catholic religion had always been Hebraism, but the Church from its beginnings had shown the greatest respect for Hellenism. By the fifteenth century it was felt that full

91

freedom for the pre-Christian classics necessitated an emergence from religion, and this brought forth the Renaissance. With the expulsion and the expropriation of the Roman power the new Church inherited its traditions—including the Hellenic expression, and Anglicanism came entirely under the control of the Renaissance: the indifference of the Church of England to theology was expressed by the statement, "with our feet planted firmly in mid-air"; and for the first time in the history of Europe Hellenism dominated Hebraism as within a national ecclesiastical jurisdiction. The Establishment's avowal of Hebraic influence was fundamentally Roman; yet some concessions, even though mostly grudging, did have to be made to Reform. In the old faith the church grounds and edifice were consecrated, and it identified religion with art, which brought an emphasis on esthetics. The sacred edifice, with its architectural designs; its contents—paintings, sculpture, crucifixes, musical instruments, furniture; its clergy—with their vestments, and their surroundings; everything in the churches of Rome and England savored of the costly—at times even of the sumptuous. And "such a daughter of the Renaissance as Elizabeth", from her formative years, had found herself in a bedlam of controversy over religion; she was caught up in the modernist atmosphere of the Tudor court, which had been established by her father; her

> "cold, entirely humanist outlook, nourished by classical study, kept her apart from the deeper spiritual currents of her time";[11]

and, "It could even be maintained . . . that she was not a Christian at all".[12]

In 1521, when the Pope dubbed Henry VIII Defender of the Faith, his Cardinal Wolsey presided at a great bonfire of heretical books outside of St. Paul's Cathedral; but defiant Reform was determined to fix it in the mind of the English that Catholic and idolator are synonymous; and they anathematized each other as "anti-Christ". During the nebulous interlude that was the transition from Roman to Anglican everyone with an anti-Papal bias tended to be identified with the new Establishment; there were the dangers of dereliction, as the ideological heirs of John Wycliffe for the first time experienced the exhilaration of release and power; and there took place a precipitous drop from the heights of sacredness to the

92

depths of profanation—"the altars have been made into pig-sties".[13] The local church was often a museum of the Christian faith, as well as a house of worship. It is said that:

> "the pioneers of the new Christianity (found) justification (for) their savage and barbarous destruction of a whole world of beautiful things, manuscripts, paintings, sculptures, goldsmith's work and jewelry";[14]
> "England when (Henry VIII) came to the throne had been a treasure-house of art; he left it a chaos of fragments".[15]

Bishop Gardiner, aroused by the rampant vandalism, denounced the "beastliness" of men who think the art of the sculptor and engraver as something per se sinful. However, the much greater part of the iconoclasm was perpetrated upon objects considered by the ancient faith as sacred, rather than as art. As the Church of England was moving towards definitiveness it was achieving an identity different from everything Wycliffite, and it eschewed and condemned the Levelers and their iconoclasm. In 1560 Elizabeth uttered a Proclamation,

> "against breaking or defacing monuments of antiquity being set up in churches or other public places, for memory and not for superstition".

And Anglicanism continued the traditional principle of Christianity in identifying art with religion.

ANGLICANISM: REFORM

The Reformation in England, Tudor Puritanism (Wycliffism and Calvinism), brought about a revolt against the Roman authority in religion. The New Christianity took it for granted that God had revealed Himself and His divine plan to man through the Bible—which was a collection of ancient Hebraic writings, and was regarded as infallible and as final.

"The Bible is the record of God's revelation to mankind, the

93

abiding witness to the fact that God has Spoken. This is the message of the Bible. There is a Word from the Lord which makes known the very heart and mind of God in relation to the world and to man. Light has shone upon the mystery of man's life, a divine answer has been given to the problem of sin. The Book is the record of His Self-communication at different times and through diverse agents."[16]

The Bible, which consisted of the Old Testament or Law, and of the New Testament or Grace—"the Book where God meets man", "the Book of books"—was the Christian's most precious possession: the Hebrew Scriptures are man's sole, fundamental source of religious knowledge and teaching; revelation is wisdom transcending simple human truth—it is qualitatively superior; it is divine cognition concerning the mystery of a Reality beyond reality—the spiritual darkness is illuminated as God is perceived everywhere; reason is the truth of man, revelation is the truth of God. And the Bible was exalted as the highest and profoundest knowledge and wisdom in the possession of man. The Reformation accepted the Athanasian creed, the triune Godhead—Father, Son and Holy Ghost. Grace was always primary to all Christians, while the degree of emphasis on Law—and on rationalism, varied with the denomination. Despite the contrast between the remorseless Jehovah of the Old, and the indulgent Heavenly Father of the New, Testaments—the Bible continued to be accepted by all as representing the principle of *final*, rather than of progressive, revelation; thus the true religion—the attributes of God—was identified with finality, which rendered all Christians tradition bound.

And divine doctrine—Scriptural inspiration, continued as the essence of their thinking: the foundation of man's life was the revelation of God—His Word, Holy Writ and His Work, Nature; it is through His Word, rather than through His Work—that we gain a knowledge of God; and they all regarded Scripture as subject to human interpretation, which is theology. Tradition and Reform both thought of knowledge as sacred and profane; there is knowledge in the world outside of Holy Writ— nature, but it is vulgar knowledge; nature in religion, the concept of a natural order of life—is paganism, which is heresy per se; and the supernatural is always above the natural. And they held on to the organizational principles of church, clergy, laity. The wider knowledge of the universe had not yet impressed itself on the mind of man to the extent of basically altering his view; and they thought in terms of geo, and of anthropo, centricism—the earth as the center of the universe, and man as the central purpose of creation. The scene of man's spiritual origins was laid in the Middle East, in the "Holy Land": it is the timeless story of this cross-roads of the world that tells of the rise of three of the great religions of mankind, and three Hebraic faiths—Judaism, Christianity, Islam; the Holy Land is not a matter of geography—true places never are; the home of the immortal is not on a map, and the Holy Land to the Europeans was never more than a state of mind. It was this area that was the scene of Christianity's sacred triune epic of creation, fall and redemption. All Christians were agreed that the Scriptural doctrines which offend rationalism are to be accepted nonetheless; and God, in some faiths, is a legitimate source of irrationality. From the day man first thought of God the world has never seemed pure enough. Social morality was regarded as within the province of the Church: the ethical teachings of the Bible were based on the economy of scarcity—"the poor shall never cease out of the land"[17]; the goods of life were the supreme value, the basic form of reward—the Lord's Prayer says, "Give us this day our daily bread"; and the relation of man to God was also economic, as He was propitiated with "burnt offerings". And they accepted the principle of qualitative difference as between—God and man; the souls in heaven, who were on a status of hierarchy; the various writings of antiquity— they regarded the Hebraic writings as divinely inspired and sacred, while all other writings were merely human.

Thus the world was a divine creation, and supernatural power was man's constant companion through life. The world within which God put man is inherently evil, and man is helpless against it: in Tudor-Stuart England all sorts of imaginery malevolent beings haunted the atmosphere; the witch inhabited the world, and was part of the Christian's daily life; and witch burning was taking place on a most extensive scale in the midst of unimaginable popular terror. God's infinite power was necessary to counteract the evils constantly menacing man, and he can invoke His aid through lamentation and prayer. Christianity alleged that there is in human nature a native tendency toward evil, which it called "original sin"—and this put the welfare of his soul into jeopardy. Yet man wants to save his soul from eternal damnation—every Christian's first concern was, "what must I do to be saved"? The Orient's spiritual gift to the West was the Hebraic concept of Messianic redemption; man's alienation from God could be terminated only by God by His Own willingness to do so—by the redeeming act of Self-sacrifice incarnate. All Christians accepted the principle of salvation; God gives man the opportunity to save his soul and win eternal life in bliss by dedicating himself to faith and works—and by regular worship of Him on His Day, Sunday. Thus all men sinned in Adam, and all men could be saved in Christ.

The Reformers intended the retention and the perpetuation of Christianity. And they inherited an expression of the faith which resulted from the fact that "in scholastic theology tradition had assumed equality with Scripture". The Puritans, however, were dedicated to Bibliolatry—the worship of Holy Writ; "the Bible, the Bible alone, is the religion of the Protestants"; and theirs was the geo-anthropo-centric, universe. They were Christo-centric—Christ is the Life and the Light of mankind, and He is both divine and human as He partakes of the attributes of God and of man. They were inspired by, and they based their life on, His authoritarianism—which they held the essential source of divine truth; His teaching was their ultimate index to the knowledge of God, of the world, of man; it was the foundation of their being, the source of their values and ethics, and their infallible guide to the present, as well as to the after, life.

"A doctrine of tradition not based on Scripture was no more than a human convenience . . . Hence, ancient practices, however fine; pronouncements of ecclesiastical authorities, however wise; or even decisions of Church councils, however universal; were authoritative only in so far as they reflected the clear teaching of Scripture. This position was distinct from that of the Roman Catholics, who placed the traditions of the Church Fathers and the pronouncements of ecclesiastical councils on a par with the Bible . . ."[18]

God alone can reveal His Word to man; He alone can answer man's most anxious questions—what was the effect upon human nature of Adam's sin? how shall one come to any certainty as to the way of salvation? how does the reconciliation effected by the redeeming death of Christ become operative? "Scriptural authority" was the cornerstone of the Reformation, and of its teachings. The faithful must obey God, not man: the

96

Church cannot establish laws that are outside of and beyond the Word of God; whatsoever is not faith is sin, there is no faith save where there is an appeal to the Bible, and all religious practices not ordained in Holy Writ are per se worthless. They rejected the combination of Scripture and Church Tradition then accepted in Europe, as they relied solely on the former; God's Word—not the Church, is the ultimate Christian authority, which renders church incidental; and all rite and ritual not expressly commanded by God in His Word were to be eliminated. The new religion abjured the tradition that the way to the truth about revelation is through a congress of Christian learning, through the authority of the teaching Church; it detached the Bible from its intellectual framework that was the product of the experience and the reflection of the fifteen Christian centuries—from the "fallibility" of all Church tradition, authority, teaching; it removed from Christian worship all medieval and sacerdotal accretions in order to achieve the simplicity and the purity of the primitive rites; yet all the teachings of the papal ages having Scriptural authority were to be respected. Thus did the Reformers repudiate the millennial doctrines of Roman Catholicism or Christianity of the sacraments; they emphasized the ethical teachings of the Bible, they postulated the doctrine that the foundation of salvation is ethical—not ritual, and they based their spiritual life on works rather than on faith or simple conformity.

The Roman Catholic church services were conducted in Latin, which gave them an aura of mystery and awe, rendered the atmosphere unintelligible to the worshipers, and kept them in the status of passive participants; and this caused the service of the sacraments to be regarded as dull routine. The Bible was thought of as the essence of sacredness and truth, and was revered: it was published only in Latin, which confined its content to specialists in religion—priests and scholars; its study by the masses for their own edification was dismissed, as they were held mentally unprepared for the comprehension of the profound and the complex— "let the shoemaker stick to his last", and their speech was confined to the vernacular; such translation of the holy was shunned as vulgarization, which was desecration; and the illiterate uncouth were traditionally thought incompetent to meddle with church and state affairs. And tradition was apprehensive of folk interest in Holy Writ as it could lead to schism, maybe even to heresy, and possibly also to sectarianism— the sect was regarded as a separation from the community. Episcopacy continued to be fundamentally the religion of the sacraments: yet it was characterized by a theological uncertainty, and it was capable of concession—although grudging, to Reform; the Bible was confined to the priest, but some respect did have to be shown for popular attitudes and demands in relation thereto. Dissent wanted the church services to be so conducted as to enable the worshipers to feel themselves personal participants in the solemnities; it held that the Roman clerical power over the laity was absolute, which rendered them a nullity. With the coming of change the people acquired potency: it was declared that Scripture is within their competence, although the great majority of them were illiterate—William "Shakespeare's own father could not write his name";[19] and the Bible as the initiative and the responsibility of the masses brought the development of a general interest in the conduct of church services in language intelligible to all. The Holy Word would cease to be the monopoly of a few theologians, as Reform intended to spread the knowledge of "Godde's laws" throughout the realm, and it was to become the property and the concern of the multitude. This was an expectation that prelacy could not ignore, and the Establishment therefore abolished confinement to Latin in the church services, so that everyone could understand what was transpiring; and this introduced a two-fold problem—the Bible had to be translated, and the masses had to be rendered literate. The translations were to be prepared for the edification of the people, whose language was not cultural and they had therefore to be made in the vernacular. This seemed like a move towards the possibility of commonalty admittance into a realm of which they had traditionally stood in reverential awe, and from which they had always been excluded. There were several undertakings for the first time to translate the Bible from the Latin, and to publish it in English; after several such efforts were eliminated by the Marian interlude a Book of Common Prayer was adopted from Elizabeth in 1559. But Reform objected to the hierarchical-sponsored Book on the allegation that it was not intended as a manual of congregational worship, as no effort was made to put it into the hands of the people; it was maintained that the popularity of the Bible was enabled by the ability, as well as by the freedom, to read and to study it; and this presupposed a mass literacy that top blood was not enthusiastic about.

The Roman and Greek Churches were based on the age-old conviction that the acceptance, and the explanation and understanding, of Holy Writ are one and the same—they go together, per se; the communicant takes both or he leaves both; and the principles of theocracy, and of institutional and theological uniformity, were taken for granted as the laws of God. Their acceptance of the Scriptures—Old and New Testaments—as the Word of God, rendered them all Christian; their differences in explanation and understanding of the Scriptures gave each of them its own particular identity. The Reformation began with the acceptance of the traditional doctrine of the inseparability of Scripture from its explanation and understanding: but Protestantism thought that God's Word had been falsely interpreted throughout the papal ages; and it was going to add another interpretation—it was at first convinced that popular study would soon reveal the true meaning of Scripture, and bring a unanimity of basic understanding which would eliminate anti-Christ, and substitute and establish the true monolithic doctrine and Church. And Reform in England did not immediately constitute a complete break with tradition.

The confidence of pioneer Reform that popular Biblical study would reveal the divinely ordained monolithic faith and church did not come true; the protagonists of the new Christianity had considered this crucial matter for several generations, but they had never been able to agree on just what God had commanded. This introduced a free-for-all condition: teaching had hitherto followed a traditionally beaten path of Biblical quotation and ecclesiastical authority; but the affirmation that Scripture is the sole source of sacred doctrine, and that there is no final human authority on God's meaning—created the possibility of an endless variety of its interpretation. Sixteenth-century or Tudor Puritanism was Christianity of the Book: Holy Writ was wide open—for the people, for everyone, to read and to know; the Reformation was a doctrinally amorphous mass, within which was included a multiplicity of sects with divergent convictions; and although its renunciation of tradition and of Episcopacy did not confine it to negativism, its initial positive haziness caused it to be referred to as "Dissent". Thus the separation of Dissent from traditional religion tended to the introduction of a vast open domain without a foundation; it created a condition of vacuity concerning specific doctrine and organization for a large part of the population; and there were no definite standards to go by—no sacred doctrine, and no fully acceptable house of worship.

The Roman principle of clerical divine quality enabled the blend of Scripture and Theology as a monolithic entity. The separation from the traditional authority brought chaos: it accentuated the dangers of dereliction, especially from the ideological heirs of John Wycliffe; the absence of definite worship brought a precipitous drop from the heights of sacredness to the depths of profanation; and uniformity in religion, a traditional part of the realm, was being succeeded by a tendency to anarchy. The realization of the hopelessness of achieving unanimity concerning what God means in Scripture could lead either to the return to the traditional principle of an ultimate monolithic inspired authority, or to the principle of the atomization of Dissent into innumerable sects—with everything that each alternative implied. Reformed Christianity had developed to the stage where it could not return to the heritage of authoritarianism; it was willing to sacrifice unity to doctrine—it accepted the principle of atomization. Protestantism therefore gradually became identified with the renunciation of the traditional attitude that the acceptance, and the explanation and understanding, of Holy Writ are identical—and it had to postulate the unprecedented idea that they are distinct propositions. Scripture is in essence divine; its explanation, theology—which was being increasingly thought of rather as interpretation—is the true belief, yet it is in essence human and hence qualitatively subordinate. A definite doctrine is identified with a definite Church: the Reformation as such never had a theology or a monolithic Church; the Scriptures are divinely inspired but the new Christianity had no specific explanation concerning them—it was the one faith with varied expression; it had general principles *on* religion, but no specific principles *of* religion; and its devotees had the freedom to evolve their own doctrine.

In the earlier days there was as yet no birth or baptism *en masse* in the Reform groups, and there were no Dissenter seminaries: the few ordained clerics identified with Protestantism were originally Roman and Episcopal priests who had been converted; and the leading Reformers were mainly lay preachers, men who had risen from the illiterate levels of commonalty. They were immersed in Holy Writ: they represented the disciple type of mind—chapter and verse; they had a profound sense of responsibility in the cultivation of God's gifts. Each of them was anxious to walk in the way of the Lord, and the preacher was fanatically convinced that he too had a direct relation to God, which rendered him

100

divinely inspired—"he who finds the Truth must obey it, love it, live it"; he identified his being in the world with a deep "sense of mission"—he was an inner witness to the Holy Spirit, and God transmitted His message concerning sacred doctrine through him to the congregation; and this gave him a messianic complex, and he was always converting and saving someone—showing him the light. Each therefore took it upon himself to give his own interpretation to Holy Writ: in his enthusiasm the Reformer viewed his undertaking as a great re-discovery of the true faith, which with Bible study and discussion would soon be clear to all; and each in all fervor and zeal called upon the people to recognize his claims, and to accept his teaching and follow him.

The consistent increase in commonalty literacy, and in the availability of the Scriptures in English, put the meaning of God's Word within the interest and reach of any literate person—of "the People". Hierarchical authority was challenged by Scriptural preaching; religion was becoming a private affair, in which one's individual faith—one's convictions about God—was more important than any Church teaching. Each of the Reformers felt free to be his own interpreter, and to arrive at his own conclusions: they became ambitious to penetrate the "purer doctrine" in the Bible itself, concerning the divine-human relationship, which created a zeal for its direct study—they wanted to become "built up in Christ"; all of which was beginning to give rise to the "preacher" as a social force.

Illiteracy has no media of communication—no source of enlightenment, other than the spoken word; the masses thirsted for the Word of God, and the hortatory harangue was their one oracle of learning; they perforce approached the Bible through the preacher, and they generally learned what God had made known by listening to him and his interpretation; they were convinced that in the sermon God literally communicates His truth through a human mouthpiece, and it was concluded that the understanding of Scripture does not add new truth to that which was revealed; the sermon only sheds light upon some phase of the everlasting truth and applies it with spiritual warmth to the actual needs of the listeners; all of which brought an emphasis on the principle of the sermon—of preaching; and in their church services the sermon from the pulpit supplanted the ceremony and sacrament of the altar. The commonalty of the Tudor and Stuart centuries took its preaching seriously—the preacher was all-important; the self-assured optimism, and the certainty

101

that his teaching alone is the eternal truth—that characterized each of them, created a tendency to sectarianism. Man as a social being tends to form, and to identify himself with, an ideological group—a sect; during the transition in religion the mass of spiritual-starved people, seeking satisfaction for their divine yearnings, developed varying tendencies inspired by the Bible, each of which created an ideological community of interest in Christ; this led towards the spontaneous formation of each into an independent group—the preacher founded a sect; and a multiplicity of sects began to make their appearance, which brought a tendency to stress differences—to separatism. Most of the sects were as yet shifting and amorphous groups of people, uprooted and confused by change, social revolution and civil war, congregating loosely about individual preachers and flocking from one to another; when social despair is too great messianism is tempting, and given a leader with the necessary qualifications the group soon consolidated itself. An important device of organization was some form of covenant, binding upon all, to which all must agree: it was a primary essential that the preacher evoke in his disciples the sense of having shared an experience which set them apart from the generality of men; the sect offered its proselytes the sense of distinction and security to be found in becoming one with a peculiar people, called to enter the ark of salvation in a doomed and perishing world. The covenant was a particular interpretation of Scripture: it constituted the framework for the development of the sect's own body of sacred doctrinal thought; with time tendencies to grouping within Dissent were developing a plethora of systems of spiritual doctrine; Biblical thinking—the product only of divine inspiration—was an inherently slow tortuous process, and the complex of ideas and practices of each finally crystallized under a given name; this gave each sect an identity that enabled it eventually to organize its own church, and to achieve the status of a "denomination" within Protestantism.

The Reformation in England differentiated between the faith, and the church. It accepted the principle of the church, yet the Bible is the ultimate authority for Christians: God's Word specifies no particular church appointed by Him to teach His revelation; the principles concerning a house of worship are impliedly but not expressly, set forth in Holy Writ; and it provides only general principles on faith, practice, church organization—monist, pluralist, hierarchical, conical—for the guidance of man. Holy Writ is above ecclesiastical authority: the Holy Christian

102

Church—whatever form it may take, is born of the Word of God; as such it remains forever subordinate, it abides therein and hearkens not to another voice, it has no reciprocal effect on its Creator; and the allegation that "the Gospel is nothing without the approval of the Church" is thrown out as it is giving the latter precedence. The Reformers gave church a two-fold expression: "Church" as the Christian religious community; and "church" as the building used for Christian worship, which is under the management of both its clergy and laity. They were convinced that the visible world is but a symbol of the invisible world: they thought in terms of the Invisible Church, whose existence is in eternity; Christ is Spirit forever—before, during and after His Being in the flesh; there was the spiritual tendency inspired by the Bible or the Community in Christ; and there was the visible church—a shelter for the gathering of devotees, a house for worship and prayer—or, a social institution. The emphasis was on the principle of the Invisible Church, from which was deduced the concept of "the gathered church"—a voluntary group brought together by the voice of the preacher; this was the visible fellowship, or the community—"where there are two or three gathered together in My name, there am I in the midst of them"; this comprised a group of faithful—totally committed believers who gave evidence that they are "Christ's men and women", Christians by conviction rather than by birth—who voluntarily and in complete independence, were associated in what they regarded to be the only true visible church. The heart of man is the fortress of Christianity; the heart of the Christian—not the structure of stone, is the consecrated temple within which God must be worshiped—"He dwelleth not in temples made with hands". The church has a definite place as social institution, but it is never more than incidental:

"Structure is structure: it neither constitutes, nor is the essence of, the Church; it exists as the servant of the Community of Christ to enable the Community to function most effectively, while fulfilling its God-given mission under the Lordship of Jesus Christ."

As within the Reformation there were varying degrees of emphasis on the importance of Church, yet there was full agreement on the rejection of the principle of "Churchianity"—the worship of Church for its own

103

sake; church exists only for the sake of Christ; its being is always derived, never inherent—it does not exist in its own right; the church and its grounds are not consecrated; church attendance is not indispensable to salvation; and worship is based on the sermon of the pulpit, not on the sacraments of the altar. The Reformers were in great fear of the exaltation of the church and the priest, rather than of God and Christ—"those who prefer the Pope's kingdom to Christ's kingdom"—and they alleged that the traditional clergy and laity served their Church better than they did the faith. Piety was identified with the fundamental doctrine of justification by faith and salvation by works, with sincere acceptance of sacred doctrine and with walking in the way of the Lord—not simply with devotion to an institutionalized religion, with obedience to the Church and its ritual; and their confinement to Holy Writ minimized the efficacy of the external or social manifestations of religion, which rendered incidental the authority of church, theologians, councils.

The Roman and Anglican clergyman was a priest, whose status was hierarchical; the spiritual—theological, preceded and was superior to the temporal; and the clergy was confined to the supervision of the canon law. And their power was triune: jurisdictional—legislative, judicial, disciplinary; magisterial—decisive in explaining sacred truth; minis-terial—potent in transmitting divine beneficence through the sacra-ments. The Reformation kept—although under well modified condi-tions, the first and the second, and eliminated the third. Protestantism was convinced that Christianity has to have a clergy. The clergy comes within the canon law, it is subject to church discipline—but this is incidental to the civil law. Scriptural exegesis is entirely confined to religion, and has no relation to the state. It was concluded that there are differences within clergy, and as between clergy and laity, but they are wholly quantitative; there was a rejection of the institutional qualitative difference, of the principle of the indispensable intermediary—the priest, only through whom the benevolence of God can flow to the worshiper; God alone can grant salvation—can save men from eternal punishment, and no human being whatever can pretend to usurp divine power; the clergy is *ministry*, it is not *priesthood.* Reform accepted the principle of quality, but confined it to divinity—to God and Scripture; there are qualitative differences between God and man, but not as between man and man.

The renunciation of clerical quality took with it the principle of hierarchy: it was alleged that ecclesiastical status, prelacy—"Prince of

104

the Church'', brought with it prestige, property, power, pride, indolence, and a change from apostolic simplicity to ostentation; and the vestments were donned for the sake of the rewards, rather than for service. To Protestantism "The Lord Jesus Christ is the only Head of the Church of God": status is nothing, function is everything; the leaders of each sect held weekly meetings for the purpose of "prophesying", or exegesis—an exposition and discussion of passages in the Bible; they wanted to share with one another their deepest insights into the central realities of the common faith. The priest was concentrated on the sacerdotalism of the altar, while the minister was identified with the sermon— the preachments of the pulpit. The Reformation clergyman—a minister of the Gospel, was specialized in the sacred writings and in the conduct of the prayer meeting, and he took the pulpit; and the congregation in prayer developed from passive participants under absolute control of the priest, to active participants in *direct* relation with God. Reform held that religion must penetrate the whole of human life: it understood the spiritual life as an intimate and mystical—as a direct and meaningful, contact of the worshipers with God; God and Christ only should be addressed in prayer. During worship the spirit of Christ must suffuse the human heart; the prayer meeting must be a baptism of the spirit, not simply a dull routine ceremony; while to worship the Father in spirit and truth need not exclude ceremonial, the latter is not of the essence of worship, and the clerical sacramental performances around the altar can be dispensed with. "God alone is Lord of the Conscience"—all souls sincerely sorry for their sins are fully absolved, without the confessional; salvation springs from the experience of faith through one's deep mystical love for the Savior; and they emphasized direct communion with God in prayer, for whenever a penitent thought piously of the Savior He was at once present.

The Reform sects had their origins from within the third estate; they were subsidized by the traders, who were predominantly commoners— while a few were of the gentry, who had some schooling and endowment. The master did not confine religion to his establishment; a number of the households of a particular denomination organized themselves into a parish, and they grouped around a separate building—a church. As within the new way the preacher was chosen and paid by the parish, which constituted his "living"; this freed the man of the Gospel from the restraints imposed by hierarchy, but it committed him to the congregation—which tended to render it independent, and emphasized the

105

democratic relation; during the Elizabethan Age the layman was free of clerical control, and "in the new Discipline the ultimate decision in all important matters rested with the Congregation". And as their church organization developed it became the center around which their social life revolved. The minister of religion was closer to life's realities than the celibate priest; his interests were primarily confined to the church, which elevated the authority of the lay heads of households, and reduced the influence of the clergyman in society.

Under feudalism the commonalty had been in a condition of serfdom; during the ages they had established certain patterns of living, and they developed rights in relation thereto for which quality had to have some respect. The social revolution brought the interim period—the destruction of the old, accepted ways of doing things before the establishment of the new—which had to be borne by those at the bottom of the social edifice; and their way of life became deranged. The move from the open-spacedness of the countryside to the congestion in the town slums was an effective separation from water, which interfered with cleanliness and sanitation—and the "perfumer" was a person of some importance. The radical changes left the commonalty helplessly bewildered: they had to begin again from the bottom to build up certain patterns of living in terms of the new way, and rights in relation thereto; the economic condition of the uprooted was such that they had to resort to anti-social behavior—crime, vice, vagrancy, beggary—in order to live; they were identified with poverty, drunkenness, brutality, and with sex promiscuity—which brought bastardy, infanticide, social disease; life became cheap, and the age developed a callousness towards human suffering; and they were not considered as strictly within moral respect. Patricians found diversion in the atmosphere of the ale-house, and commonalty furnished the outlet for their "wanton merriment".

With the coming of the Reformation, the commonalty began to emulate the values of quality, whose diffusion tended to the principle of equality; and there slowly developed a tendency towards the achievement of commonalty religious and economic integrity on a social scale, which laid a foundation for marriage, home, family. The basic unit of the developing Wycliffite and Calvinist sects was the household, which was organized on the principle of paternalism; it consisted of the

106

master, his home and family, his workshop,[f] and the servants and workers in the home and shop. The Reform household was based on discipline, which was strict; the master had the responsibility of family, economy, religion; he was a godly man, the lay religious leader of his unit. Commonalty had the opportunity for the first time in history to emerge from a background of impoverishment into the light of economic integrity, but this was based on a frugality that verged on miserliness. The fortunes of economic endeavor were determined in heaven, and success and failure were the result respectively of piety and sin. They were moving from caste-consciousness to class-consciousness; the social differences in kind in the master and servant relations in the life of Reform were necessarily changing towards degree. They were people of the book; the Bible for religion, the Ledger for economy—which rendered literacy of word and numeral mandatory. A knowledge of the Bible was a duty from which no one was exempt; the catechism was of primary importance in the Reform household, and they believed in worship and prayer—there were prayers regularly at meal, and at bed, time. They developed a hyper-sensitivity concerning morals, and there was a reaction against license as sex was confined strictly to within marriage—they objected more to a single night of adultery than to the slaughter of a battalion of men; marriages were usually arranged and based on the dowry, and they often turned out to be happy; and the rising commoners were characterized by the simple virtues—by the joys of the life of austerity, which was hardly as costly as "playing wanton"; and the religious festivals furnished practically the only opportunities for recreation. The Reform preachers of the Gospel were humanly zealous in practicing the strict life which they enjoined: merriment was regarded as per se immoral, while religion constituted the foundation of mass discipline in good character and clean living; they opposed all sports events on the Lord's Day, and theirs was always an emphasis on less play and more church. "Sabbatarianism" became pronounced, as organized amusement and Sabbath profaning were synonymous; and the sanctity of the Dissenter's Sunday, as an antipodal reaction to past conditions, made it a gloomy institution indeed.

It was inherent in the Reformation to introduce the principle of popular education; it was declared that the object of worship is to edify, which elevated teaching; the church became the institutional medium for this endeavor, and Protestantism established the house of worship as also a temple of mass learning. There was faith in the power of education, and it became a commonalty value; "the People" learned to want to learn, and they accepted the proposition that "learning is the heart of life". There was an attempt to inscribe the Scriptural message on minds virginal in their ignorance of all religion—their move from illiteracy to the Holy Word was the logical first step. The English were becoming a Bible people; the Geneva Bible was at first the most widely read version. This was followed by the King James Authorized Version of the Bible which was published in 1611, and was a book of, for and by the people. This brought about the mass discovery—the popularization, of Holy Writ: for the first time Englishmen could examine the Word of God for themselves and come to their own conclusions about it without benefit of clergy; and the Bible has been described as,

"one of the towering monuments in our literature, a poetic masterpiece that has colored the thought and speech of the English-speaking world for more than three centuries".
"At a time when there was as yet no English literature for the common people, this untold wealth of Hebrew literature was implanted in the English mind as in a virgin soil".

The Bible was their whole education, their intellectual universe; they were zealous for the Scriptures in English, they listened eagerly to the sermon in the hope of achieving edification, and as newly literate they were reading Holy Writ without a sense of history;

"A great literature which comes to us in translation and across an undeniable culture gap must always be something rich and strange";

and this constituted,

"a revolutionary innovation with consequences that have come thundering down the ages".

The Book immediately became effective, evidently because of a pre-disposition to accept it—and it became the faith of the people; and every aspect of the Reform life was immersed in Scripture—it was the

108

atmosphere within which they moved, breathed and had their being. Their study of, and life with, the Bible—gave them an Hebraic outlook, they gave the Old Testament a greater emphasis than any other Christian Church, and they equated the English with the Chosen People; and their religion has been described as "visions Judaica". The preachers were developing the art of discourse for common folk, from whom they stemmed and were one with; they were speaking *with* their people—not down to them; the style in preaching was plain, not florid—it was far removed from the theological complexities; and the purpose was to awaken the masses, to render them sentient, rather than to appear to them as scholarly. They developed a sense of responsibility towards their flock, and were concerned about their present, as well as their after, life; they regarded them as normally vigorous, and as at least potentially intelligent, individuals—who were to participate actively in the church services; they must understand everything, and play a personal part, in what transpires during worship. Their worship was in terms of communion, not of mass, and their singing was congregational, not choir; and they led them through Bible reading, prayer, singing, sermon, into a direct relation with God. The pulpit was based on the appeal: the training of the young had to be no less in virtue than in knowledge—to be good as well as to be wise; the sermon was a guide to moral conduct in human relations, in life—family, sex, economy, peace. And the sermon was also a source of information on, and interpretation of, current events—a medium for the molding of political views. All of which created a community of interest between clergy and laity—an atmosphere of association and interaction, as they developed a sense of belonging together; and this had its effect on the content of the church services.

The invention and improvement of printing began to have its influence: paper printed and bound in book form was much cheaper and more enduring than scrolls—loose-leaf script; mankind endows the printed page with nobility, reverence, eternity, and it resulted in a diffusion of knowledge. The Reformation brought a literacy and education explosion; it created a great increase in the number of presses and printers, and with the translation of the Bible and the spread of literacy books in the vernacular began to gain circulation. The change from a religion of ritual to the ethical appeal—to one in which sermons held first place, was a stimulus to knowledge and virtue; the sect regarded all its believers as missionaries, and each communicant became an evangelist; all

109

of which furthered the education of the illiterate as it gave the mass mind something to feed on, emphasized reflection and edification, and influenced society as it promoted mental advance. Reform maintained that the sacredness of Scripture is surely consecrated by its universality; by the people's saturation in it, by their reading, studying, knowing, it—indeed, by their living it. The new faith gave each congregant the feeling that he counts as it introduced the principle of lay participation in the church services; it developed the reading man, the man of the book; and he was a man of gravity, not given to levity—his humor seldom went beyond the grim grin. The Reformation had control of the religion and the education of the people; preaching became a mark of the true church, and it had the power to censor books, and to pass on the expression of thought and opinion. Scriptural treatises and notes on sermons—and manuscript replies to Establishment sermons—were being distributed among, and taken home by, literate congregants; these were read, discussed, emphasized, pro and con, by the common folk—which introduced mental contention, and a tendency to faction; they held to contention for truth, not for victory; and they acquired in time a sufficient knowledge of Holy Writ, and with it the temerity to stand up to and confound their betters, which encouraged many to become lay preachers. In addition, there took place a multiplication and accumulation of printed books on all sorts of subjects which the pulpit and all its works had brought into English life; this was developing a great body of ideas about man—his nature, history and place in the scheme of things; and it was giving rise to an increasingly literate articulate breed of thinkers and writers—of a reading, discoursing, reasoning, disputing public.

The commoner was spiritually potent in his own right; for the first time in history he was literate, and Holy Writ was available to him in his own language. Some of the leading Reformers were learning the ancient tongues: they were reading the Bible in the original Hebrew and Greek—they had their philological and textual difficulties with the Scriptures, yet "he was reputed for his Hebrew learning"; and from the light thereby thrown on the meaning of Holy Writ they were each convinced that they had "re-discovered" the true primitive Gospel of Christ; there was an attempt to purge the faith of all the non-Hebraic "pagan" influences that had allegedly infiltrated during the ages of tradition, and to restore the basic religion of the founding days—the essential features, and the manner of worship, of the "ancient church". Scripture was to be studied

110

not in the classical scholastic sense, but in terms of God's Word as directly revealed in Holy Writ; and the era stands out for the intense passion with which men wrestled with God, the central role that religious belief played in their lives, and the determination with which they formed churches and sects that could speak directly to their lives—a severe life indeed, but one made bearable, even beautiful, by an abiding religious faith. The re-evaluation of the Scriptural message would present the world with another approach to the essence of Christianity; this would introduce an altered view of God and His ways with man—a whole set of new religious motives and habits;

"the re-discovery of the infinite love of God which came with the Protestant Reformation";

a different set of beliefs on all the fundamental points of man's duty to God—a revivified sacred doctrine, form of worship, code of ethics; all of which would be enabled by the establishment of a re-organized Church dedicated to the purity of God's true revelation. And this brought a doctrinal crisis in Christianity. The Reformation has been regarded as a transitional movement linking the ancient teachings with the modern world: Protestantism's disinterred primitive Gospel of Christ, as applied to modern conditions, would introduce a different way of being a Christian, and produce a new type of European; the new species of Christian must either supplant the old one or be himself eliminated; and civilization as the Briton had always known it was repudiated. And the Reformers thrilled to the prospect of the resurrection of the true divine revelation, the purified life it would introduce, and the better world it would usher in.

With the introduction of the principle of popular education freedom of mass teaching became an integral part—it was the life, of the New Christianity. There is a qualitative difference between the illiterate and the literate: it was held that the Reformation did not have to depend for its being on clerical ability to terrify the benighted with threats of damnation; rather was it based on mass literacy, Bible reading, catechism, open discussion, and on lay influence, and even decision, in church organization; all of which could tend towards a measure of popular intelligence, understanding and appreciation, concerning even complicated theological thinking. In addition to the spoken word, Reform believed in the printed word; its printing was hampered by insufficient funds, illiteracy

111

of communicants, and fear of outlawry; yet Protestantism thrived on the condition of practical freedom of discussion that it did have.

NOTES

aThe New Testament is essentially biography, centering on the life of an individual—Jesus Christ.

bThe Inquisition never took hold in England.

cPalace erotica and court intrigue have existed everywhere throughout history; cataclysmic sociological phenomena cannot be traced to individual caprice—Cleopatra's nose, Martin Luther's frustration, Anne Boleyn; and the emphasis on Henrician erotica has obscured the sociological implications of his time.

dCardinal Richelieu, probably the wiliest diplomat of all time, is alleged to have said—"language was invented for the purpose of hiding, not for the purpose of revealing, thought".

eHe succeeded to delay the definitive rise of capital in the realm for over one and a half centuries.

fBefore the separation of industry from the household unit.

CHAPTER FOUR—EPISCOPACY VS. REFORM

The Reformation in Europe, although it had varied expression, was a protest against the Roman Catholic Church. Protestantism had risen from within the bosom of the traditional faith, which answered with what came to be known as the Counter Reformation; the cleavage was therefore fundamentally doctrinal, rather than geographical; and this brought on a series of bloody, but indecisive religious wars—which tended to mingle nationalities. Both sides finally realized that mutual respect was the only alternative to reciprocal annihilation; they were obliged to find some way of living together in the same world; their willingness to negotiate implied the recognition by each of the other's right to be; the Papacy was anxious to secure toleration for its surviving faithful, and the warring Christians concluded the Peace of Augsburg in 1555. The Peace introduced a new principle, and it ushered in a new Age in the annals of the western world; the Papacy concluded that "heretical" governments had come to stay, and Rome for the first time recognized as existent the plural interpretation of Scripture—of Christianity. From the Peace of Augsburg the princes of Europe were recognized as having divinely ordained powers to decide on spiritual as well as on secular matters; it was agreed that "the ruler's choice determines the established religion of his subjects"; he had to accept Christianity, but he could choose between Catholicism and Protestantism. A Protestant Council became lawful; it was under secular auspices, and its success required harmony among rival princes as well as among the clergy.

POLITICAL ASPECTS

In England the principle of divine right of kings was traditionally

113

subjectively taken for granted; from during the Tudor regimen this principle was brought into question and it became a problem in issue, which rendered men objectively conscious of it. The Tudor era was a time of bitterness, when everyone felt the existence of Church terrorism—"the Church's iron hand", and persecution was either experienced or expected; its ecclesiastical vicissitudes created the English *emigré*, the exile to the continent—Roman, Anglican, Reformed; the protest was not against the act of religious persecution—rather was it on whom it was being perpetrated; and it brought a constant fluctuation in the faculty membership of the Universities, especially through deprivation, flight, execution. Elizabethan England was predominantly under the spiritual guidance of Anglicanism, which refused to recognize the Roman Catholic Church as the sole custodian and representative of Christianity in the world. Elizabeth[a] as the daughter of Anne Boleyn caused Rome to question her legitimacy; in February 1570 the Pope pronounced on her the sentence of ex-communication; and he preferred her dethronement in favor of Mary Queen of Scots. Queen Bess bent every effort to save her Crown: it brought "that blind, anti-Catholic hatred"[20]; it was a time "when hatred of Spain and Rome seemed to be the only bit of religion left in the English Church"; and the Catholic priest was regarded as per se an heretic and traitor. The new Church, following the Marian interlude, constituted the realization of the Henrician program; it was Elizabeth's purpose,

"to teach the people, by the example of the archbishop of Canterbury, that in England religion is nothing more than a consent given according to the necessities of the time, to be revoked or changed according as the occasion arises".[21]

The Bibliolater *emigrés* developed the accumulated bitterness of years of exile; they were kept informed on home doings by their country's traveling traders. They lived in the atmosphere of continental Protestantism: there was "a real sense of intellectual dependence"[22] on Geneva, which was under the mental domination of John Calvin; Calvin was a second-generation Reformer, and he had a greater international influence than any of the other anti-papal leaders—he impressed many people, although only few of his own. The Swiss city became the Protestant world's center of learning—of the exegesis and understanding of

114

the Scriptures; almost all the returned exiles were Calvinist, and the sectarianism of the Reformation in England was very much under foreign influence—the influence of the "English Genevans".

Every religion has its underlying human attributes; a Christian Church is influenced by the teachings of Jesus and Moses, as well as by its particular national tradition and by the current social tendencies. The Reformation in England had its share of "Genevans", yet all its varied adherents were devoutly patriotic—they were convinced of England's primacy in divine favor; they knew few non-Britons and they advocated no allegiance to, or expected material assistance from, any foreign state; they reflected their country's insular mind as they emphasized her power on the high seas; and they were loyal to their monarchy—their foremost ambition was to increase the greatness of Great Britain. And the Reformation produced many denominations, all of which had their ties with the ancient culture of their land, and each of which was to some extent also involved with the peculiarities of the locale of its origin. The Roman resurgence brought out the power of Protestantism in the realm; the bonds of togetherness could be welded by persecution; and the new Christianity took a good deal of its courage from the consistent growth of the Reformation on the continent, which reached its crest with the Peace of 1555—in the reigns of the Queens Mary. During the Tudor Anglican doctrinal nebulosity the Reformation opposition was concentrated on the Roman Church; there was a patent advantage in having a record to attack but none to defend; and during the Marian interlude the factions within Anglicanism—Episcopalian, Calvinist—tended to draw together, although Episcopacy was never displaced[b] in its control of the Church of England.

The Church monolith—uniformity of sacred doctrine and of ecclesiastical organization, and unanimity of mass faith—was a traditional value; the union of state and church—the state church or the Establishment, was implicitly taken for granted by the English as the foundation of social structure; and Anglicanism could not separate Reform attitudes on religion from social revolutionary implications. Episcopacy was the force for Rome's Counter Reformation in England; there was an inherent incompatibility of individualism in religion with an Established Church —anything divisive was anathema; and conservatism was doctrinally much more at home with Rome than with Dissent. Episcopacy concentrated on the altar, which was spiritual and dedicated to prayer;

Reform was based on the pulpit, which emphasized the sermon or preaching. The sermon was a move from the holiness of the altar, which is strictly church and *priest*—to the pulpit, which is susceptible to histrionics, to the ways of the theatre and the *actor* ; the oratory of preaching became more appreciated than the humility of praying—and it did impugn, and did tend to be regarded as a substitute for, sacredness. Tradition elevated prayer as against preaching: it saw an antithesis between the altar, which is confined to the spiritual; and the pulpit, which could be political; and it was declared that prayer is communal, includes everyone, and that it brings devotion. Preaching is a sword to divide: it emphasizes matters that tend to contention rather than to edification; the great power of words, the persuasiveness of the orator in his mass appeal, could be politically potent—preaching could be an opportunity for the demagogue; and it breeds factionalism, and leads to upheaval. The Reform Church was seen as the natural ally of the commonalty against their lords, and there was the old Anglican thesis that Puritanism and rebellion go hand in hand. The minister in his sermon was both educational and hortatory: he had a great deal to teach his hardly literate listeners, although his chief purpose was to imbue them with spiritual and moral fervor; yet the borderline between the spiritual and the political was often indistinct, and the preacher could—unconsciously, or otherwise—use the pulpit of religion as a cover for revolutionary incitation.

Elizabeth was inherently hostile to the Reformation; she was very much uneasy about the people being rendered literate. The Scriptures as the sole source of divine truth, and the individual's freedom of their interpretation—could introduce a condition of unresolved, hopeless disagreement; it could bring about the atomization of spiritual belief; and a condition of chaos and license in religion would follow. The Crown was always in great fear of the sermon as controversial: it was uneasy about "the people, that many-headed monster"—it objected to the Biblical arousing "especially of the vulgar sort"; it held that much of the contentiousness was really inflammatory demagoguery under the cover of religion; and it emphasized that popular education bred "fantastical" notions of equality, and that Dissenter gatherings savored of conspiracy against monarchy. There was fear also of sectarianism: the sect appeared like a separation from social unity; under the conditions of the union of church and state opposition to the one was per se opposition to the other; a

116

rival to the Establishment was like a rival to the Monarchy—they thought of a church within a church as they did of a state within a state. The Elizabethan Age was "exceptionally rich in spiritual and intellectual achievement", and power was always surrounded by ability and talent; and the existence of quality was justified as a necessary check on the "many-headed hydra of English dissent"—with its insolent upstarts, and their demands for freedom of assembly, speech, press. On the continent the Roman Church compromise was jurisdictional, but Episcopacy could yield to the Reformation only doctrinally, and only what it felt it absolutely had to. The pulpit was identified with political power, and monarchal distrust of demos was much more likely to support repression than rebellion. There had to be official licensing of ministers and preachers of the Gospel, and of teachers; loyalty-to-monarchy requirements from churchwardens, teachers, printers, were absolute; printers were few and were well known, and the censorship was severe.

The Reformers charged the Queen with the attitude that men can be ruled only by fear and violence—she was seeking order, not justice; she wanted obedience rather than intelligence in her subjects; and they insisted that under her system there could be only the uniformity of dull ignorance, and that where there is no popular education a high standard of moral discipline cannot be expected. Yet the Reformation in England was fanatically anti-papal; the Crown could regard it as an ally—which brought leniency for it, even in its most radical manifestations, the Queen realized the difficulty of re-introducing basic doctrinal uniformity in religion, and she tolerated differences so long as they did not menace the basic *status quo* in the realm. During her reign a new generation had risen under a new dispensation in religion: little Genevas—autonomous centers of Biblical discussion—were rising in the land, and youth was flocking to them; printing was almost entirely devoted to polemical denominationalism; merchants had the money to purchase patronage, and to choose their own Gospel ministers; and from the later sixteenth century the popularity of Bible reading begins. During the last of the Tudors Reform was "regularly able to command a majority in the House of Commons". Elizabeth built up a denominational faction of her own, complete with creed, form of service, party loyalty, and the respectability that comes with time; she was unalterably committed to the traditional feudal landed, cultural values; she introduced, maintained and in every

117

way protected Episcopal control of the Establishment; and she tolerated no Parliamentary interference in ecclesiastical affairs. Yet something unprecedented had occurred: conduct begets a law which, though unwritten, may be more powerful than any code or body of statutes— such as the common law, which evolved by itself from within feudalism; the principle of "public opinion" had developed in the realm, and it became a force to be reckoned with; and it was realized for the first time that the mainstream of a country's life can ignore its government, and really determine events.

In the Roman and Anglican faiths Church is fundamental to salvation—if one does not go to church he does not to go heaven. Where the Church, as well as the faith, is thus inherently potent the question of the relation of the Church and the State is primary, as each is a top power in society and cannot ignore the other. Where there is a union of the temporal and spiritual powers they are theoretically in cooperation as equals, each supreme in its own sphere, assisting but not dominating one another; in pre-Tudor days in England there was a tendency for church and state to blend in the mind of the populace; yet the record of mankind establishes that it is inevitable for the problem of which is ascendant at some time to come up. During the intellectual ferment anent the Reformation there developed the idea of "Erastianism, the doctrine that the state is a divine institution", which controls the Church; temporal power belongs only to laymen, spiritual power only to clergy—the theologian is to make, the Crown is to enforce, Church law; and in the event of an impasse the supremacy of the State in ecclesiastical affairs prevails. The Roman Church rejected the principle of Erastianism, while the Anglican Church accepted it. To the Tudor state "the religion of the ruler is the religion of the people": the state may regulate the church if it engages in anti-social behavior, but the church alone is concerned with problems of heresy; religion prosecuted the heretic, while government punished him.

To the Reformation the Bible was the sole index to everything essential in religion: the absence of Scriptural instructions concerning church rendered it incidental; church was simply a shelter or meeting house for the devotees—having no intrinsic spiritual content, no meaning in relation to salvation; and it is therefore without inherent social significance. The Reformation accepted the principle of state supremacy:

"the Bible was to be determinative for both Church and State.

118

The Church, comparable to the soul in man, was by nature spiritual and eternal, autonomous in spiritual affairs, and designed to serve as mentor and conscience of the State. The State comparable to the body of man, was transitory by nature, autonomous in temporal affairs.";[23]

but the conditions and the extent of church subordination varied with time, and with the denomination. John Calvin held that the "State was ordained by God"; the state when concerned with morality and justice is God's agent in establishing and maintaining order in the world; and the government as the protector of the church has a say in its affairs. The attempt of ecclesia to reach after temporal power is a traduction of its true sacred calling, as spiritual ends cannot be attained by worldly means. Where the church is impotent the problem of the relation of church and state is non-existent, as there is no church for the state to be in a union with or separation from.

England was sharply divided between two forces—the government and the governed; "the king can do no wrong", and his ministers were held responsible for policy failures. The Reformation brought several synchronous revolutions; the movement for reform of the church was transforming itself into a movement for reform also of the state, and even of the society. Dissent gave the commonalty a structural organization, the church—as a medium for their spiritual expression, and as a stronghold of political ideology and social protest; for the first time in history the third estate achieved a voice as an organized group under their own leadership. They maintained that the Laws of God are transcendent: everyone, including royalty, was bound by God's Word; it was a cornerstone of Dissent that "we ought to obey God rather than man", and "the divine right of men must take the place of the divine right of kings"; in Kipling's famous lines,

> "the people, Lord, the people
> Not thrones, nor crowns but men"

"the people" is what's beautiful. Towards the end of the Tudor era it seems to have become dimly prevalent among the masses that royalty can err; there was no intention as yet to obtain exemption from the obedience of subjects, but objection was developing to an "exaggerated" deference

119

to superiors; and it was declared that the Scriptures contain a perfect rule of life for all to follow—in state, church, mart, family, school. Trader values were transforming the mind of the realm; and the principle of the contract as between men, and even as in their relations with God, was becoming paramount. Subjects are bound to obey their rulers, but they have to obey God first: the basis of the state is a covenant binding upon both rulers and ruled, and terminable by either; that which concerns the people must be approved by the people—government is dependent upon the consent of the governed, for "the voice of the People is the voice of God"; and the Crown must be essentially devoted to Reformation principles, not merely to be anti-papal. There was the theory of the right to revolt, based upon Biblical and historical considerations; rulers are "God's subordinate executives", and subjects have a right to resist their rulers—Bishop John Ponet in 1553 "set out in print the doctrine that for the oppressed citizen to kill a tyrannical ruler is not murder"; there is the right to revolution in the name of religion—if authority refuses to conform to the divine moral precepts the people have the right to follow the Biblical teachings literally, even if it involves the dissolution of the prevailing societal order in preference for another. Thus the commonalty class won recognition as human, having rights for which all, including even royalty, must show respect—which gave them the feeling that they count, and even that they are as capable as their peers; and in denying the qualitative role of the priest in religion they proclaimed the revolutionary Protestant anticipation of the equality of man.

DOCTRINAL ASPECTS:
RENAISSANCE vs. REFORMATION

The Renaissance was a development from within Hellenism, and it emphasized *humanism*: "the proper study of mankind is man," and this found its ultimate expression in the exaltation of the natural man—"in the emphasis on man as man, rather than on man as an object of salvation"; and man is distinguished from the beast fundamentally by his ability to be creative—with pen, brush, chisel, sound. Humanism is the doctrine that everything in life—including also ethics, is subordinate to cultural creativity; if thousands of people have to die to enable the creation of a work of genius, they are expendable.

120

The Reformation was a development from within Hebraism, which is dedicated to *humanitarianism*, the conviction that man's superiority to the beast is determined first and foremost by his reliance on ethics—by his aversion to brutality in the resolution of quarrels within his own milieu. Yet the prevalence in the ancient Mediterranean world of the scourge of war is as evident in Judaea as it is anywhere else; of the Hebraic writings the Old Testament is full—although the New Testament is clean—of the hate, and blood, and death, of war;

"Then Menahem smote Tiphsah, and all that were therein, and the coasts thereof from Tirzah: because they opened not to him, therefore he smote it; and all the women therein that were with child he ripped up.";[24]

and the teachings of the Bible have not discouraged the Europeans from being the world's most aggressive people—the Occident is hardly any more ethical than the Orient. Evidently, the identification of Hebraism with ethics is due to its humanitarian teachings—it sets human life above all else, above also mental creativity.

Man as an end in himself, his attempt to understand himself—is the fundamental difference between human being and animal being. Man's systems of thought resulting from this endeavor—humanism and humanitarianism, cultural values and ethical values are mutually inclusive, the difference hinging on which is considered more important. However, the actual operation in life—in experience, of a given teaching can never be mechanically understood; there is a difference between dedication to a value, and its achievement—the real can never more than approximate the ideal.

And the Renaissance was anathema to the Reformation. The exhortation of St. Paul in the New Testament;

"Beware lest any man spoil you through philosophy and vain deceit, after the tradition of men, after the rudiments of the world, and not after Christ"—[25]

created the heritage of an irreconcilable opposition between godliness and secular learning—the difference between knowledge as "sacred" and as "profane." With the Will of God confined to revelation in Holy

121

Writ, man's reliance on the trained mind—reason, intellect, philosophy, "the wisdom of the heathen Aristotle"—concerning the meaning of the world, of life, may be dispensed with: there is the arbitrary subordination, and even the dismissal, of mind, of rational inquiry; and there is an emphasis on the emotions, as intuition asserts itself without reason; and the prayer meeting is sufficient—it may even supplant the school. Sir Thomas More—and William Tyndale, who was a pioneer in translating the new Testament in the Bible from the original tongues into English, engaged in a literary debate on behalf respectively of Rome and Reform:

"More stated that reason was not an enemy to faith . . . (while) Tyndale thought of reason as a deceptive thing which if trusted turned one from faith";[26]

and it was held by many in the New Christianity that philosophical speculation is dangerous to faith.

Yet the atmosphere of Hellenism with its emphasis on rationalism, humanism, and on naturalism (paganism)—was spreading; and as it was realized that Anglicanism was coagulating as an intermingling of classical and biblical motives a determined, organized reaction against the Renaissance in Christianity began to rise among the Reform trader elements; and this introduced a doctrinal crisis within the Establishment. They accepted all of Episcopacy's objections to Rome but they regarded it as a superficial departure, as it continued the essential Catholic theology; and they even accused the new Church of conspiring with "papists" to keep the people in "superstition." They opposed prelacy because of its commitment both to the traditional theology—it consistently supported the Morean view, and to the Renaissance: they regarded the biblical and the classical as absolutely incompatible; and they demanded the erasure of "heretical" influences—the "purification" of Anglicanism from the "adulteration" of Holy Writ with natural—with "pagan," motives. And there was Episcopacy's seeming indifference to, and at times even depreciation of, Scripture. The Church of England had to be built on, and confined to, revelation: they demanded a complete return to Biblical authoritarianism—especially to the simplicity and orthodoxy of the primitive Hebraism in the Old Testament; and they thought of their identification with the Church as purely of spiritual value, or a matter of believing.

Scripture is Hebraic, Theology is Hellenic: Christianity from its inception was based on theology—the European never knew anything else; while it regarded revelation as superior to rationalism, they were both—intuition and reason—inwoven into the texture of the Christian religion. Bibliolatry confined itself strictly to the revelation of Hebraism, and everything alien thereto—Hellenism in all of its implications, was expunged. The confinement to the Bible—to revelation as virtually, and even as literally, the sole index to divine truth—was regarded by tradition as very much circumscribing. And the commonalty freedom of Scriptural interpretation led to the introduction of what appeared like a new principle in the history of Christianity—the principle of Biblicism as differentiated from theology, to the elimination of theology and the substitution of Biblicism. The ancient faith maintained that religion is a study in ultimates—where do we come from, where do we go to, why are we here?, which leads to the fundamental postulates of God, immortality, free will, teleology—and is based on intuition and reason; this study involves both theology and philosophy, which necessarily leads into metaphysics; and it was held that the experience of mankind establishes that it is given only to a rare few to penetrate the atmosphere of metaphysics—to enter the empyreal realm. The confrontation of the Renaissance and the Reformation created the consciousness of a qualitative difference between cultural values and popular education—they are fundamentally antipathetic, rather than sympathetic; cultural endeavor is always scholarly, while popular education is susceptible to demagoguery; the priest is the theologian—while the lay preacher, and even the minister, are confined to Biblicism. Hierarchy saw the New Christianity as an uprising of the immemorially submerged against the majesty of scholarship: there was a feeling of alienation and uneasiness on the part of extrovert nascent literacy in the atmosphere of scholasticism; the empyrean is forever closed to mediocrity, and commonalty was regarded as a menace, as it allegedly preferred to destroy what it couldn't understand or dominate.

The Reformation could not accept humanism as pre-eminent: the scholastic tradition—the theologian discussing an abstract concept of God in detachment, as cold logician—was unacceptable; God is not simply a matter of the universe as Intelligent—a fascinating problem in intellectualism; man is not brought to God only by pure, empyreal reasoning—by ratiocination; the head is instructed, but the heart remains unmoved. God is intuition, and He is emotion—love: religion is fundamentally a matter of inspiration, not of learning—to know God involves far more than intellectual comprehension; true knowledge of God cannot be that which flits through the brain—rather is it that which takes root in the heart; prayer, evangelical exhortation, come from the heart, not from the head; and they thought of religion as within the realm of feeling, as emanating from the innermost depths of the human being, as a personal emotional experience in which one feels himself transported. The exaltation of the natural man appeared like man worshiping himself—man as God's rival; the essence of human goodness is to be God-centered, and the essence of human sin is to be self-centered. And the exaltation of quality man—as a god amongst men, mentally superior, culturally creative, inherently good, wholly independent—had to be rejected. The Gospel taught humanitarianism: the Christian religion was to be purified of Hellenism; Reform ascribed all righteousness to God as it regarded man as morally naked, blind, weak; as before God all men are equal—they are childlike, helpless, sinful, who should be taken by the hand and shown the way to salvation; and the preservation of human life is man's first consideration.

To the Reformation reason was always subordinate to revelation: some Reformers were willing to accept the principle of pure or abstract reasoning, but only as a means to an end, as a help in arriving at divine truth—exegesis, Scriptural interpretation; yet many in the new Christianity denounced reasoning in problems spiritual as "carnal," and dismissed it completely. They were steeped in the wisdom of pre-science: they were carried away entirely by faith; their religion was fundamentally emotional, and they eschewed rationalism and Deism—religion is never a matter of metaphysical objectivity; they were convinced that revelation is superior to logic, science, art; there was an aversion to art in religion, and even to art as art; and rational evaluation, philosophical speculation, scientific experimentation were unhesitatingly thrown out if they appeared vitiative of faith. There was an emphasis on the sufficiency and the perspicuity of the Scriptures; and it was held that all truths necessary for salvation were to be found in Holy Writ, and so plainly expressed that the ordinary devout reader could discover them for himself. To the Biblical saturated mind logical consistency was no value, as revelation is based on divine inspiration; fundamental Christian beliefs which are unintelligible or untenable in rational-

124

ism were regarded as primary truth, on the allegation that their understanding transcends reason; acceptance was on faith—for which there was precedence in tradition, as fidelity dictated their sacredness none the less;

"reason teacheth, that God is both to be believed and obeyed in the things for which man can see no reason."[27]

In view of hierarchy tendencies to Deism it does not appear that Biblicism was ever in basic issue between Episcopacy and Reform: they were in a state of conflict, but their differences were concentrated fundamentally on their espousal of opposing doctrines—respectively the Hellenism of the Renaissance as against the Hebraism of the Reformation; whatever differences existed between them on problems of sacred doctrine and church were secondary. Thus Tudor England experienced the following confrontations in religion: Christianity= Romanism vs Anglicanism; Anglicanism= Episcopacy vs Reformation; Reformation= Wycliffism vs Calvinism; Wycliffism= sectarianism; Calvinism= Presbyterianism vs Puritanism. Episcopacy in the succeeding Anglican Church remained essentially loyal to the Roman religion, and it recognized the legality of the Reformation.

The Renaissance was concentrated on the good, the beautiful, and the true; the Reformation was concentrated on the good, the true, and the useful. Their reciprocal influences had profound social implications: with time England emerged as an original contributor—after the ancients, to basic human progress; she is the progenitor of science and empiricism on a mass, practical—on a social, scale; to the inherited basic principles of ethics, rationalism, law, she added the principle of— utility.[c] The Reformation—the revolution in religion, was very economy conscious: its adherents stemmed predominantly from commonalty, which had a tradition of pauperism; improvement in life was fundamentally economic—it was based upon the accumulation of capital for investment, which could be achieved from an abstemiousness that often meant miserliness; this brought rationalization—the principle of the budget, or the calculated intent to get the most for the least. In addition, Protestantism stressed the Old Testament conviction that there can be no physical image of God as He must not be presented to the senses; divinity must be strictly conceptual, confined to mind—Idea; this forced the

125

total exclusion of images from worship; and visual expression of anything identified with religion—statuary, picture, stained glass window—was condemned as idolatry. In terms of the way of life of Reformist Christianity with its penurious values, everything about the old faith appeared expensive to the point of profligacy. Art—the principle of esthetics, was a proper expression of the traditional religion: it was denounced as both luxurious and sacrilegious; it was declared that in worship the expression of beauty detracts from concentration on God, and that "pictures are the staves of the weak"; and they eschewed the seven arts—literature, theatre, painting, music, architecture, sculpture, terpsichore; the drama and the dance in their contemporary expressions were condemned almost to extinction; and they moved from the principle of deity as reinforced by material image, to pure emotionalism. The arts of the courtier were beyond the new Christianity, and its tracts on religion were devoid of rhetoric as they were presented in the plainest style. And they were also fanatical in their denunciation of nature as the inspiration of, and the foundation for, religion; and the celebration of the Christmas and May Day holidays was associated with the worship of nature and was condemned as "paganism."

The new way was potentially eliminative of qualitative distinctions between men: its fundamentally ascetic maxims for daily conduct were a prelude to the move towards utilitarianism; and its attitude on Scripture and on economy brought on the "vestiarian" controversy, which was a clash between esthetic and use values; it was held that there is no Scriptural authority concerning vestments, and there was a denunciation of clerical "popish apparel," "lordly titles," "pompous livings"—as artistic expressions of quality, and as wasteful and violative of thrift. And Reform was unyielding on points of worship and ceremony: the clerical dedication was to the good of souls, not to earthly vanity; divine love is to be found in the quality of character, not in temporal power and material splendor. The elegance and ritual of Episcopacy vied with the effort of Reform for simplicity and directness; and the commonalty church and its services were drab, worship was stripped of all ceremony and ornament, and for the music and color of the old services preaching was the main substitute.

CALVINISM

The French Reform discipline expressed itself in England as Calvinist, Huguenot, Presbyterian, Puritan. The theologians of Geneva were concentrated on the Scriptures, and on the classics: they were convinced that reason is a God-given guide for Christians, and that it may be applied to revelation; John Calvin's sacred doctrine was a combination of intuition—and of reason, both pure and practical; Calvinism was well developed rationally—it had attained to the intellect, and this rendered its sacred doctrine theology, rather than simply Biblicism. Calvinists thought that the Scriptures are at best not always either clear or consistent in what they purport to reveal for man's guidance, and this brought them to the age-old question—where to look for an authority by which to determine finally what the Heavenly Father intended to be understood as truth. And they had to fall back on the theologian, who relied on mental effort for the resolution of religious problems; the theologian is inherently the priest, concentrated on the divinities—as well as the philosopher, concentrated on the humanities. In the concern with the ultimate problems of life pure reason may be used to supplement the authority of Scripture; the same may hold true in the absence of definite Writ concerning ethical conduct and church rite; and there was an attempt to popularize the identification of the rational element with religion by encouraging exegesis, congregational catechetical teaching and discussion. And there was respect for the principle of logical consistency in the avoidance of contradiction when making modifications of, and changes in, sacred doctrine—although consistency could never be mechanical; and rationalism was an important factor in the attempt to define orthodoxy, heterodoxy, heresy. Yet there was an underlying distrust of pure, "carnal" reason; Reform was convinced that revelation is divine and reason is human, and the human is necessarily subordinate to the divine. Faith comes from the heart, reason from the head: the heart is primary—reason is never more than a means towards an end, the end being an understanding of divine truth; the devotee must never contravene God's Word in the name of anything, and reason, art, science, were unhesitatingly discarded if they were regarded as tending to vitiate revelation and to promote Deism.

Pioneering in social phenomena is individual, not institutional; there is a move from one ideological condition to another—which seems to operate from nebulosity, to the individual theoretician, to the organization. Protestantism was a dominant type or form that more or less imposed itself upon the whole, but underneath there were variants; the new Bible induced a recognizable distinction between the various sects within each of the major doctrines, and also as between the several cross combinations of them that subsequently followed. Dissent in England rose out of a social revolutionary condition—it was something new: it developed from the general, the Reformation—to the specific, the denomination; the leaders of the general movement, and of its resultant sects, were without the great name—the father-figure, of traditional religion.

The Reformation in England—which came to be identified as, and was synonymous with, ''Tudor Puritanism''—began as a vast ideological formation, which introduced a condition of chaos and confusion in religion. The publication in 1611 of the King James Authorized Version of the Bible introduced a new principle in the history of Dissent in England; the new Version was accepted by all Reform groups as the voice of God, and it gave them the definitive source from which they could draw their doctrinal conclusions; it created the foundation for the practical crystallization of Scriptural interpretation, and this had a centripetal effect as it became the source of a seminal flow. This was followed by the slow emergence of leading preachers from within the opacity, each of whom achieved a tendency towards doctrinal coagulation, and gained a following that clustered around him; and the essence of his doctrine eventually acquired solidity, and laid the foundation for the development of a Protestant sect, and in a few cases even of a denomination. The seventeenth century has been described as ''the century of genius''—the golden age of English religious literature. And underlying this tale ''full of sound and fury'' were the two discernible mainstreams of Reformation thought—Calvinism and Wycliffism. From these fundamental doctrines varying forms of Scriptural thinking began to develop, take shape and follow definite patterns—and Reform was evolving different systems of religious understanding. And there developed the Stuart era Reformation categories: ''Nonconformity,'' whose teachings were inherited from John Wycliffe, and whose expression was both doctrinal and structural—from which sprouted a plethora of sects some of which developed into denominations, and produced

128

variants that in time brought sub-variants; and "Presbyterianism" and "Puritanism," whose expression was at first simply doctrinal—and which drew their inspiration fundamentally from John Calvin; all these doctrines had broad areas of underlying agreement, which had constituted the Tudor Puritanism of the previous century. By about the end of the Elizabethan era the Church of England had achieved sufficient crystallization for the realization that the Calvinists were definitely included within its organization, while the Wycliffites were as definitely outside of it or independent.

Presbyterianism in England belonged to the great Calvinistic tradition: it saw a distinction between the Bible and theology; it declared that the Bible is God's gift to man, and regarded it as an eternal mystery; and it accepted the principle of theology, which is the human attempt to explain the divine meaning. Holy Writ itself is eternal: there can be no addition, no detraction; it stands, forever—unchanged. But Presbyterianism was moving towards the principle of a teleological—of an evolving, developing—revelation: Scripture is always increasingly self-revealing, which renders the content of theology subject to constant change; and this brings an understanding of God's Word which is progressively better. There is a constantly improving profundity of Biblical insight over the generations, which is in obedience to the fuller light that the Holy Spirit forever continues to shed upon the Holy Word, and whose penetration and grasp are the chief concern of the clergy. Thus it is man's supreme effort to burrow in the depths of Today in order to discern God's unchanging purpose for Tomorrow—to scent eternity in the present; the Reformer feels called upon to be "an active human agent of the divine purpose running through the ages."

The principle of theology as subject to constant change was an important modification of tradition, and it had its effects on Presbyterianism as Church. It was declared that no living institution can go on without change; *Ecclesia semper reformanda*—"the Reformed Church must always be reforming." The Church, like any other social organization, is always being challenged to answer new questions, and to make decisions about new problems as they arise; and the Presbyterian theology is a creedal confession of faith as deduced from Scripture by the Church Elders. Thus it accepted the principle of theological judgment in understanding the Word of God: spiritual inspiration and authority are ecclesiastical, whose interpretation of Scripture had to be accepted by the

129

laity; yet their conclusions are never on a par with the Bible, and theology is therefore at all times amendable, and parts of it can even be excised in the light of later understanding—all of which renders it in essence of secondary value. The differences between all the people within Presbyterianism were always in degree, and its vertical ecclesiastical structure was conical—never hierarchical: Calvinism was identified with the doctrine of collectivist worship which stressed the authority of group experience—the congregation *as a whole* is in a direct relation with God; and the worshipers in prayer developed from the traditional passive participants under absolute control of the priest—to active, self-assertive participants.

Calvinism was together with Episcopacy in the Anglican Church, and they had to have broad areas of underlying agreement: they both accepted the principle of a monolithic sacred doctrine and structure, a common creed in one united and comprehensive church—the "true religion" of the Scriptures, which was considered essential to a well-ordered and stable national existence. And Anglicanism walked in the path of tradition: a departure from the accepted theology was "heresy"—which was tantamount to rebellion and anarchy; this committed them to the principle of the "Establishment," or the union of church and state; both were ready to employ the secular power of the state—it was a proper duty of the civil magistrates to enforce and protect the integrity of the state church; and execution for heresy was an accepted instrument of unity. Thus the Calvinists were sectarians of doctrine alone: they were, and they intended to remain, within the Establishment; they were achieving an adjustment which gave them a sense of belonging within Anglicanism, whose Episcopalian theology they hoped to purify. But from the Restoration of 1660 Presbyterianism left the Establishment and set up its own distinct Church, and Anglicanism became synonymous with Episcopacy.

Puritanism first emerged in England as a social force from about 1565, and it evaporated about a century later—with the restoration of the monarchy: its first fifty years were under the Tudor influence, or before the appearance of the new Version of the Bible in 1611; and its second half century followed into the Stuart era. There were fundamental differences between these two expressions of Puritanism. "Tudor Puritanism" was a nebulous doctrine virtually synonymous with the Reformation in England, as it was understood to include all Dissenter

130

groups. The recent Bible was promotive both of divisiveness and of fusion as within the Reformation; Calvinism and Wycliffism each tended towards an intra divisiveness, and the new Version facilitated also the tendencies to an inter-cross fusion of the sects as they were emerging from the parent doctrines. The expression in England of Calvinism took the form of Presbyterianism, from within which there soon crystallized a variant group, which tended towards the acceptance of certain Nonconformist tenets, and may be identified as "Stuart Puritanism"; this constituted a compounding of Calvinist and, to some extent, of Wycliffite, doctrines—it was not a merger of the membership of respective groups. Yet Stuart or seventeenth-century Puritanism considered itself as doctrinally and politically fundamentally within Calvinism. Its devotees were mostly from East Anglia and the neighboring shires, and they evidently stemmed chiefly from the descendants of the Huguenot textile weaver *emigres*, who had brought their Calvinism to England; and they comprised commonalty people—together with some members of the gentry, who had acquired substantial manufacturing bourgeois interests.

WYCLIFFISM

John Wycliffe, and his disciples—the Lollards, were the pioneers of the Reformation in England; they taught that the Scriptures are the sole source of divine truth, they have a full sufficiency in all things, and the commonalty folk have the ability to know and to understand Holy Writ and should read it for themselves. The Lollards had a century and a half of history and experience outside the State Church, which was Roman; if it was correct and proper for them to withdraw from the traditional Church, it was no necessary part of their doctrine to identify themselves with any successor. Lollardy from Tudor England achieved several forms of expression. "Independency," which was confined to Church organization, to anybody outside the Establishment—Lollard, Roman Catholic, Jew. "Separatism," or the political principle of the *right* to freedom from membership in the State Church—the Roman Catholic in Elizabethan England was an Independent in fact, but he was never a Separatist in principle. And "Nonconformity," which is doctrinal: it held that conformity with the prescribed ritual of a given Church is not

131

fundamental to salvation; it involved the problem of faith and works, and it had its profound implications concerning the teachings of religion. All three of these propositions were inspired by the ideas of John Wycliffe, and developed from within Lollardy. They represented the most extreme form of Bibliolatry: Scripture is the foundation of life—there is nothing important for man outside of the Word of God; some of them pushed this contention so far as to insist that no action in daily life could be regarded as righteous unless expressly warranted in Holy Writ.

The essence of the doctrine of Nonconformity is the election of the individual—it is a call to dedication: each man has the ability to go to the Bible on his own, to consider himself directly "taught of God," and to interpret and to understand Holy Writ for himself; the individual may, for the salvation of his soul, properly rely on his own judgment in understanding Holy Writ; and they stressed the principle of individual worship, of the proposition that each supplicant—spirit, soul, mind, will, ego—is in a separate and *direct* relation with God. Each man has also the *right* to be a Bible student, to worship God as he chooses, to propagate his faith, and even to found his own Church. There is no traditional institutionally established authority, spiritual or temporal, in religion; however, the principle of spiritual authority was accepted as the individual, either cleric or layman, could try to win popular recognition as such; thus spiritual authority could be lay—everyone was on his own. The purity of doctrine must remain inviolate: the foundation of religious belief is one's right and liberty to guide his life in terms of his own conscience; a man's life with God is really his own personal affair, for which he is answerable to nobody.

Nonconformity was intuition without ratiocination: religion revolved around the individual, and was entirely intuitive, within the realm of feeling—it was "the culture of the heart," and full reliance was placed upon divine inspiration. The devotees engaged in practical reasoning: they stopped with the immediate, the shallow—there was no mental depth; the spiritual expression of many of the recently literate preachers —with their simple-minded understanding of the Bible—took the form of a mechanical, unimaginative literalness; God was thinking like the barely literate commoner—"why doesn't God do away with the devil?," "because his time has not yet come." And their worship was at times accompanied by an emotional overflow; they felt rather than reasoned, and ideas did not flow in smooth currents but in troubled cross

132

currents. Rhetoric tended to undermine the empire of reason, and as within the Nonconformist worship emotion was capable of an intensity that gave religion a positively hysterical character. A few of the preachers developed a practical insight into mob psychology: with religion as a stimulus that was all feeling—no thinking, they could resort to a set of devices for moving the emotions of their listeners; they developed a tendency to ranting—to rhapsodical moaning; they wrung their hands and beat their breasts—and there were those who thought themselves "prophets," and who were prone to whip themselves into fits of hysteria and to fall into trances.

Man's subjectivism may express itself in terms of the insight of the head, mind; or of the heart, feeling; or of both. The insight of the head may be understood in terms of popular education, and of cultural creativity; these two forms of learning are often non-sympathetic, and at times they are even antipathetic.

To the Nonconformists the concept of God as cold rationalism—as a study in philosophy leading into metaphysics, was untenable: they were misologists; they were in great fear of, and they hated, abstract "carnal" reasoning, which was entirely eliminated as dangerous to faith—"the most depraved and cunning of all harlots, Reason";

> "the masses, to whom abstract thought is both boring and impious, for whom the fiat of Revelation renders all speculation superfluous."[28]

This discouraged religion of the head, and it was confined to the heart; the spirit alone is sufficient—and sheer emotional fervor was infinitely preferable to the least degree of intellectual discipline, from which religion was completely separated. And there was a move away from the outward forms of faith, and toward the "inner reality": the Church Father St. Augustine said, "it is the inner master that teacheth"; it is the inner spiritual experience—the Light of Christ shining in one's conscience, that constitutes knowledge of God and certainty of faith. Individualism in religion was convinced that spiritual insight is something very different from the belief in historical facts: the religious experience gives one a deeper and truer understanding of, and makes him a sacrificial witness unto, Christ; "the Christ of experience" is one thing, "the

133

Christ of history" is another; there is an insufficiency in a faith that is merely historical. The Inner Light of each man is the only true guide for his conduct: he may dispense with outward miracles as the direct illumination in the heart is primary, while the witness of others is only contributory; the truth of revelation does not depend upon external evidence. Theirs was an attitude of pure emotion—bereft of thinking, and Biblicism never attained to the intellect.

Men thought in terms of absolutes—all evil, all good; and they could be transported from the depths of despair to the heights of ecstasy. The sermon preferred generally the themes of denunciation and terror: there was the pronouncement of a Biblical knell of doom on the land—the deluges of destruction, death, desolation; men were in fear and trembling of Armageddon, of catastrophe or the end of the world—everything annihilated in one fell swoop; this was aggravated by the urge to overseas exploration—the call of the unknown, the drive to back of beyond—which brought an emphasis on nature, and men wondered whether their artifacts were equal to the challenge; and there was an inner feeling of impotence, of complete helplessness before nature—astral and climatic phenomena, pestilence, flood, earthquake, famine, ocean, jungle, wilderness, savage, war.[d] Yet the sermon was also given to the kindred emotions of love and sweetness: they thought ecstatically in terms of Apocalypse—the heavens opening up, and God and His celestial hosts descending to dwell forever among men—bringing heaven to earth, as He abolished all evil and ordained everlasting life; and their expressions were full of Hallelujah and Hosannah.

To elementary men everything in the world, in life—is anthropomorphic; theirs is the geo-anthropo-centric mind. They create God in their own image—He is a man-like deity. The Bible men were confined to Christianity of the Book: they experienced the religious awe, the sense of wonder man had once known in personal communion with his Being; they knew what it felt like to be alive in the first morning of the world, to look in on the creative beginnings—"the joy of creation and bestowal of life";

> "But he, being full of the Holy Ghost, looked up steadfastly
> into heaven, and saw the glory of God, and Jesus standing on
> the right hand of God";[29]

134

there is the universality of the Light of Christ, and His influence on man in his daily life. God is transcendent, having separate individual identity; God is Jehovah, having human attributes—"I am a jealous God"; He is quantity—an aggrandized, glorified man. Holy Writ emphasized man's basic alienation from God, his hopeless worthlessness, his dependence upon divine assistance; and there was the tendency to flagellation, breast-beating, self-depreciation—"miserable sinner that I am." And there was exaltation of the practical, common, pioneer faith—"give me the old time religion"; and life was the simplicity of the pastoral scene.

The Reformation introduced the principle of mass literacy, especially to enable Bible study; and while it was thought that general secular knowledge has its place, it was considered of secondary value. Yet it took several generations for a practical condition of popular education to be attained, and in the meantime a good deal of reliance had to be placed on insufficiency—in the pioneering days of Scriptural nebulosity Wycliffism was not without the illiterate preacher; he was convinced that the Lord speaks through him, and he could not clearly understand the importance of being fully literate. As the various doctrinal interpretations were moving from amorphousness towards crystallization the Protestant Seminary with its ordination of ministry was becoming practical, yet Dissent continued to accept the preacher. It was maintained, especially by nascent literacy, that a true knowledge of God—the divine contact in prayer, flows solely from familiarity with the Bible; everything rested on divine revelation. They were given to "the Great Awakening, the passionate harangue that depends for nothing upon college training or book learning."

During the nebulosity of the transition to Anglicanism the Reformation did not have a clear-cut sense of "In" or "out" as in relation to the Church. The Wycliffites became convinced that it is impossible to overcome the Episcopal domination within Anglicanism: as they began to emerge from the ideological fog, they developed a consciousness of themselves as fundamentally different from the coagulating mass; and they were carried away by a fanaticism to the extent that they introduced a revolutionary principle in the history of the realm—they developed a sense of alienation from, and felt themselves outside of, the state Church—the Establishment. Thus the Nonconformists were sectarians of both faith and church: they were good Bible Christians, but they

135

were not churchmen; their appeal was to the individual heart—they forgot the social character of Christianity. The confinement of religion to the Bible and to the inner man depreciated the principle of the social institution: the idea that "the best ministry comes from something deeper than learning" rendered incidental the external or institutionalized manifestations of religion—church, clergy, ceremony, council, and also secular education; God can reach man under any condition—the operation of the Spirit is in no way limited to any specific time, place, person; and they renounced the principle of exclusiveness, or the setting apart of any man or building as indispensable for divine worship—the world is his cloister; man can go out into nature, the wilderness, into the open field, and make personal contact with God through prayer. The idea that the individual soul might commune directly with God—without the medium of a priest—lent man integrity, and emphasized in thought and religion the doctrine of individualism. The principles of private judgment and of toleration necessarily go together—they imply each other, and this means the elimination of church heresy as a social evil: however, the freedom of conscience of Nonconformity was political, it was not Biblical; the independent church is wholly free of institutional—state, church—interference, but the sectarians condemned each other to perdition as apostates and heretics for "perverting the Scriptures." Nonconformity continued in its tradition that individual interpretation of Holy Writ is the one and only true God's meaning, but with the multiplicity of such understanding a new principle had to be introduced—that erroneous explanation, if sincere, is not fatal to salvation in the eyes of God.

The fact of the monolithic faith and church was inwoven in the Europeans' subjective being: Christian England never knew of a time of separation of church and state; and Reform was at first convinced that popular study would soon reveal the true meaning of Scripture, and bring a unanimity of basic understanding which would substitute and establish the true Christianity. The idea of Nonconformity—of independence from the Church monolith, of individuality in religious conviction and expression—was a strange doctrine also among the Reformed; the principles of freedom of conscience, and of separatism, in religion—did not spring full-blown into the mind of John Wycliffe or of any of his disciples; rather were they the result of a slowly developing process in experience and thinking over several centuries. Freedom of conscience

136

in religion brought a good part of the realm into conflict with the traditions of the ages; the Nonconformists neither anticipated nor wanted the controversies that resulted from their teaching—the obstinate individualism, the move from a sense of awe to license, from religious uniformity to chaos, and the disintegration of Christendom into dozens of sects. The sectarian anarchy was thought unnecessary as it was held that the Word of God is normally its own interpreter, and light on its dark places could be derived from the texts whose meaning is clear; the Scriptures were fundamentally an example of harmony, not of strife— revelation's seeming inconsistencies are due to man's faulty understanding; and there were negotiations looking towards uniformity of Protestant belief;

> "Truth as revealed in scripture was one and the same, intelligible and without mystery, for all who would read. The only thing that could obscure knowledge was sin."

Yet with time it had to be concluded that difficulties remained; and during the Stuart era the Nonconformists settled to the conclusion that the Scriptures were at best not always either clear or consistent in what they purported to reveal for man's guidance, and that there were to be permanent divisions within the Reformation. Moreover, some of them were thought guilty,

> "of extravagant nonsense in speculation, of conceited and ignorant dogmatism, of sentiments hostile to public order, of refinements in morality which ended in escape from the sense of moral obligation, and in libertinism and universal license . . ."[30]

This brought the devotees to the age-old problem—where to look for an authority by which to resolve what the Holy Spirit intended to be understood as truth; since they had no such authority, no court of last resort, they decided to allow the individual's conscience to be his guide, and they eventually accepted religious individuality or atomization on principle—it could exercise men's faith, and it could be considered a mark of freedom that is socially desirable. Thus it took the Reformation in England more than a century to develop to the stage where it could

137

think of church and state as distinct, and formulate the idea of their separation, and eventually move towards the principle of religious toleration.

John Wycliffe had enunciated a set of teachings which laid the foundation for the concept of the state and the church as distinct entities, and led to their eventual separation;

> "Nothing came to birth in the sixteenth century that had not been in embryo, in Wycliffe's time, under the common heart of England";

his principles were propounded and continued as a viable doctrine, and were crystallized as a social movement, by Lollardy; and this took expression in the seventeenth century as Nonconformity. The Nonconformists introduced the principle of individualism: the foundation of religious belief is one's right and liberty to guide his life in terms of his own conscience; a man's life with God is really his own personal affair, for which he is answerable to nobody. Their leading figures were mainly lay preachers, men who had risen from the illiterate levels of commonalty. Each of them was immersed in Holy Writ; and each found a passage which gave him a fresh insight, and which he attempted to justify. He was anxious to walk in the way of the Lord, and as preacher he was fanatically convinced that he had a direct relation to God, which rendered him divinely inspired; he identified his being in the world with a deep "sense of mission"—he was an inner witness to the Holy Spirit, and God transmitted His message concerning sacred doctrine through him to the congregation; and this gave him a messianic complex.

Nonconformity, as its name implies, was per se the enemy of ritual conformity as the sole way to salvation. It was the normal foundation of the life of Wycliffism; it was not a matter of liberalism or of legislation for numerous individual doctrinal diversionary tendencies to exist, a few of which eventually achieved sufficient crystallization as sects and even as denominations; the right to toleration of each sectarian strand was based upon that of the others, and the principle of religious freedom is inherent in Nonconformity. Oliver Cromwell pushed through a measure in Parliament establishing the right to dissent in religion. From about the time of the Restoration the Reformation in England began to settle to the conclusion that divisions within itself are permanent; religious toleration

138

became a conscious Nonconformist demand, and the maintenance of civil peace forced the legalization of Dissent. And the Toleration Act, the principle of religious freedom, was officially accepted in 1690—for the first time in the history of Christianity, of the world. All differences within the Reformation in Stuart England could be serious and disruptive; sectarianism resulted in the atomization of organized religion, and liberty of conscience did tend towards anarchy.

NOTES

[a]During 1553-87 the sovereigns of England and of Scotland were women; for the first five years both queens were Roman Catholic, and were named Mary.

[b]Except for the decade of the Oliverian Interregnum.

[c]The recent developments in sociology, psychology, anthropology, mathematics, take their fundamental inspiration from the empiricism of science.

[d]John Bunyan's Pilgrim's Progress, which is evidently based on The Revelation of St. John The Divine in the New Testament of the Bible, seems to be a reflection of the Nonconformist mind.

CHAPTER FIVE—SOCIAL CHANGES IN STUART ENGLAND

FEUDALISM vs. CAPITALISM

At the beginning of the seventeenth century—when kings ruled as well as reigned, the Stuart family became the royal house of England, represented by James First as king. On their accession the Stuarts found themselves at the crucial stage in the "long contest which ultimately transferred purse and sword from Crown to Commons."[31] The struggle was between feudal landowners and traders for control of the realm; their differences were fundamental, being based on sociology—on institutions and values.

Land, trade, labor—the man of the soil, the man of the mart, the man of the factory—had co-existed within the civilized milieu from time immemorial: they had all along been engaged in a struggle for power, as each of them wanted to organize society according to his own pattern; yet they had an underlying need for one another, and the existence of each was never in question. Land succeeded in constituting itself the foundation of the social order—feudalism. In the seventeenth century England was organized on the vertical system of society; there were no horizontal divisions. The realm found the trader indispensable to the well-being of the *status quo,* and there was generally no opposition to the altered methods of production of wealth; but he had to remain subordinate—to stay in his place. And there were confrontations concerning economy as between feudalism and capitalism, and also as within each in itself. Different laws for lordly and lowly were accepted as a normal part of life: the word of honor in lieu of an oath was a privilege of the peer; and medicaments, more and less expensive, were prescribed respectively for rich and poor. The differences as within the commonalty or the third estate were quantitative, based on economy—banker (gain) interest and dividends, entrepreneur (profit), worker (wages).

Aristocracy was a hierarchy: its primary divisions were nobility and gentry, each of which had its own inner gradations; the membership in each grade increased numerically downwards. The infeudated estate in the countryside, the manor, the title, the coat-of-arms, the leisure necessary for the achievement of the university degree and of the values of cultural creativity—all this constituted hierarchy, the symbols of social prestige. Traditional elite was based on the principle of blood and land—*sangre y terra*. The men of quality were hypnotized by their past; everything was station, the blood of family—they were obsessed by their ancestral line. And they were rooted in a reverence for the continuity of the sylvan atmosphere; they had a voluptuous love for, they yearned for the joys of intimacy with, nature. They wanted to live according to a land ethic—they had a profound regard for its innate wisdom;

"to smell of green grass and woods where shadows lie,
and the sun shines down through the trees";

they were dominated by a mystic sense of the land; the observation of the landscape in all of its fullness was life; and they felt deeply the beauty of the countryside, and they drank in its dewy freshness to the point of intoxication. The home—castle, mansion—of the blooded was hidden in a clump of trees, as retired as one could wish, and the family coat-of-arms was carved on the front door. The universal reliance on land of that day accentuated its indispensability; realty—lands, tenements, hereditaments—is immovable, and it was the foundation of life, which gave it its social meaning. The alienation, the physical transfer of personalty—livestock, produce, furnishings—is simple; but the fee simple independent title in the alienation of "reality," was beyond the comprehension of the feudal mind.

During the forty-five years of the Elizabethan regime some Presbyterian merchants, through the acquisition of church expropriated lands and through purchase of title, had achieved unprecedented economic and political power in the realm—and a conflict of interest arose between the Episcopacy of the land and the Calvinism of the mart. The rise of the Stuarts found the monarchy under virtual trader domination. James First, evidently in an attempt to create good will, was openly

141

selling titles of nobility, and everything that went with such title—power, prestige, perquisite—at £10,000 each, for which he found ready purchasers; this was fabulous money in the seventeenth century, and it could happen only, it seems, in England—which was indeed the land of "merchant princes." The capitalists who had bought their way to social recognition acquired the external habiliments of station—the life of the country gentleman in terms of title, manor, mannerism; and to the elite of blood and land—*sangre y terra*—was added that of capital or, really, plutocracy. Thus inherited traditional Episcopalian title was *aristoc*racy—the best, which was fundamentally of the countryside; while purchased revolutionary Presbyterian title was *pluto*cracy—the richest, which was fundamentally of the town. The economic potential of capital or personalty is illimitable: the newly titled had industrial enterprises in the towns, foreign investments, ships at sea; and their manors could be given some adjustment with a view to the raising of produce for profit. The Presbyterian had, together with the Episcopalian, achieved power in the government: a few of the richest succeeded in buying their way into the best families; and land and trade managed on the whole to strike a balance of power under the Tudors. Plutocracy tried to make the ways of capital applicable also in rural life; the lord of trade, on achieving the status of local sovereign, introduced the principle of exercising personal supervision in the economy of his manor—"the best manure is the foot of the master"; and the business man was beginning to appear also as landlord.

The scions of the upper patriciate who had been disinherited by primogeniture generally entered the professions—defense, medicine, law, teaching. The younger sons of the lower gentry were quality without a household, which was the depth of misery; money was the only means to the achievement of their supreme ambition—the estate in the countryside; and money could be acquired only in the trades of the urban centers. The move from nature to artifact was fundamental—it was a change in the way of life: land was static, while the mart was dynamic; the gentleman who moved into town had to do so as apprentice, under commoner mastery; and he would have to acquire, if he was to succeed, the basic trader values—the man of honor in the mart would soon be devoured. As many of those of lesser quality were becoming masters in the trades there took place a commingling of gentry and commonalty; yet although a portion of trade acquired some landed characteristics there was never an ideological blend; it was inherent in this relation for trade always basically to prevail; and the scion of the land, once caught up in the dynamism of the capital economy, was forever lost to his heritage. Quality was welcomely received by commonalty, and accepted as in a position of leadership within trade; and the denigrated had the choice of remaining the tail of the gentry, or of becoming the head of the yeomanry. Many of them went to the city and became apprentices in the trades; some in time made enough money with which to go back to their native landscape and found a country family—they managed to achieve, and then to maintain, "the mansion that cloth built." There were also instances of interclass marriage—blood married into money; with time and the changing social conditions substantial commoners and the lesser gentry were increasingly penetrating each other's lives; and the trader becoming elite did not materially affect his values.

And with the translation of the Bible into the vernacular, and the rise of mass literacy and of printing, the commonalty became identified also with the Reformation. Thus trade and Reform revolved around "the People," from which followed its socially crystallized expression— Puritanism. All of which tended towards the creation of a fluid or dynamic society, and the development of a move to vertical class mobility. The class differences were becoming quantitative: the "bourgeoisie" were based on the masses—their values included everyone; and this gave them a sense of power they never had before. The Presbyterians wanted to establish the rule of capital, which meant the introduction of a new sociology—the capitalistic state, with its own institutions and values; this was unprecedented in the history of mankind, and the social revolutionaries had to grope; and the "new Society" had yet definitively to supplant the basic *status quo*—feudalism.

The social shift from land to trade—the rule of capital, which brought a mass separation of man from nature and towards artifact, introduced a change in mental attitudes—in values. The differences between them in way of life—hopes, ambitions, pursuits, interests—were real and profound: land was economically local, politically federal, spiritually national; trade was politically and spiritually national, and it was economically international—Puritanism was laying the foundations of Empire. The principle of internationalism was traditional in England, but it changed its expression from religion to economy. Immemorial values unconsciously taken for granted were being rendered objective as they

143

were brought to the fore, and made issues of. It seems that land always had an underlying fear of capital; the feudal realty laws—really institutions, were evidently established with a view to protecting land against capital absorption. Land in a corporeal sense—as agriculture, continued indispensable: but land in a sociological sense—as feudalism, began to feel itself menaced; a change was slowly overtaking immemorial quality land as it was moving from *sangre y terra* towards capital, quantity land—towards organization in terms of trader ways. The institutions and the values of the feudal society were adjusted to scarcity but not to reserve; and the general increase in productivity and in the distribution of the goods of life, called "wealth"—tended to derange the cooperative serenity of medieval organization. The system of wealth distribution—of economic ends and means—under feudalism had achieved social sanction; it had become spiritually, morally and legally standardized over the centuries. The coming of economic reserve, with its socialization of the methods of the mart, violated traditionally accepted norms; the values of the land economy could not be projected into the capital economy; the dynamism of capital was eliminating the staticness of land—the feudal values of stability, security, serenity; this brought a revulsion from the new ways of sharing wealth, and there were doubts that capital could rule successfully. The top traders had sufficient accumulated capital—a surplus of money, to become bankers: this they could use for investment in economic enterprise, and to lend to others at interest on good security; thus they became creditors, which began to give rise to a creditor and debtor relation. Money is a characteristic of trade, not of land: the feudal landowner—the knight, was not exactly a "rich" man, nor was the serf exactly a "poor" man; land always had a dearth of cash, of which trade always had enough; and this rendered land often beholden to capital. The power of banking had achieved the enactment of necessary legislation to insure its loans, the government became a staunch defender of creditor rights, and the credit system developed into a pillar of the capital economy. And the quality debtor was also liable to imprisonment for delinquency.

Yet the stability of the traders' social order was involved with that of tradition, and their purpose was to modify, and to subordinate—but not to liquidate, the feudal institutions. The economic insouciance of land set the social standards; all classes loved the trappings of dignity—and aristocracy continued as the summit of social life, to be looked up to and

144

emulated. To the landed elite trade and labor were per se base and corrupt: life in the congestion of the mart in the town was *contra naturam*; it was dysfunction, which brought mental and physical deformity; the city man was "a treeless ghost"—he was interred, buried alive; the world of the Puritan was a nightmare, and tradition disdained the plutocrats—with their displays of financial affluence and cultural poverty—as interlopers or pseudo-aristocrats. Yet in the economy of scarcity all men were grasping for money, and those whose station made them contemptuous of trade were not without cupidity. With their social position assured, the nobility of tradition took advantage of opportunities for their emolument; they were beginning to take an interest in the benefits of capital; and the members of the royal court were sharing with merchants in the investments and profits of commercial enterprises to an unprecedented degree. The patricians were characterized by narcissism, they were avaricious for sterling, but they felt entitled to it per se—by virtue of place, and they never wanted it for its own sake; money to them meant prosperity, but their sense of power and prestige was rooted in land—which was the foundation of their way of life; they never had the values of the business man, and they had never developed a talent for making money; they were interested in the new way only to the extent that it did not interfere with the fundamentals of sacred tradition; trade had to be tolerated as a means of livelihood for commonalty, but the idea of it supplanting land as the social foundation was anathema. They would not under any condition exchange land for trade, and no member of original top quality ever did so: money was never an *end in itself*, and they spurned it if it meant engagement in pursuits leading to a separation from the open-spacedness of nature; the tradition of chivalry called for fame and glory—not for gain, and to the man of nature, to the "man of honor" money was not the supreme value—he had no such stimulus to resist. And the changes in ecclesiastical structure did not materially affect this attitude: the differences between Roman and Anglican were relatively incidental; the latter was much more economy minded than its predecessor, yet both were unalterably opposed to trade supplanting land as the way of life.

The interaction of permanence and change in the field of social phenomena expresses itself in terms of stratification and fluidity, which can be vertical or horizontal; the staticness and the dynamism of mobility

145

are universal and eternal constants, their interaction being complementary and varying in degree with time and place. In the hierarchical society those at the top can be either haughty or condescending towards inferiors —both are attitudes of contempt. There was the disdain of land for trade, and the emulation of land by trade; the appreciation of excellence was universal; all participants in the struggle for domination—traditional land and revolutionary capital—accepted, and intended to continue, the principle of the vertical form of social organization; and the presence and potency of quality within rebellion preserved the cultural values.

Under Elizabeth First the trader had reached a pinnacle of power beyond even his own anticipation—he had just about achieved political and economic control of the realm. This had its societal implications: Reform was determined to contract religiously; it was opposed to political and economic localism on the one side, and to ecclesiastical supranationalism on the other. Land was traditionally committed to the principle of federalism in government or local autonomy, which tended to centrifugalism; while the centripetalism of capital preferred to shift power to the central government, which paved the way to the introduction of nationalism or political integration. Puritanism accepted the principle of monarchy, as the power of both tended inevitably towards the center—communications, towns, *citiz*en, *burgh*er; and there was a consistent move from numerous local independent economic entities, to one national interdependent economy. The trader bought a charter from the Crown for the commercial companies he organized in order to achieve certain rights and privileges; the king was much more sensitive to disorder in the cities than in the countryside as they were the chief source of his power; he generally supported the towns against the Church, and with the substitution of Anglicanism and the acceptance of the principle of Erastianism, the State acquired ascendancy. England's shires were to be integrated into a political whole, and the principle of a strong centralized government was to be realized in the monarchy. They preferred to broaden from localism to the inclusion of all of the realm's inhabitants; from the *shire* man—language, outlook, to nationalism or "the People," to England as a nation—to the "Englishman"; there was a consistent tendency towards the nation meaning more and the locale less; and the masses were expected to shift their allegiance from the leadership of home neighbors to that of remote national figures. The

146

population of London was growing out of all proportion to the rest of the country, and the substitution of nationalism for federalism appeared to localism as royal domination or tyranny.

The Tudors had inherited the traditional view of monarchy; the Crown and the king were thought of as identical, and the principle of rule by divine right and royal prerogative was implicit. Yet "the changing shape of English life," from the institutions and the values of land to those of trade, caused the caste antipodes—from many persons of quality to the disinherited submerged—to begin moving towards the capital way, towards industry or intensive economic expansion; the principles of the Crown, and of local autonomy, were to be retained, but subordinated— government was to exist for the benefit of the nation, instead of simply for an elite; and there was a revolt against the doctrine of the divine right of kings, which made them responsible to God rather than to "the People"—to the country. The radical shift in social organization could not be comprehended fundamentally within the framework of the Anglo-Saxon common law, which was based on precedent and was therefore inherently feudal; thus the promoters of change, in an attempt to avert the violence of imposition, had to rely on an emphasis on statutory law that it never had before; statute is enacted by legislation, and this began to make the English legislature—Parliament, for the first time the decisive force in governing the country.

> "Never in its history had parliament been . . . so continuously (1529-34) taken into account as a factor in the king's government of the country."[32]

This represents the beginnings of Parliamentary potency: the principle of "the consent of the people" appears authoritatively in the reign of Henry VIII; and his Succession Act is the first ever enacted by a legislature to regulate the continuity of the Crown. England was a powerful monarchy, unlike the "toy republics" on the continent; the royal authority was severed from tradition and rendered statutory, as the power of the Crown became predicated upon an act of Parliament; it meant the dynamiting of the traditions that had supported a way of life—feudalism, for a millennium. The beneficiaries of the dissolution of the monasteries were determined to keep what they got, and the successive Parliaments were very sensitive to any suggestion for the restoration of Church ex-

147

propriated property. And the penetration of land by capital was bringing tradition into question: Crown and king began to appear as separate principles, respectively institution and person; there was an introduction of the principle of Parliamentary monarchy—the constitutional, limited monarchy, a chosen king with a legislative title; Parliament—"the People," rather than Prerogative, seemed to be becoming the foundation of the royal power; the monarch's *popularity* was beginning to become important, and opposition to the king was not per se opposition to the Crown; and men were changing their thinking from the supreme authority of the king to that of "the government."

The rise of the trader subordinated the state to capital interests; the great merchant plutocracy and financial adventurers were in the saddle, the physical rule of arms was supplanted by the mental rule of law, and there was an increasing liaison between government and the men of money. The state ceased to be an expression of royal caprice, as it became an instrument of responsible government; all subjects of the Crown, from the heights of quality to the depths of commonalty, had rights for which it had to have respect; and rule was based on the law of the country, rather than on royal whim. Elizabeth's financial policies were those of business; and there was an introduction of the principle of sound finance as the foundation of responsible government, which led to taxation—what benefits all should be borne by all. The independent revenues of the Crown were becoming inadequate for the normal operations of the kingdom, and it was from the monarch's need for money that Parliamentary power—and eventual supremacy, grew. Queen Elizabeth's House of Commons had a strong trader tone, and she allowed them to discuss matters of state; it was a normal and almost unconscious step from criticism of national policy to the demand of its control, and the history of Puritanism was for a time the history of England. The capital-controlled realm was "preferring the monied interests before the landed," and it promoted the policy of governmental encouragement of private enterprise. It empowered the joint-stock company and corporate forms of economic organization, and it granted the principle of the monopoly, which made the source of profit a guarded privilege; and it legalized and regulated the various activities within the concern of business—contracts, capital gains, income brackets, interest percentages, unearned increment. All of which brought an impatient rejection of traditional restrictions on economic initiative, and was

148

accompanied by the enrichment of the bourgeoisie through the release of their pent-up energies; and the mystic sense of sanctity was shifting from the blood of quality to the gold of property. What had been known as a royal undertaking began to be regarded as a "national" effort, and the martial power of the state was supplanting the medieval feudal levies and private armies. And this was followed by the political integration of the British Isles, which was the indispensable first step towards overseas settlement and empire; and the realm was beginning to be thought of as "Great" Britain.

The basic societal *status quo* is *weltanschauung*, which runs far deeper than logical conviction or political doctrine—one lives it, feels it; the essence of one's ideological being is sacred, there is a hyper-sensitivity concerning it—man is rendered uncomfortable when the ways he lives by are brought into question—and a purported rationally objective analysis of it is intolerable. Man always had a suspicion and fear of basic change, an instinctive compulsion to resist social upheaval; the revolution is seen by the involved generation as the incursion of another life into the old one—the alternative reality simply usurps, erases the present. Interference with tradition is disruptive of the routine habits of life, the foundation is pulled from under one's feet, and it endangers the peace; there is a drop in morals, and a breakdown of law and order, and there are tendencies to treachery and terror; people are displaced as though by magic, alienated, plundered, exiled; times are transformed, and there is an anarchy of values as they fall into new perspectives. And the doctrine which constitutes itself a challenge to the basic societal order appears like a conspiracy, and it does not have normal political freedom.

The trader rule of land in terms of sociology was without precedent in the annals of mankind. To the landed elite the bringing into question of the fundamental values on which their society and humanity were based, the idea of the decline and fall of their way of life—was per se absurd. They had the habits of power, and the fear of losing it; they were under the iron hand—the oppressive weight, of the past; and theirs was an inherent aversion to social revolution. The men of yesteryear disliked the new society: there was the urban version of the pastoral condition, a myth of "the good old days," Paradise Lost—in which the transition from the one social condition to the next, became a kind of Fall; they loved their old hallowed ways, they were horrified by any required change in their

149

habits of life and thought—they disdained experiment; and they refused to believe that their country was on its way out of the antiquity of feudalism. They set themselves up as a bastion of conservatism; they developed a blind resistance to new ideas, and an attitude of misoneism—of sullen hostility to change; and they did not hesitate to advance military answers to social problems. And they took their confidence from the communion they had with a time when the ideal of a pastoral society was strong enough to withstand the emasculating materialism of money. Thus land was not to be passively pushed from power: centuries of landed dignity had established revered medieval precedents; the new way ran up against the traditional stratification of rural society—"the life of the land changed least"; the English were rooted in the principle of local social organization, which held together; local custom was opposed to centralism—to the modification of institutions and values to the end of one body politic; and it clung stubbornly to the past.

Puritanism was a dynamic force, and economic discontent began to take on political expression. When land awoke to the direction in which the realm was moving it determined to resist the trend; the Tudor attitude was reversed by the Stuarts—the new monarchs resolved to espouse the cause of tradition, and preserve the agrarian way. This rendered capital more overtly self-assertive in the seventeenth century than it had been before; the members of the upper patriciate were divided politically in terms of their caste origins—*aristo*cracy versus *pluto*cracy; and as the revolutionary trader power was succeeding that of traditional land a struggle for control began to take place between them to determine the realm's basic social organization. A way of life cannot be contained within the framework of statute; and in the attempts of the opposing forces to prevail they had to resort at times to unorthodox methods, and tendencies to harshness began to develop between them as they were moving towards civil war. Yet at bottom man has an inherent aversion to violence, and land and trade each tried to have its way on the whole peaceably. As the opposing sides began to take shape it was realized that the Crown—King Charles First, was still the actual head of government, and that in his House of Commons were concentrated the wealth and power of England. The quarrelling between Prerogative and People was at first constitutional, and was confined to peaceful protest—which gradually moved from legal to political. From about the time of Sir John

150

Winthrop (c1630) Puritanism had acquired a political cast, there began a move from passive to active resistance, and it was becoming militant. War came as a last resort, after each had exhausted all rational efforts; in fact, physical resistance to social tendencies had been postponed to the extent that when war did come it broke out with pent-up fury.

England had her alien monarchs—"James I did not understand the English." The king sided with tradition in the attempt to curtail the gains that the traders had made. The supporters of feudalism—called Cavaliers, were dedicated to three basic principles; no country without a king, no church without a bishop, no land without a lord—which established a union of state, church and property (realty). They were for an absolute monarchy as modified by the federal political doctrine—the autonomy of the shires was not to be infringed. The Establishment—the Church of England, was to be preserved, on the basis of the Episcopalian theological system. The union of property with state and church was to be continued by the feudal realty institutions—primogeniture and entail. The Cavaliers comprised the royal house; the traditional land-based aristocrats—who included the large landholding nobility and the smaller landholders or gentry; and the Anglican Church conservatives or Churchmen. Loyalism is essentially monolithic; it is dedicated to the continuation of the past, and it has precedents to go by—the Cavaliers had no recognizable variations. The king's position was challenged, and the struggle between the two ways of life began to take on political division as the traditionalists were identified as the "Court" party and the capital people as the "Country" party. During the four decades of bickering that took place the royalist position came to be known as "Royal Prerogative," while that of the traders was known as "Rights of the People." The king claimed that the people had privileges, not rights, of which the Crown's grace was the source. The traders held that "a people may be without a king, but a king cannot be without a people"; they declared that the people is the source of the Crown's power, and "the voice of the People is the voice of God."

By 1642 the loyalist Cavalier and the rebel Parliamentarian cleavage had taken definite shape, and Stuart England's civil war was at first a confrontation of land and capital. The conflict was fundamentally ideological; the differences were based on *values*—they did not follow exact class lines. The country took a general political division geographically, in terms of the loyal northwestern part including Wales, and the rebel southeastern part including London. The alignment was predominantly one of town and countryside: each of England's political units—the shires, had a town; and each town had a gate—which it lowered, when news arrived that war had begun. The war at first took the form of a series of sieges—each town was invested by the men of the surrounding countryside, and dissident elements in both places were easily overcome. Both sides accepted help from their sympathizers on the continent. The commerce of the country throughout the centuries had been confined to the east and south—towards civilization, which concentrated economic power within this area; a statement of 1537 says—

"For London is the common country of all England, from which is derived to all parts of this realm all good and ill occurrent here";

experience had shown that the countryside could not stand against the center of wealth and administration, and "whoever had London had the country." Within two months after the king had raised his banner he tried to take the capital, which brought the campaign around Edgehill; after some serious fighting the king retreated—he gave up the attempt on London, and never tried it again; eastern England remained an invincible rebel bastion, which was used as a base of operations for the ultimate liquidation of the Cavalier army.

Loyalist and rebel were fired respectively by the values of royalty and of divinity: the Cavaliers were characterized by a traditional habit of mastery and command, while with the Roundheads the habit was one of subservience and obedience; the rebel feeling of innate inferiority was overcome by religious fanaticism, as they were motivated by a "higher" law—the law of God, which steeled them in their convictions. God takes a hand in human affairs, and He was on their side: the experience of mankind teaches that "no moderate revolutionary ever overturned an established government"; the influence of doctrinal objectivity—of rational conviction, never made one militant; Pericles in his Funeral Oration found it necessary to say, "we cultivate the mind without loss of manliness"; yet it is the emotions—the "emotionally charged mass"— that drive men to physical daring. For the first time in history the commonalty—shopkeepers, apprentices, laborers—"the People," proved in experience that they can, under their own command, stand up to, and even defeat, quality in pitched battle; the common man emerged potent. The Puritans introduced the principle of economy as decisive in winning the war—they went from romance to profit, from fame to fortune; while the feudal mind was concentrated on glory in winning the battle.

Land had sufficient power towards the middle of the seventeenth century to fight a war for almost four years; the Cavalier endeavor was a gesture of futility yet, although inherently weak, it was exceptionally embittered—the past dies but it dies hard, and there were many fields of hate, blood, death; and the conflict transcended the realm's boundaries—it was carried into Ireland, and even across the ocean into North America. Yet England was a law abiding nation: the combatants had an underlying sense of responsibility for their country and people; the imported mercenaries were always under complete native control, and the war was fought generally in disciplined fashion. This struggle is the first example in history of a clear-cut, all-out war—for mastery, as between land and trade; and the unexpected, the unprecedented occurred; by 1646 the Cavaliers were beaten—capital overcame land.ª

Throughout the war the Presbyterians had dreaded total victory almost as much as they did total defeat, and with the achievement of power the Parliamentary forces underwent a split; and a conflict arose between the conservatives, and the radical Puritans and Nonconformists, for control of the British state. As it became evident that the radicals would triumph a union took place between the capital and land based elite; the Presbyterians were joined by the Cavalier remnants, and together they began "the second civil war"[33] to resist the radical supremacy. Thus there was a qualitative difference between the two civil wars; the first was between land and trade, while the second was confined to within trade. By 1648, however, Oliver Cromwell, who had emerged as the radical leader, overcame the conservative coalition. Cromwell now proposed the abolition of the monarchy—through the execution of the reigning king, Charles First—and of the House of Lords, which would leave the House of Commons as the sole legislative body. This brought another split among the rebels; the Puritans were monarchists and opposed to Cromwell's program, while the Nonconformists were republicans or Oliverians. The extremists had their way by purging the House of Commons of royalists, the king was condemned to the block by the "Rump Parliament"; and Charles First's condemnation by "the People"ᵇ

153

set the precedent for the right of subjects to sit in judgment on royalty. The English republic—the Interregnum, the hiatus in royal government —which began as the "Commonwealth" and developed into the "Protectorate," continued until 1660. The Protector initiated the rise of England as a commercial power when he made trade the paramount object of foreign policy, sought a favorable trade balance, and enacted the Navigation Act which introduced the principle of the protective tariff. During the Commonwealth the Puritans laid the foundations for what eventually developed into the capitalistic society.

Meanwhile the Presbyterians or titled merchants had entered into conversations with the exiled heir to the throne, from which resulted an agreement known as the Declaration of Breda. The merchant plutocracy agreed to restore the monarchy with the Stuart family as the reigning house, as well as the House of Lords, provided—in effect, that it be accepted as the power behind the throne. In 1658 Oliver Cromwell died; his son Richard, who succeeded to his position, resigned a year later; and the Restoration of the Crown took place in May 1660, with the Stuart heir becoming king as Charles Second. Thus the restoration of the monarchy —which was regarded as the end of usurpation, of illegality—did not constitute a reversion to the *status quo ante*. England's sociology was developing towards capitalism, but the Stuarts soon began to become self-assertive and to plot against it. The merchant interests then made the Glorious Revolution of 1689; and they enunciated the "Bill of Rights," whose contents assured them undisputed control. They kept the Crown, but changed the reigning family by expelling the Stuarts and importing the Dutch House of Orange in the persons of William and Mary—no British subject could attain royalty.

And out of the political chaos—civil war, Interregnum, Restoration— there emerged a change in the sense of direction. The royal authority might be questioned as easily as the Parliamentary, since both were now statutory rather than traditional; the new royal family was invited to reign by Britain's lords and commons; its powers were therefore derived—not inherent, which predicated monarchy upon the will of "the People," repudiated the tradition of the reigning family as hereditary, and insured the Protestant royal succession. And it also revealed something inde-structible in English life: the monarchy was a political constant fact, whatever the transient shiftings; and the Anglican Church with every-thing it implied was taken over entirely by Episcopacy, as the Calvinists left it to set up their own denominations. Thus the feudal institutional forms—Crown, as well as aristocracy and church—were retained, but their content was adjusted to the interests of the new society. Parliament—comprising Crown, lords and commons—was definitively established as the British state: its summoning and dismissal became its own power, and a member could not be arrested during its sessions; the royal succession was predicated upon its act, and the royal negative was rendered innocuous; and it took control of taxation, of the armed forces, and of foreign affairs. The oath of allegiance and supremacy, which confined the final authority on all political and theological questions to within England, continued to be the *sine qua non* of office holding. The Toleration Act was introduced, which legalized Dissent and gave it some rights. Nationalism began to displace the federal concept of government, the policies of mercantilism and colonization were strengthened, and the Bank of England was established in 1695 and the Board of Trade in 1696. The substantial victory of the rebel elements made England the pioneer of social revolution in the modern world.

Thus the opposition to nationalism in government and economy proved deadlier than to nationalism in religion, and support for localism was sufficiently powerful to require a civil war and several subsequent revolts fully to overcome it. The English introduced a new principle in the long, complex story of man—the rule of a country by capital: they established the fact that civilization is flexible; social revolution is not per se inimical to it; it is adjustable to different forms of social organization or ways of life, and it can continue despite basic social changes. Capital for the first time had gained definitive mastery of a potent realm: the trader had a positive practical program of his own—the capitalistic sociology, with its institutions and its values—with which he could supplant the agrarian way of life; and capital set its own stamp on every aspect of society, which made it one vast market place. Thus capitalism—a type of sociology, a way of life, differing in kind from the one preceding it—is historically recent, and was confined to a small part of the world.

155

STUART CAPITALISM: THE STRUGGLE WITHIN TRADE

Capitalism was the doctrine of urbanism, which was becoming a symbol of victory over rural coarseness; several generations of town life had brought physical and ideological adjustment for commonalty, as it was developing a sense of self-respect, pride, confidence; a revulsion was setting in to what appeared like the brutality of nature in the raw, and to an alleged insipidity of agricultural life. And from the rise of the traders in the Tudor era, and especially with their victory in the civil war, England began to emerge from within its enclosures; the people enveloped in the castle, walled town, monastery, cowl, came out of their shells and into the open world. The Reformation had its sociological implications for the realm, which were fundamental: it was based on the worship of commercial success; it intended to subordinate feudalism— the way of life of land, and to substitute the way of life of trade; and it moved towards supplanting the traditional feudal blood relations between men with the revolutionary economic—the cash nexus, of capitalism.

Those who fought for the new social order—the Parliamentarians, were predominantly town folk: they constituted an alliance of the Calvinist wing within the Anglican Church, Presbyterians and Puritans—and the various sects within Wycliffite Nonconformity; their doctrines revolved around the problems of state, church and economy, whose status they wanted to change. The realm's chief sources of wealth in the seventeenth century were agriculture, cloth, foreign trade, colonies. As the power of land waned and that of trade waxed differences within the third estate began to develop; the rebels were thinking more or less in terms of the future—they were stepping into the unknown. As the theories on the complex social institutions tapered towards detail trade was beginning to betray fissures: its devotees revealed profound disagreement concerning the kind and degree of change that should be made, which was taking on qualitative characteristics; and Parliamentarianism took on divisions—to which there could be no military answers—in terms of its three component groups, each of which in time achieved a prominent identity. Religion and politics were inseparable, and the particular church was an index to political affiliation. They were agreed on the principle of nationalism: they wanted the abolition of federalism, or the subordination of the shires to a strong central government; and this brought the corollary doctrine of the limited—the controlled, monarchy. But the areas of disagreement were much broader and more complex: a percentage of the trader people had achieved vast capital accumulation as industry consistently grew in size, complexity, power; and essential differences developed in economic function and attitude which took expression on a social scale under capitalism. Yet the Presbyterians were confronted with the rising menace from the Restoration, and they thought it best to warm up to their former allies.

The Presbyterians were concentrated on banking and commerce, which before specialization generally centered in the same Company. Their mind on economy ceased to stop with the daily budget, as they moved from current entrepreneur activity to capital accumulation for investment; they became the bankers who lent money on interest—they represented "the genitalia of money," for they engaged in breeding money rather than in earning it; and they constituted the new "man on horseback"—they participated in gold-crazed, "get-rich-quick," speculative ventures with a view to collecting "dividends."c The calculation in banking and in commerce had to be gross: there were the risks inherent in subsidizing colonizing ventures; and commerce was menaced by the ravages of nature and of man—the dangers of the seas, and of piracy; the gains were huge, and the losses were huge. They transformed acquisitiveness—the mania for money for its own sake—from a sin into a blessing; this led them from the *profit* of need to the *gain* of mammon— which move was largely successive. And the attitude of paternalism in master-labor relations was disappearing as the economic dealings between men became impersonal, and acquired the characteristics of the soulless machine—the worker tended to become a cog in the wheel of a "Corporation."

Presbyterianism in England was essentially a church organization with its own theology and clergy—it had no large popular following. Its devotees were a small minority of capitalists with powerful political and economic interests, some of whom were money-based noblemen who had recently bought their titles. They were for the subordination, but not the elimination, of feudalism: they were honest brokers as between the

157

old way and the new; they were hugging the illusions of medievalism into a different age, as they hoped to go on having the best of both worlds—feudalism and capitalism. They revealed a neatness in balancing tradition with innovation; feudal terms and provisions were distorted to express concepts no longer feudal, and they introduced the principle of "muddlin' through." The estate in the countryside—fundamental to the aristocrat, was to the plutocrat only incidental to his commercial enterprise in the town. Although at bottom they remained Hebraic, the capitalists showed great respect for Hellenism; they were fired and illuminated by the principles of the Renaissance, and this saved England's traditional aristocracy from extinction; and the medieval manor continued to signify social status long after it had ceased to represent political and economic power. The Presbyterians adhered to the principles of monarchy, uniformity of church doctrine and structure, union of state and church, and they preferred to retain the basic implications of the feudal realty laws.

The Presbyterians and the Puritans both had their origins in Calvinism; they were united in their acceptance of the new society, and they were fundamentally agreed on theology and government. They were not averse to the continuation of a good part of the past: they wanted to perpetuate the monarchy, although limited to constitutional controls—the substitution of the republic was achieved in the face of intransigent Puritan opposition; they were both members of the Church of England, as they accepted the principle of the Establishment or the union of state and church; and they both had great respect for cultural values, endeavor, creativity. Yet as within their acceptance of capitalism they had differences in economic outlook serious enough to give rise to rival classes within the mart: it was held that the acquisition of money for the sake of livelihood, the attainment of wealth through profit as the fruit of labor in a calling, is one thing; and gain—the pursuit of mammon, or money for its own sake through interest on money-lending, and through speculation—is another; that the attempt to achieve meteoric economic success involves great risks, is a form of adventurism or gambling, and that it is usurious, predatory and causes its devotees to be blinded to all human values beyond dividends.

The Nonconformists were commoners who were beginning to develop as merchants: they were for a complete break with the past; they demanded the separation of the three basic societal institutions—state,

158

church, property (realty). They wanted to supplant the monarchy with a republican form of government; as outside the Church of England they were for disestablishment—separation of state and church; they wanted to be masters of their own land and to have the freedom of its disposal, which would result from the immediate introduction of the fee simple independent title to realty; and they were vandals, as it is alleged that during the civil war they destroyed works of art—statuary, paintings, stained glass windows. The Oliverian

"soldier expressed religious zeal by invading churches and destroying altar rails";[34]

the masses thought themselves the victims of elite oppression, and they hated the aristocracy together with everything associated with it, including its cultural values—the esthetics of art, which they did all they could to destroy.

The Puritans and the Nonconformists had been allied in the second civil war; they had together constituted Oliver Cromwell's Interregnum, and this gave them a sense of kinship—a community of interest, which they transferred from government to economy. Both doctrines had their social implications as each had a mass base. They were committed to the bourgeois organization of labor, the economy of need—to the activities of regularly established industrial enterprises; before specialization the master was usually both manufacturer and merchant, the increment from which is *profit*. This kind of activity was based on a paternalistic attitude—the relations between owner and employees were personal: it was beginning to be realized that a workman's employment should be also for his own good; and the master—himself usually of immediate proletarian antecedents—in addition to having the responsibilities of management, was more often than not bending over the same tasks with his apprentices and servants, which gave him an understanding of the life and problems of the working class of people. Moreover, both groups were independents of the land: they resented the idea of man's occupancy of land as in a hierarchical relation to other men, they chafed under the fetters of the feudal realty laws, and they wanted the immediate separation of property from state and church; this expressed itself in the fee simple independent title, which brought them ownership by right; the full life was identified with one's own acreage—introduction of the principle

159

of the "mortgage," which gave rise to the independent farmer; and they accepted the principle of taxation. They had all the petty bourgeois virtues and vices: they thought in terms of the ledger dichotomy—assets and liabilities, profit and loss; they were prudent to the point of niggardliness, penny-minded, and given to exact calculation; they were intensely self-reliant, each dedicated to the preservation of his small holdings—he was the self-made man who worshiped his creator; and their ethics constituted an untroubled combination of ruthless aggressiveness and fundamentalist piety. Freedom for them meant primarily delivery from the fealty of feudalism; they associated freedom with enterprise in economy—complete mastery in the ownership of land, in farming and in trading, which they did not have.

Feudal proprietary contempt for commonalty and trade forced drastic measures for the protection of capitalistic enterprises and estates: it took civil war and social revolution for nether caste to establish its legal and moral right to gain, dividends, rent, interest, profit, wages; and *the divine right of private property* was substituted for the divine right of kings. It was an age which worshiped property as the foundation of the way of life: the traditional vertical social organization and the great law of subordination were taken over by the new order, and were sanctified in terms of sacred Scripture, and were made to serve the purposes of the quantitative values of economy; property was inviolable, and contracts were secure; and the reasoning of litigation in the court of law replaced the brutality of feudal warfare.

The land area of the globe is better known than its water surface, but it is smaller and not as rich in life. The presence or absence of water has formed the character of many nations. The Atlantic Europeans were strongly influenced by the sea—one can hardly imagine an England without sailors! There is the beautiful, fertile paradise of the sea; the call, the gift, the rigors, the sound and fury, the mansions—of the sea. On open water and out of sight of land one is enveloped in the atmosphere of the lonely sea and the sky; there is the sense of seclusion—the thrill of the limitless horizons with their freedom and movement; one is in a constant fight for survival against the perils of the sea—burial at sea; there is the perpetual motion of the ocean and its life, and the alternation of calm and turmoil—voyeuristic impulses and ventures were commonplace; their literature is rich with tales of oversea and undersea adventure, rule by the sea, family legend of watery escapade, the sea as a school of crime and vice, the discovery of islands of bliss; and they abound in proverbs and sayings inspired by the sea—"meet the Old Man of the Sea," "pounding at a crumbling sea wall," "one leak will sink a ship," "the appearing of the moon and the stars to them that are sailing upon the seas." And this, together with the seamen's experiences in warfare and their spartan life, created in them an arrogance—a towering contempt for the static town-dweller and the earth-bound peasant; only age forced them ashore.

Astronomy had been the chief science of the ancient world: geography, with emphasis on oceanography—was the leading interest in sixteenth-century Atlantic Europe; the Iberians excelled in this knowledge, and they were the ones who discovered the new worlds of East and West. These discoveries had a vast impact on the imagination of the western peoples; their curiosity was aroused, there developed a passion for sight-seeing, and expeditions into the world radiated from Atlantic Europe; it became the Great Age of Discovery, and this shifted the center of gravity from the Mediterranean Sea to the open-spacedness of the oceans. The advent of the New Age had its effects on the mind of the Europeans: their military penetration up to then had been virtually confined to areas of civilized settlement; the chasm in basic values between civilized and savage—the inexorable absence of mental contact, precluded rational understanding and moral relation between them; the Caucasian had to take it for granted that Christians were per se at war with heathens; it was therefore moral to appropriate their lands and goods, and to take them captive. Gold was the *raison d'etre* of trade—precious metals and stones, and also specie, were primary objects of civilized appreciation, although they were of little value to the primitive; there took place the rise and spread of the idea of *El Dorado*, which identified various raw areas with an abundance of the precious metals; the undeveloped continents were considered legitimate areas of civilized advantage, and greed for wealth often resulted in instances of international brutality. The New Age also brought a struggle between Europe's Atlantic nations for the domination of the new worlds; Spanish, French and British imperialism were competing to bring home the riches of remote continents, which presupposed mastery of the waters of the world; this tended to divert trade from inland waterways, and ocean traffic began to become more important than riparian. Areas of economic opportunity— ocean, jungle, wilderness—were without tradition: there was

161

no accepted international law to regulate navigation on the high seas, and everyone felt free to act on his own; it was the age of *conquistadores*, the world became an amoral free-for-all as between the sea-going rivals, and fabulous wealth flowed in a steady stream to western Europe.

Everyone was in complete ignorance concerning everything about the primitive continents; in view of the serious and numerous risks involved navigators were thought of as per se "adventurers"; men had to use their own judgment and make immediate adjustment to unexpected contingencies which, in terms of definite knowledge and normal ethics, could appear as "piratical."

The ocean in the history of England—an island state, had always been important: her people had the island mentality—a sense of separation; between the two infiltrations from France—the Norman conquerors of 1066 and the Huguenot expatriates of 1572—for over half a millennium, England lived her life without any fundamental external influences; and during this time she and the continent had important differences. England was the periphery of civilization: she was generally behind European developments, although quick to catch up; the Englishman had fundamentally to learn for himself as few Europeans traveled through his country, which led nowhere; and the continentals regarded the island as a country apart—as provincial. She was insulated from the world, which gave her a feeling of comfort—but she was not isolated; she always had been ambitious to play a leading part in the affairs of Europe; and her people had developed from an essentially defensive, to an aggressive, attitude towards the world around them. Under the Tudors England began to discover herself, to achieve self-consciousness: her people were born and bred to—they lived by, and from, and they identified their strength with—the sea; she began to realize that her destiny lies upon the oceans; and the subject of oceanography began to grip the mind of Englishmen especially from the Elizabethan Age. This broadened her interests—the world was becoming the theatre of her aspirations as she began to seek a leading position in it; and from Queen Bess this development attained fruition—the English mind turned definitely from the limited horizons of channel rivalry, to the oceanic struggle for access to the world. The endurance of the ship at sea was the primary concern in the pioneering days: with the capital acquisition of state power industry began to receive an emphasis and an impetus it never before anywhere had; England began to excel the world in the sea

162

communications and in the firepower she produced; their fusion brought forth a weapon—the first ocean-going, gun-carrying man-of-war—that overcame all before it; and this enabled her most successfully to engage in open ranging—to encompass the globe; and she introduced the principle of the island empire. All of which was bringing forth a new type of Englishman—Sir Francis Drake, the man of the open world.

The traders were convinced that God had given man, as the only souled creature, the earth and all nature for his unlimited use and enjoyment—he had acquired open windows on the riches of the world; moreover, the Caucasian—as civilized and Christian, is the Biblical master of the heathen;

> "thou hast made me the head of the heathen: a people whom I have not known shall serve me . . . they shall obey me: the strangers shall submit themselves unto me."[35]

They were confident of the future;

> "Our sons shall rule the empire of the sea,
> Their mighty wings shall stretch from east to west";

and they began wondering, "to what strange shores shall be sent the treasures of our tongue?"

During the reign of Elizabeth First England's commercial interests— the Calvinists, achieved great power in the government: they were committed to the policy of their country's unlimited expansion—which is the normal impulse of any healthy society; and this in pre-technology had to be fundamentally extensive. They had an inexhaustible initiative and drive—they were always concerned about economic advantage; this was predicated upon command of the high seas, and they bent every effort for the creation of a naval power second to none. England went from the local economy of land, to the national economy of industry, to continental economic interests, to international enterprise—to the establishment of the British Empire; her knowledge of and contact with continents made her people of capital the masters of her political life; and the foundation of the little Isle's prosperity began to spread beyond Europe, which introduced the principle of capitalistic domination of the world—the Puritans became history's first internationalists.

163

The trans-oceanic ambition expressed itself in terms of commerce, which was mainly for the spices of Asia; of looting, especially the world beyond Europe for precious metals and primitive labor; and of colonization, which was chiefly in America; and it was the foreign endeavors that created opportunity for "get-rich-quick" ventures. Her economy became predicated upon export and import; and acquisition of foreign markets for the export of her surplus manufactures, and for the import of indispensable non-indigenous materials, became fundamental to the realm. Englishmen became allured by the profits from tropical spice trading; they were looking for a short cut to wealth by the discovery of a western route to the East; and it took them some time to realize that America is not—that she is, in fact, a barrier to communications with—Asia. Yet capital's primary interest always was to find more customers, with indifference to their race or religion; there were important foreign commercial undertakings even during the Marian interlude; the trader member of Parliament had invested in sea-going ventures, and he yearned for what to him was "the fairest mistress in the world—trade"; according to Sir William Pitt—"when trade is at stake you must defend it or perish"; and trade had ideas concerning commercial policy which were not those of the feudal state.

The capitalists were convinced that their country's future greatness depended on her gaining a foothold especially in the western hemisphere, and they therefore began to make plans for overseas settlements; they were determined to found colonies for purposes of economy—ascertaining the natural resources, procuring raw materials they had to import, search for gold; exploration—the discovery of a passage to the East; defense—establishment of a base of operations in case of war; labor—social improvement for the unfortunate of the home country. The globe was *terra incognita*, especially as knowledge tapered to detail: the oceanic undertaking of the time had to be based on a very rough aggregate in the balance between profit and loss; it was subject to the ravages of nature and of man, and its investors were known as "adventurers"; their adoption of the joint-stock company system enabled them very successfully to wage war for profit—they could maintain their enterprises and make good profits despite huge losses; and they developed the great companies. Naval power presupposes centralized government; capital laid the foundations for the commercial supremacy of England—for a *modus operandi* which in time brought about the establishment of the British Empire. The future of England was no longer thought of as internal: rather was it becoming fundamentally external—dependent upon spices from Asia, gold from America, labor from Africa; and civilized men began to develop a confidence in their ability to master the ocean, jungle, wilderness. Colonization ran parallel to empire building—the future was with the seamen on the oceans, and they at first had to be also traders and fighters, and sometimes even colonizers. All of which increased the economic opportunities also for the disinherited masses at home.

The nations competing for access to the primitive continents asserted a respect for ethical conduct as in their own inter-relations; they made claims that followed a *fait accompli*, for which they tried to create a moral right—which boiled down to "right of discovery" or "right of settlement." Britain was well behind the Latins in the field of discovery, but she was quite potent in establishing settlements: while she pre-empted North America by virtue of the Cabot discoveries, she based her claims fundamentally on the policy of the open door to the new worlds; and she made the doctrine of actual possession—of effective occupation, the foundation of ownership by right. But England's inexperience as an empire builder and her lack of sufficient sea power frustrated her colonizing efforts. Meanwhile, the English men of capital challenged Spain's oceanic supremacy by subsidizing expeditions under Sir Francis Drake and other sea captains to prey on her shipping. In 1588 Spain sent her Armada—which up to then was the most powerful array of sea power in history—to obviate her "English problem," but it was defeated. The future began to be identified with Albion as she was emerging as ruler of the seas, and primary world power was shifting from the Mediterranean to the north Atlantic waters. The ability of England's commercial economy to produce much more surplus wealth or capital than the feudal economies of her rivals made her people successful empire builders. Trans-Atlantic activity was initiated by the buccaneers; they had paved the way for the traders and colonizers, and by the end of the sixteenth century the English were well familiar with the North American Atlantic coast.

NOTES

[a]In the Latin countries, which had been faced by similar problems about a century before, land easily prevailed: in Spain the trader elements were primarily alien, and they were emasculated; in France they were native, yet the triumph of land did not have to go beyond St. Bartholomew's Eve.

[b]"What men didn't dare to say, Oliver Cromwell dared to do."

[c]A contraction of the phrase "divide at the end."

BOOK TWO—THE MASSACHUSETTS BAY COLONY

1620-1690: THE BIBLICAL COMMONWEALTH

CHAPTER ONE—LAUNCHING

INTRODUCTION: METHODOLOGY

There are conditions and events in the life of nascent Anglo-America that are inexplicable in terms of its twentieth-century standards. The history of colonial life and times has been thoroughly studied, but its sociology is little more than green pastures; the limited extent of the application of sociology to early America has thrown a flood of light on many of its dark places; yet the colonial condition remains fundamentally the "unknown period" of American history. A study of the societal life—as well as of the history, of each colony must be made if it is fully to be understood; these are cognate fields, but they are different disciplines. The importance of contemporary data lies in the appreciation of their content, from which alone insight may be developed. Research in primary sources, without a knowledge of the conditions and the mental atmosphere which dictated their content, cannot result in understanding.

Quantitative values do not appreciate the fact that the social microcosm is as profound and complex as the macrocosm; a knowledge of the bibliography, of the facts and the statistics of a given time and place in history, is in itself never conclusive. Social worlds are separated by far more than space and time; they are separated by mind—values, which can render them light years distant. The colonial's world is a thing apart to the people of the space age; "his voice comes from far away in time"—"other days, other ways." To wander through the past is to live in the past; one must be totally engrossed in a world remote from his own; he is there as participant, not as tourist—"I am the man, I was there, I suffered"; what was it like to live in that particular time and place? Thus this work is an attempt also to prepare the student for the proper appreciation of primary source data.

169

It is said that one gets as much out of an endeavor as he puts in it; the creative work requires an infinite painstaking in terms of time, interest, patience—the intention to stop and think things out. The attempt to recapture the mental atmosphere of a bygone age, to see the situation through the eyes of its denizens, is based upon the ability to get at the underlying principles involved; and this follows from the accumulation of a wealth of small insights, "moments of dazzling minute observation, the telling detail"—from a mass of details arranged to become a meaningful portrait, rather than from a sweeping overview. And the comprehension of an era for its seminal implications is much more important than knowing it simply for its own sake. Yet this is a pioneer work, with all of the assets and liabilities inherent in such an endeavor, and it can at best be only exploratory. A definitive work on the sociology of any phase of American life and times will have to be the result of a study in pure sociology, to be succeeded by research in comparative sociology, from which ideas and principles may be deduced that are at present unknown. And this will have to be the result of cumulative scholarship over several generations.

The studies of genealogy, biography, history, are based—in this declension, on original sources; the individualist approach in American life has thoroughly developed these disciplines. In the study of institutions and values the emphasis is on social forces—the individual personality is incidental. The origin—the founding, and the development, of a colony—of a social organism, is "something like what the blossom is to the fruit." In the field of history the facts of colonial New England are well covered: in the study of sociology an attempt is made to get at the principles underlying the events; this can be done only by making an abstract from the available contemporary data, which renders quotation minimal; the fact of research, original and secondary, is implicit in the text. Thus the organization of this work is topical—chronology is respected, but it is secondary. And the treatment of a given social order in terms of values must be based principally on a cultural background, rather than on sources.

EURO-CENTRICISM

The land continents of the earth are separated by oceans, which made

170

the water ship the basis of communications. During the fifteenth century the aboriginals of the continent of Europe, especially of her Atlantic areas, were the world's most energetic and enterprising people; and her ability to produce sea-going craft and firearms made her the nucleus from which movements could radiate all over the globe. The Columbian discovery of the Western Hemisphere in c1500 AD was man's greatest single maritime achievement, and it took the Europeans quite some time fully to realize that an entire new hemisphere had been brought to their knowledge. This introduced a new era in the history of man: it resulted in a complete revolution in his understanding and thinking about his planet Earth; it broadened his horizons as it gave him a feeling of freedom concerning planetary ranging; and in 1521 the Portuguese Magellan became the first man to circumnavigate the globe. The planet was then a geographic mystery: yet the tenor of life in the Atlantic nations was dominated by an urge to explore, by a compulsion to venture into the vast uncharted regions; they began to think and talk in terms of thousands of miles—to comprehend vast distances; it stimulated for the first time a movement encompassing the globe; and they regarded as practical the attainment of distant, exotic lands. This resulted in a competition among them to bring home the riches of remote continents; "the sea kings" of Europe became caught up in international involvements as there followed a struggle between them for mastery of the world's sea lanes; and this set them off on a course of expansion that has continued unabated for five centuries, and enabled their domination of the world. And Europe from the sixteenth century became the pivot of world activity, which introduced the principle of Euro-centricism.

This created a free for all condition on the ocean highways as between the Atlantic sovereignties, which introduced the act of "piracy" as they preyed on one another's commerce. Yet it was felt by all concerned that law and order—that certain rules and regulations, for proper use of the sea lanes, are necessary; and there developed the principle of "the rights of the seas," which each of the disputants accepted—and understood in terms of its own basic interests. This resulted in wars between the contending trader imperialisms for control of the world's seas—"who rules the waves?," and for the power to determine what constitutes the "rights" of the seas.

The Atlantic Ocean and the western hemisphere—"this vast addition to the resources and the opportunities of the Old World," appeared to the

Europeans as another—a new, "world"; they were unknown vastnesses, which abounded in tales of bottomless pits and horrible monsters. Evidently due to the total absence of organized government in the newly discovered areas imperialism concentrated its ambitions in that direction, and success pre-supposed mastery of the Atlantic Ocean. They thought of the New World especially for its great wealth in natural resources, and there soon developed movements westwards for purposes of settlement —which was the foundation for discovery, traffic, religious mission, and possession. They were wholly without colonizing experience; and these attempts, which are a story steeped in failure as well as in success, made them empire builders and introduced the principle of modern imperialism. The colonies were regarded as "fragments" of Europe: her type of civilization—western Occidental culture and ways, was found to have general application and value as it became the model for the entire world; and this introduced the need for—the new principle of, a universal language. Thus Europe invaded the newly found continents for the permanent projection of her civilization, and America—Latin and Anglo—is an extension of her culture and way of life; this was done in the full daylight of modern history, and it is well covered by a variety of many contemporary writings, together with some drawings. Europe's colonizing endeavor in America is modern civilization's first potent experience with primitivism both in terms of environment, and of man— Indian, African. Their coming together *en masse*—permanently, within the Christian community has its lessons in human relations; it brought out the influence of the primordial macrocosm on the civilized microcosm. There was a patent mental chasm between them which no human effort could immediately span; the primitive was ideologically outside the mainstream of the civil society, he could not readily adjust himself to life apart from his own milieu, and he had therefore to be under constant supervision and control. This automatically forced a master-slave relation between white and hue, and the slave labor system was unavoidable wherever the primitive existed *en masse* within a civilized society. The development of the colony may be regarded as a capsule recapitulation of the social evolvement of man to civilization. The disappearance of primitivism within Europe itself precluded the rise of the slave labor system. The Caucasians soon evinced a sustained rational interest in the primitive, which in time developed into the study known as

172

"the science of man"; it was eventually concluded that he is a person, and that slavery is a phenomenon, in anthropology[a] —not in history; and an understanding of the civilized-primitive relation is intelligible fundamentally only in terms thereof. Thus the anthropology of American life and times is fundamental to an understanding of the beginnings of American civilization.

The Spanish were the first to rule the seas, and they had been active in America from the sixteenth century:

> "the medieval Spaniard, the best armed man of the time, balancing his sword with crucifix and rosary, had laid an iron hand on the fairest and richest Americas, intending to grasp and control the destinies of the New World";

they were mainly conquerors and explorers—their explorer Balboa had discovered the Pacific Ocean in 1513. But they were not colonizers, and their role in America is comparable with that of the British in India. In Mexico and Peru they had discovered the most populated and prosperous parts of the New World already organized on a master-serf basis, so they simply threw out the aboriginal masters and installed themselves. Soon cargoes of precious metals were being sent home. Says Fiske;

> "By the year 1609 . . . Spain . . . had taken from America more gold and silver than would today be represented by five thousand million dollars."

The French were also active in America—especially in Canada, but they too were not colonizers. They were mainly explorers and fur traders spread thinly over a vast area who never achieved self-support, and whose gregariousness discouraged the life of the frontiersman. They took easily to the free life of the wilderness, learned the continent well, understood the natives' ways and dialects, didn't bother their occupancy of the land, and accepted them as racially assimilable; and the two were always allied against settler whites. The Latin governments promoted and protected their enterprises in America, and there was little private investment and initiative. By the end of the sixteenth century the

173

Spaniards were gradually working their way up from Mexico, and the French were moving southward from Canada. The intervening area was unsettled.

In 1496 King Henry VII issued "the first English royal letters-patent under the great seal for discovery"; a royal proclamation had the force of law. Yet it was soon realized that simple trans-Atlantic trading trips were not the real way to tap the primeval wealth; and it was concluded that this could best be achieved by the establishment of permanent Anglo-Saxon settlements in the newly discovered areas. And from this the idea followed of the New World as important to the Britons for its own sake, as an extension of their civilization—in terms of race, nationality, language, religion, economy. They took their cue from their Latin predecessors in discovery and settlement, and from the Spanish Armada England developed the principle of emigration as a matter of national policy. This brought problems; the promoters of such endeavors, the capitalists—Elizabethan "merchant adventurers" who made the necessary investments—had to have state backing, and they employed seamen of experience as navigators and explorers in the new unknown regions, and as advisers in the undertaking of colonizing projects. Their reports were necessarily very generalized and unreliable. England had the people—the dissident groups, who early thought of America as a refuge and a home; Britannia as Mistress of the Seas encouraged a feeling of self-confidence; and the Stuart accession brought peace with Spain, which made the high seas more secure for Englishmen. "The reign of James I was a time when England faced the problem of readjustment in almost every field." The British Crown pre-empted North America—it asserted a monopoly on all its contents; all the rights of its subjects in the New World were ultimately derived from the Crown; and it was entitled per se to the "royal fifth" of all precious metals mined. A study of colonial America is perforce a contribution to the English past—"it is a history about the people who made history."

The organization and launching of an enterprise for trading or colonizing outside the realm was unprecedented in the history of England; and the Crown, by virtue of Royal Prerogative, acquired an overall monopoly on all foreign economic interests and endeavors, the benefit of which it could extend to its subjects. During the reign of Elizabeth First permits were officially issued—sometimes in terms of monopoly—to corporations organized on the principle of "the joint-stock company,"

174

that had interests in, and that wanted to make investments for trading towards, the East; the company could achieve status by getting royal permission through the issuance of a document—a license, which had statutory integrity—and was understood variously as "grant," "charter," "patent," "warrant"; and the acquisition of such a license was tantamount to assurance of governmental protection for the grantee in case of complications. And the same principle was applied to the group of people who went to North America to found a colony; royal permission was granted to companies of adventurers, and to proprietors of several kinds, to establish a colony; and they took with them a license—a royal written instrument, which provided the general plans and limits under which they could direct their lives by making their own laws. Thus there was a sovereign power that could grant, and alter, and also revoke, a license for overseas endeavor.

From around the beginning of the seventeenth century the British Crown made land grants in North America—well removed geographically from the Latin settlements, to its colonizing enterprises. But the continent was a thinly-populated wilderness; colonization had to begin from the ground up, and with such expense too much even for the royal treasury capitalistic enterprises, private share-selling monopolies—each organized as a joint-stock company—undertook responsibility to finance it. Edward Rider, a member of the Virginia Company with investments in the colony, declared;

"there was a material difference between the Spanish and English plantations. For the Spanish colonies were founded by the kings of Spain . . . out of their own treasury and revenues, and they maintain the garrisons there, together with a large Navy, for their use and defence; whereas the English planta tions had been at first settled and since supported at the charge (expense) of private adventurers and planters . . ."

Thus the enterprise of private capital, protected by the power of state, was the foundation of England's colonization in the New World—which was her greatest achievement in the seventeenth century. And from the settlement of the North American eastern seaboard western England was turned from back door to front door, and the Atlantic Ocean from frontier to highway.

175

First-century Anglo-America—which comprised several colonies on North America's Atlantic coast and in the West Indies—is incidental to, and can be understood only in terms of, the social upheavals which were revolutionizing life in England. These enterprises were projected under Stuart hegemony, although the merchants had a determining say depending on the degree of their influence. The colonies were founded separately at various times by different interests, who received from the Crown[b] vaguely demarcated grants to land under conditions which made them either "royal," "proprietary" or "chartered." The royal colony was the property of the king, who appointed the governor to whom he *delegated* the pre-emptive right within the colony area with power to make individual land grants. The proprietary grant was the property of one or of a group of royal grantees and their heirs forever, and the chartered grant was the property of a joint-stock company, to whom the Crown *transferred* its pre-emptive right to a section of the continent. The grant to land in America had meaning in terms of title, not of territory: wilderness has no intrinsic value per se; it achieves economic value with capital investment for its reclamation to arable land, which transforms it from a condition in nature to man's social purposes.

The Monopoly, i.e., the owner, whether king, proprietary or company, had to swear allegiance to the British Crown. Thus the colonies were members of a federal union headed by the Crown to which their inhabitants, as subjects, owed allegiance and from which they expected protection; the federal form of political organization respected, and remoteness from authority necessitated, local autonomy. The Monopoly had the right to transport British subjects to its grant; and it could alienate, bequeath or encumber the colony in whole or in part and sell or lease special interests in it, such as fur trade or fishing rights—although only to British subjects. Whether it remained in England or emigrated to its colony the Monopoly had complete immediate power over its grant. It could organize a government; regulate the Church, which had charge of morals and education; organize and command armed forces, suppress insurrection and declare war on and make peace and trade treaties with Indians; draw up a civil code and inflict capital punishment, arrange its own economy, issue legal tender, levy taxes, charter municipalities,

176

decide on franchise requirements, admit or exclude immigrants, etc. It appointed the settlement's governor and other officials, usually from its membership. For anyone within the grant to impugn the Monopoly's pre-emptive right to its land was a capital offense; all title to land was predicated upon its *bona fide* grant and reverted to it, and unauthorized purchase of land from Indians was forbidden. Under the federal political organization the colony was not involved per se in Britain's wars, and its trading with the enemy was not clearly treason.

The Monopoly's title compared with the Crown's was the same in degree but different in kind. The former's right was derived, not inherent; it could grant land only to British subjects, its legislation could not contravene the fundamental law or interest of England, and a share of the precious metals found on the grant belonged to the royal treasury. Thus the Crown had ultimate power: land in America by whomever granted originated from its grace; it could transcend colonial law to protect British creditors, and reverse colonial judicial decisions; its banking laws were enforceable in the colonies whose money values were determined on the London exchange; it had the power of intercolonial arbitration, and extradition; it could take command of the Monopoly's armed forces, and order it to refrain from or to participate in war.

The principle of the "chartered" colony was established in 1607 in relation to Virginia; that of the "royal" colony followed in 1624 also in relation to Virginia; and in 1632 came the "proprietary" colony in relation to Maryland. The chartered type of colony represented fundamentally the mind of pre-Restoration; the charter was obtained while the merchants were an influence; the grant to the company was a private estate, owned by it in fee simple independence;c its economy was commercial, and it was politically Puritan. The Presbyterians governed the British Empire during most of New England's dependency; when they began to rise to power from about 1640 their newly launched and acquired colonies in America were given either the royal or the proprietary form; the new masters did not object to the Stuarts' sociological pattern—all England's post-Restoration settlements were infeudated; they were in a relation of fealty to Britannia sovereignty; the institutions of primogeniture and entail governed their real property, and they tended to be politically traditional. A colony's status could be changed, and it was the Stuart policy to make the chartered royal; these kinds

177

of colonies instituted the union of state and church, being respectively Puritan and Anglican; some of the proprietary colonies had no state church.

THE PURITANS

It is declared that,

"the four great factors upon which all American civilization is based—(are) foreign inheritance, local conditions, continued contact with Europe, and the melting pot."[1]

"From her first discovery, the emptiness of the New World made it the field for social experiment." In the days of the economy of natural scarcity—before science and technology had solved the problem of the production of wealth, and enabled the economy of abundance—the distribution of the goods of life, the sharing of wealth, was man's most perplexing problem; and its shortcomings constituted the fundamental cause of the rampant anti-social conduct—crime, vice, beggary, war. The inequities during scarcity were evidently inevitable: some capable, sincere men grappled with the problem of distribution and came up with various theories for a solution—some of which were actually put to the test, but they all failed; wealth somehow always tended to gravitate into the hands of a few, and there was a constant condition of great economic disparity between what were known as "rich" men and "poor" men. Yet the ethics of religion—the common destiny of man, did have its effects as a brake on selfishness and greed.

The sociological struggles between feudalism and capitalism in Tudor-Stuart England created a period of shifting loyalties and values of unprecedented turbulence, and this brought Anglo-America into being. The social organism of each colony was determined by the political confrontations obtaining in seventeenth-century England as represented by the Cavaliers, and by the Reformation—Presbyterianism, Puritanism, Nonconformity—each of which had its own sociological implications. Finding themselves uneasy at home, for reasons of tradition, economy, conscience, they were willing to face the risks of ocean and wilderness in

178

order to found a colony so as to build their own way of life. At home their differences were confused, but with their establishment of separate settlements in America they each acquired a clear-cut distinction. The colony transplanted its way of life through its own legislative enactment, so that each of them had a statutory sociology. And they were all entering into a wholly new experience—anthropology, the world of the primitive.

Sir Humphrey Gilbert is pointed to as,

"the first in the series of colonizers from among the British nobility and gentry who desired to see the aristocratic system in state and church, with which they were familiar in England, reproduced in the new world."[2]

In the feudal colonies the sociology was traditional and static.

The Puritans were the Founders of a trans-Atlantic—of a "New"— England; they established the Massachusetts Bay colony, and they brought the Reformation to America. Reform was immersed in religion, which involves the ultimate problems of life; this dedication is exacting—it requires utmost mental concentration. And the settlers going to New England were embarking on a new economy—a new way of life, new institutions and values;

"the Colonists . . . shaped for permanency a social system of their own."[3]

The Puritans had a positive, practical program with which to supplant tradition; they were convinced that their way of life is a qualitative improvement, and their settlement is civilized man's first total separation from feudalism. It is declared that "men's control over the forces which shape their destinies is limited indeed": their "new Society" constituted a process of development, rather than a definitive system; it was a newly evolving—a dynamic, condition; they were groping in the dark, themselves unsure of what they wanted and where they were going; they had generalized ideas of what they intended but they were at a loss as their principles tapered to detail. Yet the Puritans had confidence in the rational proposition—"chaos conceals order."

179

"It is to New England we must turn if we are to study the true Puritan state."

Puritanism was an explicit doctrine covering all aspects of human existence, and New England's meaning and mission encompassed the world.

The Puritan mind was intense: it generated tremendous energy and compelled its release; there have been efforts to reach its innermost recesses—its essence; it can be penetrated only qualitatively, and the intent on rational analysis of it has yet to plumb its depths. Puritanism was the creed of men in deadly earnest; they believed in themselves with an intensity of conviction that amounted to ego stupefaction; their doctrine was a force of immense potency, to create or to destroy—they strove for keeps.[d] And the great bulk of its good lay in the realm of the invisible, in the future—in its potentialities.

New England was the product of a creative era; it was a giant step forward in the rise of man, the introduction of a qualitative departure; its founding is a story about men and ideas that changed the world. The Puritans were doctrinal adherents by conviction, not by tradition; they were working for a great cause, which also happened to be the wave of the future; they are the world's pioneers of the trader way—they set the precedents for its manners of living and thinking. Its most enthusiastic supporters fell far short of full understanding of its ultimate implications. It established the principle of social revolution as creative, and it introduced the unprecedented principle of the commonalty mass man as potent revolutionary. Puritanism, the way of life of the trader—capitalism, produced transoceanic colonies; it overthrew the feudal monarchy, and it set up England's First Republic; it introduced a new sociology which spread in the Occident; it was the first imperial entity in history to achieve international power, as it dominated the world for several centuries. The social change in the virgin wilds from tribalism to feudalism was imitative, but the social change to capitalism was creative. And capitalism over the generations led towards the achievement of mass democracy—equality, individualism, and towards the development of science and technology as social factors.

Sir John Winthrop, who led in the establishment of the Bay colony, is the Puritan stereotype in American history;

180

"The life of John Winthrop is the inner life of a new community, of which he was the leader and guide in its first critical decades."

He appears to posterity as the founder of a colony: yet his was a creative solution—he thought in terms of a "new Society"; he founded a sociology, a way of life—the trader capitalistic system. And he was Calvinist, a member of the Church of England; while his contemporaries—William Bradford and Roger Williams, and their people—were Wycliffite, Independent. And Sir John Winthrop may be regarded historically as a composite figure—essentially himself, together with his two Nonconformist compeers.

The Puritans represented Place—New England; Folk—underlying homogeneity of race, nationality, language, religion, economy; Work—uniformity of purpose, from which no one was exempt. They made the pragmatic test, and it proved admirably workable. Their life pattern in the colony was founded on three documents: the Bible, which was universal; the Charter, which was English; and the Ledger, which was unique—each man had his own ledger. The sociology of the Bay colony in terms of community relations—economy, religion, morals, school, came from the Bible; but her form of government was an evolvement from within the Charter—from within the principle of the joint-stock company type of organization, which was legalistic. Colonial New England is the world's first example of a clear-cut trader social system; she is the first political jurisdiction fully to experience the future, and to set an example to mankind. The "new Society" as originally planted by the Puritans in the Bay colony—the worship of economic success, has continued essentially unimpaired in principle—there was never an attempt against it from within; there is an underlying unifying element that runs throughout her being, a sense of continuity; and hers is the longest uninterrupted tradition in American history. And the Puritan sociological pattern had a seminal flow; it captured, it enchanted—the imagination, and it eventually spread all over the continent, which made New England the prime mover in Anglo-America. But the Puritans did much more—the seeds they planted in the colony were destined to sprout and flourish throughout, and even beyond, the English speaking world.

There is a continuum in history, the present is rooted in the past;

colonial New England is an era in which many of the patterns and conflicts of our own day had their origin; we see at work what we find in the minds of men who lent to their succeeding generations particular powers. One's origins constitute a thread that is never wholly lost, whatever the condition; yet exile has been emphasized as an immense influence in the breakdown of traditional relationships. The Puritan life and mind under the complete freedom for it in the new world is a clear index to its principles and intentions at home, where its seventeenth-century expression was a leading factor in the Reformation. Colonial New England presents us with a rich and complicated tapestry of political and ecclesiastical affairs. The colonists had a subjective attitude to-wards—they unconsciously took for granted, certain conditions and thought patterns in their social world, that constitute a body of objective knowledge. It is declared that,

> "no one has before made a study of the history of the Puritan State in Massachusetts as an experiment in a unique and interesting civilization."[4]

The Massachusetts Bay colony was originally founded on the charter that was issued to Sir John Winthrop and his Company, and in earlier days the settlement was referred to at home also as New England. During the founding century the Bay colony became the nucleus from which proliferated other settlements, and together they came to be understood as comprising New England. This migration was a protest against, it was an attempt to escape from, alleged objectionable conditions in the parent settlement. And the reputed advance of the Bay colony in population and economic power—her success and wealth, also encouraged additional colonization in her region from home. The territorial boundaries of the jurisdictional divisions in earlier days were hardly distinct, and they generally operated as a unit.

THE PROJECTION OF NEW ENGLAND

Man is a being full of curiosity—he wants to know what lies beyond the ever-present horizon, yet as a land animal he has an inherent fear of water. His battle against the elements is a universal theme—ancient

182

peoples everywhere told tales of a great flood. And his attempt to cross the ocean in the pioneering days was an ordeal, as he was up against the imponderables of wind, wave and watery unknown. The European monopoly in ocean communications, and the Columbian achievement, opened the civilized imagination to the new and the unexpected; the unknown is man's most attractive danger, there is joy in discovery, and they developed an interest in seafaring exploration when hopes were high, vistas were misty, and the planet was still full of undiscovered islands. Concerning the world beyond their own "little Isle" the Elizabethans were still a wide-eyed simple folk: the earth was flat, and the problem was how best to prevent falling off the edge; this grim knowledge could not be gained without risk, and the heroics of legendary forebears were often more potent than solid facts in enticing men to venture their lives across the seas.

During the seventeenth century there began the development of trans-oceanic communications—which introduced new principles; the world had shrunk to a point where the contact of the aboriginals was forced, and there followed an inter-continental mass movement of people. There is a disparity between thinking, or theories of what the world ought to be—and acting, or making the world what it is; the trans-oceanic movement was set in motion by the European; he was becoming mundane minded—he took for granted the safety of his native continent from alien invasion, and he was leaving it for settlement in remote areas. The way of life of Europe was civilized, while that of Africa and America was primitive; hence the contact, association and interaction of the continental aboriginals was entirely physical—it couldn't be mental; and the relations that followed between them couldn't have been fundamentally other than they were. The Puritan was concentrated on overseas commerce—he was primarily sea-minded, and he made his country a seafaring nation; the buccaneer had paved the way for commerce, which continued for some time to be very hazardous; and the pioneer trans-oceanic trader had to be also navigator, fighter and colonizer. To the western person of that day the world was a very big place, the greater part of it was a primitive state of nature inhabited by strange beings, and there was little hope that civilized man ever would contain it. Colonization in the New World was a national undertaking as it meant the conquest of the ocean—it was a "journey into night," as the "adventurers" were reaching into the uncharted recesses of space. The European, for the first

183

time in his history, was embarking on a "voluntary exile" from home—he was undergoing a physical, and to some extent also a mental, separation from his nativity; he was leaving the civilized society—England, "a little sea-girt garden"—for primitivism; and there was no turning back. The basic way of life of Europe—civilization, was regarded by its denizens as potentially universally applicable; America was an untamed wilderness, and its aboriginals were characterized by tribal values; civilization and primitivism are natural enemies—on contact one must in time give way to the other. The settlers had brought with them their basic way of life, which they intended to transplant in the New World: pitting the social against the natural appeared at first as novel; one's own pioneering is always exalted, and it was thought heroic and dramatic that a handful of men with a few implements were undertaking to establish and to expand a civil community in a wilderness—for the attempt of the European to sink his roots in a state of nature meant constant struggle to overcome primitivism. Thus civilization in America was at stake—and the settlers were its pioneers, embattled in its cause.

Throughout the Ages of Tradition in Europe religion was the fundamental source of man's values, while economy was a matter of routine. Feudalism was based on land, and it had also some trade: trade was permitted throughout the ages because it was needed to supplement agriculture, and it was not regarded as a menace to the basic societal *status quo*; yet trade developed to the point where it intended to supplant the traditional way. In England the manorial estate was in a transition stage: it was departing from past ways, as its occupants' relation to the land they worked was moving from "holding by grace" to "owning by right"; and the farming system in agriculture was slowly evolving from within the bosom of the manorial system—the two forms of title in land occupancy had no contiguous co-existence. Feudalism's primary value was "blood"; this expressed itself as *title*, which was proprietary; it alleged differences in blood that are qualitative and fundamental; this resulted in the *caste* system of society, which is static; vertical status was hierarchical, and social mobility was minimal; and it was politically centrifugal. The values, ways, laws applicable to trade or movable wealth, which is personalty, were qualitatively different from those applicable to realty; and the medieval feudal mind couldn't conceive of

184

realty, of immovable property—lands, tenements, hereditaments—as transferable.

The Reformation was the kind of Christianity which thought that religion is concerned with something more than personal salvation: it can be active, not merely contemplative; it is not confined to other-worldliness—economy also flows from God; and it "encouraged the shift of emphasis in theology and philosophy from contemplation to action, from beatitude to utility." There began an emphasis on the Biblical tradition in which work was the first great "curse" laid on man—"get you unto your burden."[5] With the abolition of monasticism the spiritual qualitative values were beginning to evaporate; and the third estate was moving towards elimination of feudalism and the introduction of its own sociology, its own institutions and values—capitalism and mass democracy. The new society was based on trade: its primary value was money; the fee simple independent title was universally applicable—everything is alienable. The differences in wealth are quantitative and incidental; wealth is dynamic—the vertical status is conical, which introduced the *class* system of society and maximal social mobility; and it is politically centripetal. With time, industry began to grow in size, complexity, power—which gave rise to different and conflicting classes within the mart; this brought a clash of various rival interests—but all as within capitalism, which created its own inner contradictions; and social differences among men continued, but they were developing towards confinement to degree. And with the Reformation economy became a primary conscious purpose of man, on a level with religion.

Puritanism, as it originated at home, wanted utmost efficiency—the full use of the natural and human resources of the country; its devotees rejected the confinement of man's basic economy to land, and their economic and political power rested on and flowed from the mart, the mart in control—trade as the foundation of life, created the capitalistic sociology; the principle of intensive development of economy had taken root; industry was getting a maximum yield from a minimum area, and the ability to get more from less constantly increased. Trade had practical freedom, and it took free rein; the trader type of mind, with its ends and means, organized and set its own stamp on most every aspect of society, which made it one vast market place. And the mart, which was based on the unlimited lust for wealth—money as the supreme end in itself—with its denizens, its ways and its values, became a mass phenomenon as it moved towards taking over the body social. The mart introduced the principle of economic dynamism—it was a fluid quantity in ceaseless process, in terms of improvement or of deterioration—and stratification was regarded as stagnation. Economy was the source of commonalty, of "the People's" potency: the individual became conscious and proud of the fact that he can produce more wealth than he can consume; private property was considered an extension of the integrity of the person— everyone was becoming property conscious; they thought that a rising standard of living is desirable, and more people were becoming ambitious to lead a more satisfying material life; and they were convinced that ordinary people are also meant to be rich—that they too have a stake in their country's fortunes. They had faith in the business system with its free enterprise, and the business man was looked up to as a symbol of success; and the *right* of the commoner to a private property estate was beginning to be taken for granted. The political alliance of Puritanism with the masses and with the principle of private property, brought capitalism—which proved invincible; the "new Society" was the opportunity of the common man to attain mastery in economy.

Land as topography is the foundation of any social system, and as sociology it is subject to various forms of organization. The wealth of nations in pre-technology rested on land: there was the land system of pre-civilization, tribalism; and that of early civilization, feudalism. The populations of the world were concerned chiefly with subsistence, and they tended to concentrate where the soil was good; to make the wilderness blossom like a rose had been, since Biblical times, man's most anodyne achievement; and the territorial jurisdiction—one's nation, was thought of as "my *land*," "my *country*." Agriculture necessarily precedes industry in a colonial endeavor;

"land was the greatest inducement the New World had to offer
. . . land had always been identified with security, success,
and the good things of life."

The seventeenth-century world was predominantly agricultural, and in civil war days "England was still a country of scattered hamlets and tiny

186

market towns.'' The Stuart Englishman still savored of the soil: the colony founding generations were not yet entirely out of the ways and practices of feudalism; the Puritan settlers were mostly from the largely rudimentary small towns, with their modes and outlook; the land and its life were easily visible in them; and the insular mind of England—where land-hunger was rife, was brought to the colony. The settlers had come from the atmosphere—the culture, the euphoria—of civilization in Europe, to the primitivism—the wild land, people, animals—in America; and they hoped to make the best of both continents, and of both ways of life—of the feudalism from which they had their origin in the old home, and the capitalism which they intended to build in their new home.

Tudor-Stuart England was an age of sociological sensitivity and revolutionary ferment: she became the pioneer in the introduction of a move from social statics to social dynamics; and a tendency was developing towards the general realization that civilization is adjustable to different forms of social organization—the end of feudalism is not the end of the civil status. Some men were sanguine of the miracles that could be performed by a Prince who would take counsel of philosophers; and there was an unusual interest in Plato's Republic, Sir Thomas More wrote his Utopia, James Harrington his Oceana, Puritans in their writings used the phrase ''new Society.'' But this was in the days before science, when there was a total lack of understanding of social phenomena; and the theorists of the time were generally considered impractical, even visionary. The Tudors did not think in terms of social dynamics: they had no intention to subordinate the feudal way of life; they meant to give in to trade only to the extent of precluding a repetition in their country of what was happening on the continent; and they seem to have had the confidence that they could contain the upsurge of their own capital elements.

Capital is as old as civilization—trade was traditionally a means of livelihood; the Puritans were the first to see it as fundamentally also a way of life, and they gave rise to the eventual *rule* of capital. This dedicated them to social revolution: it necessitated the introduction of a new system of society, which was to be based entirely on their theology—on their own interpretation and understanding of God's Word. Thus Puritanism from the beginning presented itself as theology, and also as sociology—as way of life, institutions and values; it was economy, rule of the trader, or what in time came to be known as—

187

"the capitalistic order, (which) was a creative development of Calvinistic principles in the world of business."[6]

Puritanism was theology as ordained of God, and it was sociology as brought into being through man; its ethics, ways, motives, ambitions were sacred, as they were sanctified by God in His Holy Word. The new Christianity was an organic inter-relation of doctrines and practices, so that an attack on any one phase of it involved the whole: since the New Jerusalem was to be founded entirely on the devotees' system of theology they had to have complete political control of their home location, which they lacked in England; they therefore constituted themselves a community of their own—in an alien society, within which they tried to the fullest extent possible to live in terms of their own way; and Puritanism as part of a complex traditional social structure defies clear understanding. They were in great fear of a possible Roman Catholic succession to Queen Elizabeth. With the rise of the Stuarts there began an emphasis on feudalism, which brought a move against the Reformation, and freedom of opportunity and hopes for worldly success for tradesmen were diminishing; their expansion began to be circumscribed—they were beginning to lose the rights and powers they had gained under the Tudors; moves against Puritans in terms of economic penalty, dissolution of Parliament, imprisonment—were increasing; decisions were constantly being made for capital by alien interests; and it began to appear that England could never be the site of the New Canaan.

The Puritan had identity—a mind of his own, about which he was grimly determined: he believed in himself with an intensity of conviction that amounted to ego stupefaction; he was fanatically convinced of the truth of his theology, and of the inevitable ultimate success of his economy—his way of life; he projected a better future from a wretched past, and self-confidence concerning one's values is contemptuous of physical obstacles. He wanted to adjust the societal milieu to his own purposes—to get away from the *status quo*, and this rendered bourgeois Reform mentally escapist; and he could do this either by staying home and changing the sociology, or by separation. The experience of generations had convinced the faithful that life at home is an exercise in futility; they were up against the dead weight of custom, of vested interest; tradition was impregnable to basic change, and they therefore turned their minds to leaving home.

188

The Puritans had a "lusty love of life"—life is to be lived, not feared; they preferred to live in this world, not leave it. Yet they need not—must not, take it as they found it; the world within limits is plastic, and they were beginning to feel that they should lend a hand in shaping it. They were opposed to feudalism: they had visions of a better social order, and they were for the trader way of life—they wanted a condition of pure, clear-cut capitalism; they wanted the freedom "to live as a distinct body by themselves"—to be masters of, and in, their own community. They were convinced that they can create something that could have a complete existence by itself; and they felt more strongly than ever that one epoch was ending and another—more complex, was beginning.

To the traders what once felt like a home began to feel like a prison, and they were settling to the conviction that the "new Society" could be truly achieved only when they acquired a jurisdiction entirely their own. Crowded in by their seeming lack of space and by a rigid social order, they thought vaguely about the continents of land in the world having no civilized settlements. The trans-Atlantic world was beckoning, and its call was undeniably compelling; if their way in all of its pristine purity couldn't be realized at home then they could find "a shelter and a hiding place" in a virgin world provided by God for His children; and in such a place—in a chaste, primitive environment, they could attain what they wanted. Their thinking geographically was latitudinal—westward; America appeared like a lost continent, and they looked longingly across the ocean as they concentrated their efforts on trans-Atlantic colonization.

> "The whole earth is the Lords garden and he hath given it to the sonnes of men 'And God blessed them and God said unto them, De fruitful and multiply, and replenish the earth, and subdue it . . .' Why then should we . . . suffer a whole continent, as fruitful & convenient for the use of man, to lie waste without any improvement?"[7]

Cotton Mather spoke of their flight from oppression as " 'inspiring them as one man to secede into a wilderness,' "[8] and they chose America as the country of their exile.

With some people the familiar oppression was easier to bear than the irritating experiences of exile—"from the frying pan into the fire."

Flight is futile, "the Promised Land is where you're at." Birth-place was home, per se and forever; exodus from nativity was unprecedented—and it was awesome, and even lamentable; and in the words of William Bradford, emigration—

> "was by many thought an adventure almost desperate; a case intolerable and a misery worse than death."

There was an attitude of status anxiety, and some prospective such emigrants were in fear that separation would cause them to drop to a lower social level. And there were those who had qualms of conscience about forsaking God's cause at home.

Yet the Britons were a dynamic people—they had experienced being uprooted; there were the enclosure laws, the Huguenot *emigres*—and men were leaving home in the periodic invasions of the continent, and as seafaring buccaneers, and with trading companies making investments in remote lands. An important spur to emigration also was the plague-ridden condition of the country; and people had had sufficient experience with epidemics to know that at such times a move from congestion to the open-spacedness of nature is helpful. And England was beginning rapidly to move towards chaos—towards the hate and blood and death of civil war.

There were those who thought that growth means stepping out into the unknown, for passage through danger is a time-honored path to man-hood. The promoters of ventures to America preferred to move from the problems of the old world, to the possibilities of the new. There were the promises, as well as the perils, of mass emigration; they realized that they were moving into opacity, into the dangers of the wholly unknown vastness of the ocean, the immensity of the gloomy wilderness, the unprecedented new society—yet the lure of profits exceeded the fear of dangers. And the Pilgrim leader William Bradford engaged in some objective practical reasoning concerning the projected trans-Atlantic removal. No doubt there were many obstacles: all great undertakings have difficulties, which must be overcome with courage; the dangers are many but not insurmountable—they are not desperate, invincible; antici-pated misfortunes are likely, but not certain—they may never occur; a good many of them can be prevented, or at least mitigated—they

190

may be borne or overcome. And with the authority of Scripture as encouragement they could take for granted the blessings of God.

Up to about 1633 the North American seaboard area was referred to at home as variously "America," "Virginia," "New England." From towards the ending of the previous century plans for planting a trans-Atlantic colony began to take shape. In 1606 King James First granted a charter to each of two joint-stock companies, one centered in London and the other in Plymouth—the London Company of Virginia and the Plymouth Company of Virginia. Each Company was roughly bounded—between certain "degrees north latitude," and was to be a separate jurisdiction: the London Company territory was concentrated towards the south, and the Plymouth Company towards the north; each had the right to control, and to grant title to land, within its allotted area for the founding of settlements. By 1620 the king created and organized the "Council for New England," which superseded and inherited the rights of the Plymouth Company. The Council remained at home; it held its huge domain by "free and common socage"—the fee simple independent title, "as of the manor of East Greenwich."[e] It had the power to grant land within the northern seaboard area—to apportion the territory to colonizing enterprises for the establishment of settlements, and to exercise supervisory power over them. It could convey its own fee simple independent title to the colonizing companies; and it could grant them charters endowing them with local governmental power, as well as give them exemptions from certain subsidies and customs for various periods of time.

The Stuart Reformers were an example of quite recent potency in literacy, Biblicism, economy; they had developed the financial integrity, the competence and the confidence, to organize their own colonizing company. The intention to establish a colony in North America necessitated an organization for its promotion and undertaking, as well as the acquisition of a sovereign grant to territory. Title to the grant had to be made secure as colonization was based on huge investments, and such an enterprise could not be risked without a guarantee from the ultimate power—the Crown, of protection against domestic and foreign rivals.

A number of people, who eventually came to be described as "Pilgrims," got together in 1620 and organized themselves into a joint-stock company for the purpose of founding a colony located on the upper Atlantic coast of North America—in the most remote frontier of the century. The carrying out of such an enterprise—the transportation to the grant, and the preparation of the primitive terrain for civilized settlement—presupposed substantial capital investment, a good part of which had to be borrowed. The organization gave itself a name—the "Plymouth Company," and it issued shares of stock which were sold to its members at a given amount per share. The Company then applied to the Council for New England for papers of incorporation; for a grant of land within the Council's jurisdiction, to which the Company was entitled as its property in the fee simple independent title—in full ownership and mastery, by virtue of its colonization investment; and for the issuance of a charter containing the articles of incorporation, the boundaries of its allotment, and its rights and powers in relation thereto.[f]

After some vicissitudes in grants to territory in the New England area, and the organization of various groups in relation thereto, there finally emerged the powerful joint-stock company known as the Massachusetts Bay Company; and in 1629 King Charles First approved the grant by the Council for New England of a charter to the Company[g] giving it title to and sovereignty over a tract of land within New England, for the purpose of founding a colony—which transformed the Company into the Massachusetts Bay colony. The Bay Company was under the control of Stuart Puritans, who had achieved an ideological and organizational crystallization; the venture as a trader colonization enterprise was given powers of ownership and government over the area specified in the grant and the corporate organization as such—company, charter, governor, settlers—was moved to the place of settlement. The established community is founded on the continuity of family life, which means the presence of both men and women. From the launching of the colony to its founding the social institution of economy played a predominant role; some direction of operations was necessary, which constituted the principle of government; but church, family, defense, were virtually taken for granted—they were no problem. The Puritan emigration sailed from England in early April 1630; it was among the largest peaceful English sea-going expeditions up to that time—"seventy days they were at sea"; and it was led by Sir John Winthrop, who was designated governor of both the Company and the colony.

And they tended to become refugees, as the principle of mass emigra-

192

tion was introduced; and this started a population movement—"the unceasing emigration of the period." Theirs was no flight from responsibility: they left home to achieve the good life—they were willing to endure the utmost for the realization of their values; and thousands of capable, energetic men and women were departing to settle in the New World. From a quarter century after the founding of Jamestown to the beginnings of the civil war,

> "about 21,000 persons, or 4,000 families, had come to Massachusetts in 300 vessels, at a cost of £200,000 sterling."[9]

The emigrants were proud of their origins, and it was not easy for them to turn their backs forever on "all that past"; yet—the present was enmity, the future was hope; they preferred to risk their future in order to escape from an unbearable present; they were leaving nativity—and they were organizing, and settling in, the colony as home.[h] And those who regretted emigrating soon became reconciled, especially because of the chaos at home.

To the Puritans the human being was body and soul compounded; and in addition to their physical weal, they were convinced of a peril to their souls—at stake also was eternity. Their escape route was two-fold: vertical—the sky as flight from earth—in the after life, in heaven as a place which is purged of the evils of this world; and horizontal, in this life, removal to a primitive terrain distant and chaste, where there were no traditionally entrenched interests to contend with—and they could organize their own way of life unhampered. And they evidently did not clearly understand the differences between the vertical and horizontal escape routes; their colonizing enterprises were endeavors in relation to religion, as they were in a search for the New Zion—the Promised Land; they were still living in the village-and-myth stage, where there was a blend of the natural and the magical—of reality and fantasy; and there seems to have been a confusion in the Puritan mind of their earthly hopes and the Christian hereafter—heaven. Thus New England was regarded by its settlers as an investment and as a haven; the Massachusetts Bay Company from inception was thought of as both an organization committed to the pursuit of trade, and as a refuge for people of a particular religious outlook; but to the Puritan mind this duality of purpose was compounded—it was not understood as dichotomous.

193

They were fired by the thought of primitivity as representing the Biblical Promised Land, which they identified with freedom; and this contributed towards dignifying the Bible, especially its first section or the Old Testament, into the unique authority that it became—for it had a peculiar application in a pioneering atmosphere. They had crossed the ocean filled with religious zeal and a profound sense of mission; the professed chief aim of their colonizing enterprise was "the propagation of the Gospel," which they understood in both a theological, and in a sociological, sense—as merged; they intended to establish in a state of nature a civil community in terms of their own way, the Commonwealth of Christ in exile—capitalism was a holy experiment; and for the emigrants the working out of the "new Society" in a chaste environment offered the excitement and the challenge of a great adventure. The Puritans isolated themselves from the mainstream of history: they intended to introduce and maintain certain principles and rights in the settlement that were denied to them at home; they were pioneers in terms of habitation, and of society—they were fleeing from Europe and also from feudalism; they regarded America as the New Canaan, set aside by divine Providence for them; they were founding the Massachusetts Bay colony so as to change from the fetters of feudalism to the freedom of capitalism; the Church must "fly to the wilderness," and they saw themselves as pioneers in introducing the principle of the godly social system.

In its early days—as a pioneering entity, the joint-stock company appeared as basically monolithic, having no apparent differences; but with time and consistent growth it began to evince functional divisions. With the introduction of the policy to found colonies in North America the practice of royal issuance of a charter to a joint-stock company was continued, without anyone being conscious of a difference in principle between a trading company and a colonizing company. Each of them had many of the features of the other; first impressions emphasized their similarities, and contemporaries were hazy concerning clear-cut differences between them. With time and the accumulation of experience they began openly to diverge, until their differences gave each a distinct identity; there was a development from the practices—from man's actual doings in life, to their theoretical implications;

"very much of the experience upon which they (the patentees

194

of 1606) could draw for examples had been gained by purely commercial companies, which had limited their efforts to the founding of trading factories in the East.'';[10]

and there was an acceptance of the principle of pragmatism—a thing is what it does. And there was taking place a slow development from a generalized condition to specialization: it was beginning to dawn on the participants that there are qualitative differences between a trading company and a colonizing company; the trading organization is a private business enterprise—the colony is a social organism; it was concluded that the chartered colony is very much more than simply a business investment—colonization is per se the establishment of a way of life, as man is a social being; and Englishmen were beginning to move towards the achievement of full sociological consciousness. The Age was not unfamiliar with the fee simple independent title in realty ownership, yet its full implications were overlooked: it took some time for all concerned in the charter colonizing grants, including also the settlers, to realize clearly that a new way of life—a new social system, was coming into being; and no one anticipated the serious implications that a challenge to traditional sociology could have—that it could lead to civil war. Thus the royal grant of a charter to a colonizing enterprise was equivalent to a license for the establishment of a social system; and this could take the form of the traditional old, or it could follow in the pattern of something new; the way of life established in the new settlement could be revolutionary—it could be a renunciation of tradition.

The Stuarts at first followed in the way of the past: they granted charters to trading joint-stock companies who intended to establish permanent settlements on the coasts of North America; there was such a grant in 1606 to the Company that founded Virginia, and then to the Day colonization endeavor in New England. Both companies were controlled by Puritans: they intended to introduce in the settlement a new, a hitherto unknown, system of society—the "capitalistic" system; and they were both organized with a view to give each stockholder an economic start as master in an enterprise in agriculture, trade, commerce. Yet the king's mounting political experiences soon brought an awareness of the principle of social dynamics: his evident naïveté regarding the fundamental differences between a charter for a trading company, and a charter for a colonizing company—came to an end from the Maryland grant in 1632,

195

when he took official cognizance concerning the societal organization of a projected colony;[i] and the grant to the Calverts stipulated that the settlement be organized on the feudal proprietary system. In Virginia the liquidation of the Company in 1624 had no effect on her basic way of life, and attempts made by Charles First to infeudate her failed.[j]

There were important differences between the two colonies in America that were eventually established by the "great joint-stock company" of 1606; between the Puritans who founded Virginia in 1607, and those of nearly a quarter century later who founded Massachusetts Bay. At the beginning of the Stuart reign the atmosphere of the Elizabethan era was still dominant, and the Puritan felt himself a power in the government—he was not menaced; he was not yet clearly distinguished from what was to become his implacable enemy—the Cavalier; and he was temperate. The Virginia Company was Tudor Puritan; it was Calvinist, although it gave evidences of tendencies towards the division that later crystallized as Stuart Puritanism; it was primarily conscious of itself as English, it had a community of interest with the Crown, and its trans-Atlantic endeavor was regarded as a national undertaking. It had no background in successful colonization to benefit from, and the Company with its charter remained at home when the adventurers left to found the colony. The appearance of the new Bible constituted the enunciation of the Puritan's way of life—it rendered him articulate; and it gave him the foundation from which he could operate in practical matters, and from which theological deviation and merger could develop. It wasn't until some time after 1611 that the Puritan became definitely doctrinally differentiated from his fellow Reformers, and future allies—the Presbyterian and the Nonconformist; thus he found himself together with the former in the Virginia Company, and he also tended at first to a measure of latitude in worship. The Massachusetts Bay Company of 1629 was Stuart Puritan; it was primarily conscious of itself as such, and it was independent and self-reliant. The state of mind from Charles First had become radically different: the power of the commercial interests was definitely menaced; feudal opposition deprived the Puritan of his temperateness; the revolutionary ideology had lost its amorphousness, as an apparent delineation had taken place between foes and allies; and the Puritan emerged as he has come down in American history—lean, hardy, embittered, narrow-minded, militant; and the colonizers led by Sir John Winthrop—whose Puritanism had achieved an ideological and organiza-

196

tional crystallization, and who thought in terms of the "new Society"—encouraged and edified by the experiences of Jamestown, took their entire organization and its charter with them to the settlement.

The Tudor and Stuart adventurers had no maps, and they were in complete ignorance of the geography of the world, of the ocean, of the newly discovered areas; and they had to sail the seven seas "by guess and by God." Yet after over a century of experience around the world the demons of doubt and despair had virtually evaporated, and the "gray and melancholy waste" that was the ocean was losing its dread for navigators. But the land-bound emigrants were unaccustomed to the hardships and terrors of a ten week voyage—to the rigors of life, at sea; the enclosure of the time was narrow and cramped, and the ship could be a floating hell; they felt themselves going to "the outside of the world," and they were afraid to cross the Atlantic; the ocean as highway was still full of dangers, and it was not idle wonder as to "who shall be meate first for ye fishes?";

> "Such a storm arose when the Talbot (c1628) was thirty-three days out and 'ye wind blew mightily, ye sea roared and ye waves tossed us horribly; besides it was fearful darke and ye mariners made us afraid with their running here and there and lowd crying one to another to pull at this and yt rope.' "[11]

Many of the emigrants were skilled men in various occupations. "One leak will sink a ship"—and each vessel carried several trained shipwrights, with the necessary equipment for replacement and repair in case of emergency; and the other craftsmen brought with them the tools and materials of their particular trade. Yet it was not infrequent for ships carrying leading persons and valuable cargo to be a total loss at sea, due to the ravages of nature and of man.

Even less was known about the continents of land; everything was wrapped in obscurity and danger; the topography of strange regions was non-existent—there was no surveying and no mapping; and the more the interest tapered the less the certainty. It was a time when one could easily be marooned—isolated forever from civilization. America was identified with grains, gold mines, forests, fisheries, furs, flowers; with rejuvenation, the fountain of youth; and it was described as a Garden of Eden, "the land that flows with milk and honey"—the New World was

197

the wonderful promise of tomorrow. The Puritans were in a condition of virtual blackout concerning the path to their goal; they were unfamiliar with their whereabouts, there were always the chances and changes of pilgrimage, and theirs was a trip filled with the adventure that comes from facing nature. The long trip across the ocean, the fear of straying and the necessity of maintaining proper direction, fighting the elements, and finally, what awaited them on arrival—all this had to depend too much on luck, for which "God" was a synonym. The Puritan mind was in a constant condition of torture as it identified religion chiefly with cataclysmic occurrences—Armageddon, Apocalypse, Limbo. It was thought by many that the New World is "Enchanted Ground," which tended to make one drowsy;

"an enchanted arbour, upon which if a man sits, or in which if a man sleeps, 'tis a question whether ever they shall rise or wake again in this world."

In their dreams their advance was often blocked by a water crossing, of which they were afraid; they were always in unknown places full of labyrinthine passages; they met characters on whose guidance they had to rely, and were usually falsely directed; they had nightmares of horrible experiences as they went through a succession of pitfalls—nets, ditches, bottomless pits, dens, iron cages—they were stepping from one trap into another; and they constantly encountered strange beings—giants, monsters. John Bunyan in his Pilgrim's Progress is animated by,

"nightmares and horrors inexpressible; in sleep we fall from precipices, are assaulted by wild beasts, murderers, and demons, and experience every variety of distress."

What was known was hardly the tip of the iceberg; the colonial undertaking especially of the earlier Stuart days was, in both space and time, wholly problematical—a venture into the unknown. The

"assembling of the saintly in England. . . , the stilling of the waves so that they might cross the ocean in safety, the conquest of the wilderness, the growth of prosperity, the victory over heresy . . ."

198

all this was in the hands of God. Moreover, the Anglo-Saxon world was in a state of social revolutionary ferment; old ways of doing things were being challenged, while the succeeding new ways were still in a nebulous condition.

The Atlantic coast of North America in general, and that of New England in particular, were well explored by 1630; settlements, trading posts, fishing areas, had been tried, established, experienced by Englishmen from some time before their country's emergence as mistress of the seas; and regular communications with home had existed for nearly a half century. To the Reformers of the early Stuart days the New England region was a scene of fabulous potential wealth; everything was overflowing—the virgin earth with fertility; the dense forests with lumber and with scampering furs; and the sea—with the abundance and variety of its creatures, which were often ejected as they were washed up on the shores by the storm-tossed waves, and were good for domestic consumption and for sale—"The Sea is better than the richest mine known."

Colonization is a commercial undertaking, which is based on collective planning: it presupposes sufficient capital accumulation for the achievement of transportation, and of preparation for establishment— which means long-term investment with no immediate returns; and it is dominated by the ledger mind—assets and liabilities. The Puritans created an organization for the colonization undertaking, which took the form of the joint-stock company; the Company accumulated its capital by selling shares of stock to its members. "Private property" is a social, not a natural, phenomenon; a state of nature has no economic value per se, and the substance of private property is non-existent—America to the Englishman was an opportunity to invest for potential profit. It was the pre-technological world of the economy and the values of natural scarcity: practical considerations precluded philanthropy from being part of a business deal; nobody—whether man, king or God—gave away anything for nothing; the early days of ocean navigation required maximum investment for minimum returns, and each venture had to be made to pay for itself. The ship sailing to the settlement, which had to be bought or rented, was a unit of capital owned by the Company—people, animals, and implements for laboring and fighting, and also food—without which there could be no settlement. New England was a natural economic mint, but the processing and shipping of its raw products to overseas markets

199

took a heavy overall toll. And the initial preparatory organization for the actual building of the colony—for the laying of the cornerstone, of the economic foundations for the efficient exploitation especially of its natural resources—required huge capital investment, and took several years; and this too could be accomplished only by the planning and effort of an organized group—by a Company.

The Reformers as shareholders had invested a good deal of their money for colonization, but it was insufficient for the implementation of the enterprise; they therefore had to obtain substantial financial backing from banker interests who had the cash money to advance, and who were looking for investment opportunities; and they were granted such a loan on the understanding that the debt, in terms of principle and interest, was to be liquidated within a given period of time. The risks of colonization were unduly great in every way: the honoring of agreements concerning precise installment payments on the debts to the promoters was based on the future, which introduced many imponderables; would the emigrants reach their goal? would the venture succeed to establish itself? would its economy produce sufficiently to meet the needs of the inhabitants, as well as to pay its backers at home? Capitalism in England had introduced the principle of "bonding"—of everyone and everything, of quality, of royalty, even of God—"into strict Bonds with God"; debt was a criminal liability, and the average person from birth lived his life through as debit per se. The bankers who advanced the subsidy were regarded as "adventurers"; they had to take every possible precaution in relation to their gamble—they became members of the Company, with a controlling ownership in the shares of stock; their interest rates were necessarily exacting; and they tied up the settlers in a bonded relation as security for their cash advance. The Bay Company was a rich organization: everything depended upon, and everything was free and wide open for, the man with money; its leading members had a sufficiency of capital, with which—although it was not easily come by—they unstintingly backed the enterprise.

The promotion and organization of a colonizing undertaking was based on the concurrence of many factors: a few propertied folk had the responsibility of leadership; the emigrants had to comprise a certain number, and they had to make up a necessary, practical complement in terms of particular occupation—husbandmen to till the soil, handicraftsmen of all sorts; and they had also to be fighters, if necessary.

Communications within England at the time required long periods; final arrangements—concerning the ship with its content of necessary supplies, the financial advances, the meeting of all intended emigrants at the designated time and place—could seldom be completely arrived at; according to William Bradford—

"as in all businesses the acting part is the most difficult, especially where the work of many agents must concur"—

and they had usually to act on partial concurrence, with differences subsequently resolved after interminable wrangling.

As the emigrants set sail and soon lost sight of land they were suddenly overcome by the realization that a new principle had been introduced in their lives; the move towards America was a leap into the unknown, as it instantly and totally cut them off from their milieu, and plunged them into the very night of time and space; they were moving into an atmosphere, into the twin expanse of water and air, within which they were virtually blind, and this gave them a sense of "wherelessness"—they were "all at sea," and entirely on their own. Yet they were fully prepared to make decisions, and to take responsibility for their consequences: this brought with it a feeling of freedom and power they had never before experienced; and the bound servant also felt himself a part of, had a sense of belonging in and concern for, the civilized values—for the defense of which he too was armed. There were instances of sea sickness, for which they brought remedies; and there were "the nutritional deficiencies of a sixty-five day sea voyage." Yet it is to "the iron, not the gold, of the Puritan character" that one must look—to "that small amount of carbon which, added to iron, makes steel"; the Founding Fathers had a sense of mission, they had a feeling of self-reliance, and they had the confidence in their ability to adapt themselves to new conditions. And the settlers did not bring with them to natural America the epidemics that are identified with human congestion; during their passage across the ocean wind and storm sent clean, fresh, healthy air through the wooden ships; and subsequent scattered settlements in a state of nature maintained the same condition.

Although several previous costly ventures had foundered, the traders had built up a background of encouraging experience in the intention to found colonies; the understanding of "success" and "failure" was not polarized, and each undertaking had its lessons; confidence concerning trans-Atlantic endeavor had measurably increased, and upper North America was not altogether a strange region when the first serious large-scale attempt at permanent settlement was made. New England, like Old England, had "to live by the sea"; it was a move from seacoast to seacoast—the interior was forbidding. English settlers from before 1630, militantly committed to the trader way of life, had lived in the area—in the Plymouth and the Salem colonies—for up to a full decade. They could act as pathfinders; the Pilgrims had plied the coasts as fishermen and navigated the ocean all the way from Cape Cod to the mouth of the St. Lawrence River, and they ventured inland to trade with Indians—they brought the coast and its immediate hinterland into the realm of practical and permanent affairs. The new emigrants could avoid many of the pitfalls of pioneers as they were well advised on topography, climate, on the most suitable place to found a settlement, and on the dangers from natural enemies—aboriginals, beasts; they could have full directions on the natural resources—agriculture, fisheries, furs, lumber; they had from whom to purchase at least some produce—grain, cattle, fish, as well as horses and small seacraft for communications. But most important of all—Sir John Winthrop's people were encouraged by the previous successful establishment of several colonies on and near the continental seaboard area; and they had general sociological principles to go by—a pattern of political and economic organization.

PRIMEVAL AMERICA

Man takes it for granted that primitivity existed before him, and he has to subdue it in order to mitigate the rigors of life. Puritanism came from an atmosphere of struggle, where its very right to be was in question; its devotees thought that the American wilderness is a proper medium within which to plant European civilization; as emigrants they had to be seamen, and as colonizers they had to be both laborers and fighters. Founding settlers have to lay the foundations—to build, for the future—for their descendants, rather than for themselves; the pioneer is present at the creation—"I like the creation of another world." The Puritans were English, in which language they dreamed, and they intended to continue

202

being British subjects—they never thought of themselves as anything else; they came to the New World as colonizers, not simply as conquerors or traders; and they brought with them the basic values and the culture of Europe—civilization, to which the wilderness about them was to be adjusted. They planned to build their social system in terms of their own way—on the principle of private property, which was to take the form of the trading kind of economy. They were masters of the scene, uninfluenced by anyone around them; there were no people of entrenched social interest with whom they would have to compromise; their way had full freedom as it was wholly by itself, but the struggle for existence was by no means over—it simply took another form.

Pioneer New England comprised a number of small clearings on North America's upper Atlantic coast; she was a microcosm, a candle light of civilization in an infinity of primordial darkness—wilderness on one side, and water on the other. Yet the colonists had the mettle from which pioneers are forged;

> "The members of the early American settlements must have been men and women of most admirable versatility, endurance and courage."

Psychologists say that,

> "Isolation from familiar groups is one of the deadliest perils. We keep our sense of identity and composure by constant reference to friendly groups. . . .Long term confinement with a few people is experienced as intensely stressful."

In traveling across the ocean they had to match their wits against the elemental forces of nature—and they wrote a heartening narrative of man's ingenuity and stubborn courage in defying winds, storms and raging seas; most of them never knew where they were going, and why they were going there; the hazards of the voyage were many—at night they could see only by the light of the moon; the atmosphere aboard ship on the high seas, especially on a stormy night, was one of helpless terror—everything malevolent was in a conspiracy against the adventurers; it seemed that only a human sacrifice could appease the forces of evil—and a number of women were tried aboard ship for witchcraft, and were hanged. It was an exacting responsibility to guide a ship, and especially a fleet, across the vast expanse of water—and they had a sense of accomplishment in having mastered it.

There are the "back to nature" aspects of human life, yet seventeenth century civilized man had had hardly any experience as a settler in a primitive environment. When the adventurers arrived at their destination they first beheld the wild-looking northern land—the stern and rock-bound New England coast, "the most inhospitably bleak coastline in the world." Yet they were happy "to set their feet on the firm and stable earth, their proper element"; after weeks of nothing but water, land was indeed a welcome sight; and debarkation relieved them from confinement and gave them a sense of freedom. There was no civilization in their new habitat: the land was lovely but savage; they were struck by its difference from the green and cultivated England they had left; they were overcome by the strange feeling of having been suddenly thrust into a wild world; and they were immediately rendered aware of the correspondence between the human and the natural processes. They found themselves in a state of nature—soil, forests, hills, sea, sky, beasts, natives: in nature's chain of life it is usually a matter of the quick and the dead, the predator and the prey; it is a world of beak and claw and fang—blood flows, tooth and claw are bare, death is common and often violent. The settlers came as the competitors, not as the imitators, of nature—they were intruders, in nature in the raw. They challenged, they meant to come to terms with, the forests—massive, dense, dark; and they immediately felt themselves caught up in its life and death struggle; they were alone in a universe of bleak wilderness, with its domineering unearthly vastness and silence, its remorseless indifference to everything, including man—its immense, brooding, lonely emptiness. Man has basic links with his environment—with nature: his life is confined within a world of air, earth, water, fire; his foundation comprises ultimately land, wood, stone, metal, grain, meat. The denizens of civilization and of primitivism were born into and brought up in an atmosphere that constituted their life, towards which they each had a subjective attitude; the first sensation that those transplanted experienced in the abrupt change from the one surrounding to the other was loss of the foundation, which seemed pulled from under their feet—what they implicitly took for granted in their native atmosphere was non-existent in the new one.

The emigrants were going into a new world: they were penetrating the vast open spaces and the unbroken forests through which the white man never before roamed; they were in the pioneering stage of a new habitation and a new society, and they were wholly concentrated on the problem of survival. Their ways of living at home—they had been primarily town dwellers—were no preparation for life in primitivity; they were destined to be among the pioneers in the writing of the first chapter of the American epic, when men faced an unconquered wilderness; society was contained in, and subordinate to, nature; they found themselves abruptly transported from town and countryside into naked forests, into a world of trees—they had never seen so many trees; they knew nothing about life in the wilderness—survival within which was more exacting than anticipated, and as pioneers they were confronted with problems they had never hitherto experienced. The ecological balance was precarious; theirs was the plain agony of dealing with nature's blank intransigence—the probability of the contingent and the irrational in human affairs, always a factor to be reckoned with, was at its worst. When men find themselves back in a state of nature they lose the sense of mastery they have in the environment of their own creation—the artifacts in the town; the abrupt change from a social to a sylvan atmosphere—from the congestion of England to the open-spaced infinity of water and wilderness—had its effects on the mind; untamed nature—the primeval wonders of America ("the vast forest with its silent majestic beauty," earth, waters, valleys, mountains, heavens, aboriginals, animals) before which they had a feeling of complete helplessness—was ubiquitous, and anything but hospitable.

They were oppressed by a consciousness of space: distance was a problem, usually a barrier, and there was frequent reference to "world's end"; the adventurers in colonization felt themselves enveloped in the hush of the ages; they felt themselves alone—even abandoned, within a primordial macrocosm; this gave them the sensation of being lost—and each thought himself to be verily, "The voice of one crying in the wilderness." They were caught up in the unimaginable solitude of primeval America: to be alone in stark nature, especially after sunset!

"Thou makest darkness, and it is night, wherein all the beasts
of the forest do creep forth.";[12]

205

and the forces of evil take over. Man, a social being, is out of his element when caught alone in the primitive atmosphere—especially at night: the difference between day and night in stark nature is like the difference between life and death—"in the dead of night"; the night created a baleful atmosphere, and gave them a feeling of weakness and resignation; they were practically without artificial illumination—the "lanthorn" or kerosene lamp, and the candle, furnished the interior with a feeble light; and the stillness all about them—"oft' in the stilly night"— was awful. They were immersed in the murk and scariness of the wilderness blackout; the conjurations of the pioneer's mind in gloomy darkness, the shapeless terrors of the night, are bound by no limitations; and they were under the spell of "this fear-ridden land"—primitivism, if not always present was always a presence.

The climate in New England is hard—this "cold, foggy, mournful country"; the winters are arduous—long, bitter and bleak; "the snow is deep and the night is long," and the wilderness soon becomes a snow covered panorama; and spring can hardly be expected before May. Especially during the long freezing nights the howl of wolves could be heard often enough not too far off in the distance, and this—together with the screaming of the winds through the leafless trees, created a concatenation of weird, uncanny sounds. And set within this inexorable wilderness winter were a few lonely wooden houses, out of touch with one another, each sheltering a man and his wife and several young children, huddled together in helpless terror; the house of wood—with its stove, "lanthorn"—alone stood between them and the remorselessness of nature. A feeling of hopelessness before the natural brings emphasis on the supernatural: religion has an encouraging effect, and God is imminent under such conditions; and they found comfort in the Word of God—"Thou shalt not be afraid for the terror by night."[13]

Theirs was an unpolluted land, an unfettered way of life, a sense of untamed frontier, a realism as absolute as death; they were down to earth, if not a bit lower; leveling is real where life is raw. Nor did they lead a dozing life; to be human is to live, labor, love, pray, fight. Nature is amoral—she knows no good and evil, and man is no favorite of hers. And they lived dangerously; there was an abundance of wild life, both human and animal—the Indian, the wolf, the bear, gave plenty of trouble. They were in a world where atrocity is met with atrocity; in Tennyson's intrepid phrase, they were determined "to strive, to seek, to find, and not

206

to yield''; they hoped, labored and loved in the shadow of the wilderness—unseen eyes were watching them. Theirs was a fundamental break in human connections; they were abruptly plunged into a universe of meaningless fury—fear, blood, death; all life is cheap, and small causes make large effects in the beginnings of a colony—life and death depend on incidents. "The breaking up of virgin soil always brings on malaria and fever''; in blood and mud and excrement, they suffered and died
   "the paths to colonization are whitened by the bones of the colonist.''

In the nascent civil community paternalism—labor's bound relation with a master of capital, is necessary for the survival of both: yet they were unable fully to engage in the normal economic pursuits of producing and consuming; wealth is substantive, hidden—it is the accumulation of several generations of constant labor; a pioneering community has nothing beyond what is visible—and this gave the settlers a feeling of economic emptiness. And the insufficiency of material resources to enable survival tended to an emphasis on the intangible values. The earlier settlers were without a sense of permanence, and even of duration; they were not sure of the future, which discouraged long-term planning —and theirs was a day-to-day existence. And fear was a dominant emotion, which applied equally to all classes and conditions of people, and man has a tendency to fear especially the unknown, which he associates per se with evil. They lived with sickness and death; the wilderness was full of disease-breeding swamps, and insect vermin abounded; various endemic ailments were prevalent, and medical attention was unavailable; liquor deadened the sensibilities and was regarded as a medicine, and there were grandmother remedies. A feeling of helplessness towards nature degrades religion to rank superstition: to the witch-ridden, tortured mind of the Puritan the atmosphere was full of malevolent beings; the coastal islands were said to be the abode of the Evil One—they were the haunts of, and were enchanted by, fiends and demons.

The Puritans were not nostalgic—they never sighed for "the good old days''; yet they could be haunted by a gnawing sense of solitude that one might experience away from familiarity. Their writings express a feeling of remoteness from home—and an ignorance of, and loneliness in, a strange land; westwards was "world's end''—America was a nebulous expanse of the mysterious and the unexpected; the transplanted Britons

207

were without a sense of location, they did not know where they were at, and they knew nothing about the impenetrable spirit-haunted forests which always everywhere towered over them, and pressed on the mind, and gave them a feeling of insignificance; a few did claim to have ventured inland, but the reports they brought back were vague and were not wholly credited. The world westwards was "back of beyond"—a place of terrifying alternative: evil beings were always prowling beyond the bounds of observation and experience; up to well into the following century they imagined the interior of the continent to be inhabited by horrible monsters;

> "Strange stories were current of marvellous and abnormal races of men beyond the mountains, which were supposed to be washed on the other side by the waves of the Indian Ocean."

They lived with and were highly sensitized to, danger; the ship was a speck on the ocean, the wooden cabin was a speck in the wilderness— each was isolated, a tiny world in itself. Theirs was the legacy of the aboriginal "presence": they were very much concerned about "wild" men, animals, lands; survival within the atmosphere of the wilderness can never be taken for granted, for where the vegetation is thick and the trees are tall armed enemies might be lurking—death is always poised nearby; men become characterized by a nervous fear, and they develop a tenseness—which they carry with them through life; and they tend to behave in terms of fits and starts, and they develop the instinctive crouched posture of the hunted. Yet the settlers were acquiring the "sixth sense": they slowly grew accustomed, or were born, to the atmosphere of naked primitivity—the faint chorus of the forest's ordinary night noises, the rustling of unseen animals in the brush, the howling of wolves, the sudden sight of bears and wildcats. They never knew what may rush at them from the forests: the urge to survive developed resourcefulness—a readiness for the unexpected emergency, and they became masters of improvisation; the building—home, church, warehouse— was erected with a view to defense; and experience in the wilds brought a feeling of confidence. And they had to rely on civilized labor, as they could not risk the introduction of a primitive force in their midst. The home was a clearing in the forests; farm animals could not be fully domesticated, and it happened often that a colonial awoke from sleep in a condition of perspired terror, having had a "nightmare" about being chased across an open field by a horse at night.

The first frontier is the most trying—there is nothing to retreat to; transplantation tends to a weakening of tradition—of social order; and man in a primitive world is bound to have ethical standards peculiarly his own—his is the wild justice of wild times and places. The first concern of the men and women comprising the civil community in a primeval setting is protection—the security of person and property; their struggle is fundamentally as against the forces of nature, not as against those in society; leadership is based upon physical prowess—and the courage to take responsibility, and to make decisions; this kind of courage is called forth more often and in much greater seriousness on the frontiers; the reliance on strength tends to the depreciation of the ethical appeal, which is per se associated with physical weakness—and to the solution of problems by force rather than by right; there is the development of a self-reliant individualism which expresses itself in initiative, daring, enterprise; there is great pride in the ability to take care of oneself, and the pioneer can hate with a virulence known only among those who struggle for existence in an amoral atmosphere—hate proved its efficiency as an instrument of survival; and the Briton in America became an armed man, and he also brought watch dogs to help him. Yet the settlers never departed from the old maxim that "in union there is strength"; their basic defense was collective—the stockade; and they always had an underlying respect for the self-restraint that is imposed by custom and law.

The commonplace variations of their life were the seasons, day and night, weather, sex—the continuous succession of generations, of birth and death; "in the dead of winter" they looked forward to the coming of spring, when most everything around them turned green—a symbol of rebirth, of coming to life; wherever there are green and growing things there is hope. They were experiencing the pervasive quality of the gloominess, yet also at times of the tranquillity, which the virgin wilds convey: the denizen of unexplored nature was not without his indifferent, carefree moments—wandering through the great green world of land and trees, beholding the beauty of the sylvan landscape with its feathered life, watching harmless wild life playing in the forests, seeing lazy chimney smoke stretching into the dark, star-dotted sky; all of which creates a kind of quiet calm that warms the primeval atmosphere. There was a consciousness of the Work, as well as of the Word, of God: man is a child of the sun, and dawn in the vast expanse is like coming to life again; and with the coming of light all nocturnal beings—spooks, instantly vanished.

From their embarkation at home to their establishment in the New World the experiences of the colonists constitute a saga of perseverance, of ingenious and unaided courage. When they came to the new land they were overcome by a sense of discovery; they found the geography of the region extremely harsh, and their first purpose had to be the taming of land areas from wild, to rural, to countryside. And during civilization's beginnings in America—the Puritan Odyssey—the settlers were caught up in a constant arduous struggle for survival against disease, accident, death—which took up the best part of their time, mind, effort; there was no escape for anyone from the dung heap of this life, they were with their faces in the earth, and there was an absence of self-consciousness in performing the natural functions; many of them forgot who they were, and individual motives were submerged as all men felt, thought, and even looked, alike. Yet they wanted survival, not rescue; "man's infinite capacity for endurance" has never lacked emphasis; and fanatical conviction creates self-confidence, which facilitates the need to overcome physically. There was the rusticity of life in pioneer New England; and it was a struggle for them to develop a sense of sacredness in their relationship with the land, and in their intent to found a family.

It is said that places of mutual danger bring intense camaraderie—the highest forms of human solidarity and loyalty arise among lonely and desperate men; survival in a natural setting—"the bleakness of wilderness, winter, and an uncertain future"—dictated that they can best do so in basic cooperation; they were reminded of the iron law of life—"man is a social being"—of the obligation men owe one another to work in togetherness; they thought primarily of themselves as a group—they were individuals sharing a common experience in the fearsome unknown; the struggles of the pioneer settlement are essentially as against nature, and not as between social forces within it. There was a steady application of common sense to the problem of living; they were alive to their surroundings, which rendered them masters of resourcefulness—the price of survival in the wilderness; they were the kind who know "how to suffer without being unhappy," and theirs was the sophistication born of experience—they learned from suffering. And the primitive milieu is leveling: distinctions of wealth and status form no real part of the traditional picture of earlier Reform colonial society; there was an underlying equality of poverty—the simple life in a simple world; they were equals on the level of humanity, if not of power; the striving of the pioneering days was killing, and the daily life of the average master was little different from that of his servants.

A colony is inescapably recessive: the endeavor to project civilization into a primordial environment brings a tendency to return to previous social forms, and its beginnings in Europe and in America are not without similarities; and pioneer New England may be regarded as an example in capsule of social recapitulation. Pioneers are rendered immediately aware of a separation from the atmosphere of home and its customary ways as they find themselves abruptly thrust into an alien world and life. Nature is always threatening, it is invasive; man's exposure of himself and of his works brings reversion. The wilderness has its influence on the civilized mind, both in terms of the community and of the individual; violence is as human as man, it has its effects on human life—it tends to kill the human in man. They were under the dominion of fear and death, and this inclined them at times to revert to the fury and bloodlust of the savage. There was a return to man's tooth and claw nature—not as an atavistic gesture, but as the retention of a necessary primeval wildness;

"when individuals, or even considerable groups of men, are segregated from the higher industrial culture and exposed to a lower cultural environment, or to an economic situation of a more primitive character, they quickly show evidence of a reversion toward the spiritual features which characterize the predatory type. . . .the American colonies might be cited as an example of such reversion . . ."[14]

It is said that at bottom man is physically and mentally a hunter—"the hunter that lurks inside each of us"; hunting is an atavistic impulse, and the denizens of a pioneering community are perforce closer to their naked origins—"in a people at bay the primitive rages."

The civil milieu was an island—isolated, in an ocean of space and wind; theirs was a small world—rural, having a relative compactness within itself; and its economy tended to revert to some extent to the

211

hunting stage. They went from the freebooting rover, from the reckless exploits of the adventurer on the unknown waters and lands, to the tawdry plodding of the settler; after the hunter came the farmer, and then the trader; the pioneers were never wholly farmers—they engaged also in hunting and trapping, and fishing, in gathering timber for fuel, in trading and fighting with the Indians. There is a romance involved in man's use of wood since the time when he first learned how to use a club to defend himself; at home there had taken place some development from wood to stone, but in the colony it was back to wood. They had to provide as soon as possible the absolute requirements of civilized living—clearings for arable, human and animal habitations, warehouses, fences, roads; few men really relish the Spartan life which pioneering imposes, and the frontier conditions forced them to build rapidly rather than permanently.

The standards taken for granted in a traditionally established social organism cannot be applied literally to evaluate the nascent community: the life of the mind is the last aspect of civilization to be developed on the frontiers; the disoriented Europeans were confronted with the problem— shall we aim primarily for righteousness, to be good? or for power, to be strong? There is a fascination—a magnetism, in nature: they were caught up in, and they seemed to be succumbing to, the spell of the forests; there was the urge to go native, to blend with the macrocosm—rather than to attempt to remake it; there was a tendency to weaken towards "the call of the wild"—they felt themselves in danger of deteriorating into barbarism. But man has values, which distinguish him from the beast, and which are dearer to him than life: the settlers were convinced that civilization is superior to barbarism; the most terrible calamity that could befall them was the loss of their values; their greatest dread was of the forbidding interior which, as had happened in previous attempts at colonization, could abduct them forever from the world of civilization; and there was a determined, both conscious and implicit, resistance— which elicited all their strength and courage, to the dead weight of the primordial vastness about them; they were enabled to prevail only by the invincibility of their values. Civil man immersed in raw primitivism is bound to emphasize natural law, and to exalt the physical qualities—but at bottom he never ceases to be an ethical being. He develops the characteristics of the pioneer—a dogmatic narrowness accompanied by a courageous candor and an intense originality. The Puritan in America was a "babe in the woods": he was a member of a small group of civilized people who were isolated in a wilderness—and they used the Bible as their way of, and their guide to, life; he felt himself "a stranger in the earth"—he had "to wander in the wilderness, where there is no way"; yet religion was always there to draw rein on the lure of the untamed—he was comforted, "Thou shalt not be afraid for the terror by night"; and he was the kind of man who carried the Bible in one hand, and the firearm in the other. There were humans in his environment that were inimical to his way, and with whom he could not make mental contact; the firearm symbolized his earnestness to preserve his way of life; he sincerely longed for peace—on his own terms.

New England was established by the Puritans; their clergymen at home made earnest exhortations in its behalf through the printed and spoken word—"fortie yeeres were expired, before Israel could plant in Canaan." The Puritans inaugurated the British Empire: no matter how small and lonely, the colonists did represent a firmly planted foothold of empire; a development towards population sufficiency took place as there was a consistent increase in arrivals who survived the first fatal years' pitiless test of adaptability; the venture swallowed up many thousands of pounds sterling—yet the London merchants, despite costly initial failures, unstintingly backed it. They achieved for the settlement stability of existence—the first great prize wrung from the wilderness, and their success was due to the fact that work and frugality were their supreme values. The settlers identified their salvation with what may come from the direction of the ocean, and their mind was concentrated towards the east; they were more communicative on water than on land, and they tended to hug the coast. The Puritans set the precedent for modern colonization and empire.

NOTES

aA work on The Anthropology Of The Sixteenth Century—which may be confined to the continents of Europe, Africa and the Western Hemisphere—is indispensable to an understanding of Anglo-America.

bThe king was an individual, while the Crown was a social institution.

cIn 1612 the Virginia Company of London sold for £2000 sterling the Somers Islands (Bermudas), which were included in its grant, to a group of merchants.

dThere is a reference to "the intrigue to transfer the Puritan virus full strength to

New England."

ePre-Norman England, like aboriginal America, had vast areas of uninhabited forest land; the commonalty settlement of such land created problems of tenure; in England this was known as "allodial" tenure, and in America as the "fee simple independent" title—both as in contrast to "feudal" tenure. The "manor of East Greenwich" served as a model in some colonial charters of a form of ownership freed from feudal practices.

fIt is said that the Pilgrims had a legally doubtful patent; in view of the heavy investments and the anxiety to found colonies, this could never have been more than a technicality. And subsidy had to have a sophistication in this respect.

gThe Company wanted the additional assurance of the succeeding king.

hLike leaving earth at present forever to settle on another planet.

iThere were no grants of charters for new colonizing enterprises after 1629.

jIt took a civil war—Bacon's Rebellion, 1676—to erase the capital way of life in Virginia.

CHAPTER TWO—FOUNDING

ECONOMY

The Crown organized, and it delegated certain rights and powers to, the Council for New England, which the Council was authorized to transfer to the colonial undertakings for their own regulation. A central governing board located at home and appointed by the king was to have general supervision over the entire project. The Council transfer of powers was accomplished through its issuance of a charter to a joint-stock company: the corporate organization, the Massachusetts Bay Company, was transported as a unit from one part of the world to another — from a traditionally established societal atmosphere, to a wilderness; and the act of moving and of planting was highly successful. And the local Council of settlers, appointed by the Company, would have immediate jurisdiction over each colony.

The Massachusetts charter of 1629 was technically that of a commercial company, and was not clearly thought of as the foundation for the establishment of a social system; yet,

> "It is impossible to treat what was a political entity from the moment the settlers landed . . . in the same way as a commercial corporation . . ."[1]

Man is a social being: the founders of a colony are necessarily sociologists—they have a positive practical program; they go to the place of their intended settlement with a plan of social organization, institutions and values, in their mind—the colony is per se a planned society. The settlers' primary purpose was to project civilization—the way of life, the values and the culture, of Europe—which they regarded

215

as potentially universally applicable, into America. When the Puritans first set foot on the soil of New England the whole problem of man as a social being—state, church, economy, family, class, race, defense—was before them: the Bay settlement was a quantitative microcosm and a qualitative macrocosm—they were confronted with the universal and the eternal; and they immediately moved from custodial to innovative roles as they had to solve their problems in terms of the "new Society"—everything was unprecedented, which perforce resulted in groping.

The iron law of the life of human beings is the obligation they owe one another—social cooperation. This is especially so under conditions of colonization, whose burdens have to be borne in common; survival requires an emphasis on the whole rather than on the part, and mutual aid has to precede the competition of the struggle for existence; the community is more important than any one of its inhabitants, there has to be concentration on collective need rather than on private property interests, and freedom is subordinated to membership in a social organization.

Reform was opposed to feudalism; the members of the Company were all for the trader way of life—for capitalism, which was in a pioneering condition and could find only rudimentary expression. The banker share-owners who subsidized the Company and who remained at home were Presbyterians, and they were known as "adventurers[a] of the purse"; while the shareowners of modest investment, who comprised the bulk of the membership—and who were Puritans, went to the grant to settle, and they were identified as "planters" or "adventurers of the person". It took a good deal of experience for the participants to achieve full clarity on the differences between a commercial company and a colonizing company; and the tendency at first for both to be involved in the same organization brought a good deal of haziness among the promoters on the primary purposes of the trans-oceanic venture, which caused some division of emphasis concerning immediate goals. To the creditor share-holders in England, to those committed fundamentally to the dividends from banking and commerce, the Company investment was inherently speculative, and its purposes—trader colonization, had to be with a view to *gain*; they saw the colony as a business enterprise, a source of immediate wealth—as a base of operations to facilitate privateering expeditions, locate sources of precious metals, engage in the search for a northwest passage and find a trade route to the East. The settlers who went to found the colony were committed to the principle of

216

"the People's" capitalism: they were concentrated on the *profit* of the bourgeois organization of labor; they saw the colony basically as a permanent settlement—as home, dedicated to normal daily life, where a man could found a farm, dwelling, workshop, family, church, fort; they had to be concerned primarily with the routine responsibilities of their new home and new way—with instant objectives, and they were concentrated on profit from labor in the earth and work in the handicrafts, rather than on gain from speculative ventures.

The Company had been originally organized, and empowered as the sole authority, for the initial achievement of two concomitant objectives: colonization—to transform a wilderness area into a civil community; and sociology—to give this civil community a certain social form. The share of stock, its cost to the shareholder, and the benefits derived therefrom, constituted the nucleus for the social organization of the colony. The free enterprise system was inevitable at the beginnings of commonalty economic integrity: yet in the initial stages of colonization there had to be the introduction of communal economic patterns, the necessity of cooperation or the subordination of the individual to the general good; the natural abundance of the country, once properly organized, could easily stabilize the colony and pay off its debt; and it was thought that the communal organization would facilitate the efforts to achieve these objectives. The Company, which was under the effective control of the bankers, had a monopoly on the natural resources, and the colony at first operated as a collective: "money for the expense of the Pilgrim enterprise was to be raised on a mortgage of the labor of the emigrants"; all property, and all profits and benefits accruing from the venture, were to be held in common; the principle of unrestricted individualism in economy on a social scale was unknown to mankind at the time, and individual enterprise was excluded. The preparatory period—sufficient reclamation, distribution of land, necessary adjustment for the exploitation of the natural resources—took several years, during which there could be no private profit; and from founding everyone worked for the Company and consumed from the common storehouse, and the ship was at first used for shelter. With the coming of stability and the economy of profit the settlers had to continue in their communal endeavor—everyone was to work for the *common*wealth, and the entire output of the colony was to be common property; and the "dividends" from the economy—everything over and above what was necessary for the subsistence of the

217

settlers, was to be paid to the London capitalists until the debt was extinguished.

Thus the exigencies of settlement forced communal property—it was never accepted in principle. The infant colony was a liability, she was in debt—hers was "an age of deficit"; but merchants had money, and they could buy—they didn't have to fight—their way out of bonded obligation. The terms for release from the money lenders—duration of the loan, amount of interest, installment payments, penalties for delinquency—became subjects of prevarication. The founders were none too clear and too sure concerning the future of capitalistic ways and methods, especially as they tapered to detail; and there was some uneasiness that certain money relations may create a danger of bringing the debtors and their posterity into a form of bondage. However, after interminable wrangling the settlers managed to extricate themselves from debt, and absentee landlordism was never a problem.

The Puritans brought their mind with them to America: the founding of the Massachusetts Bay colony was organized and directed by capital interests; their social organism with its embryonic institutions and values, and their program for its establishment in the settlement, can only be gathered from their attitudes and expressions at home. The atmosphere of the past—of tradition, in Anglo-Saxon life was non-existent in pioneer New England. Colonizing Reform was confronted first and foremost with a problem in sociology—not, as yet, with the problems of conflicting categories as within a given social organism; the differences between the rule of land and that of trade—between feudalism and capitalism, went to the very roots of everything. They were in the pre-technological days of man's development, and this put capitalism—which is in itself an economic term—within the economy of natural scarcity. And with the official acceptance of the principle of the new society, the colony's developmental processes became fundamentally quantitative. It was an age in which men thought in terms of certainty: the principles of commercial policy—of mercantilism, were as hidebound and sacred as theological doctrine; the trader had undisputed power, and capital—not land, was decisive.

It is inherent in the colonial venture for nature to precede artifact, and the primary and basic economy intended by the colonizing Puritans had to be agricultural; they were the torchbearers of sociological revolution as they had experienced it; and they intended to introduce in the colony

the principle of the "Hundred", which was a territorial layout—a jurisdictional division, existing at home. And they had to have full control of
their own settlement location as their new society was to be established
entirely in terms of their own way. The Company was the only organized
venture: the colony was an abstraction, and the capital sociology had no
clear cut objective existence anywhere in the world at the time; it was
only in its initial stages in England, and in the colony it had to be
experimental—a pattern of social organization that existed fundamentally in the mind of the Reformers. They got their immediate practical
social pattern from the theory and practice of the milieu of their origin,
from which they more or less veered—either intentionally, or from the
force of the new conditions they found themselves in, or both.

The Massachusetts Bay colony was started off on the community
system; it was settled by groups of people, rather than by isolated
pioneers. A number of Puritan families within a given town were knit
together as a congregation under the organizational headship of a capitalist, and under the spiritual inspiration of a minister—and they emigrated
to New England as a unit; and sometimes a scattering of Puritan families
were brought together under such leadership for the same purpose.
Founding settlers have to bring with them ordinary household utensils
and everyday items, and implements for laboring and fighting, and they
brought also their Bibles, and their town name. And Reform introduced
the vertical system of society in Anglo-America; the group of emigrants
going to the grant to settle were organized among themselves on a class
basis; their organization was to correspond to the intended economy—to
its territorial layout, in the colony; and the unit in terms of its full social
implications was moved intact from England to the place of settlement.
Sir John Winthrop, as governor of the Company and of the colony, was at
the head of the entire expedition; and he, together with his several
assistants, had the initiating responsibilities.

The people who went to found and settle the colony were all English.
They were mainly small town folk who planned their settlement in terms
of the only world they knew—their world back home. They had their
vertical divisions; they were of different social status—gentlemen, commoner country folk and town craftsmen, and unskilled laborers; and they
introduced in New England the vertical system of society. Situated at the
top of the social pyramid were the local elite; they had sufficient capital

219

with which to acquire estates, and they were entitled per se to leadership in the founding and governing of the colony, and to the best that their world had to offer. The ordinary folk, who made up the vast bulk of the inhabitants, were economically of two kinds—those who could finance their own transporation, and those whose transportation had to be financed for them. This forced colonial society into a retrograde move, unknown at home—the division of its commonalty class into the primary categories of "freeman" and "bondsman", each of which had its own inner gradations. The freemen, who had to be British subjects, were identified under the Puritans as "the People"—the public: their social status was that of "goodman" and "goodwife", and they had rights to property in land; most of them owned realty property in varying amount, which earned them the classification of "freeholders". While the bondsmen, who did not need nationality and were known as "indentured servants", had no social status and no rights to property in land.

The country folk and town craftsmen were classed as commonalty. Many of them had enough money to emigrate on their own and get themselves a good start. But there were also many skilled workers without funds, and the colony needed them badly. Arrangements could therefore be made for well-placed colonials to finance the start of such emigrants, on the understanding that it would be repaid by their skill over a period of time. Skill was respected: the master's investment was well protected but the agreement was a contract, not an indenture; and the assisted craftsman came in as a freeman. So long as the accumulation of a labor class had to be subsidized bondage was inescapable: the ordinary laborers had neither money nor skill; they could come in only as bondsmen—owned by the Company and afterwards by the tractowner— and their status came to be subdivided as temporary and permanent. The creation of arable land rested on the back of the man who wielded the axe: clearing tangled forests with an axe is excruciating labor; most of the bondsmen, who were gathered from the distressed elements of England's population, had never been workers or of the wage-earning class; and stringent laws had to be imposed on the settlement, under which severe measures were sometimes used to coerce the men into laboring.

Settlement of and within a colony was based on the land grant. America was a state of nature. A state of nature is not land, and it has no economic—no sales, value per se. Land—in the sense of ground ready to the hand of man for agricultural settlement—is a social phenomenon

220

created by man through capital investment; it is not found in nature. The foundation for the establishment of a colony—an arable land area—had first to be laid since people, like grains, cannot be planted in a wilderness. Wilderness is natural resources; it can be turned into arable by reclamation, which was then based on the axe.

When the Puritans came to New England they did not find "a continent of land"—the foundation, upon which to build; they had to create it. Their first confrontation was the primitivism of their new habitat, which made them conscious of their civilization: the economy of the former is based on the wilderness, which is found in nature—hunting is man's natural, instinctive way of getting necessaries; while the economy of the latter, agriculture—is based on arable, which is man's planned way of supplying his wants. Arable, the clearing—is the base of colonization, the symbol of civilization; thus the civil community cannot be established in a wilderness, and the settlement had first to be prepared for the European way of life as well as for the private enterprise economic system. Starting from scratch—the necessity to create the foundation upon which to build—therefore means reclamation, which requires the investment of abundant capital and can be undertaken only by organized collective effort. The work consisted overwhelmingly of reclamation— the alteration of nature to suit the needs of man. The processing of a primitive area for civilized living means that everything wild—humans, beasts, and most plant life, has to be cleared away; Indians settled in the area were herded to the shore and packed into ships for transportation to, and sale as slaves in, the West Indies; a premium in pounds commodity—not sterling, was paid for each wolf head brought in; many trees and bushes had to be uprooted, boulders rolled away, marshy places dried up. The capital way was predicated upon the fullest freedom for economy productive development; the colony's agricultural base had to be everything the period was capable of—the purpose was to dot the wilderness with prosperous farms. Civilization was able to reach the soil tertiary layer in its creation of arable, which was beyond primitive ken; some areas within the Bay grant were found already cleared, but this Puritan arable inheritance was quite limited in breadth and in depth. The neighbors, the woods and the waters, provided some food, but the consumer goods—most food, and all clothing and implements—were imported since local labor could not produce them. Plant reclamation was based on the axe: wilderness land was limitless and free; yet the

221

forest has its own laws, the soil is rock bottom in its primitive simplicity, and the "tree planted by the waters" defies uprooting; arable land had to be wrested from the forests at cruel cost in capital, and in human blood, limb, life; and the acre of virgin arable was gold—it was the settlers' most precious possession.

"Land" may be understood in terms of the colony territory, which was thought of in units of square miles—and of the individual estate within the colony, and of the plantation or arable area within the estate, both of which were measured in units of acres. The first two were wilderness areas having no economic value per se, while the last—arable land, had economic value. Accuracy is unimportant in an isolated pioneering community: time, weights and measures are usually estimated, as professional skills and instruments—surveyors, compass, scales, calendars—are lacking; and wilderness "land grants" are demarcated by natural landmarks rather than by surveying. The unit of measurement is indifferently understood, and acreage numerals as in relation to a state of nature do not have literal meaning.

The economy of the Reform settlement in its genesis had to rest on whatever the primitive world the colonists found themselves in offered— the natural resources, the raw materials—the things ready to hand. The Founders had the economic opportunities of first settlers in a virgin territory. The New England region was the golden mean, it was indeed the land of milk and honey: agreeable and healthy climate; controllable aboriginals; fertile soil, well wooded; plenty of edible plants and wildfowl, and animals for food and furs; mineral resources, everything necessary for the building and rigging of ships, and convenient harbors, abundant fish. The Puritans invested their capital in the products of soil, sea, forests: in the land, from which they could get grains, meat, furs, lumber; in the ocean, which yielded its marine life, and enabled commerce; and their economic activities were essentially confined to their locale—planting, fishing, hunting, native trading, and also some importing.

There had to be the attempt to establish the settlement, to get a start, take hold—and this must be understood as a daily grind, not as a grand effort. The order of their concern was survival, greed, profits. The story of man is essentially the struggle for the economic necessities of life; the immediate purpose was to render themselves self-sustaining, provide food and shelter; and they concentrated on,

222

"the soil of Mother Nature 'where all nations and races that ever succeeded have gotten their start.' "

In the words of William Bradford;

"they saw the grim and grisly face of poverty coming upon them like an armed man . . . and from which they could not fly."

Destitution is inherent in a new settlement; they were concerned about "our poverty"—and its fears, as life's constant companions; there could be no settlement without a practical economic foundation. The founding mind could not be on how to make profits, but on how to survive; they were alone, forgotten by all—except by rain and hunger; they felt themselves standing on quicksand. Yet although a few colonists were returning home, and there was some disaffection—jealousy, malice, spite—which caused sabotage and forced several expulsions, the great majority of the settlers were loyal and cooperative.

There were the initial hardships; it took about three years for a colony to get itself practically organized—to be able essentially to feed itself. Agriculture was predicated upon arable, which had to be created; reclamation required living labor, both human and animal, and also tools—axe, saw, chain; and they had to be confined to subsistence farming. Natural foods pre-supposed hunting and fishing equipment—firearm, trap, boat, net; men engaged in necessary non-productive activities, such as guards—and in necessary non-consumer work, various crafts—had to be properly provided for; and for a pioneer settlement there had to be a regular flow of imported supporting stores for several years—food, implements, clothing. Settlement on an island was a defense against Indians, and it facilitated fishing. And they had to fall back on improvisation, of which they became masters; they did with whatever they could make from available materials—they settled for the good, if not for the best. They took the step backward to gain momentum; they copied some of the primitive ways, especially as in relation to shelter, and how to pound corn with rude pestle and mortar, how to tan deer skins. And they had to face up to the problem of acclimation; New England, like the old country, is a misty region but the extremes of heat and cold seemed greater.

The Company had a three-fold responsibility—to transport, to seat, and to establish. The act of "seating"—preparing the tract for private establishment or potential occupancy and producing—presupposed reclamation, which had to follow a plan; and the plan was determined by the intended initial economic layout of the colony—which was based on the parcel of land, or the individual farm unit. Thus the reclaimed area was not one vast mass of arable: rather was reclamation carried out in terms of scattered small patches; forest tracts of roughly one hundred acres each were set off contiguously—on each of which four acres were reclaimed and fenced in, and a plank cabin was thrown up; and each of these was considered an individual farm unit.

Pioneering in colonization—man's challenge to nature—makes man conscious of the limits of his physical strength, endurance and courage. It is a practical impossibility for any one man working by himself to reclaim an acre of land with an axe, or to throw up a plank cabin of any degree of comfort even with tools. A colonial writing of 1682 says;

"six men will in six weeks time, Fall, Clear, Fence in and fit for planting, six Acres of Land."[2]

Thus it took one man, fully provided for and supervised, almost a half year to reclaim and fence-in four acres of land—the throwing up of the wooden cabin took additional time. The individual could not by his own efforts acquire a base to start from; this could be achieved only by forces outside himself—by an organized group, created and directed either by a company or by a person with sufficient capital. The principle of unrestricted individualism in economy was unknown to man at the time: people had to think primarily in terms of "we", not of "me"; the settler could not act on his own—he had to exercise his initiative only as within the limits of membership in an organization. Thus planned settlement on the group basis was necessary: sufficient capital was accumulated at home with which to organize a colonizing unit for the establishment of a Hundred in New England, to which it emigrated *en masse*; and the principle of collective responsibility—of which the nucleus was the Reform household—as preceding and laying the foundations for individual effort and reward, had fundamentally to be relied upon. The transportation and establishment of an individual presupposed a cash outlay; the necessary sum—whether through the company share, by the emigrant's membership in a projected Hundred, or by a colonial's advanced subsidy—constituted the unit of capital required for the emigrant's settlement in the colony. With the acquisition of a shelter and several acres arable the individual can by his own work produce enough to feed his family. Virgin soil remains fertile for about ten years—and once started off the settler has a base to work from, and he can clear more of his tract at his leisure. Thus a one hundred-acre wooded tract is far more than enough to enable a farmer to support his family for a natural life span. The company took the responsibility to throw up a wooden cabin and to reclaim sufficient of the area within which it stood; this meant capital investment—the putting of economic value into a state of nature, which rendered title automatic. The invested area was regarded as "realty"—and there was a practical exactness, consciousness of private property, and trespass sensitivity, concerning it. On its activation—actual occupancy and producing—the government put on a tax, which was restricted to the producing area.

The group leader—the capitalist, of each company of emigrants was a "Head" of Hundred; he selected a given area of primitive terrain, which could be had for the taking, for the establishment of the layout; he then proceeded to organize the hundred-acre prepared units as an economic entity—the Hundred. It seems that the Bay colony enterprise soon introduced a system whereby those already there agreed to prepare the territorial layout for the next expected group of settlers. The shipment of the emigrant, and the creation of the farm unit on which he was to be placed, were enabled by the share of stock—which was the unit of capital. Each member's grant was in accord with his stockholding; a few of them owned each several shares, but the great majority owned only one share, and the conveyance of the individual farm tract introduced a new principle in agriculture—the family farm system. And an individual family could also emigrate to the colony, as each Hundred always had some ungranted prepared strips which could be singly conveyed. The fundamental problem for the prospective colonist was to get a start, which involved his transportation and establishment, and the Bay Company maintained an office in London for information and help to intended settlers. The capitalist could be Head of several Hundreds, and with the consistent improvement in communications, and with the constant immigration, he could continue to seat additional tracts within each layout.

The Hundred was planned, and it was organized on what may be called the "corporate farm" system; it had been successfully introduced in the previous New England settlements, and it became the nub of the Bay colony economy. After the first few years the Company had a solid period of labor behind it: a number of layouts, a sufficient arable area, up to a thousand farm units—which was the basic substance of private property, had been created; the reclaimed area was the only unimported socially valuable article in the colony, since capital had been invested in it; there was now a consciousness of difference between wilderness and arable—which gave the founders a sense of accomplishment, and of value as inherent in the settlement; and a foundation had been laid upon which to build what the Company had intended from its inception—a civil community. The settlement took on perforce a social pattern; a government was set up, and there was fundamental harmony concerning the economic organization of the colony. As yet, however, it was a matter of all investment and no returns.

After the Company had discharged the responsibility to transport and to seat, it undertook to establish or to activate each strip; and the Puritan shareowners in the emigrant group were transposed as a body on the prepared territorial layout—on the Hundred, as they took it over and settled within its skeletal framework. The corporate farm system was organized and maintained primarily with a view to domestic subsistence, and it presupposed substantial capital investment. The Head of Hundred was the largest shareowner in the emigrant company: the center around which the life of the territorial layout revolved was the "domain", which was his property; and its creation required the merger of several of his farm units to make it economically possible. And the layout had to be limited to a maximum number of farm units; with communications primitive, each location could not be unwieldy as its occupants had to be within practical reach of the center. The Puritans were town builders and dwellers, and the domain was the nucleus for the development of a town. Its area was to quite an extent cleared of natural growth; within it was the Head's "plantation" or sown arable that was cultivated by his laborers; he had his place of residence, and shelters for his people and his livestock; and there had to be communications—pathways. And radiating from the domain were the remaining units. The Head's property within the entire layout was his personal "estate". The farm tracts, each of which included the necessary personalty—a cow and some farm implements, were allocated in terms of "fee simple by socage tenure",

226

the fee simple independent title or complete mastery; and this constituted the activated farm unit. The individual family farm was essentially self-sustaining, but it could not be autarchic; many goods and services for the proper maintenance and operation of a farm could be available only on the domain, which had to be organized with a view to accommodate several hundred inhabitants as well as some animals.

On each propertied tract—an isolated clearing in a wilderness—there was a house made of wood usually having one room, sometimes two rooms and, rarely, more: in the pioneering world of nature, the house was the outstanding symbol of civilization—economy, power, responsibility; it was a unit of viability—family, husbandry, maybe some handicrafts; and the man in charge of a house—"holder", "keeper"—was a person of consequence. The basic unit of economic and social organization of the realty owners in the Bay colony—the principle around which their life revolved, was the "household", whose owner—regardless of the number of acres or of encumbrance, was classified as its "head"; and their freedom to act in relation to it was strictly regulated by the statutes. The Puritan household had a broad meaning: if it was, or it approximated, the estate of a Head of Hundred, it usually had several rooms— for living and working, and a room for prayer and study; and it had many members—it comprised the master's family, his kin, and whatever laborers and dependents he had; and it was so organized as to be essentially self-sufficient. The family was unified around economic tasks: the household spread—with its tract, workshop, religion—was engaged also in cloth making; it had the necessary implements for carding, spinning, weaving, knitting; and it was the center for the manufacture of homespun.

Pioneer recessiveness rendered land of greater importance in New England than it was at home; the settler had to start from scratch, and reclamation—the creation of arable, was the most expensive, the most back-breaking task of all. There are important differences between arable land in a traditional civilized settlement, and in the primitive wilds. Home had its advantages: the proximity of towns tends to a rise in land values; and experience brings certainty concerning the nature of the soil, the kind of crops it is best suited for, its fecundity, and the use of proper fertilizers. Moreover, agriculture existed as the basis of a business, rather than simply for subsistence; the town markets were well developed, and some produce was exported. Yet home also had its disadvantages; a grant

227

of land was very difficult to come by, title to it was uncertain, the acreage was very limited, its cost was virtually prohibitive, and its fertility was questionable as it had been worked from time immemorial. With arable in the virgin wilds the advantages and the disadvantages of home were reversed; a land poor community in America was the one without the necessary investment capital; in England they had the capital, but the territory was very limited. A tract of land in the colony could be had for the taking: it was wooded and it required reclamation, but once cleared it was virgin soil of top fertility; its cost was comparatively minor, as labor was coerced and cheap, the title was in fee simple independence or complete mastery, and the acreage could be unlimited. There were also disadvantages: the human casualties especially in the initial days of the founding of a settlement were appalling; the absence of well developed towns and their markets tended to suppress values; and there was uncertainty concerning the nature of the soil, of the suitable crops, and of the proper fertilizers. The differences between Old and New England concerning tract owning opportunities for the impoverished were real, but they were not utopian; the creation and viability of a farm pre-supposed investment, and full ownership resulting from the liquidation of the mortgage did not happen often. Yet with arable prohibitively expensive at home, the percentage of tractowners in the colony was much higher.

There was a hierarchy of land grantors: at home the king to the Council, which conveyed to the Company, and in New England the colony government to the head masters, who passed on to the family farmers as freeholders or as tenants. The Bay colony government had the monopoly, the pre-emptive right, to all the territory within its grant—it asserted the right of eminent domain; it alone could grant title to land,[b] and all new settlements—territorial layout, plantation, town—had to have official permission. The right of eminent domain applied to a state of nature, and was identified primarily with the principle of sovereignty; it had no economic meaning since the wilderness was vast and bare, had no sales value, and was not taxed. The colony powers were anxious for it to expand: their issuance of a patent—a grant to land, was really permission to settle in the area as it certified the grantee's financial risk; the jurisdiction derived part of its revenue from a tax on realty, but this presupposed productivity or private capital expenditure. The government's power over its territory is remote from everyday life: it cannot

228

grant anyone an estate; all it can do is grant whoever has capital the right to create an estate. Natural land (wilderness) is transformed into social land (arable) by reclamation. This was by far the most arduous and expensive problem; there was no farm machinery in pre-technology; the creation of arable was based upon the sinews of living labor—men and animals, and also on implements, and they had to be imported and maintained, which meant capital investment; the man of capital had to get consent (title) from the established authority before he would risk his money; and the government grant of title simply authorized and secured the investment. Thus the acquisition of land was a double process: it had to be received from the government through title grant, and reclaimed from nature through capital risk. The legitimacy of title, and of the source of title, was paramount for it involved investment—and the colonial authority had to be empowered by the London government, whether royal or republican, to grant title to land.

The foundation of the agricultural nucleus of the colony economy had to be the fully cleared terrain in order to get the period's utmost from the land, although there may have been a few instances of improvised farming especially towards the frontiers. The Europeans, and their imported livestock, throve well in the new environment. They learned some things from the aboriginals: the use of fish to manure the soil; and the cultivation of the "invaluable maize or Indian corn" as a substitute for wheat, which did not grow as well. The nature of the soil, and its produce, were about the same as at home; and the seeds of non-native plants were imported and sown, and they flourished on the whole equally as well in the new hemisphere;

"it took only a few seasons to cover the mowing lands with a rich growth of the herbage of England"

Yet the small area of level land and the short summers and long winters in New England discouraged concentration on the agrarian economy.

In England at the time the fee simple independent title to realty was clearly understood in theory, but its application was hedged in by the traditions and practices of feudal landholding. The establishment of the colony was the first opportunity to introduce the complete separation of property from state and church, which enabled the fee simple independent title to flourish in full freedom; the settlers had a general

229

knowledge of its practice, but there were no precedents to go by, and the detailed understanding of its operation within a new social complex—rights and obligations of parties in relation to alienation (sale, gift, exchange); encumbrance (trusts, mortgages, principal, interest) which leads to banking; inheritance—had to wait on experience for clarification. And there began to develop a complication of realty laws; all such holdings had to be recorded, and there took place the introduction of a system of registration of deeds, and of testamentary instruments, for the conveyance of realty property.

The fee simple independent title in realty and personalty ownership prevailed throughout the jurisdiction, but it was in its introductory stages, and there was a good deal of groping concerning its practical operation. In the absence of certainty a reliance had to be continued in some of the traditional ways of landholding which, in modified form, were still apparent. In every emigrant group there were a few members each of whom had a measure of investment capital, which enabled him to own several shares; this entitled him to as many individual units or farm tracts in unencumbered ownership or full mastery; but he did not own enough with which to create a domain of his own as a profitable economic entity, and he had to attach his property to another's domain. The jurisdiction granted such an owner the status of "commoner proprietor", and his property came within the meaning of "estate". He had the choice of keeping all his farm tracts for his own use, or of holding the best and conveying the rest. His conveyances through mortgage or tenancy to individual farmers gave him the status of landlord,c and brought him an income from the labor of others—which distinguished him from the rest of the commonalty, and could possibly enable him in time to achieve a domain and admittance into the gentry.

It was inherent in the Purital social organism for a large class of small property owners to develop; the farm tractowner was entirely a question of capital, not of land—natural land for reclamation was inexhaustible. Each Hundred had quite a number of unoccupied prepared individual farmsteads that were created and owned by the Head and by the lesser multiple freeholders; the seating of these tracts was capital investment, the owners could not allow them to lie idle, and they were anxious to activate them so as to make them economically viable. The fee simple independent title in realty ownership enabled, and the paternalism of the Puritan way necessitated, the introduction of the principle of the

230

"mortgage": the conveyance of a family farm unit by the owner to an occupant could be made under a mortgage arrangement; the man without capital could enter into an agreement with the man of capital whereby the latter advanced the former the increment necessary to give him a start, on the understanding that the advance subsidy—in terms of principal and interest—would be repaid over a period of time, after which the mortgagee owned the property in clear title. Clarity concerning the problem of owning land in colonial New England is predicated upon an understanding of the principles of the fee simple independent title to realty, reclamation, and the mortgage. And a settler could be a tenant farmer, one who had been rented a farm of which he did not have the ownership potential as he paid rent in perpetuity.

In the time of pioneering capitalism the commoner's condition was a slow development from deprivation; he moved from the status of dependent, to interdependent, to independent—the emigrants to America did not bring with them the principle of bold, clear-cut economic individualism. Included within the status of freeman and freeholder was the non-shareholder, to whom a farm fully prepared and equipped had been conveyed—mortgaged: this could be done for various reasons—the grantee had paid his own passage to the colony; he was able to make a partial down payment; he was a bondsman whose promise of responsibility won him manumission; as dowry in consideration of marriage. Thus all realty property owners in fee simple independent title, whether encumbered or not, and whatever the acreage quantity, were classed as freeholders; they were all in law regarded as owners of property, on which as security they had the right to borrow money. The capitalistic principle of the mortgage[d] raised some economically destitute to the status of freeholder. his home lot created the fascination of private ownership; it was a vision of utopia—he was beginning to lose his immemorial sense of social alienation, of rejection—and he was developing a sense of belonging as a matter of right. The farmers paid off their mortgage in kind, at the rate of fifty percent annual increase of stakes. The corporate farm system consisted predominantly of the commonalty family farmers: they each owned one farm on which they lived and worked; and they were a laboring class of people, with a capitalistic ideology. A very small percentage of them had each, through cash or skill, acquired ownership of his farm in clear title; he kept the full product of his labor, which could enable him to buy a horse or a servant,

231

and maybe eventually another farm; the mass of the farming commonalty never achieved mortgage emancipation, yet they all enjoyed the civil rights status. The multiple tractowners, who were in one way or another subordinated to the Head of Hundred, had each at least a family with several members, and some also owned one or more servants.[e]

The settlers brought with them to America, and they at first made their plans in terms of, their "little Isle" tradition of land shortage: the potential fee simple independent family farmer, clear or mortgaged, would be made a grant of a one hundred-acre primitive tract on the principle of the "head right"; this meant that a fifty-acre tract would be granted to whoever paid for the transportation of any individual, including himself, who entered the colony—and on the grant's seating a contiguous fifty-acre tract accrued. Before long the settlers began to comprehend America's Atlantic seaboard area, which appeared to them as a vast continent, and this—together with the sparseness of population, caused their inherited fear of land shortage to evaporate. The fifty-acre tract was sufficient for the family farmer's normal lifetime economy; fewer acres facilitated communications with the domain; and the accrual's occupancy by another settler gave everyone a greater sense of security. He began to take for granted wilderness terrain, and the head right was soon ignored as superfluous.

GOVERNMENT

During the Tudor-Stuart regimen a struggle was going on in England between traditional feudalism and revolutionary capitalism to determine her sociology—her fundamental way of life. The Anglo-Saxon world was in a state of anarchy: it was experiencing an unprecedented dynamism—it was expanding, both internally and externally, and this brought serious repercussions; the Stuart realm was in the throes of social revolution—in the chaos of radical dislocation, of political and economic transition; fundamental changes were taking place in institutions and values, as people were evolving over the generations from the old ways to the new; and political extremism was alternating in succession to governmental power. The capitalistic expression was dependent upon legislative enactment or statutory law, which at first was a compromise with the feudal traditional or common law. With the restoration of the

232

monarchy the Presbyterian-Cavalier coalition of 1646 took over the British state, with the king as the front figure and the merchant princes as the power behind the throne. Parliament—as expressed by the purchaser plutocracy in the House of Lords, and by the House of Commons—was struggling to achieve sovereignty: under Henry VIII there had taken place the introduction of the principle of Parliamentary potency; and for the two decades to 1660 there was no royal rule as the king Charles First was embattled, and his heir was in exile, and England was developing from the federal political principle to the nation state. During the two centuries of societal commotion the merchants were under serious challenge by royal self-assertiveness as it persisted in its attempts to maintain its own traditional way of life in the realm.

In this time of sociological uncertainty "the crown issued all charters under which settlements were made"[3]: there was as yet no general practical familiarity with the national political doctrine, and the charter was a compact in which Parliament did not figure; the colonists held fundamentally of the Crown, and it was implicitly taken for granted by all that a political connection on the federal principle does exist as between them. British sovereignty was a part and a condition of colony existence: the principles of imperial policy towards the colonies—the influence which was directly exerted over them, and over the proprietors who cooperated in founding them—are fundamental in understanding their relations; the London government was the political power under whose initiative and protection Anglo-America came into being; and her control over her trans-Atlantic possessions did not come from conquest, but was an incident of their settlement.

The differences between land and trade were qualitative; and the transition from feudal values to capital values implied a measure of carryover, to the extent that traders were characterized more or less by both, and there was a reciprocal modification. Yet colonization was inherently a capitalistic venture; there had to be the organization of a company, and the accumulation and the investment of capital; the Reformers—the projectors of trans-Atlantic serttlements, were "at the outset merchants, or knights and noblemen who were acting under the commercial impulse", and "the colonies were by-products of English commercial activity".

The Council for New England and the Companies it chartered for the settlements in America, were part of the Parliamentarian cause at home;

they came into being and engaged in their activities long before the political division into branches—executive, legislative, judicial— became clearly delineated, when the powers of government were interdependent and confused. The Parliamentary political principles in all their haziness were extended to the New England colonization endeavors; and this uncertainty within settler Reform was further aggravated by its inexperience in governing, and by the opposition of tradition. With the founding of the colony the Company soon became absorbed in the government, and the charter came to be regarded as in the nature of a constitution for the "new Society".

The Massachusetts Bay Company was given the right of government over its grant, and it had the pre- emptive right to—and the right of realty ownership in the fee simple independent title in—the area specified in the grant. And the corporate organization as such—Company, charter, governor, settlers—was moved to the place of settlement. The Reform state was patterned on the charter: the principle of the joint-stock company— the corporation form of business organization, was the immediate instrument in law for the practical implementation of the government of the Bay colony; an historian declares—

> "There was a marked similarity between the government of the colony and that of the Company . . . which suggests that the latter's organization may have been a model."
> "The 'popular government' . . . was really that of a joint-stock company".

The charter as understood by all was granted to a trading corporation; with the appearance of a settlement the Company managing personnel manifestly drifted into, and in time became aware of itself, as a political entity—as governmental authority; and the Puritan state was an evolvement from within the principle of the trading organization. Thus the charter was the framework from within which the colony's government was a logical emergence: it constituted the Company's mark of legitimacy; it recognized and gave integrity to the colony with everything it implied; and it was a warrant for the new social organism's claim to, and enforcement of, the loyalty of its denizens.

According to the charter the government of the colony was to consist of a "Governor", a "Deputy-Governor", and the "Court^f of Assistants'' which had eighteen members; the Assistants were in the nature of a Privy Council, who were to act in an advisory capacity to the executive. This body of twenty men was originally chosen by the Company from its elite: it was made up wholly of quality gentlemen, some of whom were titled, while the rest merited the upper class designation—''Mister''; and it was to constitute the summit of colonial officialdom, as it was given full and final power in all aspects of government. Nominees for the filling of vacancies in the Court of Assistants were to be chosen only by, and from within, the Court—which made it self-perpetuating, and the candidates were to be elected by the votes of the Assistants and of the freeholders. And the charter of the Company empowered the executive,

> ''and such of the Assistants and Freemen . . . assembled in any of their Generall Courts . . . to make, ordeine, and establishe . . . orders, lawes, statutes, and ordinances . . .''

The top twenty—the Court of Assistants, governed the settlement in two distinct ways: in terms of themselves as a Privy Council, in which they engaged in inner consultation and arrived at decisions; and in terms of their open session, which was known as the ''General Court''—to which the ''public'' or all of the stockholders were admitted, and where as the ''generality'' of men they participated as a self-assertive entity.

Thus was introduced the grade of elite, ''the more important sort'', to which, from wealth or hereditary position as well as from personal qualification, belonged an eminent responsibility in the conduct of affairs —and it became firmly entrenched in the Massachusetts Bay colony; the members of this ruling order were the leading figures, the Heads of Hundred, the richest the New England ''blue blood''; ''we should more respect him that ventureth both his money and his person, than him that ventureth but his person only''. During the transition from qualitative to quantitative values some nebulosity concerning leadership status was unavoidable, and there could be no abrupt change in the group differences of men from caste to class—from blood to gold. The Court of Assistants—the top twenty, evidently despairing of achieving quality status from home, intended to create a local hereditary hierarchy: it therefore decided to reward and punish individual freeholders through bestowal or deprivation of such honor; and colonial station, although it was always included within the meaning of "the People", was in a category by itself, as it was in an official—in a leadership, capacity per se. The respect of the nether elements for mastery had to be fully maintained, especially in an atmosphere remote from the traditional compulsives of home; on matters of state there was a display of the pomp of power, and the governor was attended by an armed honor guard.

The settlers intended to establish towns, and the domain of the most important Hundred in the colony was chosen as the capital—which was named Boston, where the land office was located and the government met periodically. The settled area was divided for political purposes into counties, which were "a reflection of the old Shire system of England". Defense is of paramount importance in a pioneer community, and it was the principal item of government expenditure; the settlers were in fear of Indians, political malcontents, bondsmen; and the county served especially as the defense unit. Thus the colony's organization was essentially military, and each county had a "county commander" who was its supreme head. Forts also were built for the colony's defense.

The protagonists of the trader economy had at best an extremely generalized idea concerning the institutions and the values of their way—capitalism, and as the new principles tapered towards detail there resulted an impractical haziness. The charter content was clear in theory but inescapably vague in fact: definite understanding of pertinent documentary content—of the articles of incorporation, had to be determined substantially by the settlers in the colonizing region, who had to conform to its realities—to the logic of geography, the sophistication of experience. The instructions in the charter had to be adjusted to life; practice effectively modified—it formulated, theory; and to the extent that agreement of the contracting parties involved problems of ocean navigation, the new economy, the boundaries of the granted area, flora and fauna—understanding had to be extremely generalized. Little could be undertaken with full, positive concurrence: practical attitudes had to be dictated by objective conditions; definiteness *de jure*—in principle, was impossible; there could be no action if it had to be predicated upon certainty; and everyone concerned in the projection of civilization to America had to act first and rely on rationalization for future legal adjustment, which brought constant wrangling concerning interpretation of the charter contents.

And home was bedlam—a scene in the process of bewildering change;

236

the concessions from land to trade had to be wrung with blood, and they were at best compromised. In the colony the settlers had the freedom that is bereft of precedent; there was a condition of pioneering, with hardly anyone knowing what the morrow will bring; and the problems of trans-oceanic communications aggravated a state of hopeless confusion. Moreover, the English had their origins in a monolithic fundamental ideology—civilization: they were class conscious, but not race conscious; the European colony in America was a speck of civilization in a world of primitivism—both were present; and the settlers were pioneers in their handling of, and adjustment to, the primitive aboriginals of the Western Hemisphere; and they had to depend entirely on their own experience in the formulation of Indian policy. The Puritans were in every way European—they were hardly as yet American; and they had to be in constant connection with England. They had autonomy—they were architects of their own way; they had a community of interest with the trader forces at home, but they were often puzzled concerning the source, and the implications, of London directives. And in view of the new society the founders and their successors were for all practical purposes largely unclear on exactly what they wanted, and on how to go about getting it; they had to learn by doing—hit and miss, trial and error.

The colony soon developed a sense of identity—of self-consciousness: it had to be self-reliant in its relations with London; it had to maintain a working balance between the demands of a pioneer community and the home powers; and it soon became apparent that there were differences between the colony as it was in itself, and as it was in its relation to the sovereign power from which it sprang. It had to base itself on the principle, rather than strictly on the wording, of the charter; the political vicissitudes at home, and colony adjustment thereto, required constant charter revision, and the trader colonies each had several such documents issued to them. The document itself came to a few words; and the attempt to understand its content and meaning involved abstruse legal prevarication, and resulted in voluminous writing of analysis and interpretation.

In 1642 the principle of London regular supervision of Anglo-America was first introduced, and Parliament appointed a Commission for this purpose; from the Restoration the "Lords of Trade" took over; and this was supplanted in 1696, after the definitive capital ascendancy, by the "Board of Trade". And with each succession the predecessor's policies underwent a radical change. Free trade was the rule within Lex Britannica until Oliver Cromwell introduced the principle of the Navigation Acts: laws for the regulation of commerce inside and outside the Empire had to be formulated and enacted; there were few precedents to go by, and after a period of trial and error there slowly emerged the principle of the tariff, and the payment of customs duties. And there developed a complication of laws of commerce; there were customs officials for their enforcement, tariff manipulations, charges of smuggling, posting of bond, penalties for violation; and during war enforcement became strict.

America has played an important part in British history. The establishment of English colonies in the New World created the British Empire: this introduced the necessity for regular overseas communications, and Albion became a pioneer in transoceanic trade; this in turn created the problem of the economics of ocean traffic, which brought concern with outer and inner empire commerce. There was "an economic planetary system with England the sun and the colonies the satellites"; the colony was regarded as a source of public revenue for its owner, and "colonies . . . were viewed simply as estates to be worked for the advantage of the mother country".[4] And there took place in England, as head of an imperial system, the formulation of various economic theories concerning favorable trade balances, such as the doctrine of mercantilism—

> "which regards colonies as suppliers of raw material to the mother country and buyers of its manufactures . . ."[5]

and London adopted, and it tried legally to enforce, the mercantile theory—with its export-import, and its monetary, policies—which thought that commerce is one country's gain and another's loss; and it was accepted that "mercantile usury is less damnable than other varieties".

The leading figures in the projected colony were men of substantial property; a few had huge estates, in the management of which they were fully experienced. The colonizing endeavor confronted them with unprecedented problems—ocean navigation, primitive region, the "new Society". In the colony Puritanism was transformed from an instrument of rebellion to one of stability; capital—for the first time in the annals of man, was entirely on its own; for the first time it had full complete freedom and control—there was no need for compromising adjustment, as at home; and the new way of life was first beginning to move towards formation—it was in a rudimentary condition. Their understanding of the trader way was at best very much generalized; there were no clear distinctions as between the social institutions, and as within each social institution. The full implications of their responsibility as governors of a societal entity—not simply of a commercial company, had not been anticipated until they were actually confronted with it; and the exacting complexity in the attempt to grapple with the unprecedented problems before them—which was exacerbated by their inexperience as officials of state, brought them a measure of fright. The common law at home had emanated almost entirely from the feudal way: legislative enactment or statutory law had to be used for the capital way, which gave the Parliament in London integrity; and in pioneer New England the development of capitalism introduced new ways having no clear background in English law. And they had to rely essentially on the Biblical law for guidance.

With the introduction of the principles of private economy and of government the initial objectives were considered achieved. The Company had striven for permanence, and it succeeded well; and as it was fading from view as the visible active head of the venture, as policy was being translated into practice—the government took over the management of the colony. The Massachusetts Bay Company had definitely failed as a commercial enterprise, and it had as definitely succeeded as a colonizing venture. This introduced a new principle: with all the arable land apportioned and beginning to produce the settlement was started towards self-sufficiency; the civilized society was emerging from the wilderness—Massachusetts as a jurisdictional entity was a fact. The Company had given the colony its social pattern, along which lines it continued to develop after the former's withdrawal and eventual disappearance. Authority ceased to be monolithic, and there took place a separation of powers: property became independent of state and church; the government had nothing to do with the creation, stocking and conveying of farm units as this became the responsibility solely of private capital. Now came the problem of expansion: a land office was set up; areas ungranted were public property reserved for the people, and men turned their gaze westward to the forests; and private capital could now undertake to do what had previously required the efforts of a government-chartered Company—to furnish the unit of capital, and assume the responsibility to transport and to seat and, in addition, to establish.

The colonies in America had definite relations, and they had to arrive at specific understandings, with the top powers in the government in London, whether royal or republican, to whom they always had access; they had relations with the Council for New England, especially as concerning the charter; they had to liquidate their debts to the merchant adventurers, who had substantially subsidized the overseas ventures; and they had to respect the requirement of the royal fifth concerning whatever precious metals were mined on the grant. The colonial government possessed full civil and criminal powers as within its own jurisdiction; it had the right to admit new emigrants, to inflict capital punishment, to repel by force of arms all invaders of its territory from land or sea. But this authority was derived, from London—it was not inherent. The Reformers in New England were based primarily on, and they reacted fundamentally to, events in the old country; their policies were much influenced by the existing relations of sympathy with or antagonism to the particular principles, parties, persons, of power in the parent country; and the evolution of the trader government in the colony followed essentially in the implications of the Parliamentarian empowerment at home.

The economic development—the existence and expansion of the New England colonies, also was derived; they were constantly in need of, and entirely dependent upon, immigrant population and capital; for decades after founding, their life blood—their nourishment and protection, had to come from "home"; and the maintenance of communications was indispensable for a full century. In earlier days this domination was expected and was welcomed by the settlers—they were always subordinate per se; and in face of all the chaos "the charters forbade the passage of laws which were repugnant to those of England". And there was concern at home for the success of the attempts to establish overseas colonies; there was a sense of political and economic responsibility towards them, and they were at first virtually exempted from taxation; and London was to take leadership in the defense of her offshoots from enemy attack.

First-century New England's commercial relations were predominantly with home, and communications between the continents were

240

primitive; decisions in London were a long time getting to their destination, and events in both places moved much faster than transit. The colony had a representative handling its financial affairs in London, and there were a number of agents both ways in the service of business men; yet their instructions concerning opposite sides of the ocean could never be followed literally as conditions changed rapidly in each place, and they often had to use their own judgment. A general agreement on weights and measures had yet to be reached, and precision instruments were often unreliable. There was an absence of medicines for man's ordinary physical ailments, which brought maximum interruption of regularity; and the alcoholic beverage was identified with well being, and was extensively used. The bookkeeping for ledger inventory was not always competent, and there were tendencies to dereliction. The inherent vagueness in the relations of the colony with the home powers brought numerous accounting discrepancies, and sometimes there was outright dishonesty. Shipmasters for the transportation of goods, and agents for buying and selling, had to be put under bond: the condition of being bound was general, and everyone in the emigrant entourage was, in one way or another, subject thereto; and even quality could be so held, as debt delinquency was a criminal liability. The totality of pioneering conditions rendered everything as confused in New England as it was at home; and the nebulosity, and the irregularities, in relations were further aggravated by the general nascency in literacy and by the inebriety that prevailed.

RELIGION

Christianity was convinced of a qualitative difference between the various writings of antiquity—it regarded the Hebraic writings as divine and sacred, while all the others were merely human. All Christians always accepted as the Word of God both the Old Testament, the Law of Moses—and the New Testament, the Grace of Christ, and they all gave Grace a greater emphasis than Law; St. Paul said, "ye are not under the law, but under grace"; and the degree of emphasis on Law varied with the denomination.

Ancient Judaea, the area of the Holy Land, was the scene of Bibliolatry—as in relation to both the Old, and the New, Testaments.

Religion was confined entirely to the Bible, the "Book of books"—to authoritarianism, "I AM THAT I AM". The Bible was a slow emergence from within primitivism—the transition was not abrupt: it came into being before the days of the full contact of Hebraism and Hellenism; intuition, Revelation alone, had meaning—it was preeminent as the Truth of God, while reason was merely the truth of man; in non-Hellenic places man moved about in a mental haze, having vague ideas of a Supreme Being and of problems of good and evil; and before man became familiar with and impressed by the rationalism of philosophy logical consistency was not a value. Scripture is religion, it is not philosophy—it is not a complete system of rationally coordinated thinking. Primitive Christianity was Hebraic Bibliolatry.

The Bible is a depiction of man's complete inability to help himself. In ancient times his most serious scourges were war, poverty and disease— "the sword, the famine, the pestilence". Man was thought of as a blend of soul and body—of spirit and flesh, and the flesh was a permanent condition of pain and suffering—"the old Crazy Rotten house of the body"; he had not been brought into this world to be happy—"the misery of being". The ancients were in constant dissatisfaction with the *status quo*: their expression is inherently an appeal for delivery from life as it was at the time—a yearning for change, as they thought it impossible to be for the worse; and they had to identify their hopes for basic improvement with some power out of this world, with the supernatural— only God could help. The children of Israel were the Chosen People of Jehovah; they had to stand in His favor, and He held forth to them the alternative of a change of locale, the hope of the Promised Land, which is here on earth—there is no after life in the Old Testament.

The pagan deities were imagined, but the founder of Christianity was an historical figure; the real Jesus lived and taught in the thought patterns and Messianic expectations of the first century AD; with the coming of the New Testament and the rise of the Christian religion the principle of delivery from the suffering of this life was still identified with God, but its location became separated from this world. The early Christians thought themselves beyond all help in nature, and they couldn't be self-reliant; their only hope of relief was to be "delivered from the burden of the flesh, and the miseries of this sinful world"; Christian fulfillment was out of this world, identified with early extinction, and it was associated with an after life in another world—with heaven; only in

242

heaven could man escape suffering—there was no escape in this life, and in hell; and this brought a concentration on other-worldliness—the present life could be no more than a preparation for the life to come.

Religion felt itself divinely instructed to have a structural expression: this was to take the form of the Church, as ideology and as edifice; there was the "Church" as social institution, and there was the "church" as local congregation—which comprised a building and its grounds; the church was dedicated to worship, and to the teaching and propagation of the faith. Christianity had been traditionally authoritarian, and throughout the millennium of trans-Alpine civilization the principle of ecclesiastical monism was implicitly taken for granted. The Savior had founded "His Organization"—the one and only Church—into eternity, which represented and taught His divine revelation to man: one day of the week—Sunday, was set aside as the Lord's Day, a day of contemplation, worship and prayer in church; in a sacred place men get a feeling of worth—and the church, as well as the faith, was potent in man's hope of achieving eternal bliss, for church attendance was fundamental to salvation. Thus the Christian Church and its theology are divinely ordained; the church edifice and its grounds are consecrated; Christ is Truth, and there is only one true understanding of Christ—that taught by the particular theological interpretation. The clergy was a body of men professionally trained and ordained by the Church for the service of God; it was organized on a vertical basis—hierarchical qualitative or conical quantitative; its members were the official authority of, they constituted—the Church. The laity comprised the vast mass of the people who were devotees of the particular faith, and who were shepherded by their clergy. And all Christians were agreed that social morality emanates from religion—the principle of proper conduct, especially as in relation to values and to rights,[h] was within the province of the Church.

The religious writings accepted by the Europeans had been done and compiled as the "Bible" in the days long before the beginnings of science and technology, when the nascent knowledge of mankind—the wisdom of the ancients, was the foundation of life; and the Scriptures are without even an adumbration of the principle of science, and of its implications. Religion is *weltanschauung*—world view, it is not philosophy; to the Biblical mind rational consistency was not a value, and the numerous logical contradictions in Holy Writ did not detract from its convincing power. And the Bible is pre-Columbian, when man was wholly in the dark concerning the planet he lives on. Their religion rested on the fundamental principles of: the geocentric cosmology—the earth as the center of the universe; the act of special creation—the abrupt coming into being of life fully perfected, in all of its varied manifestations; and on economic ethical precepts that flowed from the economy of natural scarcity.

By the seventeenth century Christians knew of the Aristarchus heliocentric doctrine—they did have a glimmer of God as infinite Intelligence: yet in the early days of science the ultimate effects of the new astronomy on the Bible could not be fully realized; it takes some time for a new concept, no matter how logically convincing, to eliminate ideas that are identified as life, that are traditionally rooted in institutions and values—"we much prefer established error to novel truth"; and they were also in fear of becoming earthbound if they dwelt too long on natural wisdom. Thus seventeenth-century Europeans retained fundamentally the Biblical ancient cosmology, which precluded a clear realization of the infinity of time and space;

> Men felt giddy and insecure when they first had to think of the earth as a very small, and far from central, fragment of the observed universe . . ."

of the earth as a pebble lost in space; they were unconscious of cosmic indifference—of the loneliness and defenselessness of man in the universe; and their theology did not take into consideration the macrocosm. And religion did not have the concept of evolution, of slow development over an extended period of time: man understood life as final, rather than as mutable; the world was qualitatively static, although quantitatively it was subject to change; the principle of teleology, the consistent move towards a goal—the improvement of the world, of life, of man—was identified with the supernatural; the theory of progress as a phenomenon in nature was in the future. And in pre-technology, before the economy of abundance—the goods, the necessaries of life, came within the realm of ethics, and were identified with the problems of good and evil.

It is said that the ethics of the Bible—its ways, values, interests, language—are essentially those of an agrarian economy; that the Old Testament is fundamentally an expression of the customs and traditions

244

of a tribal society—a reflection of the ancient village mind. Its class differences are quantitative, which renders it relatively egalitarian and democratic; and its standards and myths could be used for destructive criticism of the qualitatively hierarchical medieval feudal society. All men are equal in the sight of God: the fall of the great—monarchs, nobles, bishops—moved the common people to an awareness of the impermanence of worldly things; there are the eternal laws of God as set forth in Scripture which the mighty and the lofty as well as the lowly, are subject to; and the conscience of religion is above the civil law. Hebraism expanded the ethics of a privileged minority caste into the ethics of mankind; the ancient Biblical society was necessarily a *common-wealth*—an organization of men where there are no extra-social beings; the ethical values are primary, and there is reverence for all human life; the People—everyone, is within the competence of the civil code, of due process; all are called, everyone has equal rights and responsibilities—actual or potential, for which respect must be shown by all concerned.

The particular creed—the theology, sacred doctrine—of a religious movement, is profound and complex; it is a matter of slow underlying development over several generations. By the end of the Tudor regimen the differences as between Episcopacy, Calvinism and Wycliffism were understood with effective clarity. But seventeenth-century Protestantism was not yet quite sure of itself; Rome's Counter Reformation was still a power in continental Europe, and many Dissenting sects had been suppressed as "heretical".

The Reformation inherited the fundamental religious thinking of the ancient world, the Holy Writ of Moses and Jesus—"'Revelation, God has spoken"; it was the voice of the past appealing to an alien people and generation. The translation of the Bible into the King James Authorized Version of 1611 took four years, and was accomplished by Reform theologians.[i] The Version was the Bible of the Reformation, and it was regarded as *final* revelation. Episcopacy was immediately differentiated from it. And as within Reform the new Bible was subject to varied interpretation and understanding: it constituted the source from which developed different systems of theology or sacred doctrine; it soon brought a recognizable distinction between Calvinism and Wycliffism, and between the various sects rising out of each of these parent doctrines. And it rendered Stuart Puritanism a distinct sect as within Reform. Thus

245

the Bible was the Word of God, while theology was a particular understanding of the Word; the theology of each denomination was a compound of literalness and of deduction, from—and of interpretation of, Holy Writ. Man likes to indulge himself in a constant re-invention of an innocent past: nostalgia—looking backwards, is very forgiving; he tends to detach himself from history and to enter a realm of myth, where the bounds between nostalgic fantasy and historical reality fade away— "from history to mystery". The Reformers were immersed in the supernaturalism of the ancient times and places: they thought that God's Word had been falsely interpreted throughout tradition; there was an appeal from an alleged depravity of their own time to a golden age of the pristine innocence of the prophets; they did not expect anything new—what they wanted was the restoration of Holy Writ to its original spirit and form; and they were at first convinced that popular study would soon reveal the true meaning of Scripture, and bring a unanimity of basic understanding which would substitute and establish the true monolithic doctrine and Church.

The Biblical writing was not looked upon as historical document to be read in relation to men and events: rather was it regarded as absolute and timeless—its narratives were understood as ingenious puzzles to be deciphered only in an imaginative realm outside history; and with logic regarded as that which proceeds by infallible degrees from certain premises, the Reformers could take their polity as well as their creed from Holy Writ without any sense whatever that they were exceeding warrantable meanings. They never studied Scripture with the mind of reason reading the pages of history; theirs was the mind of faith, and they studied the Bible as the pages of sacred revelation—upon which everything rested; the *raison d'etre* of man, and the sum totality of the life of man, is God; there was nothing to cast any doubt on the divine origins of the world and of everything in it. They were ecstatic about "the mighty power of the Spirit of the Word"; and they likened the clarity of the Bible to the bright beams of the sun—"the Word of God is so clear in fundamental and weighty points". To the Calvinist mind natural causes coincided with supernatural decisions; and historical processes, social dynamics, political movements, were not the result of materialistic determinism—they were miraculous divine acts.

It was an Age of Faith—religion was paramount; everyone thought that,

"The perfect happiness of man cannot be other than the vision of the divine essence".

The Reform mind—Presbyterian, Puritan, Nonconformist—was a composite of religion and God, which are universal; of the 1611 Bible, which is Hebraic; and of the theology and the Church that were peculiar to, and that constituted—their particular identity. They were God seekers, in whom religion was so deeply rooted as to defy any challenge— "everything is God"; He had revealed the secrets of eternity to mankind in His Holy Word—Scripture, from within which they each deduced their own sacred doctrine and Church. They were convinced that "The fear of the Lord is the beginning of wisdom"[6]; they thought in terms of the Biblical power, with its message of God—His Word, and also His Work, nature—as two aspects of the same reality; and their theology was the foundation of knowledge and truth. There was faith in Him as the First Cause, as the all-pervasive power from Whom everything flows; the life of humanity is a chronicle of God as beneficent—as the Good Provider;[j] He was the foundation of life, of biology—and of the way of life, of sociology. They had the serene confidence that everything necessary for divine grace is contained in the Scriptures plainly enough even for the untutored to appreciate; they were animated by an emotional certainty of salvation as the immediate result of faith; and they were convinced that their sacred teaching could constitute the foundation of a new way of life—a sociology, having its own institutions and values. Social theory was cast in the mold of religion—it was essentially mystical, rather than rational; and the Holy Word was considered an all-sufficient guide to action.

The Founder of Christianity said,

"Render unto Caesar that which is Caesar's, and unto God that which is God's":

this brought about the separation of the emperor-god identity; and it seems to have led to the development of an additional fundamental tendency—the principle of the differentiation, and of the eventual separation, of church (God) and state (Caesar). It is said that the early Church Father Tertullian thought that religion ought not to be compelled. English civilization was coincident with the Roman faith. The continent

247

was a solidly frozen theocracy—church and state were compounded. John Wycliffe was the pioneer of the Reformation in Europe. With the expulsion of Rome in 1534 Henry VIII introduced the principle of union of state and church, as differentiated from the principle of theocracy; church and state went from compound to union, as each acquired an underlying identity; the Anglican Church became the Established religion, and the principle of Erastianism prevailed as it was agreed that it is the divine purpose for the state to dominate the church.

Where there is a state church—an Establishment, the most that can be expected is toleration. The Nonconformist Biblicists of Tudor-Stuart England identified the state with compulsion; they regarded it as inherently unfit to pass judgment on religion; and they advanced the doctrine of religious toleration. But they did so as pioneers: they constituted the beginnings of commonalty integrity in religion, and they were extremely guarded in their boldness; there were among them varying degrees of permissiveness, and the few who threw out all limitations—who advocated the separation of state and church, and postulated the principle of salvation regardless of institutions—were not yet a social force. They relied on popular search into Biblical doctrine: they saw a legitimacy in seeking reciprocal light and learning; saints and sinners could very well meet together, and the resulting exegesis may eradicate pollution. Yet around the end of Tudor England no one thought that full religious freedom is possible.

The Nonconformists were Wycliffites: at home they had been sectarian adherents of the doctrines of the evangelist Robert Browne; they organized themselves as a denominational congregation, and they did not regard their separation from the adherents of different faiths—including those of other Reform sects—as religious intolerance. Dissatisfaction with their condition under the first Stuart king caused them to remove *as congregation* to Holland, and soon back again—as such, to England. In 1620 they received permission to settle in New England, in an area that was thought to be within the Virginia grant; and then—still on the principle of the congregation, they boarded ship and went to what they named New Plymouthk to found their own social organization. The founders of the colony were not conscious of themselves as "Pilgrims". About half of them were from the Holland settlement, who had become identified with a sect known as "Anabaptists"; the other half, who included Captain Miles Standish, were picked up in England, and they

248

were no doubt Nonconformists but evidently not necessarily of exactly the same sect. The adventurers were challenging the unknown; they were moving head-on into the ocean, into the primitivism of the wilderness, into the new society. Their sense of identity as civilized during the pioneering stage went deeper than doctrine. They were well agreed on most everything, but religion was regarded as an extremely sensitive—a volatile, subject; their founding responsibilities made ironclad organization dedicated to the monolithic purpose an absolute necessity for survival; and there had to be complete unanimity on everything fundamental. On arrival at the place of settlement the emigrants drew up a document— The Mayflower Compact, which is regarded as the first evidence in history of the actual signing of a social contract; forty-one members of the Company, each of whom was a prospective head of household, bound themselves together in a church—a congregation, now adapted for societal purposes; their settlement had to be "compact", and they each pledged to restrain their right to Scriptural self-assertiveness, which could be disruptive. It was a simple method of ensuring unity in a dangerous world; behind them was the ocean, cutting them off from civilization, home, friends.

The Pilgrims at first tended to extend the principle of the congregation to the community—to think of the two as synonymous: they built their colony on the concept of the congregation, from which they developed to the principle of the social organism—to the autonomous political jurisdiction, with all of its implications; the Bible became the foundation of their sociology, and from it emanated their ideas on the social institutions. There had been a number of abortive attempts to establish a settlement in the northern regions,[1] and the Founders of 1620—"Mother Plymouth", had to work on a background of failure. The colony was a candle light of civilization in a macrocosm of night—they were in a condition of stark terror, and egos were submerged; for better or for worse, everyone had first and foremost to be practical—nothing could be subversive of order; and the principle of monolithic organization was willingly accepted by all members of the community. Their monism had to include also religion: they did not tolerate non-Christians; nor could they allow freedom for the Roman and Anglican faiths, which they regarded as "anti-Christ", and from which they had fled. There are varying groups of people who cannot live with security in one another's presence, and men have always asserted the right to choose their com-

249

pany.[m] They were in fear of freedom of religion.[n] of serious doctrinal rift, because they thought it impractical under pioneering conditions—it was a threat to the success of their venture; and there is the rigidity of the colonial mentality, "the stern, intolerant ideals of the first settlers"—the pioneer is never a liberal. Yet their essential denominational exclusiveness had to be only for the sake of expediency, as it couldn't have been literally for the sake of conformity; they were never confined to any one sect emanating from within Nonconformity; there was always latitude—albeit cautious, concerning sacred doctrine; this assured them a measure of toleration from their inception, and they were never opposed to freedom of conscience in principle.

The Nonconformists' doctrines always tended to minimize the Church—they founded sects, not churches. As within their jurisdiction the church is virtually non-existent as a serious doctrinal, and as a political, factor; some of their sects regarded the word "church" as opprobrious, and used another term;[o] and the incidental house of worship has no visible union—no ecclesiastical hierarchy or central authority, and it has no amount of property to defend. Wycliffism always put more emphasis on moral conduct than on doctrinal dispute, and this gave it a tendency to sectarian toleration. The problem of the relation of state and church presupposes the potency of each as a social institution—in some faiths church is the foundation of salvation; and the question may here well arise, where is the church for the state to be in a union with or separation from? The Nonconformist Pilgrims, in their organization of the Plymouth colony in 1620, became the world's pioneers in the introduction of the principle of the secular state.

During the seventeenth century the Wycliffites had no seminaries. The Plymouth colony could not stress ordination: it had no accredited minister of the Gospel of its own particular persuasion; and its devotees had to rely on the lay preacher, who was self-trained. Problems of denominational doctrine and organization were handled by their legislature, which recognized and respected its elder statesmen as spiritual authority. They emphasized the autonomy of the community church; and on problems of organization—structural changes, preaching personnel, fiscal measures, each local church was virtually independent. Yet concerning the more constant and involved phases of religion they had to rely on the Puritan Church for guidance. According to William Bradford;

"Touching the ecclesiastical ministry, namely pastors for teaching, elders for ruling, and deacons for distributing the church's contribution, as also for the two sacraments, baptism and the Lord's Supper, we do wholly and in all points agree with the French Reformed Churches".[P]

And the ordained clergymen in New England—the spiritual figures of note, were all from the Calvinist settlements.

The principle of indifference to religious expression cannot strictly be confined to a lone jurisdictional entity—to an oasis of freedom in a desert of rigid monism. There were legislative attempts to control the tendencies to sectarian pluralism, and in 1645 a proposal to legalize the existent *de facto* condition of religious tolerance in New Plymouth failed. Yet the manifest destiny of Nonconformity pulled irresistibly the other way: its pioneers in America were for "freedom of conscience, or at least freedom for all varieties of Reformers"; they had reference to "the bloody tenet of persecution for cause of conscience", "extinguishing doctrines or practices by weapons of wrath and blood"; and they believed that the propagation of religion by "the sword may make a whole nation of hypocrites". It is said that,

"The separation of Church and State is the work of Wycliff and not of Luther or of Calvin . . .;[7]

and Roger Williams, who was active chiefly as an administrator rather than as a clergyman,

"was the first person to advocate and bring into actual practice complete freedom of conscience, complete dissociation of church and state, and genuine political democracy, all three together, on either side of the Atlantic".

Roger Williams thought that the state cannot be trusted to decide on spiritual verity; statutory decision on religion is always subject to popular indifference, and to modification and repeal—devout worshipers cannot be created by legislation; man's best hope for the attainment of true religion lies in protecting the freedom of all faiths—including

251

free thought; and with institutional separation there could follow the state's positive protection—as a matter of right, of individual liberty of conscience.

It was inherent in Nonconformity, especially in its social expression, to provoke Biblical dissension; and from this necessarily followed the eventual extension of permissiveness to other Reform sects. The doctrinal centrifugal tendencies were there throughout the seven decades of New Plymouth's existence, and they were not considered a threat to the social foundation. The attitude concerning freedom of conscience in the colony is best expressed by William Bradford;

> "And it is too great arrogancy for any man or church to think that he or they have so sounded the Word of God to the bottom, as precisely to set down the church's discipline without errour in substance or circumstance, as that no other without blame may digress or differ in anything from the same."[8]
> "The Pilgrim covenant itself disclaimed omniscience . . ."[9]

The settlers in New Plymouth had no fundamental theological discordance; there was always an underlying doctrinal homogeneity, but no neat delineation—there was unity, but never uniformity, in religion. They were never brought up in an atmosphere of religious intolerance; as the settlement took hold and prospered, and especially as civilized establishments throughout the region increased, its people gained confidence—and the toleration of differences broadened in time to include all Reformation denominations. There never was religious persecution in, and there never were any exiles for theological differences from, any Nonconformist jurisdiction; and Wycliffism constituted the foundation for what over the centuries finally developed into the principle of religious freedom.

The Puritans were Calvinists; next to Scripture, John Calvin was the source of all spiritual wisdom. And Calvinism was also committed to religious absolutism, as it was not an abrupt, complete break with the past. The 1611 Bible became the dividing line between Tudor and Stuart Puritanism; the latter contracted from the doctrinally amorphous religion of the previous regimen, to the hard-core Reformist group of the succeeding one. Stuart Puritanism resulted from a divergent wing of Presbyterianism when it became involved with a phase of Nonconformity; it was an accommodation chiefly of Calvinist sacred doctrine and Wycliffite church organization. They were concentrated on—but never confined to, Bibliolatry: there was an underlying uniformity in religion—One Faith, One Church; there could be no compromise on fundamentals, and they emphasized exactness concerning Biblical tenet. Protestantism in England in its beginnings was structurally and doctrinally in a nebulous condition: with time Emmanuel College of Cambridge University—the "nursery of Puritanism", was acquiring the characteristics of a seminary for its divines; and in the meantime the Reformation had to introduce the principle of the lay preacher—many of whom were sincere, learned, experienced men—who before crystallization took leadership in expounding the Scriptures.

Protestantism believed in the existence of an Intelligence in the universe—of an essentially beneficent God Who created man, and He created him spirit and flesh: God revealed Himself and His purpose to man through His Holy Word—the "Bible", which comprised the Old Testament and the New Testament; He is a living personal God, not simply a rational abstraction. Reform took for granted the perfection of revelation in the Hebrew Scriptures; the Bible—"the Good Book", is man's sole source of religious knowledge and teaching; Holy Writ was exalted as the highest and profoundest knowledge and wisdom in the possession of man; and mental creativity was confined to within the religious temperament. To be without the true faith and grace of the Gospel was to be without life; the study of "Hebrew . . . 'the language of God and the angels' '', gave one that kind of an outlook; they searched for inspiration and guidance among the ancient records emanating from the "Holy Land"; they regarded,

> "the children of Israel as a people of indestructible vitality and
> aggressive energy";

and they were impressed by the tremendous and continuous involvement of "the people of the Book"—a people of seemingly unlimited intensity "in a state of perpetual creation". They concluded that God no longer informs sages and kings by direct revelation—there are no more prophets; God had revealed his Word, and all future additional revelation is His decision; and the collection of the ancient Hebraic writings was their most precious possession.

> "First and certainly basic in all of Calvin's thought is a healthy Biblicism, a belief in both the authority and sufficiency of Scripture. The Bible, which shared with Nature the role of revealer of God, was the only acceptable rule of faith and practice".

Scripture taught that God is transcendent, He is not immanent. God takes an interest in man's doings on earth, and it postulated the principle of divine intervention in the affairs of man; and Reform understood history as the interaction of the divine and the human. Thus man came into existence as an act of special creation. God made man an ethical being, which is part of his subjective life; the precepts embodied in the Ethical Code of a people—their particular standards of conduct, are objective, and were determined for them and given to them, by God; the principles governing the Christian's activity in life were included in, and disseminated by, the teachings in the Bible; and the practical promotion of the good life was through the Church, which was the custodian of the Code, and the censor of its devotees' conduct. Part of holy revelation to man about himself is that he has a soul: man, by Adam's and by his own acts of disobedience to divine commandment, alienated the love of his Creator; thus man is born into a condition of original sin, and he lives his life in sin;

> "I was shapen in iniquity, and in sin did my mother conceive me"; [10]

he is helplessly corrupted by his very nature—inherently evil, not merely prone to evil; and it is impossible for man ever to be good per se; all of which condemned him to mortality. Man is eternally a compound of the material and the spiritual, of body and soul—yet although spirit and flesh are complementary, they are in a constant condition of conflict; spirit dominating flesh was regarded as per se good, while the other way it was evil; emphasis on the one was necessarily at the expense of the other—

254

"the spirit is willing but the flesh is weak"—and spiritual values enhanced, and material values detracted from, human integrity; and to indulge the spirit was a blessing, while to indulge the flesh was a sin. The good in man was expected—it was taken for granted; and there was a minimum of praise, and a maximum of blame. Good and evil were never in a state of equilibrium, and their reciprocal ascendancy fluctuated; and which dominated was determined by individual proclivities and by social conditions. Yet the concept of sin in and of itself suggests that of mercy, and God terminated man's alienation from Him through a redeeming act of Self-sacrifice—by sending His only begotten Son Jesus Christ, in the role of Savior. Thus is man confronted with his triune epic—his creation, fall and redemption: death, in a Christian universe, is illusory; the devotee never ended his life, he simply changed it—"For as in Adam all die, even so in Christ shall all be made alive";[11] and he has immortality in another life.

To the Christians Scripture was divine revelation as *final*—into eternity. Yet it presented God in dual form: He was the implacable Jehovah of the Old Testament who ruled by Law; and He was the Heavenly Father of the New Testament, full of love and understanding and forgiveness for His children, who ruled by Grace; and this would seem to suggest the principle of *progressive* revelation. The Old Testament has references pointing to the doctrine of monolatry, which postulated a condition of hierarchical polytheism with a top god, the God of gods dominating the heavenly scene—"thou shalt have no other gods before me",[12] "our Lord is above all gods";[13] the various ancient tribes had each its own god whom it thought of as in the nature of a tribal chieftain, and whom it worshiped as most potent; and its members claimed to be his chosen people, which tended towards the creation of a tribal spiritual aristocracy. And the children of Israel thought of their God of gods as "Jehovah". The New Testament also seems to postulate the idea of monolatry in the principle of the Holy Trinity, whose Members—God the Father, the Son, the Holy Ghost—all partake of divine attributes, and are presented in hierarchical order. Concurrent with monolatry was the concept of "Caesar", the reigning monarch on earth who was thought of as emperor-god; but this combination was definitely eliminated by Jesus Christ when He said, "render unto Caesar that which is Caesar's, and unto God that which is God's"—and this rendered each, emperor and God, a separate concept. With the introduction of the principle of

255

monotheism the idea developed of God as the King of kings, who ruled the whole world.

The faithful began with the premise of man's innate depravity since his fall: under the Law of Moses all men were condemned for the sin of Adam, but under the Grace of Christ they could be saved; God could be appreciated through the Scriptures as the Creator, and also as the Redeemer. In the Biblical geocentric cosmology there were two worlds. There was the natural visible world—a cozy corner, of which it drew a neat blue-print; the earth was flat—a vast table-land. And there was the invisible world—a supernatural sphere existing in space, which controlled the visible world. The devotees of the Puritan Absolutism lived their lives in both the natural and in the supernatural worlds. The invisible sphere was divided into two distinct parts: the one above the earth which was heaven, presided over by God in an atmosphere of light and good, where the saints found eternal bliss; and the one below the earth, which was hell—the eternal torture chamber of the wicked, presided over by Satan with his demons in an atmosphere of darkness and evil. The benevolent and the malevolent powers were both cognitive, and the visible sphere was subordinated to both. The human world was divided into light and darkness, spirit and flesh; and it had the principle of *good* which was represented by God, and the principle of evil which was represented by the *devil*. A constant struggle was going on between them, and each had cohorts in its support; yet the certainty of virtue triumphant permeated the moral style of the time—God is always stronger than the devil, and man took it for granted that the forces of God were dominant, and that it is inevitable for good ultimately to prevail over evil.

Eschatology was fundamental in their lives: change was identified with a sudden coming into being, as in the act of creation; they thought in terms of the catastrophic event, of abrupt supernatural intervention in the world of man, of the last days, which could be disastrous—Armageddon, Apocalypse, the end of the world; or could be delivery, the second coming of Christ—and they had the doctrine of chiliasm—the millennium, the belief that Christ will return and reign on earth for a thousand years. They were full of superstition: their world was haunted;[q] they peopled their environment with mystically endowed evil-doers— witches, wizards, sorcerers, necromancers, and they were in great fear of the "evil eye"; they filled their atmosphere with innumerable varieties of malevolent beings—devils, demons, imps, sprites, gnomes, hob-goblins—

"these demoniac angels their own inflamed imagination had conjured out of the life about them";

and doubters concerning the truth of all this were frowned on. Sickness and pain were explained in terms of demonology, the infiltration of the body or its member by devils, which must be exorcised; human help with a view to relief or cure through medical, surgical treatment—the process of healing slowly in the course of time, was unknown; the cure for a physical ailment had a mystical connotation, and was synonymous with "godsend"; and they thought in terms of magic, the "laying on of hands"—to take an ailment away with the hand. The work of the apothecary was a mystery in his time and place; and chemical compounds, and medicines—usually due to professional insufficiency—sometimes had a malign effect, and were often thought of as "the witches' brew". And there was an hostility to scientific tendencies and remedies, as they appeared to be thwarting the "Will of God". They believed in numerology, the occult influence of numbers; the numerals seven and three respectively in the Old and in the New Testaments seem to have a mystical connotation.[r] They were also guided by astrology, in terms of which they explained heavenly phenomena—meteors, eclipses, shooting stars—which they regarded as catastrophic, "portentous signals of great and notable changes". They suffered from a sense of guilt—a sin consciousness, and they felt themselves in constant danger of saying or doing something that may cause the Lord to frown on them; they tended to endow ephemera with mystic significance, to identify such objects and acts as signs of blessing or sin; and there were also inclinations towards oneiromancy, dream interpretation with a view to divination—the prognostication of future events.

Reform was in accord with the traditional images of God: it emphasized "the Old Testament, an account of kings and harlots"—with its blood and thunder Jehovah, who was part of the beastly superstition derived from primitive mythology; he was a capricious, vengeful deity, who hurled thunderbolts and commanded bloodbaths;

"For this is the day of the Lord God of hosts, a day of

257

vengeance, that he may avenge him of his adversaries: and the sword shall devour, and it shall be satiate and made drunk with their blood; for the Lord God of hosts hath a sacrifice in the north country by the river Euphrates."[14]

Jehovah, the invisible power, was the overwhelming reality in man's life: he had to be regularly appeased with blood, with the shriveling, flooding, killing off of hordes of people, "like a page from Genesis"— although a change had taken place from human to animal sacrifices; he was the kind of god who made himself known only through the punishment he inflicted on sinners.

The Old Testament aura is endlessly solemn as it emphasizes the dreadful might of Jehovah; he was the authoritarian figure—"I AM THAT I AM"; he was never a rational deity. The Calvinist God was a tyrant and an executioner, and the faithful were driven by devotion to an implacable deity;

> "Their theology was the stern, vengeful Jehovah of the ancient Hebrews, and not the compassionate and gentle Christ of the New Testament";

and they stressed the heavenly wrath towards, rather than the indulgence of, the sinner. The fortunes of men were determined in heaven; His Will brought them success or failure—He was the last word, the relentless taskmaster who always stood over his disciple's head and passed judgment. The faithful always had the sense of an unseen hand—they acted in life as if God were watching; the denizens of the invisible kingdom, both good and evil, were a constant presence—a matter of daily experience; and there was an emphasis on man's basic infidelity and his need of divine assistance. And the devotee felt himself in God's good graces if things went his way, while failure was traced to a disobedience that merited punishment. And it was fundamentally God—not man, Who pursued and punished the wicked.

Yet the Old Testament dogmatism on guilt and fear was tempered by the New Testament faith of love and mercy—the Father is stern, but forgiving; and the concept of Mosaic savagery and revenge, its retribution and its remorselessness towards the guilty, was to some extent redeemed by Christ's principles of charity and brotherhood. The

258

emotions of the faithful towards God were a complex of both fear and love: they "walked with God"—a feeling of helpless terror within a given environment makes God a constant companion, and He continued to regulate the daily life of each person; and the devotee knew the Lord as intimately as he knew his family—His presence was always felt in home, field, shop, church. The common, practical, pioneer "old time religion" prevailed, and life was the simplicity of the pastoral scene.

Christianity of the Book resulted in a literal form of anthropomorphism—of man creating God in his own image;

"But he, being full of the Holy Ghost, looked up steadfastly into heaven, and saw the glory of God, and Jesus standing on the right hand of God."[15]

Reform had the geo-anthropo-centric—the eschatological, mind: God is Jehovah, having separate individual identity and possessed of human attributes—"I am a jealous God"; He is quantity—an aggrandized, glorified man.

The Reformation as represented by Wycliffism and Calvinism—as it worked out in a wilderness—founded, took root in and developed, New England; it supported the capitalistic social set-up, and it introduced the trader form of economic organization. The Pilgrim and Puritan pioneers were an expression that flowed from a common underlying ideological attitude; they brought no tradition with them—theirs was not in any way "the faith of the Fathers". The Calvinists were concerned about the differences between the preacher and the minister of the Gospel; they very much preferred the trained—the ordained, clergyman as the interpretation and explanation of the Word of God could not be permanently entrusted to laymen; but ordination was unavailable until their denomination crystallized sufficiently to have its own seminary, and they made plans to organize a school; and they accepted the preacher, but only as a temporary substitute.

Under the Tudors there began a series of social commotions; and in the theological and ecclesiastical turmoils of the century down to the Restoration there was a general underlying haze—a definite absence of clearcut understanding, concerning attitudes in religion. The doctrine of

259

union or of separation—each of which per se suggests the other, was not in issue in England as a social force in the early days of the Stuart regimen; and the founders of the Massachusetts Bay colony brought the principle of theocracy with them as part of their subjective being.

During the chaos at home there was uncertainty in New England concerning Church affiliation, and from the Restoration Calvinists were out of the Church of England. Puritanism was synonymous with the Massachusetts Bay Colony. Reform postulated the Church Universal, of which the Lord Jesus Christ is Head: the faithful called their religious organization The Churches of Christ in New England; and in the Bay settlement it comprised the parish, church, vestry, clergy, laity. The local church was a rude wooden shelter located on the domain.

The Founders thought of themselves as Biblical Patriarchs; it was abnormal for the Puritan to live without a viable ministry, and among the first concerns of the settlers of New England was the spiritual life of the community.[s] With the establishment of a territorial layout there were immediate efforts to build a church on the domain and to settle a spiritual leader in it; they made haste to organize Harvard College in 1636 as a theological seminary—the "High Church of Puritanism", for the training of their own ministry; they never stinted on support of the Church, of its personnel, of its maintenance; and they imported ecclesiasts, Bibles, vestments, commentaries. It is said that "the spirit shown in the administration of the (Church) system was more Jewish than Christian",[16] and the Sabbath was observed according to the Jewish custom, from sunset to sunset.[t] A shelter had many uses—the church could be thought of also as a fort. An important Puritan institution was the day of fasting and prayer in church, which was really a call to arms or mobilization; thus the shelter—which sometimes mounted cannon, was a military rendezvous, attendance on public worship was enforced by law, the faithful were mustered by drum beat,[u] and armed men were marched to prayer like soldiers. The meeting house was identified with opportunity for worship, and with the light of knowledge, moral exhortation for clean living, armed protection—all of which objectives beat together closely in the heart of the pioneer settlement.

They accepted the Calvinist teaching, that Christ instituted in the Church four classes of principal office-bearers: there was the office of "Elder", which was the general term of top designation; each church had two clerical, and two lay, Elders; the clergymen were seminary

260

graduates, who were ordained by the "laying on of hands", with one acting as the preacher Elder or "pastor" for exhortation and the other as the teacher Elder or "lecturer" for scholarly explication; the other two Elders were both laymen, who were identified as "deacons". The local cleric's authority was confined to his own church. There was segregation in church seating in terms of class, sex, seniority; during the services there was a verse-by-verse reading of a passage of Scripture, and church instrumental music was forbidden, while singing was allowed. They were dedicated to the observation of the Lord's day, Sunday—and they brought with them the Gregorian calendar: this holy day was to be carefully guarded against profanation, and to be devoted entirely to worship—everyone had to lay aside all worldly pursuits, and there was no business, no work, and no play; economy was fundamental to the Puritan mind, but God was sacred—and work on His day was shunned as sacrilege.

Sir John Winthrop the Founder of Massachusetts, and the Reverend John Cotton "the Patriarch of New England", were respectively the body and the soul of the Bay colony; they could, for all practical purposes, easily perform each other's functions—they could each as competently officiate in both church and state. During the earlier days it was not easy to get a regular minister for the church: there was an absence of clear understanding and certainty concerning the formality of "ordination"; such claims by new arrivals often could not be properly ascertained, and it took some years before the local pioneer seminary could become practically effective. And they had often to employ a preacher or lay reader to lead especially the frontier congregation in worship, and he too was called upon to act variously—as teacher, administrator, military officer, and at times even as doctor. And the house of worship was also the seat of government. The ministry was hardly a potent factor in its own right; the courage to contend openly with the Founding Fathers had to stem from a religious premise; the graduates of the College were none too sure of themselves, and it is an open question whether their scholarship in the divinities compared with that of many of the leading settlers.

But it was a matter of primary and immediate importance that a competent, responsible Church be organized, and before long this was accomplished. New England colonization brought many capable and godly persons to establish the churches of Christ. The Puritans were based on the trained, professional Biblicist, on the theological seminary,

261

ordination, the minister. As within the territorial layout the ordained divine was on a level with the Head of Hundred; reverence was included among the social elite, and the *bona fide* clergyman—especially the one from home, and his family belonged by birth or position to the gentry of the land. They were the most educated and reliable group in the community, they were held in the highest esteem, and "the ministers . . . were the most powerful group of men" in colonial New England—theirs was a position of leadership per se. They could control elections, decide on excommunication, determine the attitude of courts of justice—including capital punishment; they were the teachers—all wisdom flowed from religion, and education had to be confined to its purposes; and there were movements of organic communities united in allegiance to a "sturdy pastor" and his church, who sometimes led in the founding of independent settlements. The pulpit ruled; in the new society the sacred teachings determined the life of the people—they were the inspiration, the commonplaces of experience. The theologian could also act as statesman and economist, and there were leading laymen sufficiently Scripturally sophisticated to be churchmen; and the laity felt themselves an important part of the church government.

> "The churches, with magisterial cooperation, regulated matters of the relation of man to God . . . The state, with ecclesiastical cooperation, regulated matters of the relation of man to man . . ."[17]

And the Calvinist ecclesiastical organization was a combination of intelligent and disciplined clerical leadership and lay responsibility.

The Church of the Biblical Commonwealth comprised the clergy; the laity—the elite, the propertied freeholders of the layout who alone were admitted to church membership, and who constituted the vestry; and the masses, who were not members and who had no say, but had to attend church services. The member of the church was per se a citizen of the state, and in Puritan New England such status was the door to power and privilege in this world, and to bliss in the next world. The Bay colony compelled all, including resident non-Caucasians, to church attendance; man's place in the world is allotted by God—yet the poor, the lowly, the mean, also have a chance to go to heaven where they will get their reward, and nobody was denied spiritual consolation. The illiterate stood with bated breath in the atmosphere of Holy Writ, and to them the theologian transmitted the voice of God.

The primitive communications in earlier days isolated the community, and this necessitated local autonomy for everything in it, including the church; and the local loyalty to the central power could be taken for granted. To Puritanism in the Bay colony theology was fundamental, and church autonomy was superficial: the church could choose the person of its minister and fix his salary; it was decisive concerning budgetary problems, such as assessment of members for general expenses—structural changes of the shelter in replacement, repair, enlargement; importation of ecclesiastical necessaries. The church became the town hub—the pivot of social organization around which the life of the domain revolved; it stood close by the market, the jail, and the instruments of punishment. Its accommodation was generalized, and it was used for a variety of activities: the community affairs of the territorial layout, the public functions, the gatherings of the people, all centered around the meeting house—"Judgment must begin at the House of God", which was identified with worship, as well as with the local administration of public policy and of justice, and with school, morality, defense; and church was also the center of social life. And around the altar clustered the best interests of the community, impelled by a law as imperative as the economic law.

The local Puritan church had autonomy on matters of organization, but not of theology; problems of sacred doctrinal interpretation and understanding occasionally did arise, and they were decided by the development of a "synodical council", which regulated and controlled the essential creed. The Synod as a general council comprised both ecclesiastical and lay leaders. The Biblical Commonwealth regarded differences in religious faith as tantamount to civil rebellion—the sociology had to be adjusted to the particular theology; the conclusions of the Synod were applicable to the polity, and sacred law took precedence over civil law. In 1637 "the magistrates summoned a synod of the churches" on whose "pronouncements on the heresy and blasphemy" of Anne Hutchinson she was tried, and she was declared guilty by the lay and the ecclesiastical leaders of the colony who sat in judgment. The Synod of Cambridge in the colony in 1648 formulated "the first ecclesiastical

263

constitution for American Congregationalism", which defined "the New England Way". And before the Toleration Act of 1690 there were a number of additional Synods—1657, 1662, 1679.

The "New England Israel" was a Church civilization, whose ideological atmosphere was spiritual, not secular; the Puritan social organism was an institutional compound governed by God, to which the individual was subordinate; and everything in the new society was within the Bible, within the covenant with God—which was the containing vessel. To the Puritan mind the Church was the soul eternal, and the State was the body temporal, of the Biblical Commonwealth. Their "ecclesiastical republic", as a covenant between God and man, was much more than simply a condition of Church and State as separate institutions that are in a union; as a society governed by God through its theologians it constituted a theocracy, a fused compound—"the limitations of church and state were then only dimly perceived, and not at all defined". Scripture was the source of the Puritan sociology, and Church was the symbol of theocracy; their particular interpretation of the Bible was the theological premise; and the Church was the structural foundation which, as the embodiment of holy teaching, expounded social doctrine. Church was not just another institution, as she represented a different principle—she was the Mother of social institutions, from whose womb they had their being. And ecclesia, with the dead weight of its spiritual authority, was custodian of sacred doctrine and of morals.

Puritanism was the way of the Bay colony, rather than of a group within it; learning and knowledge were based on Revelation, and to its denizens Holy Writ was routine, daily experience—life; and religion was never incidental, a thing apart—Sunday. And in the Covenant community each local congregation had a feeling of independence, which made it a church responsible not to men—to government, kings, bishops—but directly to God. There was nothing secular in the new society, and life in their world was immersed in religion; and church membership, and civil and business leadership, were one. It was before the day of clear-cut institutional distinctness; the seminary and ordination as within Reform were not yet definitively specialized; and the ministry was thought of as a desirable position, rather than as a specific profession. A few literates had made some study of the Puritan theology; they were the clergy, in relation to whom the business men were the laity, while the bulk of the population were simply church-goers. And incidental to the underlying theocratic foundation—for all practical purposes, some difference was dimly perceived as between ecclesiastical and civil affairs, with each under its own leadership.

The direction and guidance which religion gave society and the individual under theocracy were complete: it conditioned its people so that they had a subjective attitude towards their social organism, and they lived their lives normally in terms thereof; and they could not form a concept of difference between church and state, nor of the co-existence of several denominations within the same community. The pioneer Puritan settlement was to consist of a monolithic body of believers— there was no place for "heretics". The jurisdictional monism enhanced the disciplinary elements of the divine state, which insured the effectual operation of the Will of God in the life of the people—the Will of God is law eternal and immutable; all the inhabitants—authority ecclesiastical and civil, ultimately derive their rights and powers from, and are responsible to, God.

The record of mankind establishes that the foundation of a given social order, from which flow its institutions and its values, is arbitrary—the principle of First Cause is inescapable, and it must also be fundamentally monolithic; a basic premise is taken for granted, which may not be impugned; and logic may be used in its attempted justification—which renders rationalism the handmaiden of authoritarianism. The Puritan theology, its understanding of Holy Writ—was the foundation of the Massachusetts Bay colony's way of life; there was,

"a profound veneration of the authority of the scriptures, provided they are properly interpreted";[18]

and so long as the trader sociology was based on a particular Scriptural interpretation its devotees were effectively precluded from being latitudinarian. The theology of Stuart Puritanism in New England achieved complete jurisdictional power and definitiveness;

"the real reprehension of Mrs. Hutchinson and her friends,

265

and of Roger Williams and his friends, was that they struck at the foundation of the body politic . . ."[19]

There was concern about Roger Williams's,

> "doctrine of separation of church and state. Since the Bay clergy, magistracy, and deputies agreed with Calvin that the first purpose of government was to buttress the church, that the church should dominate society, and that this would be impossible without the coercion of the state, Williams in their view was trying to pull the rug out from under the entire order they had risked everything to erect."[20]

The Puritans were in fear of the possibility of "a church within a church". Where a certain doctrine is a menace to the sociological foundation, is its outlawing "intolerance"? Man has a subjective attitude as within his "gens"—as within the mental ideological atmosphere in which he is enveloped, caught up; his view of the outsider as "gentile"—as alien, stranger, seemingly does not strictly come within the meaning of intolerance. Would the Bay folk be tolerant of other sects, or would they "give others the opportunity of being intolerant to them"? The concept of toleration, of religion or of anything else, can exist only as within—it can never be separated from, the implications of the underlying principles of a given social order. The societal foundation of the Kingdom of Christ on earth was confined to *a particular understanding* of Holy Writ; and there could be no tolerance of any other premise whatever, including as within Reform;

> "The essentials of the faith and the foundations of the political system were in no case to be attacked.";[21]

an organized aggressive denomination predicated upon a different interpretation of the Bible—Episcopal, Presbyterian, Quaker—would be a menace to the *status quo* in the colony. Quakers were suspect of the Parliamentary cause, and they were regarded in the colony "as underminers of this government".[22] And there could be no freedom to bring into question the tripod upon which the Biblical Commonwealth rested— Puritanism, the Charter, the Ledger.

266

The devoutly religious are rarely tolerant; the temper of the times was extremely agitated, and theological speculation and action had its eccentricities. The Puritans' fundamental relationship with their society—their world, being divine and sacred, it was sacrilegious for anyone in any way to impugn it; compromise on the teachings of God was regarded as a menace to the purity of Holy Writ—"perverting the Scriptures", and it was denounced as heresy; their ethical conduct was to be confined solely to within their own theology, and doctrinal dissent was tantamount to rebellion and anarchy. The theological dispute led by Anne Hutchinson in 1637[v] left the infant settlement "rent by faction, and in imminent danger of civil war"[23]—it was a threat to the public peace; and the banning of other Christian sects was fundamentally an attitude in sociology, as affected by theology—it was a political, not simply an ecclesiastical, position. They consistently believed that it is the duty of the state to nourish and support their religion, with its ethical teachings; and they were convinced that it is a proper duty of the civil magistrates to enforce and protect the integrity of society as church and state merged. Religious intolerance in New England was defensive—the devotees thought themselves guilty of sinning against God if they permitted heretics within their colony; and church proscription as punishment for heresy, which brought social alienation—ex-communication, banishment, execution —was an accepted instrument of unity.

The legal system of the Massachusetts Bay colony was based on the Mosaic Law, which had integrity as divine; on legislative or statute law, on common law, and on judicial decision—all of which were promotive of capitalism. And lawful conduct in the Puritan community was based essentially on the Biblical teachings, rather than on Lex Britannica. Anti-social conduct was thought of as "sin" or "crime"; the canon law for sin and the civil law for crime cooperated to enforce the disciplines of daily normal life. The Bible was the main guide to guilt and punishment; the faithful tried to model their Massachusetts Code of Laws after the "judicials" of Moses, and

"the Pilgrims had used the Scriptures, the Mosaic Code in particular, as legal writ".

The judicial process was both Anglo-Saxon and Hebraic; there is a vagueness concerning the ancient system of court procedure—

267

jurisprudence, adjudication—and they followed the processes brought from home; the trial conduct was statutory, while the ethical imperatives were sacred. The Bible was the foundation for trial arguing. The Old Testament—the Mosaic Law, is essentially harsh and unforgiving; Jehovah appears as Judge, and He can be remorseless. Jesus Christ in the New Testament emphasizes the principles of love and forgiveness in religion—God is the understanding Father; and St. Paul taught, "ye are not under the law, but under grace". And in the Puritan court procedure the prosecution based its arguments on the teachings of Moses, while the defense was based on the teachings of Jesus Christ.

And the reaction to the manifestations of Dissent in the Puritan pioneering times and places was apt to be drastic. The heretic had the freedom to leave: if he remained he could be sentenced to ex-communication—the casting out of an offending individual from partici-pation in the normal activities and the relations which bind the commun-ity together—thus shutting him off from all business and social life; and what was much more serious—there was ex-communication also from the church, which was tantamount to expulsion from Heaven. Christian-ity immemorially had adhered implicitly to the proposition of "life for life in the present, and soul for soul in the next, world"—to thrust away a soul from God is a greater injury than to deprive a man of bodily life; and Reform consciously also adhered to this doctrine. In addition, the of-fender could be sentenced to expulsion from the civil settlement, and if he persisted in staying he was generally shown little mercy. Being "dealt with" for heresy was in the nature of an inquisition, as it menaced the social foundation; banishment was an act of divine judgment, and was not considered persecution; and return of the culprit could be a capital offense. In the earlier days the banishment of individuals from the civil community was a drastic punishment, as the only alternative was the wilderness.ʷ

There were some instances of a dissenting group within a colony, theological or political, that had sufficient adherents and capital with which to found a settlement of its own, and its departure was a matter of mutual consent. New England seemed to be a vast region, it has similar conditions throughout, and there was plenty of room for the migration of dissidents. The Reverend Thomas Hooker led a cavalcade of covered wagons out of the Bay colony which founded a settlement that developed into Connecticut. Soon some settlements of tolerant views, like Roger

268

Williams's Providence Plantations, came into being which eventually became Rhode Island. There were a few individual movements of re-settlement within and between chartered colonies; but there was an absence of clearly defined jurisdictional boundaries in seventeenth-century New England, and the inhabitants were often uncertain which colony they were in.

Yet religion in New England was fundamentally a unifying, rather than a dividing—force, for that which united them was in every way more powerful. The Puritans had an unsavory reputation at home for bigotry and persecution, to which they were sensitive; they resented such allegations, as they were anxious to be thought reasonable. The colonists usually preferred to avoid inflicting physical punishment on the offender; the spaces were vast, the civil population was tiny, the life span was short—all of which perforce combined to create an underlying sense of value concerning human life. In the decision to banish Anne Hutchinson, her punishment was delayed four months because of the weather and her pregnancy. With Reform at home in all of its expressions united in arms against feudalism, the Bay colonists felt called upon to make a gesture of amity towards the rebel cause, and they could show some cautious lenity towards their allies. If they regarded a measure of theological divergence as no serious menace to their sociological base, it was permitted; and in 1643 a few freemen who were not church members were accepted as Deputies to the General Court.

The faithful thought of themselves as participants in a covenant with God: they regarded their own society, the Biblical Commonwealth, as the ideal way of life, a model of Christian living, patterned after the ancient church—it was the City of God; they had a sense of uniqueness—of sharing an experience which set them apart from the generality of men; they developed a feeling of seclusion, of distinction and security, as within a doomed and perishing world; they were an island of purity in the midst of a world of crimes of dark and mysterious enormity—except for the saints, all men were moral outcasts. The meeting at the church was the central life and activity of the neighborhood: the terrors of judgment, the torments of hell, the delights of heaven, were emphasized from this severe and simple altar, and it held its communicants in a weird, fas-cinating thralldom; and the faithful were sent home from church renewed, uplifted—inspired with new social desires born of this warm intercourse. And they were convinced that in the godly society the ordinary evils of life would be obviated: in the "heavenly city" man's development is perforce from Satan to God, from the ways of evil to the ways of good; in the words of the Pilgrim leader William Bradford,

> "God's People are all marked with one and the same mark and sealed with one and the same seal, and have for the main, one and the same heart guided by one and the same spirit of truth. And where this is there can be no discord, and here must needs be sweet harmony."

The Puritans preached godly living; the love of God pervaded and affected the collective whole, and it flowed reciprocally as between the community and the individual soul; and they maintained an essentially monolithic theological condition throughout the Biblical Commonwealth. There was a peculiar relation of Church and People: they were steeped in "the beauty of holiness", and they developed a tendency to religious snobbishness; and theirs was a "holier than thou" attitude as they were convinced that the people who exist outside the divine compact, who are organized on the secular basis, are "a profane nation", whose state is temporal and mechanical—without a soul. The whole Bay community was in a convenant with the Absolute, proud of itself as not being like others; the theology of the covenant inevitably bred a contempt for the lesser folk outside of it; and the devotees believed that in all human history there had been only one nation in covenant with Jehovah—only one Chosen People. Thus the religion of orthodox New England was not strictly evangelical in character; its way envisaged a quantitative dynamism—in area, population, wealth; but qualitatively— in terms of the principles of social organization, it remained fundamentally static; each unit of its polity would be the church, sitting tight on its covenant and guarding the gates against promiscuous admission.

The Biblical tales of odyssey seemed peculiarly applicable to the adventuring English; "I am a stranger in the earth"—and their pilgrimage appeared like a repetition of the experiences of the children of Israel, with their leader Moses, who became the Chosen Ones of Jehovah.

"They were a chosen remnant saved out of the general destruc-

270

tion, for whom God had providentially reserved this New England Canaan."

New England, like Canaan, had been settled by fugitives; like the Israelites they had fled to a wilderness, and they had heathen for foes; they had no supreme ruler but God, on whom they relied for light to lead them on; and they derived their legislation from the Hebraic Code. There seemed to be a similarity of experience in the primitive wanderings of the ancients as recorded in the Old Testament—"to wander in the wilderness, where there is no way"—and in the wanderings of the Puritans in the vastness and loneliness of the American continent;

"Though I walk through the Valley of the Shadow of Death, I will fear none ill, for Thou art with me".

Like the Hebraic ancients, they were strangers and pilgrims in the earth; Sir John Winthrop went into the wilderness for wisdom, as did Moses and Jesus; like Moses, he had a sense of mission—the conviction that he was ordained to lead his people out of the wilderness to the Promised Land, and his aim was the construction of a Biblical state which should be to Christians all that the one of Moses had been to the Children of Israel. The power of the Bible became evident especially in the atmosphere of primitivism, where there were no environmental civilizing influences. The experiences of the ancients in reaching the Promised Land, and in building a stabilized existence therein—the establishment of the agricultural village as the center of life—could be regarded as precedents, and they could be a lesson and an inspiration for their disciples in the New Jerusalem. God's indulgence towards His Chosen Ones could be expected:

"God sifted a whole Nation that He might send choice Grain over into this wilderness";

yet "whom the Lord loveth He chasteneth", and the Puritans—who thought of themselves as the Chosen People of Jehovah—could learn from the experiences of their predecessors.

England was created by God, but New England was created by man:

271

the sociology at home had its origins in the misty morning of man's awakening, before civilization and Christianity; and most of her institutions were of slow growth from obscure origins. The Founders of New England brought their mind with them—they brought the Reformation, to America. Their society was to be planned: they were conscious of man as a social being; they had developed a tendency towards sociological thinking, they seemed convinced of a difference between sociology as a general proposition, and as a particular *type*—human society as within civilization can have different forms of organization; and they were aware of the principle of social institutionalism and of its varying forms of expression.

Reform believed in a miraculous origin of the Bible, and in colonial New England the Old Testament lived again as if Sinai were but of yesterday. It was the Gospel-intoxicated social milieu—"the Bible was present like sand, sea and sky". The Puritans rested on a monolithic theology—they had their own interpretation of Holy Writ, their own particular doctrinal system—which differed from that of every other denomination within Christianity, and about which they were fanatically sincere; and this was the seed that they planted in the wilderness. "The Word of God"—as seen through Calvinist eyes—"was the only rule in ordering the affairs of government": implicit in it were the principles involved in the movement for social change; it was the womb within which was developed and brought into being new social institutions, a new way of life, that in time evolved into the capitalistic system—the Sociology of the Massachusetts Bay colony.

The Puritans spoke out of centuries of Hebraic wisdom: they were drawing on an immemorial legacy of man—the body politic exists for the glory of God; they intended to build the City of God—to inaugurate a new conception of conduct as the positive law of a Christian community possessing a written Code derived directly from divine revelation, and sanctioned by divine precepts of reward and punishment. They believed that every social identity of humans can exist properly as such only by virtue of a Covenant with God—an agreement whereby they promise to abide by His laws, and He in turn agrees to draw their souls to salvation. The Holy Word says;

> "But this shall be the covenant that I will make with the house of Israel; . . . saith the Lord, I will put my law in their inward

272

parts, and write it in their hearts; and will be their God, and they shall be my people".[24]

Throughout the large design of Reform thinking was endlessly repeated the pattern of the Covenant—its sacredness, its wisdom; the Covenant of Grace was of the soul, the Covenant of the Church was of the community, the Covenant of Works was of the deed.

Puritanism was religion, Christian, Reform, Calvinist: its faithful were deep in the power of God; they accepted the authority of Christ as their only High Priest and Mediator, and the principle of the brotherhood and communion of Christians in Him. They were inspired by the thought of America as a renovated England, "where ideals might blossom into realities". They founded the Bay colony so as to establish in the wilderness, in terms of their own theological wisdom, the Biblical *Common-wealth*—"a divinely ordered ecclesiastical system". The trader sociology was "the Will of God"; and they intended to build the "new Society" in the image—in the truth, of God; and their

"magistrates . . . fell back on the Mosaic law for principles and precedents, when . . . English sources failed them".[25]

They based their life and their mind on Scripture; it was the fountainhead for the determination of "divine trueth" and "divillish errour"; it was their sole authority, from which all specialized learning flowed; it was their guide in every phase of this life, and of the after life; and they "found in Scripture a special rule for everything of the nature of civil as well as of ecclesiastical order and administration". There was a required acceptance of the authority of the Holy Word, and there was "corporal punishment for 'such as shall deny the Scriptures to be the rule of life' ":

"in early days a committee was formed with the power to make a draft of laws agreeable to the Word of God, which may be the Fundamentals of this Commonwealth";[26]

where there is no law all causes shall be heard and determined "as near the law of God as they can"; Sir John Winthrop is quoted as saying "Whatever sentence the magistrates give, the judgment is the Lord's";

273

and the only test for the validity of social practice rested on whether Scripture permits it. Thus in the "Bibliocracy" religion was the vessel within which all of life was immersed—the atmosphere within which men moved, breathed and had their being.

The faithful stood in great reverence of the document, the written word—"it is written", which they considered their guide to life. There is reference to the "American confidence of committing generalities to paper"—ideals, "glittering declamations", and survival of the word was then confined to paper. Their thinking rested on a tripod—the Bible, the Charter and the Ledger, as different integrated qualities of the one societal entity—the holy commonwealth. They thought the royal patent inherently of less importance as a basis of government than the "Grand Charter in Genesis"—the Old Testament was the "written constitution" of Calvinism; and they regarded the principles contained in the Charter and the Ledger as implicit in, and as ultimately emanating from, the Bible.

Their New Jerusalem was,

"a commonwealth worked by the interpretation of Scripture, actually turning Jewish history and precedent into New England law and custom";

and the purpose of their mission was the transformation of a trading company into a holy experiment—the bringing together, in an harmonious relation, of theology and economy. The basic conception of the holy commonwealth was the sense of divine mission, which transcends the principle of society as simply a contract—an agreement among people. Their colony was to be the citadel of God's Chosen People—a refuge for truth; it was to be fundamentally a community for righteous living, and they thought of it as primarily a socio-religious, rather than a commercial, enterprise. It was felt that at home the ways of the feud-ridden days had been inherited and carried over into the mart: as within the godly community the mart would no longer represent the law of the jungle, bereft of spiritual consideration and conscience; ethical practices in business and clean competition would prevail; and the morals especially of the new generation would be greatly improved. And the Covenant with God exempted their Calvinist Absolutism from the normal operations of cause and effect, as it became the object of a most peculiar

274

solicitude in heaven; benefactions and afflictions were not mere natural law—they were divine judgments; and any violation of the agreement could never be traced to God.

MORALS

In Tudor-Stuart times serfdom was slowly taking on the form of commonalty; these groupings represented a social condition which rendered life cheap; there was a callousness towards human suffering, and their members were not considered as strictly within moral respect. Patricians found diversion often in the atmosphere of the ale-house, and humble folk furnished the outlet for their "wanton merriment". With the growth of the Reformation and the rise in economy, the commoners began to move towards overcoming their traditional sense of degradation and worthlessness; they began to emulate the values of quality, whose spread tended to the principle of equality. They developed a hyper-sensitivity concerning morals, and there was a reaction against license; the status of woman was always polarized, and the line between virtue and vice was sharply drawn—she was either an angel or fallen; and they objected more to a single night of adultery than to the slaughter of a battalion of men. The Reformers postulated the truth of a universal and timeless morality: they lived their lives in the conviction that sex as nature intended it—as between man and woman, is its holiest and most beautiful expression; they taught the principle of the single standard of morality; they preferred a society which takes marriage seriously, and were convinced that it is noble and desirable to spend a lifetime with one mate; and a fundamentally frank and healthy relation did exist between the sexes. And there slowly developed a tendency towards the achievement of commonalty religious, moral, economic integrity on a social scale, which laid the foundation for monogamy—for marriage, home, family.

All Christians were agreed that morality emanates from religion, and is within the province of the Church; she is the traditional guardian of public morals, and the source of social conscience—of guidance, consolation, charity. The existent Churches at home were shunned by the devotees of the new Christianity: they were horrified by the "idolatry" of the traditional religion with its physical obeisance, vestments, sign of the cross, ring in marriage; they thought that their children were being taught a pagan morality—"this idle or idol maypole"; and the Christmas celebration was stigmatized as anti-Christian, flippant and sophomoric "pagan revelry". However, their own sacred doctrine was still in a largely nebulous condition; and the establishment of the structural aspects of their church—seminaries, ordination, ministry—had yet fully to acquire definite shape. Reform emphasized the inherent depravity of man—his tendency to stray from the straight and narrow; and it taught that religion is man's only hope, as it constitutes the foundation of mass discipline in good character and clean living. The preachers of the Gospel were humanly zealous in practicing the pure life which they enjoined, and sex was confined strictly to within marriage. They were people of the book—the Bible for religion, the ledger for economy—which rendered literacy mandatory. A knowledge of the Bible was a duty from which no one was exempt; the catechism was of primary importance in the Reform household, and they believed in worship and prayer.

A few of the offspring of the uprooted "commons"—who were huddled together in the towns, had reached a measure of economic integrity; they were characterized by their immemorial simple virtues— by the joys of the life of austerity; frugality, which was synonymous with miserliness—was a blessing—and luxury was a sin; they had plenty for simple living within their homestead, but little to dissipate beyond its snug boundaries; and the values and the attainments were utilitarian, rather than decorative. Yet they rejected asceticism on principle, and they never objected to recreation for its own sake. They emphasized abstinence from the worldly pleasures in order to save money, to maintain health, and to avoid sin; and they denounced as licentious the activities that tend to arouse the sex passions, especially revealing dress, and music, dancing. Puritanism was a "stainless religion", whose devotees were required to be "unspotted lambs"; merriment was regarded as per se immoral, and the betrayal of gay patches was frowned on as tending to "playing wanton"; and they engaged in mutual criticism concerning their conduct in piety, morals, business. On the Lord's Day everyone was caught up in a vise of holiness; church attendance was strictly required—other activities at such time were denounced as "a desecration of holy time"; and there was a general condition of severe decorum, poverty of amusement, want of humor—they couldn't associate Jesus Christ with laughter. They opposed all sports events on holy days, and theirs was always an emphasis on less play and more church. "Sabbatarianism" was pronounced, as organized amusement and Sabbath profanation were synonymous; and the sanctity of the Dissenter's Sunday, as an antipodal reaction to contempt, made it a gloomy institution indeed.

The Reformers brought their mind with them to America; their view of the world was Biblical and sacramental—their monolithic faith was the foundation of everything. The Hundred was the organizational nucleus of their colony; it was the dominant productive unit, and the foundation of the Biblical Commonwealth. The commonalty had achieved the opportunity to found their new society entirely on their own system—on the trader type of economy with its values, ways, interests, hopes; for the first time in history they emerged—actually or potentially—from a background of impoverishment and degradation into the light of social status, civil rights, manly integrity. All realty owners regardless of economic status were classed as head of household; the jurisdiction was under patriarchal rule, with the Head of Hundred as the Father figure— the model of authority, in terms of which the humbler heads patterned themselves. And on the domain of the largest and richest Hundred in the county was the parish and a church, as well as the governmental adminis- trative office. The Reformers were convinced that church and state exist to control human corruption, and to help man attain victory over the flesh and the devil.

It is said that knowledge is based on contrast; the mind is indeed rare that achieves consciousness of the all-pervasive. The settlers soon forgot the contrasts they had experienced at home: they thought of themselves as exiles, and life in the colony was essentially one of remoteness and seclusion—they existed in a world of their own, and especially with the rise of the new generations they developed a subjective attitude towards their fundamental inspiration, and Puritanism became an implicit part of their being. Their religion was the containing vessel—the underlying principle of their settlement; and this tended to render the denizens of the Biblical Commonwealth unconscious of themselves as Puritans, which made their way of life all the more binding. And the Reform mind on the institutionalism of their "new Society"—capitalism, was compounded.

The lesser tractowners, who were all in some way subordinated to the Head of Hundred, were Reformers devoutly committed to marriage, home, family; these vital institutions were divinely sanctified—they

277

were an implicit, not a conscious, part of the devotees' mental make-up. The family was the sociological nucleus of the Biblical Commonwealth—"the man forms his household, that in turn forms the state"; it was of the greatest importance in the ordering of the new society, and the Puritan state was a community of families. The family as the nub of the social institutions gave a tone of domesticity to the era: it was the unit of religious devotion, and it set the rules of moral association, of economic enterprise, of racial purity; "founding a family" was a duty, and bachelors were rare in the Reform settlement. The realty owners had each a family with at least several members, and some also owned one or more servants. The relations within the "household family" under capitalism were determined by the canon law—and by the civil law, both common and statutory, by quantitative class values, rather than by qualitative caste values. The head represented the paternal principle with its world view in family relations, and as such he was *pater familias*— lord and master; he had the ultimate responsibility for everything in his charge, both lay and sacred; all members of his household were subordinate per se—wife, children, kin, servants; and his word was decisive in the spiritual, political, judicial affairs of his homestead. He was a pious man, and the religious lay elder—especially in the absence of ordained clergy—for "every man ought to be a priest in his own house"; and the Reform families became little cells of godly righteousness. And he and his people thought of themselves as a unit representing the ancient patriarchal family.

And family unity was required for the sake of survival, especially as within a primeval environment; and the organization of the household was based on strict discipline, which could be elicited if necessary with paternal correction. The head of the unit was usually fully literate, and he sometimes had the help of a clerk; he knew his Bible, and he also knew his Ledger—which was unique (each man had his own ledger) and was identified with the principle of economy; he was very much concerned about the training of his household in the catechism and the "three R's"; and religion was a daily affair—with prayers at meal, and at bed, time. The head of household was the kind of man whom "wee folk" could emulate, he controlled his "family", and he was in turn controlled by the minister and the magistrate on the domain. There could be no unwarranted intrusion into the sacred precincts of the household.

During the economy of scarcity—in pre-technology, one had to go outside the home and into the world of nature and society in order to do his duty as family breadwinner; and there was a sharp competition and struggle in these efforts, which was aggravated in a pioneering area. Man is endowed by nature with a tendency to pugnacity, and with a greater physical strength, endurance, courage, than woman; man was therefore concentrated outside, while woman remained inside, the home—"to make a living" was his first moral imperative; there was a profound sense of the disparity in man's and woman's work, and they assigned fixed ways of behaving to individuals on the basis of sex. The Reformers were under the Biblical injunction—the patriarchate, male domination; woman was regarded as mentally as well as physically inferior to man, and incapable of making worldly decisions; she was to be commanded, and the Puritan as husband and father was absolute master. The future of girls was identified with marriage—they were to be relegated to the home; for their education a smattering of the "three R's" was considered sufficient, and the doings only of men were thought important enough to go on record. Woman's role was purely domestic: she was a symbol of centuries of rural women, whose fear of the world was bred into them; her major creative life was grounded in wifehood and motherhood, and poverty and fear were her constant companions. She was enslaved by routine—hers was an endless and mindless round of farm toil and pregnancy, a body responding joylessly to the necessaries of existence, and her purpose was to please her husband, bear children and attend to household affairs. She was a normally practical person—capable, sober, thrifty, loyal; and she was mistress of her home, which was an economic unit—budgeted, of which the kitchen was the heart; and the constant industry of woman was an essential factor in every phase of colonial New England life.

In view of her inferiority the idea of the female as preacher, or even as teacher, was absurd; custom bound woman to silence in a public assembly, and she did not have the temerity to compete with men in sophisticated matters. Yet is said that "to understand bygone manners and morals the proper study of mankind is woman": she is basically conservative, and she was not always unhappy with her place in the Reform social arrangement—she did not mind being relieved of worldly responsibilities. Her status as inferior forced her towards the development of a shrewdness tending to subtle domination; her advice was not requested, yet women do have the power to shape ideas, to force the

279

making of sound decisions, to act as conscience for the world—
"man's mind and woman's heart"; and she was not without a good deal
of prudent influence—women could play masterful parts in a society
apparently dominated by men. She was never the clinging vine; yet she
was suspected as temptress, and as capable of witchcraft, but the idea of
woman as aggressive—as the "pursuing female", was nonexistent. The
marriage institution was respected, and the married woman was rarely
approached with a view to an illicit relation. The Puritans were pioneers
in recognizing the rights of women; careful provisions were made for the
widow's dower; a marriage could be annulled, and divorce was permitted for adultery, cruelty, desertion; and bigamy rarely occurred. Women
were predominantly useful, and seldom ornamental or intellectual: colonial New England produced a few female historical figures—Anne
Hutchinson,ˣ Mary Dyer; but the Puritans meant at all costs to avoid the
universal male nightmare—the superior woman; they intended to anchor
her firmly in her place, and the woman of flesh and blood was excluded
from their literature.

The average life span was short, and the population turnover was
rapid. The decline in physical appearance and health—especially of the
women, was terrific. The birthrate was high, as was the mortality rate of
mothers and infants; disease killed many children before it did their
parents, and this necessitated many births if there were to be heirs.
Sickness was frequent, and it was virtually equivalent to demise; there
was a relative absence of doctors, medicaments, hospitals. An early
death dogged the people of the seventeenth century; this tended to render
the home unstable, and it detracted from the richness of family life; the
condition of mourning and lamentation was frequent, and people lived in
an atmosphere of death and gloom.

Marriage for the colonists—farmer, artisan, master—was an economic necessity. They were without birth control measures. Children
were considered an asset: happiness was a house filled with children and
pets; gold could not buy a child from a poor woman with a dozen of them;
and the exposure of unwanted infants was a cardinal sin, and was never
permitted or practiced. Parents were indulgent towards their children,
and they often erred on the generous side. Yet under pioneering conditions a greater degree of responsibility must be exercised by all; this
induced a tendency to harshness from which even children were not
entirely exempt; and it elicited the adage—"spare the rod and spoil the

280

child''. Puberty introduces a new principle in the life of the human being, and it had its practical implications; the act of the witnessing, and the understanding, of tragedy grinds away the tenderness of youth and innocence—and it topples wide-eyed, precocious children into unwilling maturity. They were not coddled: childhood as such was barely recognized, and their upbringing did not occupy the center of family life; there was little sense that they might somehow be a special group, with their own needs and interests and capacities; they were viewed largely as miniature adults—they too were old; and they were put to work, almost to the exclusion of play.

The colonial era had a very simple view—the necessity of the absolute obedience of children to parents as a moral imperative: the overlapping of the generations creates a partnership between past and present: and worship of the past, especially of the Bible—"Honour thy father and thy mother", anchored the offspring to ways, places, people, and ensconced the elders. Colonial New England was dynamic in degree, but the fundamental principles of the "new Society" were static; the new generation learned from its forebears, and filial love was stressed more than parental responsibility. No one thought that the son may be qualitatively better situated than the father; yet it was in the nature of the Reform way for consistent quantitative increase to take place, and children were ceasing to genuflect before their elders—which perforce brought some adjustment in this respect; and in the Biblical Commonwealth there was never an ideological inter-generational conflict. And the stern head of the family remained very much a figure of awe to his offspring; this was especially so in the instance of the unfortunate youth who was overshadowed by the crushing image of a distinguished father—"it will ill become the son to be wiser than the father".

The goody folk were first acquiring social integrity, with its civil rights and status; they thought of marriage as sacramental and as contractual—it was both divine and civil. The monolithic religion of the Biblical Commonwealth was implicitly taken for granted by all concerned, and the ceremonies of marriage and interment did not need a clergyman for their spiritual blessing. The civil phase of marriage was objective, and it had—definitely, a practical attitude towards property; courtship and matrimony had their economy concerns—the building of a home, the upkeep of a family, the proper raising of offspring; and there was a

281

delicate balance maintained of financial prudence and amorous language, as the birth of love flowed from the womb of worldly goods. And children married early; they were often pawns in the ambition of family advancement. Their ethics required that marriage should be "arranged"—it had to be based on the parents' judgment; however, the children took for granted a measure of paternal indulgence in their choice of mates. Yet personal affection was not the basis of married life: the values of economy could not recognize an essential connection between love and marriage; holy wedlock was a duty automatically determined by property values and sacred morals; there was the principle of the dowry, and hard bargaining concerning the marriage contract was a matter of course. The fathers of the principals agreed on a settlement, and the son and daughter were told to get ready for the nuptials; and family pressure sometimes bore heavily upon those otherwise inclined; yet the practical marriage often turned out to be happy. The inter-racial union was horrifying and illegal; the interclass marriage was frowned on but was not illegal; widows had preferred status on the marriage mart—the inter-generational union was acceptable, and sometimes did occur. The marriage was performed by the magistrate, who used the domain shelter for administrative purposes.

With time there developed a tendency towards social life, and travel for sociability was generally within the Hundred. The master did not confine religion to his establishment: as the ecclesiastical organization took shape the humble little church on the domain became identified with religious devotion, with the regular Sunday worship, with the festivals of confirmation and baptism, and with the performance of the holy ceremonies in relation to the vitals of life—birth, marriage, divorce, death; and church was the main opportunity for the gathering of men and women, and it became the center around which their social life revolved. With the passing of time and the rise of prosperity the bourgeois homes in town and country became commodious, well furnished, and they were the rendezvous of the colonial smart set; and they soon began to supplement, and eventually to replace, the churches as the centers of social life. The coach and pair began to appear around 1685, and a "post office" was started in 1693. Travelers as within the commonwealth on the primitive paths could find accommodation in inns and taverns along the way; the inns, those old-time abodes of repose and relaxation for its guests, and for gentle jollity, provided a form of social life; and the

282

innkeeper was the traditional genial host, and the repository of interesting information and gossip.

The Puritans and the Nonconformists had little sophistication in the governing of a political entity; and they had hardly any understanding of, and experience with, a capitalistic society. Town life with its implications was still essentially something new to the European of the seventeenth century, and authority soon discovered that it was helpless to achieve a condition of complete purity in relation to morals. Normal social conditions strained well-intentioned efforts to maintain strict morals: all shelters, in passenger ships, in hostelries, in homes, were very much circumscribed; the simple house with a few small rooms had often to accommodate a large family, and crowding is not conducive to decency and refinement. A few graduate physicians and apothecaries of English Universities came to the colonies to settle, but medical treatment and medicaments—herbs, emetics—were very expensive, and generally beyond the reach of the goody folk and servility; however, midwives and grandmother remedies were easily available. The alcoholic beverage was a necessary aid to life in colonial times: distillation tends to the purification of water, and it was used as a medicine for the ordinary transient physical aches and pains, as it numbed the sensibilities; it brought warmth to the human body when it supplemented improvised shelters and insufficient clothing; and it enhanced aggressiveness and courage in a primitive setting; all this especially in the freezing atmosphere of the New England winter. The use of tobacco by women was unheard of,y and by men it was frowned on—"that miserable weed"; and gambling was non-existent. The degraded condition of the lower classes was exacerbated in the wilderness atmosphere, and Reform moral strictness was a measure against their tendencies to license—there was "so much wickedness in this new land". There were always more men than women in colonial life: yet economic conditions often rendered the responsible wary of the normal sex life, a large percentage of men were in servitude, many of them followed the seas; and some men "hath lived long in the woods, in an uncivil way"—for furs and lumber; all of which tended to cause a superfluity of unmarried women. The town, especially the seaport, developed inevitably as the scene of vice as an organized business: it appeared as a memorial to the corruption of the flesh as it tended towards the morally lax environment; especially towards the waterfront there was an atmosphere of "wantonness"—of "wanton women, wanton wealth", of love as a commodity; and it gave rise to dens of infamy and excess, or orgiastic abandon—of abject surrender to the devil.

Yet they had to exercise extreme care concerning sternness in the repression of the natural impulses, as this brought a tendency to license on release—"this riotous prodigality and profuse excess". And the power of rank-and-riches put it above normal moral controls; it was enabled to achieve gratification cleanly, as careful extra-marital permissiveness was not unknown; and the colonial town was too small for secrets. And conditions forced the Puritans to conclude that the real can never be more than an approximation of the ideal; it was acknowledged that "one has to give something of one's self to the devil that one may live", and sinful men must be tolerated as they bring profits to the community. A general condition of drinking prevailed: on a military expedition there was to be "one hogshead of good beer for the captain and minister and sick men"; a contemporary reference declares, "he had sunk so low that he was 'content to drinke water' "; and there was a good deal of habitual intemperance. Yet overindulgence in intoxicants was definitely frowned on; it is conducive to fellowship, but it also tends to brawling; it causes physical sagging, and encourages profanity—which is a mark of moral weakening. And sobriety—moderation in its use, was a primary value of Reform life; it saved money, made for responsibility and clean living, and promoted clarity of mind especially in relation to business undertaking. Authority had to rely especially on religion to control the human passions, and there was always the hortatory appeal with its emphasis on sin and eternal damnation. Morals can be kept well in hand on land, but on the high seas conduct was virtually amoral; and for unnatural sex they relied entirely on the instructions in the Old Testament—which are remorseless. And the relation of the sexes in general was carefully regulated; there was a good deal of cynicism, especially from the Restoration, concerning Puritan rectitude—yet it did succeed on the whole in maintaining colonial New England as a community of social decency and moral cleanliness.

NOTES

[a]The founders of a trans-Atlantic settlement were called "adventurers" because of the great risks involved.

[b]The Crown always reserved the right to make a direct land grant to anybody within any colony.

[c]There was a retention of some feudal realty terminology as within the new way.

[d]The mortgage at present is regarded as a mark of oppression.

[e]The colonial tractowner planted the seed, he laid the foundation, for the development of the fee simple independent family farmer—who before the days of oil and steel was the backbone of American economy and democracy.

[f]"Court"in England was understood as an official meeting of a Corporation.

[g]Judaism and Christianity are both within the comprehension of Hebraism.

[h]A value is ideological, while a right is social; there is the adherence to a given value, and the attempt to acquire social rights in relation to it.

[i]William Tyndale was the first (1534) to translate the New Testament from the original ancient tongue into English, and "the Authorized Version of 1611 is 90% Tyndale without alteration".

[j]Colonial New England named one of its cities "Providence".

[k]Captain John Smith of the Virginia colony had learned that "several hundred Brownists had gone to New Plymouth".

[l]New Plymouth was the pioneer, the first successful settlement in New England.

[m]There will always be certain practices in the name of religion that are shocking to some people.

[n]As it is understood in the twentieth century.

[o]Meeting house, temple, chapel, tabernacle.

[p]The French Reform discipline; Calvinist, Huguenot, Presbyterian, Congregational (Puritan).

[q]The haunted world in time narrowed down to the haunted house.

[r]Numerology is an important part of some religious denominations today.

[s]The Puritan Book of Discipline—a complete outline of the system of ecclesiastical government for whoever wished to organize religious life after the pattern of Geneva.

[t]Before the importation of clocks.

[u]Before the importation of church bells.

[v]The year of the Pequot War, the first serious Indian trouble in New England.

[w]Anne Hutchinson left the colony, and some years later she was massacred by Indians in the area where she settled.

[x]The first woman of distinction in English America.

[y]The curing of tobacco of harsh ingredients to enable its more refined use was then unknown.

CHAPTER THREE—ESTABLISHMENT ECONOMY

The settlement—and the "new Society," both took hold. The Reform complete control enabled the peaceful introduction of full freedom for the capitalistic economy; its devotees were convinced that the success of the new way of life had to have full political support; the government existed fundamentally for the purpose of developing industry as the social foundation of the jurisdiction, and it encouraged such undertaking in every possible way. Yet the settlers' immediate purpose had to be to render themselves basically self-sustaining—to provide food and shelter; the initial economy had to be predominantly agricultural, and by about 1640 it had achieved self-sufficiency. Within a few years the economy foundations of the colony were substantially laid, and it cleared itself of external debt; this immediately brought the introduction of private property as everyone got the right to work for himself—"a man was wholly at his own command to tend his private affairs." Their situation in the settlement was fundamentally different from that of their brethren at home. "The New England way" was independent—it had full jurisdictional control. Revelation was the foundation of their social organization, and their religion was monolithic. Thus they were confined to capitalism; they set out to make trade the foundation of their way of life; they were committed to the bourgeois organization of labor, which constituted a planned, neat adjustment of the various parts of their economy to the ordered movement of the societal whole. This gave their new way a degree of impetus wholly unanticipated, and it created unprecedented problems.

The institutions and the values of the new order had to be arrived at pragmatically; its *modus operandi*—ways, methods, laws, had to be dictated essentially by the hit and miss chances of experience, as it had neither theory nor clear-cut precedent to go by. The Reformers firmly believed in their way; the trader society foundation was rigidly monolithic, and its protagonists were remorselessly determined to establish their own order. They were convinced that the state exists for the fundamental purpose of promoting economy; they intended to play a positive role in the regulation of, and they were wholly committed to, the fullest freedom for productive development; and they introduced the principle of the expanding economy. And New England had complete unrestricted freedom for industry—manufacture, merchandising, commerce, banking.

Massachusetts Bay was a collective of Hundreds; the foundation of the colony, of the Hundred within the colony, and of the household within the Hundred, was arable. The jurisdiction, Head of Hundred, head of household—each had to have an initial capital base from which to operate, as the creation and acquisition of realty were enabled solely by capital—which could take the form of cash, chattels or skill. Capital investment was title. The corporate farm system was the peculiar social organization of the territorial layout: the estate constituted the master's own total realty and personalty property; and the mortgaged tracts were distributed among the "goody" folk. The capitalist as in relation to the territorial layout was a Head of Hundred: the Head of Hundred—as concerning his own private estate within the layout, together with his entourage of aides, domestics, artisans, laborers; the "goody" freeholder as in relation to his own multiple tract property; the lone farm owner, clear or mortgaged—each of them was classed as a head of household. And the entire layout was rendered autarchic or a self sufficient economic entity by the domain, which in time became the head or center—the nub, of the Hundred's industrial activities.

The Puritan mind was basically on the town organization, but the intention to build a compact town was succeeded by the inevitable tendency towards agricultural economy, which meant dispersal; there had to be a delay in the full attainment of the original purpose, as there took place a decline from compact settlement; the emphasis changed from trade to farm, and agriculture became the foundation of the inhabitants' existence. And theirs was a concentration on land, household, community. It was in the era of the economy of natural scarcity, with its parsimonious values; the people of the Puritan time and place were constantly confronted with the problem of basic need, and the sombre sense of the presence of the poor permeated the atmosphere; they were "economical"—they knew how to get the most from the least; there could be no luxury, and no philanthropy—they were, they had to be, penny minded; and the jurisdiction greatly feared "to bear the publique charge."

The man with enough capital organized himself a corporate farm estate, which made him a Head of Hundred or owner of a domain; and the man with abundant capital could own several layouts. The Head of Hundred was a leading person and a rich man, who engaged in the pursuit of profit: he owned many laborers who cultivated his plantations; he received a given time of the craftsmen's skill, up to half of his mortgagees' yield, and payment in produce for use of his domain; and the surplus he accumulated from all this he could sell at a profit. And on the domain was his plantation, which was given over to the edible crops, on which the independent farmers also concentrated. The man of small capital could buy, and the craftsman through skill could in time achieve, clear and unencumbered, a fifty-acre farm; while the impoverished freed servant could get a farm on the advanced subsidy, or in terms of the mortgage. These men were the occupants of the corporate farm estate— the independent family farmers; they owned their farms—even if encumbered—in complete mastery, which made their tracts technically free of the Hundred; but they were subject to the rights of the mortgagor, and they had to use his domain; and they were economically poor men whose life was confined to earning a livelihood.

There were important differences—actual, and especially potential— between the domain, and its radiating farm tracts. The trader colonies had the grim determination to concentrate on artifact in a macrocosm of nature—and they emphasized the artisan, who would be located on the domain; and the tiller of the soil—"the hewer of wood and drawer of water," was taken for granted. It was indispensable to import handicraftsmen—shipwright, blacksmith, carpenter, tanner, brickmaker, and the records of the Company mention the cooper, weaver, plasterer, vine planter, and men skilled in making pitch, tar. The master, who created the colony ideological atmosphere, was himself usually of worker antecedents and experience; the skilled workers were regarded with respect—they were men of some standing in the community; and they had to be brought over under contract, which granted them certain inducements. The craftsman was generally a family man with wife and

288

children, and he had to be furnished with home accommodations: the Head of Hundred, with the help of a surveyor, would lay out a street within the domain; along both sides of the street he marked off and cleared home lots each of which was about an acre in size; he then constructed on each lot the necessary houses, of wood—dwelling, shelter, and also a "garden" where some vegetables could be grown—and stocked it with a cow and some farm implements; he distributed each prepared lot to a craftsman's use, and the conditions of its occupancy— full ownership, mortgage, tenancy—depended on the content of the contract. Each artisan had to be supplied with a work shed—some with a yard, and the necessary tools of his craft; and he was also assigned one or more apprentices.

Colonial pioneer industry was an isolated urban dot: it had to be generalized—it could not be specialized; the tanner was also a leather goods worker, as he manufactured and repaired shoes and horse equipment; the blacksmith was also a gunsmith, a wheelwright, he fashioned iron, steel, tin, products, and he made some agricultural implements; the shipwright made watercraft for the fisheries and for commerce, and he was to quite an extent dependent upon the blacksmith and the carpenter. And the carpenter could make hewn timber and clapboard for frame houses. The brick house began soon to appear, and it was regarded as a mark of permanence. And if the domain fronted on a river the power of falling water was accessible, and it could have the wind and water driven saw mill with its sawyer, and the grist mill with its miller. An indispensable part of the domain was the erection of a church. And with the continued systematic establishment of home lots and work sheds and yards, there slowly began to emerge a village. The Head had also to import farm animals of good stock—cows for the conveyed tracts and several bulls, work horses and some stallions, as well as sheep, hogs and poultry. And he had to build warehouses for the storage of surplus produce, a store to be filled with imported manufactured articles, facilities for shipping, and for churning milk into butter and cheese, as well as for sharpening and repairing implements, breeding livestock. And the farmers paid for use of the domain appurtenances with their produce.

Some of the communal economic patterns that "the commons" had inherited from home, and from the colony founding days, had to be continued. The freeholder's family plot on the domain couldn't include

289

farm husbandry—the growing of plant life and care of animals; and the Head of Hundred had to take the responsibility to provide these necessaries. He reserved part of the forest area within the domain for urban expansion, and the rest he set aside for agricultural needs. Behind the street front of houses he reclaimed areas which were to be used as land in common by himself and the villagers in growing various crops, especially the staple grains—wheat, corn, rye, and also vegetables; while other areas were turned into meadows and pastures for their livestock. The cultivation of fields of grass was a very important part of the New England agriculture: it was cut and dried into hay, and it became the mainstay of animal life through the long, hard winters. The settlers were committed to raising livestock; in a frontier settlement the fencing-in is inadequate, and untended animals are prone to run wild; by organizing in one herd the live stock—horses, cattle, swine, sheep, goats—of many owners, the best care was obtained with the least effort; and there was planned feeding and milking, protection from predators, and shelter from the weather. For all of which activity the Head had to provide the labor, both human and animal, as well as the necessary implements. In the heat of summer, due to the absence of ice, there was the neighborly cooperative slaughter of the bovine and its immediate distribution. Reclaimed land—arable, always had, and primitive terrain near a settlement was beginning to acquire, sales value; and in view of the value of land, of the necessary closeness in urban settlement, and of the fact that the grantee's time was committed to the master, each acreage grant as private property had to be very much circumscribed. And the property of some objects in nature, such as strewn timber—as private or common, was contingent; at times it could be either or both. Land in common gave man the feeling that he is living in his *own* world; he was in a partnership as owner, from which he developed a sense of social relation. Yet while the individual had certain rights concerning communal ownership, he was necessarily subordinated to the group; and in earlier days the associate possession of land for tillage and pasture was a step toward—was nearly as effective as, private ownership.

Man's manufacture of the goods of life is as old as man himself; and under feudalism it was carried on within his home, which was the foundation of industrial economy. By the seventeenth century in England manufacture ceased to be domestic as it was moved to a separate site, which introduced the factory system. Due to the unavoidable

290

recessiveness of a colony there was a reversion in pioneer New England from the factory system to household manufacture—home and industry tended to come together again; and handicrafts to an important extent did exist in the rural areas as part of the larger farming households. But the normal development of the domain tended towards their separation; the domain fundamentally implied trade rather than farming; there took place the production of surplus wealth, which introduced the principle of capital accumulation; and this gave rise to the "entrepreneur"—one who undertakes to start and conduct an economic enterprise, assuming full control and risk. And the steady growth of the economy brought complications in relation to the numerous activities on the domain to the extent that it did not pay the owner himself to handle it all; he usually kept his realty interests and became the local banker, but his store, warehouse, shipping and dairy business, he had to sell.

Every member of the community had to be gainfully employed; homeless able-bodied men of age were pressed into the militia; no one could be idle—on penalty, which meant definite attachment to an economic establishment. The ravages of nature and of man often created refugees—orphans, vagrants, incapacitated; there were the physically abnormal—the halt, the lame, the blind; and there were those who were mentally affected by frontier affrays with wild men and beasts— eccentric wandering persons, night prowlers. Sex as moral had to be identified with economic competence to avoid unwed mothers—bastards; Hebraism forbade the extermination of the unfortunate—the hurling of the infirm off cliffs, the exposure of infants—and the parish had to take responsibility for their care; and they were placed through the church into a household where, to the extent that they could, they contributed by working towards their keep. And there was no unemployment, and there were no beggars, in colonial New England. The Bible has reference to, "the goodman of the house:"[1] the principle of paternalism prevailed, and there was social status as within the household; the head concentrated his life on making the living, clearing land, erecting houses; and his people had to be loyal to him, and to everything he represented. And the householder had the authority to be armed, as well as to arm and to command others; the house set in a wilderness had constantly to be on guard against marauders; a feeling of xenophobia— suspicion and fear of strangers, pervaded the colony; and a newcomer had to approach a house with a good deal of circumspection.

And in the Biblical Commonwealth manufactured goods were always scarce and very expensive; and hardware especially, iron and steel utensils and tools necessary in the various industrial activities, had to be almost wholly imported—the nails and hinges in a burnt out shelter were carefully retrieved. Soon England became a scene of war and chaos, which precluded imports, and this gave an impetus to local manufactures. Trade with the Latin and Dutch settlements was of some help, but reliance had to be placed chiefly on the domain craftsmen; its handicraft enterprises were increasing in variety and in number, and some metal objects could be made by the blacksmith. The assignment of apprentices to the imported craftsmen tended to create a class of native artisans and their helpers who were hired for wages, which introduced in the colony the principle of the freeman without a freehold; and there was always a large class of goody freemen who were separated from land. Most of them continued their relation with their former masters as hired wage workers; a few managed to acquire ownership of the tools of their trade, to rent the sheds they worked in, and to set up for themselves and become entrepreneurs; and some rented a farm in the countryside and became tenant farmers—and they settled to the legal status of "housekeeper," with all of its social benefits and responsibilities. The absence of fixity in wealth ownership, both real and personal, and the consistent increase in the production of personalty, introduced a social dynamism which brought a vertical fluidity—chiefly upward—as within each class, and to some extent also as between the classes. The move from working for a living to engagement in the pursuit of profit presupposes capital, or the ability to accumulate an economic surplus; the social conditions did give the commoner freeman an opportunity to rise from the "poor man" status—to become the business man; some of the members of the upper class had risen from the ranks, and they were an inspiration to the lowly freemen.

The colony was becoming consistently richer, wealth brought a better style of living, involvement and responsibility grew, and the burdens became heavier. A few of the principal merchants had grown very rich, and a spirit of ambition in economy prevailed throughout the settlements; their laws are an index to the community as orderly, industrious, frugal, thriving—well might the contemporary English statesman Lord Clarendon say, "No person that has his Limbs and will work can starve in that Country."[2] The patent success, and the consistent growth, of the

292

trader economy inevitably increased the rate of the production of wealth; but there was an urgent need of reserve capital for expansion investment and, although there was an increase in the rate of wealth distribution it was far from proportionate to the increase in production. Yet the fluidity of personalty tended towards its diffusion among the masses; there was no glaring disparity in property distribution on a social scale in pioneer capitalism; the indications are that there were proportionately more property owners in New England at the time than in any other form of civilized society; and never had there been so much comfort for so many anywhere else in the world. By towards the end of the century—working throughout in full freedom, and in practical peace—the new way had achieved a success that exceeded all expectations; the eventual economic opportunities of capitalism for all the people, were beyond the imagination of its pioneers; the settlers became flushed as they began to sense the potentialities of their type of economy; there was success from the very start, it exceeded everything hitherto known to man, and with the succeeding generations the trader way forgot its recency as it began to take itself for granted. Up to 1690 the holy commonwealth was synonymous with Puritanism and the Massachusetts Bay colony; it had laid the foundations for, and established the success and desirability of, the "new Society"—the capitalistic system.

The Puritans of the Bay colony were in the pioneering days of capitalism, and they were little familiar with its clear-cut workings. The new society brought new problems—the problems of the production of wealth, and of its distribution or sharing; there were the vagaries of the mart, and its denizens were constantly being confronted with unprecedented complexities—prosperity, depression, unemployment, overproduction, under consumption, currency enigmas—adjustment to which was incumbent. They had brought with them some experience in the trader economy from home, but it was hardly an index in a primitive country wholly committed to capitalism. Their only alternative was governmental arbitrary action, which extended its powers into the regulation of most every function of economy—rent, interest, profit, wages, buying, selling, lending, credit; and there was detailed supervision of the crafts. This perforce introduced a condition of groping: they had their hands in the everyday business of their callings, and their eyes on heaven; responsibility could suggest only hit and miss solutions; and in their attempts at government regulation officials betrayed a lack of self-assurance, as laws were enacted, modified, repealed. Yet despite the uncertainties of the pioneering days there followed an unprecedented increase in the production of the goods of life, and the wealth of the community soared.

The achievement of the fundamental objectives—settlement foundation, introduction of the new way of life, full power and freedom for industrial enterprise—enabled the development and rise of the entrepreneur, who organized manufactures for the processing or converting of raw materials into consumer goods; and from concentration on the simple problem of survival—the sustenance of life, they bounded forward to the creation of wealth. Their economy emanated from the countryside, sea, wilderness, town; there was consciousness of, and interest in, native products with a mind on building a private property estate; and the Reformers invested heavily of their capital in the natural resources. Industries which went beyond handicrafts to expensive plants and machinery had to be dependent chiefly on British investors for capitalization. The New England region had potentialities for trade, and it is ideal for commerce; it has excellent waterways—bays, rivers, harbors—ample, accessible, deep, with convenient landing places, sheltered from storms, and facilitating defense. Agriculture, manufacture, commerce, could each achieve its utmost expression only under conditions of reciprocal influence, the government was committed to the policy of trade unimpeded; it encouraged and aided in all ways—at times even subsidized, enterprises for discovery and for artifact. It emphasized the exploitation of the natural resources—animal, plant, mineral deposits; and monopolies were granted in the fisheries, in the fur and skin trade, lumber, iron mines, salt licks. It promoted experimentation with a view to the invention of processes for easing, and for increasing the yield of, production. The quality and quantity of commodity exports were carefully checked and protected to insure the credit of the country. With the consistent growth of the economy there began a tendency to the development of industry from generalized to specialized. And experts in various occupations were at a premium, and they were imported to New England from home and also from parts exotic.

The settlers brought with them from home a sophistication in the cloth trade, and they early laid the foundations for what eventually developed into the New England textile kingdom. Workers were imported who were skilled in making cloth through the weaving of woolen and cotton

294

fabrics; these fabrics, as the base products, were worked into different combinations, which yielded a variety of cloth; and most families—especially the larger households, were engaged in this activity. They had to import some kinds of ready-made cloth, as well as all the cotton and some of the wool.[a] The implements necessary for the proper operation of the textile industry—the gearing for a fulling mill, the wheels, spindles, combs—were imported from England. Textiles were considered light industry, and women and children were put to combing, carding, spinning, weaving. Many settlers in their home activities became quite skilled at the loom: much of this manufacture was linsey-woolsey, which was made of linen warp and wool weft or filling; from this cloth making was produced homespun raiment, chiefly for private use, which the great mass of the population wore; and the homespun industry was becoming an integral part of life in New England.

Next to agriculture the settlers' primary initial—their heaviest promotional or pre-profit investment, was in the fisheries, followed by furs and by lumber. This was economy in natural resources, the much greater part of which was for export as raw material, and it came under commerce.

The fisheries required much greater investment capital than furs and lumber, as well as greater sophistication and sense of responsibility. The fishermen had to be also thoroughly experienced, hardened seamen—from ship to shore: they had to be weather wise; they had to know the "happy fishing grounds"—where and when, in what parts of the sea and at what times—certain fish tend to congregate, and the catch is best; how properly to handle sails, cables, anchors, and how to make emergency repairs on boats; how to use the catching apparatus—nets, skeins, weirs; and they had to have a knowledge of the coastlines so as to avoid accidents—rocks, shoals, beaching. Their proficiencies on the high seas led them to the development of the whaling industry in the western hemisphere; they perfected the "whaleboat," and in the eighteenth century they excelled the world in deep sea fishing and whaling; and the production of whale oil and of its other products formed an important part of New England industry. The ship's crew represented the principle of team work; each member had to be experienced in his own way, as this was indispensable in case of emergency. All of which required abundant labor; many Europeans had had experience in ocean fishing at home, and the importance of personnel reliability confined this activity to them. And there had to be facilities on shore in relation to the industry; they had

295

to build docks and wharfage appurtenances, and sheds had to be thrown up for processing and preserving the fish. The "Codfish Coast" had men who had mastered the seas—they were hardy fishermen, bold seamen, efficient sailors. Those specialized in the various phases of the industry could get government preferred treatment; it was impractical to disrupt the team work of a ship's crew, and many were often excused from militia duties. There were problems concerning the rights of fishing; the utmost exploitation in the industry could be accomplished only on the basis of coordinated, far-flung, complex organization. The conditions surrounding the fishing industry: its huge initial investment requirements; the indispensability of responsibility and sophistication of all its employee personnel; its involvement with most all other industries in the New England economy; its predication on government license; all this tended to monoply, as well as to the discouragement of freebooting. There were some instances of free fishing. New England dominated this industry in America, and it was emphasized that fishing "was the Apostles' own calling."

The fur industry, which to some extent included also skins, was based on the primitive—and was known as the "Indian trade." The pelt had to be taken from the body of the fur-bearing animal, that was found only in nature—in the wilderness, which the native roamed and was well familiar with; and the trade was irregular, as animal availability varied in periods of abundance and scarcity. The organizational investment for the traffic was comparatively minimal: the Europeans did not set up fur-bearing animal farms; they simply provided the Indian with the implements necessary to catch the animals—the firearm, steel trap, knife, string; they followed the practice of establishing a fur trading station at some prominent location outside the settlement—often at the head of a river, where the Indian could bring his load of furs in a canoe; the exchange was based on barter, where the whites gave the aboriginals additional amounts and kinds of manufactured articles for their furs and skins. There was some responsibility and control in relation to the fur trade that operated from within the settled areas; the regularly organized trading company had to have a government license to carry on its business in a legitimate way—but this tended towards monopoly. On the frontiers there could be little control; the nature of the industry—small investment, no need for skills, vast open regions, native innate simpleness—encouraged the freebooting adventurer, whose irresponsible

296

and immoral attitude debauched the Indian, especially as in relation to liquor and sex. And by the year 1700 the importance of the fur trading industry began to decline.

There was always some interest in the region's mineral deposits and the colonists never gave up hopes of finding gold mines. There were legislative inducements to those who discovered deposits of iron ore, copper and other minerals; and to those who promoted the organization of mining operations by importing the necessary machinery for the smelting, forging, refining of the metals. This brought some iron manufacture, yet first-century New England's activities concerning mining have significance only as an index to subsequent developments.

With the growth of industry and the rise of population centers—towns, there developed market places, to which farm surplus in grains, meats, vegetables, fruits, dairy, and also fish, could be taken for sale. Some articles were predominantly, and a few were wholly, for sale as merchandise. Most manufactures in New England began entirely for purposes of household consumption; after a while there remained a surplus, which could be marketed; the particular commodity then developed to the stage where it existed chiefly for the market, and it had to be removed from the home to its own separate location or the factory. The textile industry had its origins in the household, where they engaged in the weaving of cloth and in its manufacture into homespun clothing. The industry waxed in importance, employed much help, developed division of labor and need of specialized skills; and it eventually began to extend beyond the "family" as it moved from the household into the factory. The brewing of alcoholic beverages—liquor, wine, beer, cider—began with domestic distillation, and soon expanded as a leading market sales item. The fisheries made salt a necessary commodity, and the settlers found deposits of it on land, and they refined it from sea water. The local manufacture of gunpowder always had top priority. Metal objects for shipbuilding had to be imported until about 1680, when some manufacture of them was started. The business in naval stores was indispensable from the beginning—ship supplies, masts, oil, rosin, tar, rope. The carpenter also made barrels, and caskets. Bricks began to be made about 1650, and some attempts at glass manufacture failed. There was a good deal of activity in the making of pewter dishes. A colonial notes in 1639, "we began to print at Cambridge."

By making the horse an efficient source of labor power men were to some extent released from drudgery, and the settlers brought him with them from the beginning. The horse was important in colonial economy and life; he was used for labor, he was the nub of land communications, and the horseman was a symbol of status. Horse breeding was an important colonial industry, and he was also to quite an extent imported. Domesticated animals in general were well cared for and used sparingly; they had "the well-fleshed stallion, dangerous at times;" and they knew how to handle him, and how to break him to harness.

Money in pre-technology was based on the precious metals, which were the primary moving force in trade; and money always had intrinsic value. The principle of barter in trade was unavoidable in a pioneering community; it was measured by the bushel, the yard, the pound weight; it was used on a large scale, and it became the means of industry; and it always existed as between the whites and the natives, to quite an extent as between the various settlements, and to some extent also as within each settlement. Yet the trader economy rested on money as a medium of exchange; in England the pound sterling had achieved integrity as such, and the principle of money was early introduced in the settlement. The purpose of the founders was to create some form of currency that was to be based on the English banking system; and the Bay colony was progressively becoming a money economy. Her money took the form of paper, and New England has been described as "the founder of the paper currency of America." The issuance of paper money had to be based on an arbitrary regulation of standards of value; it introduced a fiat—a forced, currency—which was used as the medium of exchange. In frontier communities some commodity of value and small bulk was the usual "money;" the Reform foundation for such current money was generally grain, fur, Indian wampum, and sometimes also realty; and it became known as "country or money pay." The pound sterling, some of which was always in local circulation, was the index to determining currency value, and the pound commodity always tended badly to depreciate.[b]

In the great emigration to New England, from 1620 to the beginnings of the civil war, some of the newcomers arrived with substantial amounts of money; they immediately began buying necessaries from the settlers already there—which introduced an unexpected local prosperity, as well as a condition of monetary inflation; and with the abrupt cessation of emigrants from 1642 the bubble burst, there was a catastrophic drop in

298

prices, money again acquired integrity as exchange was taking place in terms of solid values, and many merchants were faced with economic ruin. Yet their experiences in the new society stimulated the Puritans in their ambition of "make money;" they determined to achieve a rational understanding of the principles of monetary value, and this initiated them into the mysteries of high finance. But there were unresolved capital problems: they were helplessly befuddled on currency value and exchange, and on fiscal policies with their relation to economic stability; trader naivete caused the monetary plans sometimes to appear as "schemes," and a variety of foreign coins brought by men of the seas always circulated in the colonies and added to the confusion.

With the rise of Parliamentary power at home the integrity of money—its intrinsic value, was very much emphasized; there took place the introduction of the modern system of credit, which stimulated the mighty flow of exchange; there was an extension of English capital in the form of credit to the colonies, which helped immensely in their economic operations; and this introduced within New England the custom of extending credit—on good security, which is indicative of the existence of inherent value. And the activity anent money constituted the beginnings of the development of the principle of banking in the new society: banking was stimulated especially by the realty mortgage and by commerce; its reward was interest, which is gain; its foundation was a solid—a precious metal-based, currency; and interest rates were set from 1689 at 6%. Yet banking never became practical because the colony money was based on a commodity, and the system of long credits and slow payments was aggravated by a bad currency.

In 1652 the Bay colonists took the necessary measures to mint their own metal coins. The Puritan John Hull was the first "mint-master," and he is regarded as the founder of the American specie coinage: dies for minting could be locally produced; they never had gold, but they could use silver as they had accumulated a good deal of it in the Spanish trade. This brought political problems with London, which was uneasy about the colonial minting of coin; mercantilism thought the power over the currency an assertion of sovereignty; was the raising of the commodity that was used as a money-base the operation of a mint? How was the charter to be understood in this respect?

The communications in the wilderness settlement began with the primitive condition, and there were no practical continental land trade routes. The New Englanders were ship builders—surprisingly capable, from the earliest days; and the shipwright was always a freeman of responsibility and importance. In a trackless wilderness the sea is the smoothest route; they had good harbors and abundant naval stores; the interior was accessible only by water, to which the rivers flowing over the mountains carried the seaboard travelers; and their movements were much more numerous and better organized on water than on land. The land communications for heavy industry—lumber, and iron and other mined minerals—forced the widening of aboriginal paths into roads, although they remained unpaved; and in winter after a snowfall the snow froze over and facilitated the use of horse-drawn sleds, which increased land travel. Travel as within the colony was chiefly on horseback, along the primitive pathways; it was confined to the propertied folk—almost entirely to male adults, and for economic and political purposes; they were going to church, and sometimes to trade centers, local courts, the capital city. And there were improvised bridges and ferries for streams, which rank was able to cross on the back of horses, and sometimes even of underlings. They could find accommodations in inns and taverns along the way; they tended to join the villages they passed with the news and gossip they brought; and communications revealed the beginnings of a commonwealth, no longer in settlements of isolated hamlets, but organized for social living and growth.

At the time of England's move from Tudor to Stuart there was a complete absence of tradition—of precedent, concerning the ethics—the ways and the values, of a trader society—of capitalism. The connective principle between the various units constituting the realm—the political relation, was federal; and the distances between parent and offspring gave the colonists a sense of seclusion and of freedom which strengthened the tendencies to political attenuation or particularism, and encouraged action on their own. And there were no precedents for man's conduct on the high seas. The seventeenth-century world was a vast scene—on ocean, and in wilderness and jungle—of absence of ethical and civil control. The high seas were infested with pirates of various European nationality who preyed on each other's commerce; and under conditions of scarcity of alien prizes they did not hesitate to victimize their own nativity. When Britain was at war she put the stamp of legality on outlaws by issuing them "letters of marque" for the duration of

300

hostilities, which converted them into "privateers." Yet it was in the nature of outlaw life for a condition of war always to exist: the pirate's occupation was a way of life, and he was constantly subject to the ravages of nature and of man—he lived dangerously; he was hardly conscious of himself as an outlaw, and he was insensitive to the delicate distinction between piracy and privateering.

It was inherent in trade to force its way through—lawfully if it could, otherwise if it had to. There could be clandestine transoceanic understanding; New England had a vast ocean traffic; and with Britain's naval power as yet uncertain, and her own hands not wholly untainted, an accommodation with piracy had to be made. British pirates preying on foreign commerce—Latin, Dutch—sometimes used Yankee ports as bases of operation; they had to find customers for their plunder—ship, cargo, crew—and they took it often to the traders, where they got a good price; moreover, the rovers of the seas could be a source of intelligence, as they were well familiar with the activities of potential enemies, about which their hosts could be informed; all of which created a community of interest between sellers and buyers. The traders tended to act primarily, and at times even solely, in terms of their own interests; and during Empire wars they didn't hesitate to do business with enemy colonies.[3] Yet it seems that partisan feelings were stronger than national; and during the civil war they boycotted the royalist colonies, although Puritan concern as within the hemisphere had little political implication.

The Interregnum was an opportunity for capitalism in New England— as it was at home, to entrench its power in terms of the institutions and the values of its own social order. Civil war reduced trans-Atlantic contacts to a minimum, the colonies were practically independent, and while they were in some ways hard put to it they were gratified to learn that they were essentially self-sufficient. The derangement in maritime relations disrupted English commerce especially in fish and slaves, which was taken over by Reform colonial shipping interests; Commonwealth control in London gave these interests an added impetus; first-century New England commerce was her most lucrative endeavor, and its consistent growth ceased to be confined to English initiative. The gross profits from the products of America—from its colonies, its wilds and its waters— had to be very high because of the shipping dangers; distance, theft, weather, sinking or capture through warfare or piracy, and goods spoiled in transit by water, rot, vermin. From the Restoration in 1660 it began to

301

be taken for granted that Britain is master of what was then understood as the North American continent. The Presbyterians were in the saddle at home, capital enterprise received first priority; and there took place a great expansion of New England economy, her products had become an important element in Britain's commerce and industry, and she began to become a London concern as it was realized that she had to be respected as a serious factor in the inter-empire trade.

With the advent of capitalistic power a determined effort was made to move towards the introduction of law and order on the high seas, a realm hitherto thought uncontrollable. Parliament set up the Council for Foreign Plantations, which enunciated the Navigation Acts; the Acts intended to regulate ocean traffic and, through customs and tariff measures, to control American commerce in relation to export and import. These activities—from full freedom to controls—were unprecedented; they appeared to the Reform merchants like an interference with freedom of the seas, and they chafed under the rules and regulations of the Navigation Acts. There were huge profits in freedom; and the "straight and narrow" can sincerely vary in degree, depending on conditions. English industry had to pay all government taxes, while colonial obligation could often be evaded, and there were complaints at home of being ruinously undersold. The mind of the time thought of commerce on the high seas in terms of "free traders;" the pioneering condition is necessarily generalized, and as within the meaning of free trade could be naively included the armed merchantman, the slaver, smuggler, privateer, and possibly even the pirate. It is said that "smuggling became a regular element of . . . New England commerce:"⁴ the tendencies of colonists to continue largely, if not entirely, on their own did not appear to them as "evasion," "corruption," "smuggling;" royal commissioners had to be sent to the colonies to supervise their activities; and the principle of the "bond" had to be applied to them, with its consequences concerning criminal liability. And with the consistent improvement in water communications law and order on the high seas progressively advanced, and "illegal traffic" steadily declined.

The fisheries and commerce early promoted an important maritime activity: "the sea is as free as air," it became America's highway, and the harbor was the town's livelihood. Men had to go out to the sea in ships, and it created a traditional pattern of navalism in New England thought—"this seaward-looking region." The settlers did not import

302

sea-going vessels, which means the early organization of their own shipbuilding industry; most sea-coast towns had a shipyard—with the shipwright and the allied necessary skills, and their implements and tools; and they built their own ships. The shipwright's responsibilities meant heavy capital investment; it presupposed a complicated, widespread organization; his activities had to be chiefly managerial; he had to direct skilled workers—blacksmiths, carpenters; and he had to supervise many apprentices, as well as hordes of common laborers—"the building of a large ship was a community enterprise." The shipwright supervised also the making of many smaller watercraft—the bark, shallop, pinnace, skiff, ketch, for the fisheries and for the coastal commerce; as early as 1640 they built a ship at Salem of 300 tons burden;[7] and in 1670 they made plans to build a drydock; and it was reported in 1676 that 730 vessels, mostly small ones, had been built in the Bay colony.[8] And the primitive region with its virgin forests was an inexhaustible source of timber, and of the raw materials necessary for naval stores.

Commerce, which is external relation, was capital's index to prosperity, and it thought in terms of "the fairest mistress in the world—trade." During the first few decades New England had a good deal of the carrying trade in North America; and commerce in grains and meat, and in the natural resources—especially naval stores, fish, furs—was definitely established. And some ships were being built for sale abroad. By 1665 Yankee ships were trading regularly to transoceanic lands: there were exports to Europe—mainly to the old country, and some even to Spain; they had to have purchasing power abroad, and the shape that colonial economy took was importantly influenced by the commerce with "home." New England was also developing an extensive trade within her hemisphere: there were about three hundred of her vessels engaged in the coastal trade; small craft were moving along the Atlantic colonial shores in all directions at all times with all kinds of loads. The French in Canada were feeble competition; and the Yankee skipper on his clipper was a transient huckster of the sea as he went from port to port, he was often part owner of the vessel and its cargo, and he was always a trader adventurer. And some settlements had become dependent on New England for a good part of their food supply.

GOVERNMENT

The principle of democracy as a form of government goes back thousands of years—to ancient Greece. Democracy is a phenomenon in sociology; it is freedom in a social—not in a natural, sense. Its understanding cannot be confined to politics—to the mechanics of governmental organization, and it is much more than an administrative apparatus; it is an entire social ethic based on the rights, dignity and welfare of all. Democracy is a sense of belonging—as a matter of right, within a given social milieu; all its inhabitants have benefits and responsibilities—they are under restrictions, but only in terms of degree. In the earlier days of the economy of natural scarcity there was an extreme shortage of the goods of life—there wasn't enough to provide the whole population. Full distribution, the best the society could afford, had to be confined to a very small minority; and they constituted aristocracy, which governed the polity. Included within the rights of this favored few was the value of freedom, which expressed itself as democracy—often to the point of anarchism; thus *demos* had its origins from within *aristo*, and there were varying degrees of democratic expression. In the course of the centuries the ability to produce wealth consistently increased, more and more people were moving towards the top of the social ladder, and the area of democracy proportionally broadened.

The differences between men in the world of land were qualitative, while in the world of trade they were quantitative. Land was aristocracy, caste; trade was mass democracy, class. Trade was democratic potentially if not actually, implicitly if not always explicitly; and the rule of land was static, while the rule of trade was dynamic. There were no gentlemen of the feudal values, of *sangre y terra*—blood and land, in the Massachusetts Bay Company: the emigrants to New England were confined to a vertical cross section of English *trader* life; they were from the cottages, not from the castles, of England; they were all Puritans, concentrated on God and gold—they were the elite of sterling saintliness. According to the charter the joint-stock company was to hold periodic meetings of its stockholders; and while on board ship meetings and consultations were held by the Company management, to which some of the smaller shareowners—on the basis of a restrained aggressiveness, were sometimes admitted. And the Reform communities—whose unit, the Hundred, seemed like a colony within a colony—got together, and laid the rude beginnings of a commonwealth; and from a trading corporation with its meetings of the stockholders, there emerged a social organism with representative government.

The legislature of the Bay colony was usually referred to as "Courte of Assemblie," and as "Assembly of the People;" it consisted of elite, the Assistants—who were members per se; and of commonalty, the Deputies, two of whom were periodically elected by the ballot of the people of each town—which introduced the principle of the overall jurisdictional franchise. They sat as one body. Yet the manifest initial division within it led, in 1644, to its re-organization—on a class basis, from unicameral to bicameral; the bicameral relation was vertical—as upper and lower house—their differences at first being seemingly qualitative or hierarchical, yet irresistibly tending to becoming quantitative or conical. The two houses met separately: the upper house was the Council; the lower was the House of Representatives, which was popularly identified as the General Court; the people had the right to petition the Representatives for redress of grievances, and their petitions were numerous and varied. At times the two houses met in joint session, and this was referred to as the Great General Court.

The Governor and his Council of Assistants, and the Deputies—the General Court of Massachusetts Bay, were the central source of power and administration. The government of the Reform colony was based on the developing, yet still inchoate, principle of the political trinity—executive, legislative, judicial:

"The idea that a separation of powers was possible or desirable had not occurred to the founders of government in the American colonies."[9]
"We look in vain for the classification of the organs and powers of government, and for the clear distinctions between them, which appear in modern written constitutions."[10]

The governmental authority, in terms of the theory and practice of each branch of the political trinity, was compounded: the transition from feudal land to capital trade brought an essential move from the common law to statutory law, and a good deal of confusion resulted on the

305

meaning and the interpretation of the laws; the charter included all phases of management, and in the absence of clarity concerning unprecedented instances it had to give officialdom vast discretionary power—which could create the impression of "oligarchy." The governors had executive supervision: they appointed the Secretary and the Treasurer of the colony, interpreted the laws, and exercised the veto; and they and the Assistants, who were referred to also as "Magistrates"—had overall judicial control. The colonial Code of Laws, which included the criminal and punitive laws, was determined by the magistrates and the ministry, and was derived from the English jurisprudence and from the Bible. There was hostility to a standing army; the civil power had ultimate control of the armed forces, even though they were normally more for show than for service. Colonial elite had connections with pertinent external power—it had, especially, friends at "home"—which gave it full control of "foreign" policy; and it lay within "the authority of the Council of Magistrates" to appoint and instruct ministerial officials for missions to England, and to the other civilized settlements in America.

Thus while the executive and judicial authority lay within the top twenty, the legislative power was shared from the beginning by both Courts; the colony developed from the direct, to the representative, Assembly—and the goody folk became fundamentally part of, and confined to, the legislative process; and the General Assembly—hitherto the monopoly of gentry—had been penetrated for the first time in history by the common man, as he acquired a voice in the government of a societal entity. There took place an increase in population, and in the organization of additional towns, and of counties: with the consistent increase in property owners, and in their litigation, local inferior courts were set up; the post of county justice of the peace was reserved for persons of "importance," which meant property; humbler freeholders also became eligible as local officials—selectman, sheriff, judge; and a committee comprising members of both Courts adjudicated in county trials, whose decisions could be taken to the Court of Assistants, which had appellate power. The laws and rules concerning the office-holders' manner of choice—appointment, election; duration of incumbency; frequency of session—regular, emergent; the quorum, or what has integrity as a "Courte of Assemblie;" as well as the differences between freeman and freeholder in the exercise of the civil rights—all this varied in the different New England jurisdictions, and in time often in the same jurisdiction.

The General Court sessions in the new jurisdiction began with the lesser freeholders being permitted a voice in the proceedings; they stated their complaints and made suggestions, for which top power showed respect—there was an acceptance of the principle of redress of grievances. The people's economic status in the Biblical Commonwealth perforce gave them a measure of political integrity: there were attempts from London to abolish the new society through infeudation; this spurred top authority to maneuvre in its efforts to hold power, and it had to make concessions to the people—"to give permanence to the representative power of the Commons;"[11] the ruling twenty needed, and they could get, the goodman's support by enabling his acquisition of an economic stake in the settlement; colonial propertied assurance of bottom discipline could be facilitated with mortgagee cooperation; and respect for demos was inherent in the societal set-up—it was not an act of liberalism. In the days of the Bay colony genesis the new freeholders comprised a handful of men; their participation in the General Court sessions soon shaded from permission into right, and they acquired status as an integral part of the settlement government. In 1634,

"Sir John Winthrop explained that the patent had been granted in anticipation of a small number of freemen, as in other business corporations, which would make their law-making power feasible; but the freemen—in the original charter sense, stockholders—had become such an unwieldy number in the Company . . ."[12]
"The charter had used the word 'freeman' to designate the stockholders of the company . . . Winthrop extended the term to mean citizens of the colony."

And with the increase in population and in property owners lower class membership in the General Court had to be changed from the direct action of all persons concerned, as in the ancient Athenian agora—to the representative system.

Colony denization, to "take the freeman's oath"—the goodman "free *burg*ess" or *citiz*en was based on male seniority and church membership.

307

But the application and the exercise of the civil rights—trial by jury, acting as juror, the franchise, being a candidate for, and holding, public office—were at first identified per se with the ownership of a freehold, or the property qualification, and this constituted the "popular" vote. "The theory of public office was of the nature of a freehold;" all freeholders were per se freemen, but it was not so the other way; yet both were understood as within "the People." The bondsmen, however, were not so included. The stockholder, the mortgaged—as a tractowner, had full lower class freedom; the entrepreneur was rapidly acquiring the same status; and the goodman multiple tractowner's social position had been elevated to the dignity of proprietary estate owner and landlord.

Trade had existed throughout feudalism as an incidental part of the social organism. With the rise of the Tudors the trader began for the first time to move towards the development, and the acquisition, of a degree of power and influence in the world he lived in. The emancipation of the commonalty masses was quite recent; they had inherited from time immemorial a sense of alienation from, rather than a sense of belonging by right in, the social organism; illiteracy, besottedness, brutality, immorality, were rampant among them, and they tended to irresponsibility. The absence of mass civil liberties condemned them to the condition of "the great unheard," and the expression of their protest against suffering had to be confined to "mob" action—to the riot. Slowly over the generations there began to emerge from the depths individuals of capital interests, until they achieved class proportions; and differences began to appear within the commonalty—from the brutalized proletarian to the skilled responsible worker to the bourgeois master. By the rise of the Stuarts and the introduction of the trans-Atlantic endeavors capital was securely embedded in English life as a distinct, self-assertive entity, and even as a challenge to the traditional social *status quo.*

The Puritans in New England did not have a blue print of their "new Society;" most of their plans were conceptualized, not realized—and their responsibilities were both executive and creative. They were in a mental haze concerning everything in their own way of life; its social institutions were in their beginnings, in a generalized condition, and there was an absence of refinement—of specialization. And the new way had its implications also concerning the organization and the purposes of government.

308

The Bay government during the earlier generations was based on the principle of centralized control, and there was a condition of paternalism—the dictatorship of the bourgeoisie. There is the principle of oligarchy—rule of the rich, the absolutism that is static;[c] it intends to perpetuate a *status quo* which can be improved—to freeze the few smug and the many deprived to their respective place. There is also the authoritarianism that is dynamic; by introducing a radical social change a condition can be achieved of consistently increasing the number of rich, and of decreasing the number of poor. The Puritans' settlement in an unknown region, and especially their introduction of the "new Society," were bound to confront them with unanticipated contingencies; this rendered trader unanimity indispensable—they had to be prepared for immediate efficient adjustment to any emergency. It was resolved,

> "that none but the General Court hath power to choose and admit freemen, or to make and establish laws; or to elect and appoint, remove or determine the duties and powers of, civil or military officers; or to raise moneys and taxes, and to dispose of lands."[13]

There was a concentration of political office—of power, influence, of functions of every kind, with a view to enable their unprecedented social organism to achieve full freedom of growth. There was an introduction of the principle of the patriarchate, as private and public functions were compounded—they were not clearly distinguished. The colony official tended to exercise jurisdiction as though he were a head of family—it was virtually a condition of governmental regulation of man's daily affairs; and they were committed to an order and control verging on repression, as decisions concerning perplexing problems had to be confined to a small, compact group of leaders, to the theoreticians of the new way—they had to make adjustments as they went along. The success of the entrepreneur was predicated fundamentally on the success of his way of life—it was social, not individual. And those who were developing towards the potentialities of "captains of industry" were becoming the "oligarchy" in the Biblical Commonwealth. Yet it was inherent in the values of the mart, it was in the nature of the trader way—although its pioneers had no way of knowing it—for its vertical social structure to develop from the hierarchical quality of caste to the conical quantity of class; and it was manifest destiny under capitalism for a transition in group relations to take place. And the pressure of social forces in the normal development of the trader economy precluded the danger of the establishment of a self-perpetuating oligarchy. Those at the top were unquestionably sincere, and on the whole capable and honest; yet the fundamental reliance was on the manifest destiny of sociological development, not on the ambitions of individuals. The leading reformers wanted power, but never for its own sake.

Colonial New England had three basic social divisions—the gentry, "the People," the bondsmen: the tractowner freeholder, the entrepreneur freeman, comprised the commonalty; and the tendency of the peripheral groups was to merge with and vanish into the people. The Puritan way preferred and supported only those interests that were promotive of capitalism; and the "new Society," as inherently quantitative, tended towards the conical relation—fluidity, leveling, universalization of civil rights—towards the basic monolithic political ideology, mass democracy. And the inclinations of individuals, of families—no matter how powerfully placed, could sometimes slow the process but never stop it. As the social differences in kind of the categorical relations in the life of Reform were necessarily moving towards differences in degree, the trader way supplanted them with the economic differentiation known as rich, middling, poor; included as within the designation "rich" were the top group, the freemen who had arrived with some capital, and those who became "self-made" men in the colony; and the development and rise of the bourgeoisie, the victory of the people—of capitalism, was achieved without any drastic aggressiveness at the bottom or of condescension at the top.

The goodman's assertion of mastery over a farm tract in his own right was a vision of utopia—the home lot, the common right, the propertied ballot; and to be a freeholder and a citizen, to come within the integrity of civil rights, was the object of social emulation. Yet dependent men never know their own strength: the commoners were in great fear of the freeman status—of the implications of their own ambitions; they had been oppressed for so long that they didn't know how to take what they suddenly found themselves entitled to; and there was a lack of interest in the responsibilities of freedom. They had to educate and stimulate themselves to become active in the opportunities that were immediately open to them, and toward the development of additional roles; the

310

exercise of the franchise, of the right to sit as juror, of the power of decision in local, and especially in overall, legislative and judicial procedure—all this was something new, strange, seemingly beyond their ken; they appeared as a burden rather than a privilege, and they often shied away from these new found pursuits. To economy-minded men political concerns are unimportant: office-holding had its implications— its performance generally meant separation from home, sometimes for an extended period: there were the obstacles of communications; and they were usually badly needed at home, where there was always some problem—economy, health, defense. This tended to discourage the ambition to achieve the status of freeholder; and there were instances of absence from governmental sessions, and even of refusal to accept political office. It had to be emphasized that public office is a civic duty; they had to be pressured into a sense of responsibility, integrity, morality; and laws had to be passed fining them for indifference to the exercise of the civil liberties, and to the duties of office-holding.

The population of the Bay colony in 1634 is said to have been about 3500; the Magistrates, their successors, and their families, together with those who were multiple stockholders in the Company—ruled the colony; they constituted a tiny fraction of the whole—"the title of honor, Mister" seldom occurs in earlier days; while the freemen numbered about ten percent. The colonists had come from an atmosphere of social polarization, of extremes in wealth, station—from the deified to the dregs. They had introduced the principle of the dynamic economy, with its consistent expansion and cumulative increase in the direction of mass prosperity; the channels of capital flow were opening, and there was a measure of vertical fluidity both ways—up and down; there was a slow—yet persistent increase over the decades in the percentage of property owners, and in the amount of property each owned, and room towards the top was widening of itself for those from below. During the new society's pioneering condition nobody anticipated as inevitable its ultimate complete transformation from caste quality statics to class quantity dynamics; and the earlier settlers thought in terms of social group stratification, and of paternalism—the reciprocal obligation of the economic categories to one another. Yet there was going on a concomitant increase over the decades in the percentage of freemen, which brought a pronounced uneasiness towards the top at the "multitudes" of workingmen and discharged servants who were becoming property own-

311

ers, with all of its implications concerning civil rights; and elite began to wonder, "if the multitude govern, then who shall be governed?"[14]

The Puritans thought that government over men is necessary to control the "corrupt" human will; yet they respected the principle that sovereignty ultimately resides in "the People," who have the right to choose and depose their rulers and limit their authority. "The People" were then understood as confined to the property owners, who—as such, were associated with the characteristics of responsibility. Mass democracy was something new, untried: the masses were regarded as grist for the demagogue's mill—those "rude mechanick fellowes;" and it was thought that the emotional appeal is inherent in, and must be accepted as a legitimate part of, full popular freedom. There was emphasis on the differences between the appeal to reason, and the appeal to emotion; there was no clear cut understanding of a difference between the "rule of the people" and the "rule of the mob," between liberty and license, democracy and mobocracy; and there was genuine fear of the emotionally charged—the impulsive, unreflecting, violent—mob.

The men of decision had great capital, while the mortgaged Deputies were practically without intrinsic worth; elite could not easily countenance mass democracy in the sense of a simple political majority, as this would be giving the lower classes menacing power over the top capitalist estates, especially through fiscal measures—currency policies, taxation. Inclusion within the people of tractowner, entrepreneur—the status of freeman, freeholder, was a commonalty mark of achievement. Yet those at the summit per se transcended the people; the elite Puritans were ultra-practical—"democrat" in the mass sense existed as a sneer; Sir John Winthrop thought that opposition to the Magistrates—the "slighting of authority," "would endanger the commonwealth and bring us to a mere democracy."[15d] And the Puritan big-wigs regarded public office as a privilege and an honor: they were always concerned about "sober and industrious citizens," reliability, honesty; they put great stress on the "good family," in terms of training and morals—on "the gentleman of status, of family and fortune," as it meant competence, property, capital for investment; and there was the highest respect for "estate, office, age," which were identified with responsibility—not with blood.

And there was a constant vital struggle going on in the Reform colonies between peak arbitrary privilege and the popular principles;

there were the forces of conservatism who held for entrenched power, as they opposed the aspirations of the commonalty masses; and they tried to arrest the moves towards democracy. The people were not yet quite sure of themselves, but they were picking up confidence: the Deputies in the General Court were exercising the power of excluding fellow members of questionable competence and morals; and they were taking courage from the fact that the extremist wing of the Reformation at home was patently waxing. As early as 1636, "The people . . . thought their condition very unsafe, while so much power rested in the discretion of the Magistrates;"[16] and a group was in process of formation which "appeared to comprise the elements of a party of opposition to the magistrates." All of which forced a consistently increasing respect in the settlement on the part of elite for commonalty: the top twenty ceased to ignore inferiority in the determination of their own personnel composition; they introduced the new policy of annually nominating candidates to succeed themselves from within their own group, between whom the freemen could choose; this compromised the sacredness of the summit membership as they accepted the principle that the lower class has a say—the people are consulted, however incidentally, in the staffing of the government. And the Court of Assistants had to make concessions to the freemen in relation to the coveted veto power. Yet with all the vicissitudes of life and fortune, the Magistrates remained pretty well in control of the colony throughout the Biblical Commonwealth—"the people choose but the rulers rule." Nonetheless, this was always within constituted authority: the newly propertied were not averse to monolithic government especially during emergencies; all the inhabitants of the Reform society had a sense of belonging within it and were anxious for its preservation, and "a general good understanding prevailed among all classes;" there was an underlying mental rapport—a community of interest, on the part of the governed with their rulers; and this was the basic reason for the freeman's apathy to the civil rights—they had the confidence that their governors could not betray them.

Yet the full development in values from difference in kind to difference in degree—the essential removal of Reform, both elite and commonalty, from the ideological atmosphere at home, took several generations;

"the element of leadership and the aristocratic temper from

313

which it originates, were strong among the magistrates and clergy of Massachusetts. It led them to form a clique, and against its predominance and exclusiveness a party in the deputies kept up a prolonged conflict."[17]

Men were still living in "the era of hereditary right;" they were still in the times of the legacy of medieval monarchy, and the novelty of democracy. There can be no abrupt complete break with the past in experience: under feudalism a line could be drawn between aristocracy and commonalty; some traditional values were brought to the colonies by the settlers, the principles of blood were not entirely absent in the Mayflower, and there was an attempt at the introduction of qualitative standards in the trader society. The top twenty exercised the power to create social distinctions within the Reform community, and they invested certain favored individuals with superior status so as to establish a colonial gentry. There was a consciousness of the hierarchical relation, and its tendencies to obeisance; the language of tradition—superlative and subservient terms of address, was commonplace in institutional and individual relations; everything was a matter of station, and there was an evident narcissism concerning it.

The new society was in its unique, germinal years—it was in a condition of evolvement from elite quality to democratic quantity; its denizens were well on the way out of the values of feudalism, and they were characterized by a developing—not by a static, ideological condition. The universal law of subordination did exist in the Reform colonies. The social organization of the Hundred was vertical—the place of each individual was determined by the number of shares he owned; this introduced the principle of group division, but its foundation was economic as it was based on wealth, on the triune relation—rich, middling, poor; and, whatever the terms of designation, the social differences in colonial New England were always fundamentally quantitative, conical, class—they were never literally qualitative, hierarchical, caste. The fundamental implications of caste were impractical in the sociology of the "third estate," especially in a primitive setting; the solemnity of royal investiture—with its implications of divinity, tradition, integrity, power—never took root in New England. Puritanism in America was transformed from an instrument of rebellion to one of control—dominion might be above the masses, but it must not be out of

314

their reach. The inherited subservience was carried over to some extent to the wealthy capitalists—the Puritan provincial gentry, but this status was a far cry from that of the feudal lord of the manor; and the commoners became inbued with a political consciousness that diminished the unassailable sanctity of civil authority. That an attitude of boldness—even of aggressiveness, existed towards superiors seems to be established by the frequent use of the Biblical phrase, "without any respect to persons." The conditions in the trader society enabled the lowly to emulate their betters, and also to achieve some of the symbols of status; and since inferiors could not effectively be kept in their place by traditional social custom, resort had to be had to sumptuary laws. Thus the vertical social relation had to be legislatively buttressed, which is a weak substitute for the inherited condition; the meaning of the feudal terms as within the new social complex—capitalism, must be understood as extremely modified; the blood of Reform gentry was always at best ancmic, and thc awc that commonalty stood in of the top leadership was due to quantitative considerations. It took at least several generations for the full ideological transition from the old ways to the new, and Reform elite began slowly to understand itself as within the meaning of "the People." The Puritans had laid the foundations from the beginning for a way of life that inevitably eventuated in the elimination of everything feudal.

The colony, and the local—county, town—administration of government had been fully established. The government had to make adjustments to the developing economic phenomena, which rendered it an institution constantly moving towards greater involvement; with the growth in area, population, wealth, and in the industrial complex, it became increasingly burdensome for the elder statesmen to avoid local autonomy; the political trend was consistently towards the rule of "the People," towards the *common*wealth—democracy; and the development of local government eventually eliminated authoritarian rule. And with the growth of confidence concerning mastery of regional problems, and especially in the permanence of the new society—came the beginnings of departure from the requirement of strict political unanimity.

Reform introduced the vertical system of society in Anglo-America. The vertical form of social organization could express itself in terms of the feudal aristocracy, or of the capital plutocracy. The trader world was

315

based on sociology—on the values of wealth, which was dynamic, and it was possible for the vast submerged to rise above contempt; but this was precluded in the feudal world, which was based on the static values of biology—birth and blood. The attitude of the feudal lord to the commoners was one of disdain, while that of the capitalist to the goodmen was one of jealousy—they were potential competitors.

The New England society was a class conscious jurisdiction, but not in terms of the ironclad caste system of the Old World. The Puritan sociology laid the foundations for a development over the generations from the hierarchical, to the conical, to the horizontal—social condition. The nub of the Puritan's societal organism was the Hundred, whose basic unit was the household—which revolved around the master's family. Thus the organizational pattern of England's feudal manor and of New England's corporate farm layout was basically the same, as the latter was an evolvement from within the bosom of its predecessor—there was an obligatory tie to a superior. Both organisms were vertical—they each had a system of graded social division. Yet the societal relations as between their occupants were radically different: the old condition was an eternal vassalage in a hierarchical, qualitative, caste, static, relation; while the new condition was a terminable bonded—mortgaged, quantitative, class, dynamic, relation to a conical creditor. And as within the atmosphere of quantitative differences between men there is respect for leadership, but no feeling of inherent inferiority. Theirs was the traditional trilogy of family, church, village: their *common*wealth had a conical organization, which was from church, to parish, to godly society; the parish was a federation of churches, and the commonwealth was a federation of parishes.

Full jurisdictional control by Reform was required for the eventual complete change from qualitative to quantitative values; capitalism brought an evolvement over the generations towards democracy and equality; and the underlying ideology was monolithic, as it was the foundation of all classes—the civil rights were applicable to all. The Reverend

"John Cotton argued that society consisted of magistracy, ministry, and people; the first standing for authority, the second for purity, the third for liberty. Each of these he said, had a

316

negative on the others, and the ultimate decision must be reached by the agreement of the whole."[18];

he does not differentiate his three categories qualitatively. There was a condition of dynamism, of change—*within* the social organism, but not *of* the social organism, whose fundamental institutions and values remained static; and the more things changed the more they remained the same.

ETHICS

The Reformation was a development from within Hebraism, which is dedicated to humanitarianism—the conviction that the superiority of human being to animal being is determined first and foremost by man's reliance on ethics; the Biblical ethics sets human life above all else, above also humanism—mental creativity; and there is a pronounced aversion to brutality in the resolution of quarrels within the social milieu.

The Old Testament evidently saw no fundamental contrast between the temple and the mart;

"So took the priests and the Levites the weight of the silver, and the gold, and the vessels, to bring them to Jerusalem, unto the house of God."[19]

The Jews permitted the temple to be used for commercial purposes, except on their Sabbath and on their "high holy" days when economy was strictly forbidden anywhere; and the temple as a counting house seems to have been a matter of course to the Jews. Jesus Christ introduced a new principle in what eventually became the religion of the Occident—Christianity: He taught, "Ye cannot serve God and mammon;" He drove the money changers out of the temple, and to the Christians of the New Testament the temple and the mart were necessarily in ethical contrast—they became polarized; and the mart was regarded as desecrating the temple. The temple—the "house of God," represented spiritual values and was identified with the teachings of religion; it was dedicated to mental creativity—introversion, abstract reasoning, cultural appreciation; it brought out the best in man. The

317

mart represented material values—the drive for euphoria, which was identified with property ambitions; it was committed to sophistication—the wisdom of experience, knowledge of people, extraversion—to richness; it brought out the worst in man. The temple was sacred, the mart was profane—theology and economy were mutually exclusive; they introduced the principle of total separation at all times between the two basic social institutions, and it became a strict tenet of traditional Christianity.

The Puritans were caught between the conflicting drives of Scripture, poverty, primitivism. The initial organization of the sociology of the Bay colony as the Biblical Commonwealth comprised the lean, bleak, stern years, during which Jehovah, the God of the Old Testament, was dominant. Their values were all-inclusive: all men came within the blessings of, and stood on the same footing towards, God; there was one creed, one code of laws—a person was either entirely inside, or entirely outside, the atmosphere of the Covenant with God. The Calvinists understood their doctrine as a new scale of moral values and a new ideal of social conduct; there was the intention to renew society by penetrating every department of life, public as well as private, with the influence of the true faith; and they conceived of the social order as a highly articulated organism of members contributing in varying degree to a spiritual purpose. And their "heavenly city" is the first modern social organism within which all the values of life were applicable to the entire population. Their way of life, capitalism—was based on "the People": all are called, which had its implications concerning democracy—and education was extended to all; literacy was universal in relation to the catechism—to a knowledge of Scripture, and to the ledger proficiencies indispensable in mercantile activities.

The founders of the Kingdom of God on earth considered their society as the best example of a Christian civilization—everything in life, including morality and economy, flowed from the Bible. Yet theirs was a move towards the Old Testament, which they understood as divine permissiveness for the association of the temple and the mart; and they gave the Mosaic teaching the heaviest emphasis of any Christian sect, which caused Puritanism to be described as "visions Judaica." The way of Calvinism was a departure from economic traditionalism: it dictated standards which converted economic interests from a moral frailty into a resounding virtue; it brought about a change in moral patterns which

318

sanctified material habits that in earlier Christian Ages had been denounced as evils; it was an unprecedented way of life with new virtues and vices. It introduced on a social scale the principle of "success," which was concentrated in economy and was identified with the accumulation of a private property estate or quantitative accretion; economy ceased to be simply a routine for existence, as it became a way of life. The attitude of the guardians of religion on the ethics of the mart was of supreme importance in pre-technology, in the world of the economy of natural scarcity; they considered the transactions of business also as within the province of the church; they were fully aware of the Savior's strictures concerning the two masters—God and mammon; the mart was fundamental, but it could lead to greed in economy; and this rendered it morally the most sensitive—even volatile, among the social institutions. Calvinism was revolutionary in its permissiveness, but it warned that economy—an activity indispensable to society, is fraught with grave peril for the soul.

Theology and economy, the Bible and the Ledger, became necessarily complementary—obverse sides of the same coin; theirs was a relation of action and reaction, of reciprocal influence and adjustment; a clear line could not be drawn between them. Traditional Christianity—the New Testament, regarded piety and profit as antagonistic, yet in the Old Testament and in the Biblical Commonwealth they go together. The move towards the empathy of temple and mart brought a tendency to "the pious economy"—they were coaxing a living from the wilderness, with their eyes riveted upon heaven; and the Reformers were rendered a good deal hazy concerning a distinct difference between them. The mind of the devotees was confined to their immediate time and place: they associated Jehovah with current incidents and objects; they had an understanding of God's Will in terms of their own particular need at a given moment—the eternal and the temporal did touch and vibrate. Their mind always identified religious ritual with the operations of trade: wherever the risks were inherently high, piety sought to bring God into sympathy with the purposes of the devotee and trader; "spirit with matter, piety with profit and loss, mingle strangely" as the merchant's "affections, religion, passions, all work together into pence, shillings, and pounds." A Puritan merchant wrote in 1675;

"it is best willing to submit to the great governing hand of the

319

great Governor of all the greater and lesser revolutions that we the poor sons of men are involved in by the invoice you see the whole amounteth to £405 . . .''[20]

It was in the pioneering—in the innocent, days of pure capitalism: the faithful were convinced that in their own society economy and ethics are fundamentally compatible; they never thought that there could be an underlying antagonism between them. The world to them was per se evil, yet one could be *in* the world but not *of* it: they were to meditate on the hereafter, as well as to conduct themselves ethically in their present life; they were to seek wealth, but never to love richness for its own sake— eternity was always the primary hope.

The Puritans were convinced that a man's acquisition of a private property estate is a gift of God; they thought of man's endeavor in economy as a "calling"—a sacred summons to skill in an occupation or profession; and in the holy commonwealth the emphasis on the right to accumulate a private property estate was on its divine—rather than on its natural or social, aspects. They regarded man's innate tendencies to workmanship as divinely inspired: they believed that there is a spiritual call to worldly achievement, that each person is prepared by God for a certain type of economic endeavor—a man's life's work is in response to an inner call, and this was therefore identified as a "calling;" mundane toil, the work of the artisan, became as solemn an endeavor as that of the clergyman—a man responded to the call of his vocation as he did to "the call of the cloister;" and association of the mart and the temple, of worldliness and holiness—was based on the divine call to material accomplishment. In the bourgeois world—as in the Bible, the occupational relation was conical: the goodman could become an apprentice, who was a potential craftsman, who in turn was a potential master; these basic groupings were physically and ideologically the same; they lived, worked and thought alike, having the same underlying values—their differences were in degree, as they shaded vertically from the one status into the other. And there was an emphasis on the trained occupation of the master, artisan, apprentice—as his calling, a sacred summons to skill;

"a man's duty to God was to work at his calling and improve his talents like a good and faithful servant";

320

his business was also the Lord's vineyard in which he was called to labor, and the Christian must conduct it with a high degree of seriousness, as it is a form of sacrament—of religion; and he must work at his job with the devotion that he knew God expected of him. Thus one's duty in a calling was the foundation of the societal ethics in capitalistic culture.

The faithful postulated the doctrine of implied powers: they believed that Christians are free with respect to works that are not expressly enjoined in Scripture; there is no divine objection to money in principle, or to the effort to get it; and their ethics emphasized the virtues of the work life, the persistent application with a view to achieving the rewards of industry and thrift—the worldly goods or standard of living. They never thought of money as necessarily dissociated from sacredness: man's acquisitive ambition—the pursuit of money, is in itself not immoral; the faithful may engage in bourgeois activities—employ labor, buy and sell, let and hire, lend and borrow—they may accumulate principle, take rent and interest, make a profit, collect dividends; there were tendencies to bring the mart and the temple together again, and instances of the relation—the contact, association and interaction of business and religion, their indissoluble merger, were commonplace. Spiritual values and material values compounded to create *human values*—the inherent rights of man. A private property estate for the common man on a social scale was without precedent in all history: it was a vision of utopia; it was a boon bestowed by God, a sacred trust— "riches and wealth . . . the gift of God;"[21] to the Puritan mind the religious and the economic aspects of life were not simply a dualism, with each retaining its own identity and having a reciprocal effect on the other—they constituted a compound;[a] a man is only the trustee in his ownership of what ultimately is not his property, and he must handle it with a sense of solemn responsibility to God and to society— and man in economy could be serving God for his own personal, as well as for the common, good.

Man throughout his being has based his welfare on economy, which in pre-technology was enabled fundamentally by living labor—primarily his own. "Work"—as differentiated from routine drudgery—tends to creativity, and workmanship is instinctive, and is more or less present in all men: the worker takes a personal interest in his job, which tends towards the development of a sense of duty and responsibility; and his endeavor in relation to skill elicits ability, in which he takes pride. The workingman was increasingly called upon to engage in occupations that require training and, at times, even some education. Success gave him the feeling that he counts, selectivity brought out individuality, and the principle of quality was becoming identified with commonalty—the village artisan developed a sense of worth as he began to feel himself indispensable.

The Puritan lived by "the Book"—which implies literacy; he depended on the Bible for ethics, and on the Ledger for economy—there was never a complete separation of the two. He had religious sanction for the methodical abstemiousness of mart worldliness as the way to wealth: his attempt to achieve an estate from nothing pre-supposed the accumulation of sufficient capital for a start in an economic enterprise, and this required the concentration of the sum totality of one's being; there were no precedents to go by, and the new status of commonalty forced the introduction of new ethical standards. It was concluded that a man's ambition to reach a position of ownership or management—to merit the status of master over other men, rested on his ability to acquire mastery over himself; and this brought an emphasis on the discipline of the character, especially through the virtues of industry and thrift. Trust in God could be a spur to self-help in economy, and there was an emphasis on individual initiative; the Bible says,

"Seest thou a man diligent in his business? he shall stand before kings; he shall not stand before mean men."[22]

Identified with industry were sobriety, reliability, diligence, frugality— the assumption of personal responsibility. This introduced the principles of self-reliance as social values; work was uplifting—assiduous application to one's job was a virtue, and the "gospel of work" and the "dignity of labor" became fundamental in the new social order. And in addition to the positive good—thrift, he stressed the negative virtues of self-denial, which tended to produce miserliness; he was pecuniarily calculating, and icily precise—"waste not, want not"—and he was often penny-minded and close-fisted; everything had to be budgeted, balanced and accounted for, which caused production, rather than consumption, to be regarded as the pivot of the economic system—and this brought a reliance on "the lean goddess, Abstinence." His time—his daily routine, was also strictly apportioned for labor, rest, prayer, play. Capitalism brought a de-

322

velopment of the cult of the ''self-made man'' as it created the genius, the hero of the mart—''from rags to riches;'' and its denizens were economy conscious, energetic, competitive.

TRADE & ETHICS

With the successful laying of the settlement foundation, a self-confidence developed which tended towards the expression of disagreements as among the colonists. The spread of trader interests to social proportions began to reveal an underlying conflict between theology and economy; and there developed a contrariety of conviction concerning the fundamental values—spiritual and material—both as *between* them, and as *within* each of them. The chief area of disagreement as within the Reformation concerned Biblical interpretation; while in the material sphere the differences were concentrated within economy—the profit from work versus the gain from speculation.

The problems of this world—new economy, primitivism, nationalities, ocean—the concern with sheer physical survival, tended to detract from men's concentration on the hereafter. And there were different attitudes as within the new economy of Reform; Puritanism was based on the principle of *profit*, as differentiated from Presbyterianism with its concentration on *gain*, and from Nonconformity with its tendencies to an unsocial economic individualism.ᶠ The Puritans managed to maintain an underlying control of the Bay colony throughout the Biblical Commonwealth. It was before the days of political economy as a science; they were in the pioneering stages of colonization and of capitalism, within which the activity of banking, as a social force—with everything it implied, was quite remote. Sir John Winthrop's people had brought with them from home a scale of economic values which was based on the profit of the bourgeois organization of labor, not on the gain of speculation; they were concentrated on the produce of the land, rather than on the land as real estate; and they had their instructions in Holy Writ;

''I likewise, and my brethren, and my servants, might exact of them money and corn: I pray you, let us leave off this usury.''[23]

323

"In thee have they taken gifts to shed blood; thou hast taken usury and increase, and thou hast greedily gained of thy neighbours by extortion and hast forgotten me, saith the Lord God." "Behold, therefore, I have smitten mine hand at thy dishonest gain which thou hast made, and at thy blood which hath been in the midst of thee."[24]

And with its definite establishment the capital economy was beginning to develop growing pains. Reform had introduced the vertical system of society from founding, which was based on the economic differences that were created fundamentally by the capital and labor relation—income respectively from profit and wages, which resulted in a "rich" and "poor" alignment; and there began to develop also differences in interests between town and country. And experience began to reveal a divergence of, a conflict of interest between, ethics and economics; and the pursuit of money soon betrayed the fact that the manner of its acquisition and the uses it is put to, often do not comport with Christian ethical standards. The Calvinist economy had grown out of religion, from which it soon began slowly to move away; there was a tendency for men "to escape from a teleological world into a universe of commerce and profit;" and with time they found themselves slowly moving from emphasis on theology to emphasis on economy—they were moving into a world of grains, fish, furs, lumber.

It was the economy of natural scarcity, which emphasized the acquisitive instincts: the traditionally deprived masses—the immemorially disinherited pauperized, were readily reacting to the conditions in the mart as they were rendered aware of the financial opportunities that the business wonderland held for them; the potentialities of economic aggrandizement under the new way began to appear illimitable, and the commoners were fired by its implications—wealth, power, prestige; and their entry into it released pent-up energies, which brought terrific results; and there followed a mass stampede of blind greed—"their grasping ways." The martmen were an example of a potency quite recently acquired in literacy, Scripture, economy: the dynamics of the market place with its insane and bloody carnival of greed, brought new opportunities; and their scramble to become skillful in an occupation, and—possibly, in time—to found a private property estate, were new experiences; and there arose pertinent unprecedented problems concerning popular rights in property, religion, politics, law, sex, education. And with the rise of capitalism the ethics of "the People" took on social proportions: Puritanism was assuming moral, as well as doctrinal, aspects; Holy Writ was the foundation of its ethical teaching, its *weltanschauung*—of its view of the true and the good life; and creed and code were both divine.

It soon became apparent that the world of trade is a closed compartment with laws of its own, and that its denizens are more or less at its mercy. Austerity was a fundamental quality of the Puritan's economy; his mind was on money—fiscal responsibility was the primary value of capitalism. The logic of the Age—of economic growth, was ceasing to regard money as a means towards an end, as it was becoming an end in itself—from need to acquisitiveness; its accumulation was thought a mark of "success"—it was the foundation of euphoria. Puritanical dedication—isolated hard work, meant competitive personal aggrandizement; there was an inevitable vanity and selfishness in the ambition to build, especially from a pittance, a profit-making business, and to found a private property estate. There was the hard legalism in the active enterprise of bourgeois-capitalistic entrepreneurs, which could lead to a debtor's jail; and market conditions forced them to buy as cheap and sell as dear as they could. There developed an unbounded cupidity in industrial undertaking as a field of profit and, at times—even of speculation, to the extent that the martmen were being rendered obtuse to all other considerations; the standards were becoming solely those of material success; there was a compulsive search for utmost efficiency—for profits, which subordinated all other values; and there developed the ambition to get maximum results from minimum means.

There were "men as loved their lives more than their souls," who emphasized the earthly rather than the heavenly—temporals at the expense of spirituals; these two fundamental concerns of men, instead of being necessarily coordinating were working out as conflicting. All of which brought a development away from the values of other-worldliness, and towards the values of a mundane materialism; says John Bunyan in his Pilgrim's Progress—

"heaven is but as a fable to some, and that things here are counted the only things substantial . . . look no way downwards; it is to let thee know that earthly things, when they are with power upon men's minds, quite carry their hearts away from God.''

It began to appear that wealth all too often draws people away from their faith—''they think more of earthly rewards and less of the life to come;'' ''there was commercial prosperity enough to conflict with the ancient strictures of public morality.'' The investor had—he *had* to have, his eye on profits, rather than on the salvation of souls; there was ''a growing disposition to consider not only what was religiously 'lawfull' but what was practically expedient and immediately profitable;'' there was a tendency to subordinate Biblical interpretation to the needs of economy—''base covetousness prevailed in men that should know better;'' they became ready to sacrifice every other consideration to the ambitions of the mart; and the pursuit of wealth began to be regarded as incompatible with, and even as inimical to, sincerity in religion. It was becoming a case of property *versus* ethics—men were tending to draw a line between religious and economic motives, as their ethical implications seemed at variance and at times even at antipodes.

And the Age of Faith did not render churchly principles necessarily incompatible with anti-social practices; Puritans could not clearly distinguish laudable industry from reprehensible ambitions, and in the New Jerusalem also the conduct in life of the faithful was falling far short of requirements. Man seemed corrupted by riches: there was religious indifference in the man who had become pre-occupied with material gain—''a mere worldling;'' and his actions as a member of society were no longer the extension of his life as a child of God. Everyone's reach always exceeded his grasp; sharp, sordid practices, mercilessness in driving hard bargains—were commonplace; there was the sin of extortion—usury did not stop at exacting ''the pound of flesh;'' and they were not above heartlessness in the treatment of the poor—''business is business.'' The traders were moving towards a confrontation between, seemingly even a separation of—economic realities and ethical principles; they preferred private gain to the public weal, and they did not hesitate to seek it even at the hurt of their neighbors—profit tended to stifle piety. There was a deliberate ruthlessness in acquisition together with a seeming conformity in religion: the worldliness of the trader was displacing the other-worldliness of the devotee; they were not incapable of a sycophantic gush of pietism, conscience in the temple was compensation for lack of it in the mart, and traders cheated sanctimoniously. And there soon appeared a tendency to depart from the Biblical injunction— "thou shalt have no other gods before me;" as within the economy of scarcity there developed the co-existence of God and mammon, the sources respectively of the ethical qualities and of the anti-social characteristics. And it seems to have been in the nature of the economy of scarcity—manifest destiny, for the distribution of wealth to be glaringly inequitable, for the goods of life to tend towards concentration in the hands of a few.

Thus while the Puritans were troubled by what they ought to believe, they were even more troubled by what they ought to do. The new society was baffling man with new problems. And in the world of experience the teachings of Christ concerning the chasm between temple and mart— "Ye cannot serve God and mammon," seemed to be holding true. The faithful were torn between the conflicting values of the two urges, each of which was developing as a world in itself—piety or profit, prayer or usury? which is more important—property or life? The problem of ethics in economy was expressing itself in a conflict between *property* rights and *living* rights, which were developing as antipathetic per se. Divine punishment for unethical conduct could find expression in business failure: the master of the mart was motivated by fear of God— damnation, and by fear of want—deprivation; if a given act constitutes good morals but bad business, which is to prevail? must sanctity give way to expedience? where does individual selfishness end, and social responsibility begin?

Their way of life—capitalism, with its economy consciousness, primary commitment to "making money," profit and gain, caused them to develop the ledger or quantitative type of mind—which is a dichotomy, one side marked "assets" and the other "liabilities," with the one in excess spelling the difference between success and failure in life. The ledger introduced and developed the values of system, of organized thinking in economy; the new way was adapted to rationalization—skill in making much of little, shrewdness in getting the most for the least; and the business enterprise had to express itself in terms of the precision of accounting. All of which rendered statistics important, and

327

they had to rely on mathematics—from which flows order, efficiency, exactness; and it introduced ways of doing things that eventuated in the standardization of weights and measures.

And they began to apply the ledger type of mind to religion, as God was being appeased economically;

> "And Solomon offered a sacrifice of peace offerings, which he offered unto the Lord, two and twenty thousand oxen, and an hundred and twenty thousand sheep. So the king and all the children of Israel dedicated the house of the Lord."[25]

There was the bookkeeping of God, as well as of the trader—whose systematic life of grace was calculated, methodical; the relation of penitent to God was that of debtor to creditor; he thought of salvation in terms of a balance between moral assets and liabilities, blessings and sins—of equal parts of God and gold; and holiness was never an absolute condition, as it became subject to degree—the "holier-than-thou" attitude. And as within the freedom of the colonial nascency property began to move towards an ascendancy—property rights were taking precedence to living rights. It was held that trade is one thing, religion is another; the church should keep its hands off trade; men thought in terms of all power to the trader; and there was the underlying feeling that without the mart there could be no temple—erecting churches, training and employing ministry, importing Bibles.

The coming of technology, the presence of automotive power on a social scale, began to take place nearly two centuries after the Puritans; and the advent of the machine caused the use of human labor to appear as "exploitation"—as immoral. The commonalty was beginning to achieve a clear-cut condition of respect, and it was being regarded as within human rights. In the days of Sir John Winthrop the commonalty was just out of serfdom, and the use of human labor for profit was not thought of as exploitation.

All material acquisition in the holy commonwealth was derived from God—it was His property, His gift to man: the private estate was a form of stewardship; it was felt that the divine bestowal carried with it per se the duty of social responsibility, as its misuse was sacrilege—a sin; and its beneficiary had always to behave towards his fellow man in good faith—with ethical consideration. It was in the early days of capitalism, in pre-technology: the influence of the machine on the mind—rationalization, getting the most for the least—and on the emotions, man as a "cog in the wheel;" the sophistication of discipline, the cold-blooded demand for profits, the impersonal relation in the application of system, of efficiency, to life—including also to man; all this was no part of the Reform consciousness. Although employers could be exacting, the cold, calculated attitude of the mechanical mind was unknown, and the human element more or less always prevailed. Moreover, the English-man's complete separation from the insouciance of feudalism, whatever his class, took some generations; survival of the civilized microcosm as within a primitive macrocosm dictated an underlying cooperation, which was brought from home and strengthened here; and as within the heavenly city this had to be wholly reciprocal—class differences necessitated a mutual interdependence, or the obligation of the high and the low to one another in harmony.

For the Puritans there was only the alternative of divine will or earthly vanity, and they found themselves in a condition of perpetual conflict between conscience and cupidity. The custodians of religion—the "men whose hope is not in this life," were nonplussed by the extent to which doctrine and conduct can diverge; there was the contrast between a sublime ideal and a hideous reality. But the conviction of the divine qualities, and of the social blessings, of property—stimulated the hope that wealth and piety could live well together, and brought a necessary cooperation between the theologian—the man of contemplation, and the trader—the man of action. It had to be concluded that theory can be utopian, but that practice can not—the real can at best only approximate the ideal; and there was clerical intervention in the doings of the trader—the priest of the temple asserted jurisdiction in the mart, and he was both the protector and the mentor of property.

Excessive concentration on a given objective automatically creates its own offset, and they combined an amoral opportunism with zealous devotion. It was thought that the duties of religion rendered incumbent the application of restraints on the worship of mammon, and there had to be the brake of conscience to save society from dropping to the ways of the howling wilderness about them. The problems of the mart brought generalized principles on fair economic dealing; and the unlimited lust for material aggrandizement, even to the extent of sanctioning violence

as a means of securing gain, was denounced as anti-social and immoral—
no man may seek pecuniary benefit by injuring his neighbors. Ethical
rules are binding on the master to maintain principles of good conscience
in economic affairs, he must never take advantage—and his financial
involvements are to be controlled by a moral law of which the Church is
the guardian. And Calvinism imposed upon economy an inquisitorial
discipline: there were to be the strict restraints of divine judgment—the
devotees were not to forget religion for the quest of wealth; there was no
objection to wealth in itself, but it must not traduce religion—piety was to
be a brake on profit. And the men of the mart were constantly being
reminded of the exhortation in Holy Writ concerning ''the deceitfulness
of riches,'' ''the mythology of gold''—as the holy woman being led to
the stake for Christ said of money, ''this world's trash will not pass in
heaven;'' and it was emphasized that the support of their corporeal life is
only temporal—

> ''For what is a man profited, if he shall gain the whole world,
> and lose his own soul?''

eternal salvation is primary, and the vanities of this life are at best
incidental.

A balance had to be maintained between worldly ambitions and social
responsibility; there was clerical emphasis on respect for ethical standards, especially through the fatherly exhortation—which was based to
quite an extent on the teachings of the Old Testament; and Puritanism
instilled its devotees with fear and trembling of Jehovah, whom they
revered as a Judge rather than loved as a Father. And there was also the
preacher, the sage—the gnarled-faced, bearded *pater familias*—the man
of doctrinal knowledge and unblemished ethics, and his world stood in
awe of his wisdom and virtue. Puritanism eschewed the theatre, and
substituted for it the pulpit—which, through its ministerial sermon, was
often an outlet for the tendencies in man to histrionics. The sage was
known and feared for the severity of his stare—his stern frowning
countenance, pointed knuckled finger; he was full of denunciation for the
sins of the land, brought on by its transgressing people; ''we have sinned,
we have violated the Lord's commandments—repent, the day of reckoning is at hand.'' His was a solemn warning of retribution from on high,
with its implications of the Biblical knell of doom; there was an hysteri-

cal emphasis on eternal torment—hell-fire terrors, and he was eloquent with exhortation against sin; all of which was usually effective as a substitute for physical coercion. And the penitents responded with masochism: "self-accusations were the religious stock-in-trade of the Puritan dispensation"—"miserable sinner that I am;" there was a feeling of helpless terror as men beat their breasts and women wailed; and there was the "day of fasting, humiliation and prayer."

The Reformers believed that individual ownership and social responsibility are not incompatible—they can work together in an underlying harmony. They were convinced that a man's practice of the godly traits in economic endeavor, meticulous attention to duty—will generally result in his achievement of economic self-sufficiency, and maybe even in more. They sincerely identified private interest with the public welfare—"the greatest good for the greatest number;" if each man follows strictly in the divine teachings—if "charity begins at home"—then the principle that "God helps those who help themselves" will bring mass results, and the Biblical Commonwealth will be a prosperous community.

The Puritans scarcely distinguished between the teachings of Moses and of Jesus, yet as Christians they always gave the New Testament the greater emphasis—"ye are not under the law, but under grace;" and its contrast between temple and mart was never entirely lost sight of. An amoral unrestricted economic individualism—the law of the jungle, can never be traced to the teachings of John Calvin; the doctrine of "the best man to the fore and the devil take the hindmost," was unknown to mankind at the time, and it was never a part of the Puritan world. They were convinced that the divine commonwealth is inconsistent with an uncompromising anti-social selfishness; they eschewed as irresponsible the kind of economic "competition" which results in absolute standards of "success" and "failure," of "winners" and "losers," and they shunned the wilderness freebooters who roamed the New England region as "gain-thirsty murderers." The faithful were "merciless alike to religious liberty and to economic license;" and they were committed to the profit from the honest toil of labor—not to gain from speculation, which they denounced as gambling. Salvation was predicated upon both faith and works: the maxims of that austere time emphasized that the true Christian must repress mendicancy; and economic destitution was regarded as a personal calamity, rather than as a social problem. Yet there were attempts to reconcile the self-interest of property with the

331

moral standards of religion; it was the sacred responsibility of the rich to refrain from, or at least effectively to mitigate, the oppression of the poor; and their repudiation of the traditional identification per se of Church with charity did not preclude the godly, ethical exhortation—

"He that bestows his goods upon the poor shall have as much again, and ten times more."

And no responsible person living within an established settlement in colonial New England ever died of starvation or exposure.

The iron law of the life of human beings is the obligation they owe one another. The Puritans were fundamentally social minded, and religion was established as the most powerful single antidote to the "call of the wild." There were always the restraints of group solidarity, whatever the individual tendencies; they never dismissed the values of public discipline; their community spirit—their social consciousness effectively subordinated the free expression of the individual's urge for economic aggrandizement; and there was never an essential conflict between self-interest and the social good.

The Puritan economy stimulus was dictated fundamentally by need: no doubt their new way had its full share of selfishness, greed, grasping ways; yet this is to be understood only as confined within the restraints of a given social context. They were sincerely concerned for the health of the soul, as well as of the body: their sin-conscious life resulted in a highly developed sense of responsibility; they accepted the principle of the ethical imperative—they were carried away by maxims of conduct that they regarded as religiously incumbent; and violation of precepts brought a guilty conscience, for which they had to find forgiveness. There was always the driving need to be moral and righteous, not only to be rich; the emphasis on the *good* man could at times exceed that on the caste, rich, wise, strong, courageous, man; and peace, piety and learning, were matters of serious public concern. It was their belief in the power of self-interest and in the integrity of self-help, that created the Puritan state of mind which could see no contradiction in the principle of combining a selfish economic materialism with a Biblical fundamentalism. The Puritan's morality constituted a skillful combination of economic individualism and the needs of the collective order: there was

332

"that indefinable realm where altruism and selfishness meet;" the deep genuine feeling of sin drove ownership on the whole to combine a practical ethics with a theological idealism and personal piety, and they always did maintain a reasonably just balance between private interest and public policy. Religion acted as the guardian of the institution of private property, and the sanctity of the church and of the bank went hand in hand; and the cleric had a restraining influence on the mart, as he "related his recommendations of economy to religious conceptions." And as within the atmosphere of colonial New England, "there was a communal feeling larger than any statute, and more effective than any administration;" and it consolidated the social organism as it gave all the members a sense of belonging, of responsibility, of worth.

NOTES

[a]It was not easy to protect sheep from predators.

[b]There seems to be a confusion of pounds sterling and pounds commodity in contemporary records.

[c]The ancients did not have the theories of evolution and of progress, and they thought of each type of social organism as fulfilled.

[d]Mass democracy—universal manhood suffrage, first came into being in Anglo-America more than a half century after 1776.

[e]For purposes of study—analysis, an attempt to take the institutional strands apart is necessary.

[f]The attitude in colonial New England is not to be confounded with that on the later American western frontiers.

CHAPTER FOUR—THE ABORIGINALS

It is good and it is just, in terms of civilized values, that America was settled by people from other continents.

Of the various continents in the world the aboriginals of Europe were the most energetic and enterprising: their development of communications made their global ranging inevitable; they led in the penetration of other regions, and in their exotic experiences they had seen a variety of human-like beings. The Columbian discovery—the Western Hemisphere, was a primordial world: the adventurers found a scattering of natives who were non-Caucasian, men of a different appearance—race, and of primitive society, whom they called "Indians;" and this resulted in continental contacts, from which followed association and interaction. And the natural aboriginal was an important factor in the experience of the Anglo-American colonies.

The Indian life was in conformity with—it did not go beyond, the essential implications of their sylvan environment. Those found along the seaboard lived in villages on a neolithic—a tribal, form of social organization, yet they were at bottom a nomadic people; they were mostly on the go—migratory, not rooted; they tended towards the development of agriculture, but it was in its superficial stages. Their way of life was based on the wilderness, which was to them what it was to the buffalo—a medium of ranging; they couldn't stay put, and they formed no permanent attachment to a specific land area; they simply occupied—they had no sense of "owning," the land they lived on. They had no domesticated labor and food animals—no dairy; and their basic food supply was separate from the soil, as it came chiefly from hunting and fishing. Their primitive economy required a vast land area—they had to make a maximum effort in space and time for a minimum yield; they engaged in barter, but they never planned economically for the future—

results had to be immediate. They were well behind the Africans in the development of the artifacts: they did not have the principle of the forge, did not know how to make intense heat, and could not beat iron into desired shape; and they did not have the wheel, the ladder, and not knowing smelting they were without steel products. They knew no precious metals. They were practically without implements for laboring, hunting, fighting; they had the bow and arrow, but it was crudely made and of very low efficiency—the pre-Columbian Indian was characterized by a childlike harmlessness. They could fell a tree only by burning its roots; and they did not have the implements with which to reach the deeper, richer soil. They were without the means of land conveyance, and when they hunted a large animal they drove it as near as possible to their village, so as to save transporting the carcass. But they were adept at mobility on the water; the canoe was their top achievement in transportation, and it became as much a part of them as the hand or foot. They were beyond the stage of cannibalism. They lived from hand to mouth, and had no thought for the morrow; they were scavengers, without aversion to anything—but they fired their food; they knew nothing about meat preservatives, and never used salt. Yet as within their own social milieu they were essentially self-reliant.

Their housing did not go beyond the "long house," a primitive shelter which could accommodate a few dozen occupants for gatherings, for protection from the weather, and for sleeping. They did not have monogamy: there were more women than men in the village as some men were always away hunting and fighting; they slept and mated promiscuously, Indian descent was matrilineal, and "the sons of the chief" is myth. There was no condition among them under which the sex act was forbidden, as sin or crime; they were not sex conscious, and participation was natural—as desired. They did not have the idea of rape—and their vengeance was always physical, never psychological. Epidemics were frequent among them, against which they were helpless; they knew no medicines, and their average life span was very short. They had no alcoholic beverages—they were "Destitute of the means of drunkenness until they were tempted by the stranger."[1] There were times when they laughed, and times when they wept; and they were very devoted to their children. Yet the barbarian heart was brutal, superstitious, magic-ridden; they had what appeared as "medicine men," who were all magic; and they were unconscious of sanitation—"the smell of the Indian village."

335

They identified male activity with hunting, fighting, trapping, but not with laboring; theirs was a natural individualism, which found expression in the wilderness; "they loved the chase"—they found their greatest triumph in the kill of the hunt and the war—yet they always hunted for food, never for sport; history has regarded them as per se warlike—"that yearning for martial honor that inhabited every Indian breast." They had the simplistic view; they were headlong—they charged anything immediately before them that appeared hostile and vulnerable. The act of scalping as a mark of triumph in battle was not inherited; scalping requires the kind of a knife that, in terms of size, sharpness, durability, they did not know how to make. To the savage all death is murder, for he judges the unknown by the known, and death from "natural" causes is murder by evil spirits. He was characterized by a wilderness individualism: he did not have the concept of punishment by deprivation of freedom; and his imprisoning, or chaining—was worse than death. He was an expert in woodcraft, and he had a primeval cunning in the ways of the wilds. Yet his essential safety was collective, as it lay within the group; he had no class divisions and no class consciousness, there was a relative absence of individual inner competition, and there was never a civil war as within the tribe. To the primitive mind arduous effort— waging, striving, was to no purpose; they knew how to braid animal hair and certain grasses into string, rope, mats—and this, together with labor in agriculture, was consigned to the women, the "squaws."

They had no rational development and no mental life, and they acted instinctively. They had an elementary speech expression—a dearth of words; they were confined to oral transmission as they had no alphabet and no writing, and they were without records—history; knew no numerals, and were unconscious of chronology—no measurement of time, and of space; they had no system of communications—either horizontal or vertical—and there was no broadcasting, and no handing down or tradition; were without a knowledge of geography, and a sense of direction— they thought that the "pale face" strangers had come from beneath the seas. They had a religion which they identified with a "Great Spirit," and they had a concept of an after life which they thought of as the "happy hunting grounds." And the Indian mind was a complex of primitive mores, customs, loyalties.

Europe was all civilized, and the New World was all primitive. When the European emigrated he brought his way of life with him with the

336

intention to transplant it. He had an alphabet and was literate, and he had mathematics, a system of computation, and instruments for measuring time and space—the clock, the compass; and he brought his monopoly—his ability in the artifacts. He had capital, and he took it with him for the necessary investments. He had the required implements, made of iron and steel—the firearm, axe, plow, knife, hatchet, trap, pick, shovel. And he brought medicines as remedy for physical ailments. His economy was based on arable land, and he had livestock for food and labor—cattle, horses.

The Europeans had a highly developed mental life: in the area that came to be known as "New England" there had been no civilization before their trans-Atlantic endeavor; they created "America"—they described it as they saw it, and gave it history. And in terms of a knowledge of the world, and of the effectiveness of artifacts, they were qualitatively superior to the primitives—and this dictated certain necessary relations. The continental aboriginals were both human, and as such they were both ethical beings—they had values, and codes of conduct. They made contact; this induced contrast—they were wholly without experience in mutual relation. Their underlying difference was in both mind—values, and in blood—race. Their fundamental initial practical difference lay in mind: their mental processes, their ethics—were millennia apart in human evolution, and there was a total absence of mental rapport; the naturalist Charles Darwin says,

> "the difference between a domesticated and wild animal is far
> more strikingly marked in Man: in the naked barbarian . . .
> with difficulty we see a fellow creature";

and their contact was one of physical proximity and mental insularity—the complexity of civilized thought and belief confronted a primitive simplicity. Each was in a condition of complete blackout concerning the other's way of thinking; there was an unbridgable chasm between them, and their relations were entirely physical—they couldn't be mental; each could see and understand the other only in terms of his own mind, his own values; there could be no meeting of minds, and there could never be mutuality—agreement, between them. And the civilized and the primitive were totally helpless in each other's milieu, which created a reciprocal impression of inherent incompetence. Yet they both sub-

337

jectively accepted each other as human being—not as animal being; and the records point patently to the conclusion that each never identified the other as food, as he recoiled from it as cannibalism.

The Indians were wrapped up in their own tongue, ways, customs— they were living in their own, in a wilderness, world. What was the Indian mind when he first saw the European? A history of the white settlement and expansion from the primitive point of view would be baffling, as it would belong to a frame of reference totally alien to the civilized mind. By 1620 the coastal natives already had had experience with the invader; they were in fear of his firearm, even the sight of it; and especially of his artillery, whose noise and flame were used to scare them. And the sudden intrusion of European methods of warfare into America may well have seemed to them as a natural catastrophe—like the hurricane, the earthquake, and even as a supernatural visitation. They were overawed by his watercraft, his house, and they were uncomfortable within it. Each was susceptible to the other's communicable diseases: they accepted and used the civilized remedies; the village in the wilderness was seldom without a member in grave illness, and the miracles of the stranger's medicines, at times accompanied also by some nursing, raised their life span. And use of his utensils facilitated many a routine endeavor. The white man's artifacts caused them to regard him with superstitious awe—as demigod, but with time and experience he began to appear human. After the first generation the continentals were beginning to learn to live with each other; the intruder was no longer a mystery to the aboriginals, and they lost their fear of him; they became convinced that he is mortal, and they too acquired the ability to use his implements. And they were not without reciprocity: in the founding days of a colony improvisation is fundamental; the Indian was a factor, and his artifacts were helpful—the wigwam for shelter, the canoe for communications, wampum for exchange; and the primitive female had her uses. And the colonist learned the native woodcraft; survival in stark nature turned out to be much more exacting than anticipated, and he soon learned what to do besides panic when lost in the wilderness.

The colonists' inexperience with the primitive made their mind a *tabula rasa* concerning differences in basic ideology, and in race; they had had their origins in an atmosphere of caste, but not of race, consciousness—they had no tradition in racism. They soon evinced a sustained rational interest in the primitive: in dealing with him the

338

civilized mind sensed a heaviness, a denseness, that couldn't be penetrated—it was up against a rock; they concluded that he is a person in anthropology, not in history; and an understanding of the civilized-primitive relation is the foundation for an understanding of the European-Indian relation. The differences in values between the continentals eventually became identified with physical characteristics, or race; and the anthropological solution—ideological segregation, had to be introduced; it preceded—and it induced, race consciousness. Confinement to history in the study of their relation is insufficient: the contemporary sources on the Indian, the isolated instances as reported by colonists, have statistical value; but they are inherently faulty as the whites tended to read their own mind into the primitive's head, and he is understood and interpreted in terms of civilized ways and motives—in the American story he speaks English. The relations of the continentals are intelligible fundamentally only in terms of anthropology.

The absence of global communications had hitherto precluded the contact of the continentals, and they were in a horizontal existence with one another; and the vertical human relation was thus confined to within each continent, and not as between them. The principle of caste difference had existed in Europe from time immemorial, and was inherited by the seventeenth century; and with the contact, association and interaction of the continentals there resulted perforce a hierarchical segregation, with the European as dominant. The primitive was lost in the white world—he was unable to adjust mentally; and the necessity to keep him, like the horse, under constant control tended to put the civilized under the impression that he is of an inferior race and even, although rarely, that he is animal being—rather than human being. And he was never a potent, decisive figure in his own right, as he was entirely at the newcomers' mercy, to whom he didn't—he couldn't, count.

The earliest settlers simply had no words to describe the vast forests, the strange streams, the unaccustomed cold, of New England—and the new unnamed animals, trees and flowers of America; and the invention of new words was going on apace at home and in the colonies. The Caucasians created the "tribes" and their "chiefs," to each of which they gave a name—the "Mohicans" and their chief "Uncas"—and they identified each with a particular area; thus "Iroquois" sounds French, "Delaware" English, "Navajo" Spanish. Names given to tribes and chiefs could be the contraction of an off-repeated native call phrase, or it could be a blend of white and red sounds; and different Europeans sometimes had different names for the same Indian groupings, and the English spelling of the same name often varied. Language is based importantly on values, and the natives were practically helpless in learning, understanding and pronouncing European words; they were unconscious of themselves by their alien given names both as tribes and as individuals;[a] and they were unable to differentiate between the European nationalities. The tawny and the white thought of each other as simply "pale face" and "redskin," and they were hardly able to distinguish each other as individuals.[b]

There is a qualitative difference in a treaty as between civilized entities, which is intra-ideological; and in a "treaty" as between civilized and primitive, which is inter-ideological. The native was characterized by an unspoiled primal innocence, the concept of the "man of honor" was wholly beyond him, and he could never be a "conspirator;" and he was always regarded as not responsible, as unreliable—never as disingenuous. In the founding days he was not thought of as a savage—a wild man, per se; he appeared to the Caucasian as a natural, simple being—he was childish minded, he soon forgot. It was easy for the European to slide down the centuries, but impossible for the denizens of nature to go up; he understood them, and in their dealings he had to condescend. The inter-ideological "agreement" made no impression on the tribal mind: a land "cession" was meaningless to them, and to their descendants—"the futility of trying to restrain savages by a 'scrap of paper';" a relation with them involving time limits had to be based on natural conditions, as they measured time and regulated their life by the sun, the moon, the seasons; and all references to Indian "title," "treaty," "purchase," are per se fiction. The London land grant in America had to regard the aboriginals as part of the flora and fauna; they were not included in any peace treaty made in Europe as they did not understand what it means; and practical considerations gave the whites no alternative but to create a mythical "Indian," who had to be understood and dealt with on the fiction that he is motivated by civilized ways. The act of "buying" a wilderness tract as a substitute for outright seizure created a semblance of legality for the claim, which could be used as against rival white interests. A land "treaty" with Indians could have some integrity especially in Europe; and maybe also in the colony several

340

decades later, when most everything was new—generation, conditions, problems.

With the passing of time and the accumulation of experience the Europeans began to think of the Indian as a non-Caucasian, a savage and a heathen, and his control was a matter of common civilized consent; yet the Puritans in their attitude towards him were Christian first—they saw him essentially as heathen. They considered their own way of life superior, and they had no intention to renounce it in preference for primitivism; they thought of their own purposes as exalted, while those of the primitive—if he had any, were unimportant. Rather did they intend to adjust him to their way, and it was thought at first that this could be done by simply converting him to Christianity. The Puritan was the trader, and he was also the priest; he was interested in the Indian trade—but he was also certain that the natives are human beings, and that they have souls that must be saved. He was convinced that their transformation to civilization and Christianity is consonant with the divine purpose; he thought that they were debased by the Devil, but not damned forever by God; and he regarded them as "poore barbarous people" who were to be helped, not condemned. Moreover, the numerousness of the natives in the New England region, and the settlers' experiences with them in the Pequot War, brought the conclusion that it is better to show them some respect—to parley with them. Yet the Puritan was zealous in his intentions, and he made some honest efforts to convert the heathen.

The Christian endeavor had to be financially supported from England, as the colonial economy precluded philanthropy. And there were attempts to give the Indians civilized social organization; according to Roger Williams—

"We English were ourselves at first wild and savage Britons; God's mercy had civilized us, and we were now come into a wild and savage country, without manners, without courtesy, so that generally . . . you had as good meet an horse or a cow."[2]

Colonial Reform organized the Corporation for the Propagation of the Gospel: there was a plan for combining the religious instruction of the Indians with their labor on a large farm; this, together with some help

341

from abroad, would repay the original investment with interest in up to five years, and thereafter provide revenue in support of the Corporation.

With time New England began to identify the aboriginals per se with land, fur, and evangelism. Roger Williams was engaged in the Indian fur business, and he "operated a little empire of trading posts;" and he and John Eliot, both ministers of the Gospel, became the Reform Apostles to the tribes; the religious missionary had then the attribute of heroism; together with the help of some assistants they engaged in the proselytizing endeavors, and they showed an aptitude for friendship with primitives. They stressed evangelist gentleness within the tribes, and they walked in the way of the Lord; they were also educators, and even healers of the body—as well as saviors of the soul; there were plans to train native missionaries for work among their own; and this show of consideration for their tawny charges brought a measure of reciprocity. And the colonists tended to the creation of an aboriginal likable character, the principle of the pet—and this took the form of Pocahontas in Virginia, and Squanto in New England. There were instances where some Indians were favored with civilized weapons, and they often took advantage of their fellows; and those in fear of their own kind ran to the whites for protection. The Puritans soon developed the ability to handle the tribesmen: they settled some craftsmen, especially gun- and black-smiths— among the natives, where they became Indian linguists, a help to missionaries and fur traders, and spies on other Europeans; and they acted as interpreters at "conferences" concerning land and trade agreements. Roger Williams proved himself a capable, reliable intelligence agent; he traveled among them, learned their jargon, understood them well, gained their confidence, and he was the brains behind the scenes in the colonists' dealings with them.

But to the primitives the change to white ways was the world up side down: they couldn't make a voluntary adjustment to the status of freemen within the civilized society; they could settle within it only on a coerced labor status, as they had to be under constant direction and control. The white way for the Indians was the end of a proud life as free people, and the beginning of a fenced-in existence as wards; from a traditional masculine culture, to a way where men no longer have their roles as hunters, warriors, providers. They didn't want to make the change from hunters in the wilds to tillers of the soil; they knew the region they lived in, they could easily leave, and they invariably vanished; and the whites had no way to keep them to their status. It was soon realized that the attempt to adjust the primitive to civilized ways is a practical impossibility: his Christianization was never due to inner conviction; rather was it a matter of mere compliance in the hope of getting some food, which resulted in a few frontier small settlements of "Praying Indians;" and it was concluded that religious conversion would have to be preceded by his acquisition and appreciation of civilized values. Yet the Christian mission was not wholly without civilizing influences: the religion of primitive peoples is polytheistic; the seaboard Indian's "Manitou"—the "Great Spirit," has been regarded as having monotheistic implications.

In earlier days the wooden cabin was not easily come by, and it had to be used for a variety of purposes. Reform emphasis on the Old Testament saw no sin in coupling religion and economy, and trading with the enemy was not thought treasonous. In founding days the improvised shelter was used as both church and fort, and later the Praying Indian village on the frontiers was used by the colonists both as Christian mission house and trading post. However, there was fear of the frontiersmen's reaction to enemy armed empowerment, and precautions against it required undercover activities.

When the first Caucasian set foot in the new world he automatically looked—and moved, westwards. The Indians at first did not see the intruder as a menace to their way of life. The underlying cause of Indian trouble was "manifest destiny"—civilization's inexorable push towards where the sun sets. The steadily increasing white population and its avidity for land, crowded the natives: their concept of the after life was the "happy hunting grounds;" they were losing the joys of their old free life, which to their later generations was a tale told by old men; and the menace to their lands and hunting grounds—to their way of life, tended towards their ultimate presentation of a united front. The entire New England region had to be Europeanized, which necessitated their total removal; they appeared to the colonizers as a nuisance, and an obstacle to progress—and they were thought of as "barriers of barbarism." Their elimination could be brought about through genocide, reservation, enslavement, emigration: the Corporation could be regarded as representing the principle of the reservation; the Puritan phrase "send them out of the country," was a euphemism for their sale as slaves in the island colonies; and there was also some native migration, as New England had an open northern frontier. But there was no genocide—there was never a planned, systematic physical extermination of Indians.

It was manifest destiny for the tribes to become subservient to civilized authority: the whites took pride in their conviction that,

> "property and the industry which amasses it and which it stimulates, are the instruments of civilization;"

they dominated the Indian completely, and they always had an attitude of superiority towards him. During the civil war at home the overseas settlers were thrown entirely on their own, and in 1656 New England created an office on Indian Affairs under a Commissioner; and the Bay government appointed a committee as "guardians of the tribes." As within the practical purview of their settlements the whites had to assume the responsibility of aboriginal control: they pre-empted the land, and allocated the site of native settlements; they chose tribal chiefs, and maintained native peace by making them submit their quarrels for white arbitration; and in cases of inter-racial crime the machinery of justice was entirely in white hands. The Puritan, like all Europeans, could treat the Indians only in terms of his own values; and he had to make them subject to Anglo-Saxon law—he had to adjust them to his own purposes to the extent that he could. The government asserted a monopoly of the Indian trade—furs, skins, venison—and regulated it by licensing traders; and it banned unlicensed conveyance of arms and liquor to the natives. But in sylvan America peace was hard come by: New England was caught between the French and Dutch colonies; and in this area of Caucasian settlement there was an unusually large concentration of Indians, whom settler rivalry tended to empower. In addition, there were European transients—"irresponsible whites," rovers, gun and liquor runners—who sometimes gave the Indians more in trade than did the settlers, and at times gave them defective firearms and poisonous liquor. To the Indian all white men looked alike: he was unconscious of the principle of territorial boundary; his mistreatment by one automatically involved all within a given area, and this forced the Puritans to think of each other essentially as nationality, not as individual colony.

The idea of war—the act of men slaughtering each other *en masse*, was common experience to both civilized and primitive; they fought each

344

other, and they each fought among themselves; and the European military sophistication was introduced on the American terrain. The Puritans had a serious aboriginal problem: they were not entirely unfamiliar with the home built primarily for defense; memories of feudal strife in the parent country were still vivid, and life in the vicinity especially of the Scottish frontiers was precarious. They built the stockade, and garrison and block houses, for defense against attack; and in each town militia companies were organized to which all males aged sixteen to sixty were liable—which introduced the principle of the citizen soldier. Irresponsible individual behavior especially in the wilderness was inevitable, and isolated instances of white-red depredation were constant. There were two embittered and protracted race wars in the history of New England— the Pequot War in 1637 and King Philip's War in 1676; during the intervening four decades a condition of practical peace prevailed. The Pequots were an individual tribe; they were overcome, and the survivors were transported to, and sold in, the island colonies; and the white man moved into their area and settled it. And this set in motion the ultimate extinction of Indian settlement, as well as the introduction of the slave traffic, in New England.

The aboriginal was never more than a front for the Europeans. The causes of the "Indian" wars were manifold: there were the initiative and the influences of the English, of the neighboring French and Dutch, of the Indians; where the interests and designs of the one ended and those of the other began, has yet fully to be determined. National wars in Europe had their repercussions in America, and Indians were incited, armed and used by the rivals. The Christian converts were always Indians first, and they could act as a cover for their warrior fellows. The natives preferred the Frenchman—"the superlative skill with the Indians of the French;" he was not the settler kind, who permanently deprived them of their hunting grounds. Whites on a rampage often disguised themselves as Indians, and they armed and led warriors in numerous raids on one another's settlements. The degree of organization the Indians showed took the English by surprise; they had forts—"blockhouses," about whose construction, organization and direction they knew nothing, and they had firepower: "the Pequot fort . . . covered about an acre . . . Its encircling palisade consisted of trees and half-trees set three feet deep in the ground;"[3] and there was "the second Pequot fort".[4] The fighting in 1637 was chiefly in the southern area, near the Dutch settlements. The

345

Indians fought for the preservation of their natural way—their fury was grim and determined, and their retribution was remorseless. An historian declares that there were proportionately more white casualties in King Philip's War in 1676—which was fought chiefly towards the French area—than in any subsequent American war;[5] the white settlements were pushed back southwards about a score of miles, and more than that eastwards; thousands of persons died, families were disrupted, and homes and lifetime estates were forever erased; and a number of sacked, charred towns were abandoned and given back to the wilderness. A royal agent to New England, the contemporary Edward Randolph, said that the Puritans "look at the French with an evil eye, believing they had a hand in the Indian wars."[6] Without white instigation, arms, leadership, primitive action could never have been more than incidental.

The colonists were not slow to retaliate in kind, and the natives who survived retreated to the northern Maine territory. With their elimination from the midst of settled New England agriculture took a great leap forward, the fur trade suffered a final setback, and the English were left smarting under the blows inflicted upon them; and this brought about a radical change in the attitude towards the Indians—they ceased to be heathens capable of conversion, and they became "varmint". During the British-French wars for domination of North America the Indians continued consistent in their traditional alliance; English settlement northward was slowed, and special protective measures had to be taken—the border village had to be also a garrison; and frontier ravages were a constant condition until the definitive elimination of the French continental power in 1763, when the Indians in Canada were left without leaders and supplies. The following is a contemporary portrayal, c1750, by a woman colonist;

"A detail of the miseries of a frontier man must excite the pity of every child of humanity. The gloominess of the rude forest, the distance from friends and competent defense, and the daily inroads and nocturnal yells of hostile Indians, awaken those keen apprehensions and anxieties which conception only can picture. If peaceful employment of husbandry is pursued, the loaded musket must stand by his side; if he visits a neighbor, or resorts of Sundays to the sacred house of prayer, the weapons of war must bear him company; at home the distress of his

346

wife, and the fears of lisping children often unman the soul that real danger assailed in vain.''

During this time there was some difference in the colonial and royal officials' attitude towards the Indians. The colonist had had his experiences with them, and he understood them; he and his family had to live there, and he owned property that was hard come by; and he paid a bounty for Indian scalps and prisoners that were brought in. The royal officials came and went; they were somewhat slower than the colonists for action against the tribes, and they constituted a restraining influence.

The white treatment of the redman was pragmatic rather than planned: the impact of white settlement on Indian values and ways, the relation of the ideologies, is a story of the gradual liquidation—and of the succession, by the one of the other; whatever the intention, the touch of civilization was the doom of primitivism—the Indian resistance was impotent; the transformation of nature by artifice resulted inevitably from their meeting. There are references to "the fatal effects of civilization" on primitives—their "degeneration". Yet the Puritans never had the attitude that "the only good Injun is a dead Injun," and no vigilantism or lynch law was perpetrated upon anybody in New England. Their society had a high sense of social responsibility; many of the leading figures were of sufficient educational background to rise above the simplistic view, and to refrain from rash, headlong action.

The first point of contact between settler and native was land: the white settlements per se rendered vast areas of surrounding wilderness useless as hunting grounds; the European took up Indian lands, in exchange for which he gave them his artifacts[c]— implements for fighting, laboring, hunting, fishing, snaring, cooking, as well as apparel, spirits—and also medicines, which helped a great deal in connection with sickness; they accepted and eventually learned how to use the civilized goods, although they never learned how to make them or repair them. The European artifacts were qualitatively better than the best the Indian had; their use enabled a transfer of effort from person to implement; this brought fundamental results—the products of civilization materially reduced the aboriginal economic effort in space and time, and increased the yield; a new set of behavior patterns developed around the superior implements; the change in the way of life was a move from sparseness to concentration; and the white man's artifacts created more surplus land than he could immediately take up. This caused the natural economy to deteriorate; the native lost respect for, and he neglected and eventually forgot, his own primitive skills; he gave up his wantless way of life as he became ambitious; and as within the confined area he acquired certain habits of life which became indispensable. But the Indian had lost his own old skills without acquiring the new ones; his inability to replace and repair the necessary implements destroyed his self-reliance; and he was rendered helplessly dependent upon the Europeans' good will, and upon their goods—the deprivation of which could mean his extinction. Thus did the primitive experience a millennial leap; he had to undergo a recapitulation of the many centuries required for the development of civilization in a very much compressed period of time. What the Indian eventually came to want was an association of the artifacts of civilization with the values of primitivism; he did not want to give up his own way of life—he persistently fought the westward penetration of the white way; yet, there was an essential correlation of Indian land and European implements—an avidity on the part of each for the other's possession, which implies an underlying cooperation; the axe cut deep into the roots of the tree, and of the aboriginal way; the natives' acceptance of the white man's implements was an implicit acceptance also of his way of life; "manifest destiny" was the inexorable process that eliminated the Indian as a primitive—it did not eliminate him as a human being.

The Indian never thought in terms of political jurisdiction, and he had no concept of border lines: there was no identification of a particular tribal group with any bounded area of land; thus they did not have the concept of "nationalism" with its hyper-sensitivity concerning rights of "sovereignty," and when strangers came from the water onto their habitat they did not resent it as "invasion;" and they were never racists —they had no race consciousness, as they followed the practice of adopting outsiders into their tribes. They never settled within the white man's social milieu; they were unable to understand, and to exercise, freedom and responsibility in terms of the civilized way; they could find a place within it only as common labor, which did not require the exercise of power of decision; they preferred their own natural way of life in the wilderness—and natives and colonists lived on a horizontal relation of segregation. The pioneer in America had to have help: the success of white trading and military undertakings that were based on wilderness communications often depended on the Indian's good will; he was adept

348

at woodcraft, he had mobility—and he could render valuable service as guide, hunter, trapper, fighter; and he often helped whites who were sick and lost in the wilderness. He was then much more than a subject of juvenile interest—he was sooner desirable as friend than as foe—"his help was so material and his hostility so mischievous;" and there was a good deal of rivalry between the European groups for his support. The Indian did not have the concept of private property, especially in land; he did not understand what is meant by realty, with all of its complications—title, conveyance, sale, purchase, payment; he did not think in terms of fencing in, and of trespass; he never had paper—written paper appeared to him as "the talking leaf"—and he was mentally precluded from associating a mark on a piece of paper with separation from land. His nearest approach to the concept of private property in land is hardly more than an adumbration—the natives inhabiting a given locale always tried to chase out intruders. The "right" to land by prior possession is a civilized concept; it meant nothing to the primitive; had the newcomers respected his "rights" and "paid" him for land his attitude towards them would have been exactly the same—his conduct was determined by his own values. Thus a "treaty" with Indians is per se fiction since it presupposes civilized values in the Indian; the whites understood a land cession as complete alienation, while the native thought he was granting them the right also to hunt and fish thereon.

The primitive way of life was based on the wilderness, which is found in nature and has no economic value per se—while that of the European was based on land (arable), which is not found in nature and thus requires capital investment for its creation; the Indian lost his wilderness—but the European was not thereby a gainer per se as he had to pay, with cash or labor, for every foot of land he got. Colonial records describe the acquisition of Indian or wild land as "purchase," because of the heavy investment that had to be made to turn it into arable. And there could be no rivalry between them: the bow and arrow were wholly ineffective against the firearm, even though in the early days it was crudely made and inherently deficient; the native weapon disappeared soon after the coming of the whites as the Indian learned how to use the firearm, but he never learned how to make or repair it; the European had developed a knack in its use after manufacturing it for some decades; to the Indian the firearm was something strange, he was ignorant of its proper handling, and he probably got less than half the use from it that the white man did.

349

The early colonists also brought the cannon with them, which they used as a psychological weapon; the boom and flame it made when fired caused the natives to flee in panic. Thus the Indian power was always derived—it was never inherent: the Indian as a man is about the same as other men, but the Indian as a primitive is an historical nullity; he could never be a factor in his own right, or the primary cause of anything; wherever the ways of civilization had been introduced the primitive was only too happy to have the European take leadership and exercise responsibility. The basic relation between European and Indian couldn't have been other than it was: the act of giving primitives sophisticated weapons; the existence of "friendly" Indians who acted as "spies," "buffers," "allies;" the whites in Indian disguise when on a rampage— all this was an inherent condition which existed everywhere from the first settlement to the last frontier; the most that could be expected in relation thereto was the exercise of restraint, which often did occur in varying degree. With the urbanization of the continent primitive America takes on poetical and romantic characteristics: however, convictions concerning the "noble savage" recede with civilization; the primitive is volatile—he is a minimum of logic, and a maximum of emotion; he is unpredictable, as he can jump easily and without apparent cause, from the heights of love to the depths of hate—when in contact with him the whites had constantly to be on the alert; since the relation of the races was fundamentally physical, violence had to be at a maximum; the fur trader and the frontiersman were the ones most exposed to aboriginal fury, and savage warfare in the wilderness had its horrors. The English could describe primitive life only in terms of their own values—Colonel Norwood refers to Indians as "the king, and . . . his nobles," "one of the royal blood"; and as late as 1705 Robert Beverly describes the identification of an Indian with the chieftainship as, "Accession . . . to the Imperial Crown"—and their application to the natives of such ideas as "grant" and "sale" of land, "marriage," "family," "parents," "wives," is fallacious.

NOTES

[a]There was never an Indian in New England who was conscious of himself as named "King Philip". From about the 19th century the Indians began to become conscious of their white man's tribal designation.

[b]The man of the 20th century is identified with a preciseness that the colonial was innocent of.

[c]The artifacts of pre-technology appear today as "trinkets."

CHAPTER FIVE—WITCHCRAFT

In a pioneering community there is no intrinsic wealth: civilization in New England had not yet definitively established its predominance over primitivism; and the Puritan "new Society"—the "Wilderness Zion," was without precedent, it was in an experimental stage, and it had yet to prove its superiority to feudalism. Up to the Glorious Revolution of 1689 the British state was seemingly in the hands of the enemies of the capital way, and there was fear of the Stuart regimen with its persistent efforts to revoke the colony charters—to erase the trader economy by infeudating it. In the absence of tangible self-assurance there has to be an emphasis on intangible values, which brings complete submissiveness to God. With the king against them God had to be with them; finding no sympathy in the state they had to take consolation in the church; the traders were loyal denizens of the theocracy, and they were ideologically wholly within the other-worldliness of Calvinism. Their Covenant with God rendered the Biblical Commonwealth the object of a most peculiar solicitude in heaven; the Lord's treatment of His children depended upon their obedience or transgression of His commandments; and benefactions and afflictions were not mere natural law—they were divine judgments. And God was with them when they had bounteous yields from earth and animal husbandry, and from the fisheries; when "their ship came in"—when there took place the safe arrival and delivery of goods-laden cargoes; when they had narrow escapes from emergencies on the high seas, and in the wilderness from precarious travail, and from beasts and Indians; when they achieved recovery from sickness.

To the Puritan mind the Bible was the Doomsday Book: it had black leather covers that cast a cemetery mood over it; it rings with the "wail of mortality"—the prophet speaks of "the sword, the famine, and the pestilence, among them;" it deals with the stern facts of life, with the ultimate, eternal verities, which are unalterable—and depressing; and it constituted the last will and testament—the final judgment, from which there is no appeal. They believed in the doctrine of original sin, which was inherited—they were born guilty; this created in them a sense of permanent sin, which was overwhelming—and rendered them guilt-ridden, and gave them a morbid turn. The state of mind concerning the American wilderness, as expressed in John Bunyan's Pilgrim's Progress, continued throughout the colonial period; it is a nightmare story, an eerie journey into the unknown, and Death is in the heart of the bogeyman. The Puritans were townsmen, and the emigrants had spent their formative years in civilization: they had always lived in a hostile environment, and they were characterized by a consciousness of the external world as evil; and this state of mind was aggravated in America, as they were wholly out of place in—they feared, primitivism.

The settlement of New England brought about the association and eventual interaction of the Puritan Biblical mind and the atmosphere of stark nature. The emigrants were in an unknown region, which had its peculiarities; and the natural world is highly conducive to superstition—sounds can play tricks as they drift across water or bounce off a fog-hidden island; and they rendered their primitive milieu alive with all sorts of imagined malevolent beings. Yet not all unseen beings were harmful —thus Samuel Sewall, a judge in the Salem witchcraft trials,

> "as he was journeying toward Ipswich (he) saw a rainbow, which seemed to him a special augury of good fortune."

But there was always much greater consciousness of supernatural evil than of good:

> "The fear of sorcery and the evil power of the invisible world had sprung alike from the letter of the Mosaic law and from the wonder excited by the mysteries of nature";

and the devotees' life was essentially a mingling of the civilized and the primitive, a blend of daily experience and the supernatural—of reality and fantasy. They believed in the power of the spirit to leave the body before death: there were the terrors of legendary spirits that haunt the primitive terrain—the gloomy wilderness; the atmosphere of nature—"the peopleless, spirit-haunted forests," emphasized credulity and brutality, and this accentuated the tendencies to demonology; and the colonists walked constantly in the shadow of death. Their Satan-infested mind was peopled with demons, trolls, witches, who were ready to devour the witless at the least misstep; they could never understand that "these were creatures that populated only the mysterious land of the human mind."

The colonials were given to waves of alienation and depression, and at times even of despair. There were always omens of ill in nature; evil was muted, but omnipresent. They were in mortal dread of epidemic disease. And there was fear of famine: the Biblical mind, both ancient and modern, was apt to look for divine approval in earthly prosperity; and in the economy of scarcity there were times of abstinence—the custom of ordaining public fasts, so as to emphasize through physical privation the seriousness of an emergency, as well as to save food. The Puritan mind was in a condition of constant terror: in the atmosphere of the Bay settlement—"This living cemetery," the pit of Original Sin—everybody was always full of strange forebodings; impending catastrophe was forever perched over one's head concerning this life, and there was the ever-present threat of hell-fire torment in the next. In the loneliness of life in primitive New England they were easily prone to be overcome by a Biblical sense of doom; Increase Mather said,

"I am afraid that some Awful Judgment will come upon this Land, and that the Wrath of God will arise, and there will be no Remedy."

They were "born and reared in melancholy homes;" the threat of death from disease was constant, and settler mortality rate was high; the healing sciences were hardly existent, and there were no hospitals; and the act of standing beside the beds of the sick and the dying was everybody's experience. All of which brought a tendency to resignation: the world was full of supernatural occurrences, almost all malevolent; death was not only inevitable, it was imminent; life was short, the funeral was an ordinary sight, and widows and widowers were always to be had—the person of several marriages was commonplace. All sorts of rumors were constantly flying around: there were times when it seemed that there was a curse on the land and its people—that a secret evil spirit had to be discovered so that it could be exorcised; the instances of "possession"—of a person's physical infiltration by demons, and of vengeance from the grave, were compelling; and whether or not the

354

unseen and malign presence was sufficiently palpable to make its working seem real and strong and indeed inexorable, it pressed on the mind, it could not be ignored, and it had to be dealt with. And in the terror-charged atmosphere of New England there was a constant underlying tendency to panic, which could easily be touched off at most any time.

The seventeenth century had been an eventful one for the Puritans: Anglo-America for the first time was nearing a new century—they were entering the seventeen hundreds; and there seems to have been the influence of the Biblical numerology, as the calendar changes were revolving around the number seven, with its mystical connotations— could this be a portent? And in the last decade of the dying century there suddenly began a rapid succession of decisive events that rocked the New England edifice and mind. The political commotions at home introduced tradition-shattering changes; from the overthrow of King James Second there followed 1689, that brought the Toleration Act; and all this had a fundamental impact on the colonies. The upheaval in England was the signal for a social revolution in Massachusetts; her sociological foundation changed from theology to economy, and there took place the move from the temple to the mart— the end of the Biblical Commonwealth; this brought the change from Puritan to Yankee, and from Puritanism to Congregationalism; and the Bay colony in 1692 came under her first royal-appointed governor. The colony's adoption of England's Toleration Act enabled her absorption of the Plymouth settlement; this meant a change from Calvinism to Wycliffism, and the mind of William Bradford on religion prevailed—not that of Sir John Winthrop. The monolithic theocracy was dissolving into sectarian pluralism, and church became just another social institution; groups of variant theological understanding were rising, some of which became identified as Protestant denominations; and traditionally accepted ways of doing things—hallowed customs, were being repudiated. And even skepticism—Socinianism, Deism—was becoming noticeable; religion was losing its hold on the people, and the power, prestige and influence of church and ministry were waning. The New England mind was rendered bewildered; conservative Puritanism was present, and it intended to react.

In 1690 there began King William's War, between Britain and France, which involved their trans-Atlantic colonies: the Puritans collaborated with home naval and land forces against Canada, for the erasure of

355

French power in America; their attempts on Montreal and Quebec, New England's first big military undertaking, brought them disaster; their losses in men—due to enemy action, disease, food shortage, were staggering; and they beat a sullen retreat. The cost to the Bay colony in human life and treasure was unequalled by any other event in her history; and there followed a serious inflation, which brought their economy to the verge of bankruptcy; and there were fears of famine conditions. The disaster of 1690 put the Yankees on the defensive, and they developed a fear of counter invasion. Many Indians had fled after 1676 to the proximity of the French in the Maine territory, and their fury against settler whites knew no bounds;

> "While some families were extinct, others mourned parents, brothers, children, murdered or torn from them to hopeless captivity. The settlements were reduced to miserable poverty; their trade was ruined; their houses were burned; their fields were devastated. More than a hundred miles of sea-coast, lately the seat of prosperous life, bore no longer a trace of civilized humanity."[1]

The Bay colony's northern frontiers were also exposed to the aboriginals. And French privateers were harassing New England shipping. Boston had to resort to harsh measures—taxation, impressment—in its attempts to recoup the Bay's prosperity and defense integrity, which brought threatening overtones from the inhabitants. The atmosphere was very much depressed: "there ensued a crushing mortification and sorrow to Massachusetts;" "mourning was already in many of their houses;" and many Puritans felt themselves confronted with the possibility of their world's extinction. For New England the last years of the founding century were "the devil's decade," and King William's reign was "the woeful decade"—it was a catalogue of disasters; and "they interpreted the failure of the Quebec expedition as a stern frown of Providence."[2]

In the course of the century there had taken place an influx of refugees from the social commotions at home—civil war veterans, Restoration *emigres*—and they brought a certain type of mind. In addition, the non-Caucasian primitives were beginning to impress themselves on the civilized mind: the Indian meant massacre and war, the African slavery;

356

and they had certain religious rites which seemed to the English as sorcery—''the devil had appeared before him in the form of a black man.'' The Founding Fathers had long since passed on, and they were beginning to acquire the attributes of legendary, hallowed figures—the New Englanders were becoming tradition conscious. And there was developing a generation gap—the young people were departing from the original teachings of the Elders; they appeared fallen from grace, both in terms of creation—God, and of tradition—ancestors. The belief that God had especially favored Reform received a shock: "the end of the world" was a commonplace expectation in colonial times, and periods of profound social change produce their prophets of doom; what were the portents for the incoming century—the seventeen hundreds?

The philosopher Pascal is quoted as saying, "Men never do evil so heartily as when they do it from religious conviction." The tale of supernatural terror is singularly well suited to the analytical exploration of the human mind: the essence of the Bible is suggestive of the principle of the blood sacrifice—from animal, to human, to divine—the offering of a life as expiation; the idea of Christ may be regarded as a conscious replacement for the scapegoat. In times of crisis societies may turn to odd medicine and strange auguries, and there can be an atavistic relapse.

Witchcraft had been rampant throughout Christianity: it was interdicted in both canonical and civil law; it was a crime, for which there was prescribed punishment. A witch was a person, usually an old woman, who was thought to have supernatural powers to do harm in the natural world to other persons; she derived her powers from the Devil—she was in league with the Evil One. When the Puritan came to America he brought his mind with him: he had the inflexible finality of a remorseless dogma—his "Good Book" says, "thou shalt not suffer a witch to live;" there could be "no compromise with Satan" in the Biblical Commonwealth; that "the witch has made a pact with Satan" was an integral part of public daily life, and wealth was no safeguard against such accusation.

The succeeding local-born generations had grown up in an environment that was essentially primitive; their nativity was beginning to give them some instinctive knowledge of it, and a measure of confidence concerning an adjustment to it; however, the Biblical state of mind they had inherited continued fundamentally implicit and dominant. There was a constant stream of immigration from home to New England, some of which comprised leading figures; yet as the founders died off there was on the whole a decline in the rational standards of the people, and supernaturalism was strengthened. In 1646 a trader vessel with seventy persons and a rich cargo, was lost at sea with all on board;

> "Disturbances in the natural world ushered in this extraordinary event. Circles and light about the noonday sun, three suns at evening, two in the morning, the coldest winter known, a calf born with three mouths . . . all these portents manifested clearly to the mind of the seventeenth century providential displeasure and coming disaster."[3]

Was there something essentially peculiar about the witchcraft craze of 1692?

> "when military movements miscarried, when harvests failed, when epidemic sickness brought fear and sorrow, when an earthquake spread consternation, they interpreted the calamity or the portent as a sign of God's displeasure . . ."

The Mathers, father and son

> "shared fully in the prejudices and superstitions of the times, with their continuous fasts, prayers, and exhortations of a holy life . . ."

The idea of the "haunted house" was general; its inhabitant sensed unsettling spaces at his back, a menacing presence lurking in the rooms, and he was in a constant condition of doubt and uneasiness.

There was always respect for the Anglo-Saxon civil liberties; nobody was ever condemned for witchcraft without due process of law—without a trial. The governor had the power to create a tribunal in emergencies: this consisted of judge and jury, as well as of attorneys and witnesses for both sides; the afflicted and the accused had opportunity to testify in their own behalf; they were all under the solemnity of sacred oath—"honest-to-God;" the court had to rely entirely on spectral evidence; and everything was on record—notes were taken of the proceedings by official

358

clerks. There had been a number of trials for witchcraft in New England before Salem, most of which ended in acquittal.

The Salem witch trials of 1692—which took the lives of twenty people—were the culmination of a cumulative process; they began with the most helpless part of the population—servants, children, females; the witch hunters were in mortal fear of something they could not rationally explain, which they were convinced could be expiated only with a human sacrifice. The immediate cause of the panic, the incident that triggered the outbreak—was pathetically small, a throwback to some primitive emotion. It is hardly possible that any of the testimony could have been deliberate falsehood: the differences between the inhabitants—class, generation, sex—were fundamental, yet they were all equally in a condition of deranged terror of the Evil One; "fear is merciless," and it determines punishment—witchcraft was more heinous than murder; they were in the borderland region of mental disintegration, and as within such a state of mind testimony is bound to be confused and contradictory. New England was not without its tendencies to reason—to "common sense," the mental and moral balance of a community—yet her powers were determined "to silence any incredulity that pretendeth to be rational." It was worse than futile to try to apply natural remedies to supernatural ills, and the witchcraft craze was like an epidemic—it had to run its course. Hundreds of suspects, some in the upper strata, were arrested and jailed throughout the Bay colony, although the contagion did not spread elsewhere. It is said that "the witch generally belonged to the lower classes,"[4] especially the "goody folk;" wealthy defendants contrived to escape from confinement, and from the jurisdiction.

CHAPTER SIX—RELATIONS WITH LONDON

In the chartered New England colonies there was no provision for a resident Crown official, and they were under the immediate rule of their own Company leadership. The Puritans in Massachusetts Bay boldly advanced the claim as early as 1632 that their legislature and executive together partake of the nature of a Parliament:[1] they had their start under conditions of full freedom, and they did things entirely their own way; they developed their corporation into a commonwealth, in terms of the capitalistic social system—trade as the foundation of the way of life, with its institutions and its values; and their "new Society" had taken root—it was highly successful, and it brought prosperity. The Reform colonies avowed a political connection with London, but their imperial control—being entirely from outside their jurisdiction, appeared to them remote and indirect. The members of the Court of Assistants—the top twenty, were Heads of Hundred; and they had a community of interest with the colony governor, whom they chose from among themselves. The charter gave them the power of pre-emption to the territory within the grant, and made them the sole local source of individual title to a private property estate; they wanted the separation—the freedom, of real property from feudal union with state and church; they introduced the fee simple independent title to realty, and they asserted full mastery in its ownership.

It was inherent in the colony to expect the utmost degree of self-government consistent with any recognition whatever of the supremacy of the mother country; and the Puritans interpreted their charter as giving them the right to settle their own problems without appeal to London. Did royal directives apply to the Reform settlements without their consent? New England took for granted the principle of local autonomy or self rule: the governmental system of the new society sufficed for all its purposes, without the interposition of any external power; the Puritans opposed resort to imperial jurisdiction for arbitration or settlement of inter- and intra-colony disputes; and local adjudication was considered final—appeals to London were frowned on as impractical and costly. To the settlers' mind the imperial executive was dim and distant, and the idea of its domination seemed to them oppressive; the administration of government by remote control was bound to be faced with obstacles that would render it ineffective—the early Navigation Acts were virtually nullified in practice; and all this was further hopelessly aggravated by the basic unsettlement at home which—until 1689, rendered the attitude of London towards the colonies necessarily erratic.

There was always a strong Wycliffite element in New England. There were always some Dissenters—immigrants "afflicted with a variety of eccentric theological humors," "incorrigibles," "base and unruly people," who couldn't be tolerated in the monolithic colonies, and in earlier days they were expelled—sent back home. However, with the realization of the vastness of the region the disaffected groups, each with its own form of dissent, decided on another place to go to for the establishment of its own settlement; safety dictated proximity, they had to be tolerant of each other's particular beliefs, and this in time gave a Wycliffite identity to the jurisdiction that developed into Rhode Island. Roger Williams became their spokesman; his doctrines on church and state relations appeared to lead to the atomization of religion, which gave the theological monist the impression of mental instability. Yet the political alliance that had prevailed at home continued in America; and Plymouth and Rhode Island, the two Nonconformist jurisdictions in New England, were always in an underlying harmony with the Calvinist colonies. Thus a strong sense of togetherness pervaded the Reform traders: a high degree of uniformity distinguished their social organization, as they resembled one another in all essential particulars— economy, religion, government; and they all traced their main troubles to external factors—primitives, alien settlements, interlopers, royal officials. Their community of interest as English emphasized their sense of common mission in America, and promoted joint action; and they were united per se as against non-British interests. Yet in view of their scattered settlements and primitive communications they could not conveniently live under one government. There was some friction between them over jurisdictional claims to boundary lines, and to advantageous spots relating to water connections, fisheries, furs. They were in fear that their squabbling about a charter's content could jeopardize all of them if it was submitted to royal officials for settlement, as it might cause London to send over a governor-general; and their disputes were few and superficial, and were always peaceably resolved, which precluded the need for a resident central arbitration board.

The civil war at home brought chaos, and the trans-oceanic dominions were thrown on their own resources: the challenges of European rivals, and the dangers from primitives, created fear of attack and emphasized the settlers' national consciousness; the common origins, interests, destiny, and the security, of the New England colonies all called for union; and in emergencies they were automatically together—the cause of one was the cause of all. A "consociation" of the Reform settlements—the United Colonies of New England—was organized in 1643 for purposes of mutual defense; it was the first voluntary union of English in America. Each trader colony was far from having achieved as yet a clear sense of identity, as is evidenced by the subsequent mergers of some of them.ᵃ Yet the Puritans were for a strong central government, and the counties in each jurisdiction had no local autonomy; each colony was a monolithic entity in its own right, it did express a sense of political autonomy, and the inhabitant thought of it as "my country." There was an extension of the intra-empire political connective principle—federalism, to inter-colony relations; they respected one another's territorial and governmental integrity; and the Union of 1643 is "the first federal constitution in the history of America."² The Massachusetts Bay colony was more important than the rest combined, and she was in a position of leadership as she had a sense of paternalism towards them: as the richest and strongest she was looked up to and relied on for safety by the others, and in the seventeenth century she was often thought of as synonymous with New England.

Yet in New England the settlers felt themselves surrounded by new hostile forces. They were confined within definite boundaries: those of nature—the seas on the one side and the mountains on the other; and those of nations—the French to the north, and the Dutch to the south; and scattered on all sides, and even within their midst, was the native—they were always under the anxiety of the barbarian at their gates; all of which gave them a sense of land limitation, although not of shortage. They had been abruptly transported from a condition of ideological (civilized), racial, national, lingual, homogeneity—to one of heterogeneity; they had to adjust themselves to both a primitive environment and a new society—it was in every way an example of "mankind's Fresh Start." They found themselves in a new world and a new life, with new men and new minds—where they all felt as strangers, as pioneers. The first frontier is the most trying—there is nothing to retreat to: there can be no compromise on the survival of the man, and of his values; their preservation in a wilderness setting has first priority, even if they have to be brutally imposed. This immediately introduced a feeling of togetherness, and there was the instinctive effort from the beginning to resist the temptations of nature. The fundamental concern of the Fathers had to be the perpetuation of their foundation values—civilization, Christianity, capitalism, and they were grimly determined on the necessary measures for the taming of the wilderness.

With the passing of time settlements increased, and growth created a sense of "maturing;" and during her first three decades Massachusetts Bay was in a period of transition towards fulfillment. By about 1660 the struggle for survival was behind it, and the settlers had developed a sense of rootedness, of stability, of self-sufficiency—which created a con- sciousness of permanence as a community. New England had achieved the most compact and clear cut expression of capitalism existing any- where in the world, and she had developed the self-confidence to attempt the liquidation of the aboriginal settlements in her midst.

The colony's underlying development took place in seclusion: the average settler led an isolated life subject to frontier conditions in a primitive continent; he was mentally, as well as physically, localized— his world was no wider than "hoein' and weedin' "; his thinking was concentrated on himself, on his family, farm, county, colony; and he was baffled by anything beyond the immediate world of his daily chores. With the passing of the Founding Fathers and their succession by the local-born generations, a new mental outlook developed: the North American continent as then known was enormous compared with the "little Isle;" and the settler thought of his colony as "my country", as it was beginning to acquire full identity and integrity as such. By 1675,

"There had been time for attachment to the soil to mature; for a sense of national character to be formed; for

363

society to be moulded into that shape which makes it strong and thrifty . . ."

The Puritan believed firmly in God, capitalism and country; he was a new kind of man, one who thought, spoke and acted in ways very different from his parent-country forebears; he was developing a consciousness of himself as something other than—as different from, an Englishman; and England gave the impression of a remote island, and "trans-Atlantic" began to seem synonymous with "foreign," as "home" was being identified with the colony.

There soon developed a network of land grants in the New England region, and the colonists found themselves caught up in a complication of land conflicts: as among various rival forces within the granted area itself; as in relation to its adjoining territory; alleged encroachment by aboriginals and by alien nationals; and as between it and the home powers. The grant to the Company required its members to settle the area—permanently: this meant the presence of both men and women, as well as heavy financial investment; every substantial colonist had to reclaim a land tract, and to throw up shelters—at first made of wood, some to be succeeded later by brick; he had to import labor, both human and animal, and implements. He was a responsible person, who accumulated an estate; he was married, and had a family—wife and children, and sometimes he took care also of one or more relatives.

In a primitive vastness there is topographic obscurity, precision is no value, and competent surveying was practically non-existent; there was overlapping, and at times even duplication, in grants of land from London; and this resulted in inter-colony boundary disputes. And the territorial claims of the rival French and Dutch imperialisms sometimes overlapped into the English regions, and further aggravated boundary uncertainty. There were also territorial troubles for New England emanating from home. The old country was the pioneer in formulating the fee simple independent title to realty; the new way in tractowning had been recently introduced, there was as yet little actual experience with it, and a condition of confusion prevailed concerning pertinent questions in relation to it; and where the rights of the one grantee ended and those of the other began, had yet to be pounded out on the anvil of human experience. And there were attempts to infeudate the colonies—to change their realty laws; there were powerful forces at work in England

364

to eliminate the principle of commonalty realty mastery, and to go back wholly to the traditional feudal system of land tenure—both at home and in the colonies. A land grant in America could be alienated by the grantee. There were professional informers who looked up the records—for a price, and reminded heirs at home of dormant grants of tracts of land to forebears who had failed to settle them; such heirs could prosecute their claims in both places. There were also threats by itinerant troublemakers against high ranking Puritans to expose their alleged regicide support, which could result in the bringing of serious charges—they could even be "attainted of high treason". And strict adherence to charter boundaries was impractical; investment of contiguous areas often could not wait on permission from London; they had to act first, and wait for subsequent official grant of title. And British hold on some places in the New World was at best shaky, and there were instances where London ceded such areas to alien powers in peace treaties. Certain local interests had meanwhile made improvement investments in some of these dubious locations, and they were in great fear of their title being rendered defective.

There were some instances in which a fur trading station was established within the New England region by an independent individual of money, who brought some men with him. The wilderness atmosphere tended to irresponsibility, and in his dealings with the Indians—who could hardly distinguish between the whites—he showed no restraint in giving them arms and ammunition, and intoxicants, and he abused them physically and morally. He "bought" land from them, and he then set up a fort at a strategic spot along a river to interfere with the regular settlers' freedom of movement. This brought up the problem of jurisdiction as between the colonists, and the claims of those acting on their own; there was lack of a clear-cut distinction between them at the time, and some persons no doubt were well-intentioned; and it was alleged that the former were being self-assertive concerning areas outside their charter. The legitimists held that there are qualitative differences between a colony and a trading station: Sir John Winthrop said that station masters "go and come chiefly for matter of profit, but we came to abide here, and to plant the gospel";[3] a settlement gives sales value per se to the areas radiating from it for some distance, and there is a consistent rise in realty values with time. And they emphasized communications, and insisted on their right of way—a river outlet to the sea; on the right of communities

365

inhabiting the upper sections of rivers to pass unobstructed along the lower waters to the ocean, the common highway of nations. In addition, settlers are perforce under restraint in their general dealings with primitives, especially in empowering them—"men do not give weapons to their enemies." And the tendencies of national colonies to harbor alien fugitives, and to buy from Indians European goods looted in raids, and to arm them—had to be controlled for fear of retaliation. And the alleged possession by a station head of a duly-issued "Commission" from London could never supersede the integrity of a charter-based social settlement. The legitimists saw the station fur traders and lumbermen of the wilderness as drifting, freebooting adventurers—as "land speculators"—men bereft of religion, who were in constant trouble with the natives, with the settlers, and with one another. The Union of 1643 was aimed also at them: the problem was finally taken to London and substantially resolved when regulations were made for a peaceable settlement of questions arising between the owners of lands and "irregular" occupants upon them; and it was decided in the future "to grant a patent with power to deal with 'interlopers' ".

Of one thing, however, the settler was certain: his investment could be a commercial loss, but nobody in England—under any condition whatever—intended to evict him or dispossess him of his land. There were many contract complications, and litigation initiated by grantee heirs went on at home—which was often procrastinated; things had to be ironed out in the course of time and experience, and after a good deal of bickering many problems were finally resolved.

When the royal interests became aware of the sociological implications of colonization, they found justification in English tradition for the identification per se of monarchy with feudalism; colonial legislation could not contravene "the fundamental institutions and laws of England"; and royal prerogative had no intention to countenance insurgency. They therefore made it their policy to infeudate the Puritan settlements in Anglo-America by revoking their charters, and this constituted an attack on the trader colonies—both as capitalistic, and as jurisdiction. The traders were faced with a menace to their way of life: in 1634 the king demanded that the Bay colony surrender its charter; the trader colony's power to elect its own governor and to make land grants would be annulled; and the following year he dissolved the Council for

New England, which left all wild lands in the hands of the Crown. And Massachusetts Bay received,

> "a copy of the commission creating Archbishop Laud's committee to regulate all foreign plantations";[4]

The Reformers wanted, above all else, to continue their own way with its trader institutions and values—capitalism, and to be masters of their own land in terms of the fee simple independent title; they considered the charter as the foundation of their "new Society," and they had no intention to allow themselves to be infeudated. The royal demand created panic in New England, and rumors soon spread that a—

> "fleet of soldiers might be on the way to force the English Church establishment and a governor-general upon the Bay."[5]

Yet,

> "The Puritan belonged to the militant type of humanity, and he considered the defence of his inheritance, by force of arms if necessary, as nothing less than a religious duty."[6]

The traders regarded infeudation as expropriation, which they intended to resist at any cost, and they made military preparations to do so; and they let it be known—covertly, that if worse comes to worst, they would call in and hand the colony over to an alien imperialism,[b] and that they would retreat into the interior of the continent where they could set up their own way undisturbed. But serious complications in England soon frustrated royal attempts at colony infeudation.

The attempt by Charles First in 1634 to infeudate New England unified the settlements against it; they required of their inhabitants the "Freeman's Oath," the "Resident's Oath," as measures of allegiance to the colony—even as against the king; and "a military commission was established with extraordinary powers." The Interregnum at home rendered the Reformation political and put it in control of the realm, and New England had a community of interest with it. And the anti-feudal measures continued having integrity in Reform America during the civil war and the republic in England. The trader saw the Cavaliers as an alien

367

force, and he denounced their local support as treason. Parliament asserted jurisdiction over Anglo-America, and it consented to the Union of 1643. The Bay colony resented outside encroachment from any quarter whatever; it recognized the overall government in London, and it had a sense of belonging with Parliament, but only as a self-assertive entity.

The Restoration demanded explicit colony loyalty to the Crown, and renunciation of all Interregnum favor, although it made some show of accepting Commonwealth acts *vis a vis* Anglo-America as *fait accompli*. Yet the end of the English Republic brought grief to transplanted Reform: hope of another political change at home introduced the colony policy of delay and evasion; the Puritans made attempts at adjustment without impairing basic principles, and they were tardy in their official recognition of the monarchy; and they did whatever they could to minimize their acts of rebel support—the aid and comfort they had given regicide. And from the Restoration the Union of 1643—the principle of intercolonial jurisdiction and decision, lost purpose and soon withered.

It is said that Lord Clarendon had in 1663 "pronounced the Colonies to have already 'hardened into republics' ";[7]

"the course by which that (Bay) government had established,
in all but name, an independence of the parent country";[8]

and up to 1680 Massachusetts Bay had been *de facto* practically a self-sufficient independent commonwealth.

For two full decades from 1640—during the Long Parliament, the civil war, the Republican Interregnum—the trader elements had been in practical control at home; and they introduced certain institutional and ideological changes in the realm that no royal petulance could now materially alter, let alone eliminate. Yet the Restoration began slowly to plan towards a return to its previous powers, and some moves in this direction were made concerning the *status quo* both at home and in the colonies. The experiences of Charles First's Cavaliers were not without their lessons for their successors: the traders were determined—regardless, in their opposition to infeudation; they meant to have their way, especially as concerning trade and land mastery. The Stuarts, however, had reason for aggressiveness: careful manipulation by the

368

capitalists had made some seeming concessions to monarchy; with the king's demise in 1685 James Second ascended the throne, and he was avowedly traditional; the Monmouth Rebellion against the succession in the same year was easily crushed;c and in the Virginia colony in America Governor Berkeley had achieved a definitive victory for feudalism. And the Reform traders of New England were becoming uneasy as the Crown was seemingly moving towards "reviving in America the feudal system".9

After the early introductory moves towards tradition, which were several times interrupted by more pressing concerns at home, the Crown made another overt attempt, in 1684—after a half century—to infeudate the settlements in Anglo-America, and a group of royal Commissioners endowed with extraordinary powers arrived in New England. The "royal commission" comprised the king's appointed governor—Sir Edmund Andros, with his several assistants; and many Puritan officials— "considerable men," were perforce consigned to private life. The royal succession and the rebellion caused some delay, and in 1686 the feudal governor finally undertook to put into effect the new program.

The people were reminded that there is a sovereign power that can grant, alter, and also annul, a charter. The Crown repudiated the Charter of 1629 that Charles First had granted to Sir John Winthrop and his Company, on which the Puritans had all along based their life and liberties. Soon the first church services other than Puritan were held in the Bay colony, which left its people bewildered. And the governor then instituted *quo warranto* proceedings—10 show cause why not to be infeudated, against the Massachusetts Bay colony. And he took the necessary steps to impose the medieval system on New England by bringing about the reunion of real property with state and church; he introduced the traditional principle of *nulle terre sans seigneur*—no land without a lord, and the entailed proprietary estate with its implications concerning sub-infeudation. This automatically put all the land in the region—both occupied and natural, ultimately into the hands of the Crown; the Puritans were deprived of the pre-emptive right, and they ceased to be the source of land title; and all wild areas were transformed from public domain to Crown lands, whose officials had the power to allocate. He declared all patents to realty as held of the charter per se invalid, and he required the taking out of new patents in terms of the medieval social order;d

369

"The Governor gave out that whoever wished to have his title confirmed might do so on an application to him and the payment of a quitrent".[11]

The renewal of land grants for patents having royal validity meant a change in the realty title from fee simple independent to proprietary entail; and rent was to be paid to the proprietors and quit-rent to the Crown, which changed the title in land occupancy from "ownership by right" to "possession by grace".

The Crown policies also tended to the idea of political centralization, to which Reform was not opposed in principle. London was extending the policy of the United Colonies of New England in planning their union as the Royal Province of New England; and this in time was to be combined with the provinces of New York and New Jersey into one grand "Dominion of New England". The Crown was to appoint the royal governor as head of the grand political union, as well as the commander-in-chief of its armed forces, there was also the intention to bring about the complete reorganization of the government of each of the colonies in all its phases. And there was to be the legalization of the Anglican Church, and worship in terms of the Episcopal rites.

The Stuart program to change the colonies' status from chartered to royal constituted a direct interference in their internal affairs; it meant the bringing about of a social transformation in New England—the introduction of a new life style, by replacing the capitalistic economy with feudalism. Thus the nullification of a colony's charter had much more than incidental implications; it was a problem in sociology, as it meant the liquidation of a way of life; the Reformers' power—their very identity, rested on their kind of social organization; the change from chartered to royal was the first step towards feudalism. And the institutional framework for this transformation was there; the Puritan principle of the Hundred, the corporate farm estate—was an evolvement from within England's manorial system, and it could easily revert; a simple change in the land laws could bring this about, and there was no need for confiscation or dispossession. This meant the super-imposition throughout the jurisdiction of a class of proprietary overlords—most of whom were members of the English nobility resident at home; and the liquidation of the class of independent family farmers by changing their status to

370

that of sub-infeudated tenants. And the principle of absentee landlordism would be introduced.

The intervention of the royal will through the governor's program immediately brought into question the subjects of state and church—and also the problems of the *source* of title, and of the *kind* of title, to land. Pre-Restoration New England's connective principle with London was based on the federal political doctrine, which the king had no intention to change; but the Puritans regarded the royal governor's attitude on local political power as a threat to the principle of popular government; and they also objected to the proposed changes in church status. Moreover, land was the foundation of everything; the validity of title was basic, and the idea of the king as the direct source of title caused consternation especially among those who had distinguished themselves by opposition to the royal cause during the civil war. In 1721 Jeremiah Dummer of the Bay colony wrote of this event;

> "Their Title to their Lands was absolutely deny'd by the Governour and his Creatures upon two pretences: One, that their Conveyances were not according to the Law of England; the other, that if they might be thought to have had something like a Title formerly, yet it now ceas'd by the Revocation of their Charters."[12]

However, it was understood within the realm that a colony of one's own nativity constitutes a different principle, dominion over which has its implications. The royal plans for New England did make some important concessions: the Reformation received recognition and respect—it had the right to continue, as such; and Episcopacy was to be introduced in the colonies as a denomination in addition to, not as a substitute for, Puritanism. Moreover, there were trader inner jealousies and rivalries, which brought tendencies among some New England capitalists to compromise with tradition; a few of the local bigwigs were promised admittance to the class of lord proprietor; and, while the governmental changes favored the royal power, the Puritans were not to be wholly excluded from political position.

It was in the era of the economy of natural scarcity: commoners were first beginning to hope for emergence from a traditional benighted condition; a few individuals of pauperized antecedents had managed to

371

achieve the coveted position of property owner; and they thought in terms of the sanctity of private property, which was dearer to them than life—vital possessions are not surrendered without a fight to the death. And the development of capitalism in New England was growing to irresistible proportions; by 1680 the early hardships were history, and the new generations were living in comparative tranquillity and comfort. There had been a few grants of land tracts in the wild regions to elite at home, which they intended to organize as feudal estates for themselves as absentee landlords, but the atmosphere of trader success precluded their survival. During the seventeenth century the Puritans had established a tradition of militancy, both at home and abroad, in defense of their way of life; and they did not hesitate, after all sober alternatives had been exhausted, to revolt—to resort to force and violence, in every instance, against the attempt to infeudate them.

The *raison d'etre* of the Reformers was to preserve—at all costs, their trader polity and land mastery—to live their own life: they argued that the grant of wilderness land was an allotment, not a bestowal or gift; the adjustment of the primitive condition to the needs of civilization—especially reclamation, was based on capital investment; they created New England on the investment of their own capital, of their well being, and even of their life—without any help from the Crown. Governor Andros seemed to the theocrats like a foreign conqueror, and they—God's Chosen People, were about to be led into captivity; and they said—

> "We can sooner leave our place, and all our pleasant continued enjoyments, than leave that which was the first ground of wandering from our native country." [13]

Yet their threat to abandon the coastal area and found their way in the interior could not now seriously be emphasized in view of their vast investments especially in lands and fisheries, as well as their fear that any new establishment could in time also be so menaced; and they exhorted their people—"do not give away the inheritance of your fathers".

The Reformers had an aptitude for wrangling; and, in view of man's inherent disinclination to rebel they could have compromised on the subject of state, including also the *source* of title to land, and even on that of church—but never on the trader economy, and never on the problem of the *kind* of title to land. The *kind of title to land* penetrated to the very roots of human relations—it was a problem in sociology: the Puritans' categorical imperative was the separation of property from state and church; what they each wanted above all else was to be master of his own tract, which expressed itself in the fee simple independent title. The sub-infeudated status appeared to them as expropriation, and when this seemed to be their alternative they intended to live up to the full implications of their traditions—they were "stripping for the fray:" all inhabitants of the Bay in 1677 were required "to take the oath of fidelity to the country;" and they emphasized the laws concerning "rebellion against the country".[14] And they also repeated their previous threat that, if driven to it, they will go over to the French.[15]

The Puritans secretly sent a representative to London to contact some of the top capitalists there, as well as to employ native counsel to plead their cause. At home they tried to subvert—to buy off, some of the royal agents. And they relied on argumentation, which was pressed chiefly by the ministry of religion—"the ministers of New England were statesmen and political leaders." They invoked the law: they emphasized the principle of implied powers; they contended that the Charter of 1629 gave them all the rights that were not expressly reserved to the Crown. Yet they couldn't do much with the common law, as this derived fundamentally from the feudal milieu; the Parliamentary statutory law could be of some help but it too was a compromise with feudalism; the Puritan "new Society" was essentially unprecedented in Anglo-Saxon law, and its protagonists had to fall back on the canon law. The Reverend John Higginson told the royal officials;

> "we received only the right and power of Government from the King's Charter . . . but the right of the Land and Soil we had received from God . . .";[16]

they were divines—not lawyers, and they were best familiar with the canon law; and they identified their way of life with God, Whose commands precede those of royalty.

The *quo warranto* proceedings would have to be taken to a law court in England; the judiciary was in the hands of the King's men, the lawyer of the dynamic days was still essentially in the feudal ideology, and with the decision a foregone conclusion nobody bothered to do so. The governor

373

appealed to the colonists' loyalties, and he held forth a royal pardon for all who had been in opposition. He attempted to justify infeudation as colonial law "could not be repugnant to the law of England," even though the century's societal dynamism could very well pose the question—what is "the law of England"? The persistent refusal to accept medievalism he denounced as a repudiation of the king's sovereignty, which had implications of rebellion, and even overtones of treason. And Harvard College appeared to him "to be a seminary of sedition". The governor also instituted a search of realty titles, and to the claim of Indian purchase—

"The signatures of Indians he declared to be of no more account 'than a scratch with a Bear's paw' ".[17]

And on the failure of the trader realty owners to apply for new patents to validate their property as sub-infeudated, he ordered them to be served with "a writ of intrusion"[18]—they were to be "dispossessed of their property and exiled from their homes".

The attempt to introduce in New England the feudal principles on state, church and property meant the liquidation of Reform power. This engendered a morbid partisan rancor; the king's men evidently anticipated physical resistance, and they had to take careful measures against malcontents; the feudal cause was wholly without native popular support, and the governor had to bring with him a group of armed men, who were mostly regular soldiers, to defend him in case of necessity. The Puritans were determined to have their way: they seem to have been encouraged by reports that were brought in by ship officers arriving from England and Holland; they did not hesitate to back their reasoning with a show of force, and groups of men fully armed were organized in Boston and were brought in also from the countryside. As the opposing forces were drawn up for a show-down a ship from home came into port bringing the news that the king James Second was overthrown and in flight, and that William of Orange had landed in England to take over the throne: and it brought an order for Sir Edmund Andros to return home.

England's capitalists in 1689 called in a foreign armed force—"the Dutch invader," to help put them into power; they saw James Second's flight as "amounting to a violation of the *contract* between himself and

374

his subjects"—he forfeited the Crown, for himself and his heirs. The Revolution introduced for a while a condition of uncertainty and suspense, during which governmental activity was confined to immediate needs.

The Presbyterian capital interests made the "Glorious English Revolution of 1689", which constituted the fruition of the Parliamentarian cause in the civil war. Parliament became the British state—and it was declared as comprising Crown, Lords and Commons. The doctrine of difference in organization and function of the political branches was fully introduced; and it laid the foundations for the eventual development of the triune principle in government—the separation of powers into executive, legislative, judicial. Parliamentary sovereignty introduced respect for the integrity of the legislature as the governing principle. The basic purpose of the new state was to be the promotion of the interests of capitalism, and the creation of an empire; henceforth it was a clear cut policy of commerce—the search for foreign markets, that was to determine the imperial policy of England; some practical moves in this direction had been made from before 1689, essentially by the House of Commons. The Revolution adjusted monarchy and aristocracy also to the interests of capital, and supplanted the feudal federal centrifugalism with the centripetal principle of nationalism; and the British government and its laws became clearly capital oriented.

The Stuart officials in New England were regarded as an alien force, as they promoted infeudation: the Revolution of 1689 took a mountain off the mind of the Puritan; it brought the realization that the fundamental principles of sociology in Old, and in New, England—are the same; and the upheavals in their behalf in both places created an underlying community of interest between them. The Reformers had a sense of belonging with, and of respect for, Parliament. The advent of William and Mary did not mean full restoration in the Bay colony of the *status quo ante*, and some of the Stuart changes in principle were kept by the new order. The settlers could compromise on their own traditional principles in the organization of the state, as they patterned it on the new British model; they became indifferent to the restoration of the old charter, and New England was to continue to be a royal province; and the trader power accepted the introduction of Parliamentary-appointed royal officials as constituting their resident government.

There were also revolutionary differences: attempts to impose feudal

375

tenure were forever erased; Reform's categorical imperatives—the trader economy as the foundation of the "new Society," and the fee simple independent title to realty property—were for the first time officially established as legitimate. The change of 1689 was the most fundamental single event thus far in the history of Massachusetts. With the British state definitely in capitalistic hands, and the trader economy firmly entrenched in New England, Reform achieved self-confidence and forged ahead; the nature of its societal base could now undergo a radical change, and there took place a social revolution in the Bay colony. It meant the liquidation of the Biblical Commonwealth—of its Covenant with God; the foundation of the way of life moved from religion to economy, the polity developed from the theocratic to the secular state, and the merger of these basic institutions was dissolved as they each acquired separate identity.

The colonies were to be governed according to the English common and statutory law, and also the church canon law. The principle of government, which had always expressed itself in terms of the three branches, was officially confirmed; and it was beginning to emerge towards clarity. The executive branch was to comprise the Governor, the Deputy Governor and the Secretary of the Colony, who were to be appointed from London. The legislative branch—the General Assembly, was to be bicameral and vertical: it was to comprise the Council or upper House, which was to have twenty-eight members; and the General Court or lower House, which was based on the franchise and was periodically elected by the people—the goody freeholders. Members of the Council were nominated by the lower House. The executive authority in legislative session appointed all members of the judiciary, both general and local, as well as the county sheriffs—which put the judicial branch into royal official hands. Power was also vested in the Governor to summon, adjourn and dissolve the General Assembly. And he had the veto power concerning all colony legislation: including, the choice of a resident agent in London to represent its interests; the General Court's nominations for membership in the Council; its choice of a Speaker of the House. And the right to engage in printing had to have his license. The great majority of all government officials were local born; and a system of reasonably balanced powers, royal and colonial, was introduced in the

376

governments of New England. Trans-Atlantic understanding began to improve, and the systematic regulation of traffic on the high seas was taken in hand.

The Puritans could also be amenable to the principle of religious toleration; the Revolution broadened the feudal insistence on Episcopacy permissiveness to include colonial acceptance of the Toleration Act of 1690, which extended liberty of worship to all Christian denominations—"Except Papists";[19] and this enabled the merger in 1691 of Plymouth with the Bay colony.

The Latins were the pioneers in the projection of civilization to North America. The New England colonies were at first hemmed in between the French and the Dutch settlements, and there was bound to be some mixing in the normal course of affairs; all European jurisdictions produced a few embittered expatriates, who went to and helped an alien colony against their own; and many men were not too particular about the colors they served under. With the English acquisition of New York in 1664 the imperial bisection between their settlements was eliminated, which removed a possible alien enemy. Anglo-America tended to aloofness from European imbroglios, and up to 1689 New England had contributed little to British war efforts.

The rise of the capital power at home brought with it the concept of nationalism; the policy of imperialism, in terms of its modern capitalistic expression, was unknown in Stuart England, and was not fully introduced until after trader control of the realm was established. And London began to carry out the intention to erase the continental European power in North America, which would bring on war. The wars in Europe involved the colonies, to which they had to contribute of their manpower and treasure; but this was solidly backed by the parent country with contingents of regular troops, with naval units and with materiel. And for the first time it was officially declared that colonists are to be respected "as if they and every of them were born within our realm of England," and British subjects were forbidden to enlist in the armed forces of a foreign power; this was before the full development of nationalism as a value and an emotion, and it necessitated legislation. English and French settlements were moving towards proximity; and the reckoning between

377

them for full control of the continent began with King William's War in 1690; and a struggle followed between the British and Latin imperial systems for eventual domination of the Western Hemisphere.

The English Revolution of 1689 introduced many unprecedented propositions in the life of Anglo-America. In the attempt to facilitate trans-Atlantic military measures London had to have a single center of control, and she emphasized the northern area and the union of its settlements. King William's War, which began in Europe between Britain and France, soon involved the Bay colony in a military attempt against the French in Canada. Yet the implications of the potent struggle, which were aggravated by earlier military defeats, caused her to throw herself on London support. The cost of imperial defense rested on Britain; there was the royal expectation that the colonies should bear some of the economic and military burdens in the wars of the Empire; and they were warned that they could not be independent and protected at the same time, as benefits and responsibilities go together. But when London's commercial policies became the primary purpose of government New England bounded forth, and she became fully identified with the imperial wars. It was the first time in their history that the Yankees found themselves participants in *welt politik*—in a dynastic war; this gave them a sense of importance—the feeling that they count; and they felt themselves caught up in an immensity of endeavor that had a staggering effect on them.

Britain's imperial interests had catalytic influences: she was never entirely easy concerning the development of a colonial continental view, and even of sectional cooperation; and the liquidation of French power in North America may lessen filial dependence. Yet the centralized control of trans-Atlantic was an urgent requirement if her mercantile system was ever to become a reality; she was convinced that her interests in the Western Hemisphere were menaced by the ambitions of Bourbon imperialism, and she decided to incorporate Anglo-America into her own imperial system—which is in its nature centripetal.

NOTES

ᵃThe absorption by Connecticut of New Haven colony in 1662, and by the Bay of Plymouth colony in 1691.

ᵇNew England was located between the French and the Dutch settlements.

ᶜA palace imbroglio within the royal family over the succession to the Crown, which tended to reveal the inherent deficiencies of the Stuart monarchy.

ᵈThere was a fee for the issuance of a new patent.

ᵉItalics the author's.

CHAPTER SEVEN

THE BIBLICAL COMMONWEALTH—SUMMATION

The settlers came to America: they strove to subdue the soil; they established a planned community of man for production and defense in a howling wilderness, in terms of a new social order; they were excited by the feeling that they were wholly on their own, and that they were experiencing something new—territory, society, religion. They made heavy investments, they cleared the land; they hewed prosperous farms, solid homes, substantial villages, out of nature; they raised families, planted grains, caught fish, trapped furs, sawed lumber; they went down to the sea in ships and engaged in commerce; and all this was combined into one well ordered system. The civil settlement endeavor that took root and waxed was promoted by responsible men who had a practical view of the American environment; there was careful advance planning and good motivation; they were men in earnest, with strong, positive reasons for going to the wilderness. And there took place the inevitable expansion of a closely guarded community into a *common*wealth; within two decades the "immigrants had turned barrenness into abundance, and uncertain want into constant plenty"; and the Puritans developed from the wants of settlers in primitivity to the wants of dwellers in civilization. And from the early days a pattern of life had been established which made New England throughout a land of steady habits.

Most everything in the settlement was "new," and the new society began in New England as a blur—a gross nebulous mass: in the pioneering days the household was the foundation unit from which community life flowed; the household was a return to the principle of the patriarchate, and private and public functions were not clearly distinguished —their separation seemed artificial. The fundamental institutional activities of man—economy, church, government, family, defense—were compounded; and the trader social organism as a pioneering enterprise was a basically monolithic entity, having no apparent differences. There was no fully developed capitalistic system existing anywhere in the world to learn from—it was unprecedented in the annals of mankind, and the settlers' inheritances from home were meagre and warped. The Puritans at home had had full experience with church, economy, family; they were hazy on social status—caste, class; and they knew nothing about state, defense, race, nationality. The pioneer society inherited most of the institutional forms of its predecessor but there necessarily resulted a modification of their traditional expression, and it also introduced new forms; and the differences between the social institutions of feudalism, and those of capitalism, were qualitative. The colonists thought of their trader sociology—of their new way of life, as a composite whole; they couldn't at first methodically take apart and analyze separately the social strands—the changing, and the newly developing, social institutions—as they subtly shaded into, and emerged from, one another; they had to grope as they were slowly yet consistently evolving from a generalized condition towards specialization; and they perforce developed tendencies towards novelty—towards creativity, in social organization. Thus the fundamental activities of man—industry, religion, school, defense, and to quite an extent also government, in addition to farming, home, family—had to be identified with the hearth.

Sir John Winthrop and his people took their charter with them to New England: the Massachusetts Bay *colony* could legally absorb the *Company,* and there took place an imperceptible transition from the corporation as a private business enterprise, to the commonwealth as a social organism; and the Company began to take on the characteristics of the state. The organization and centralization of government, with the right of representative self-government, was introduced; its powers were defined, and its composition was directed, in the charter; and the members of the board of directors of the Company slowly drifted into the position of government officials of the colony. The settlement then developed from the private law of a corporation to the public law of a social jurisdiction; and the freemen settlers ceased to be "adventurers" as they achieved the status of citizens, and they acquired complete domination of the colony. With its bondage to the external bankers

381

surmounted, private property in full became practical, and individual ownership replaced communal ownership.

British law during the Biblical Commonwealth was the exemplar of Anglo-American constitutional thinking. The colony charter, as a document of state, was statutory law, and it was the precursor of what in time developed into the principle of the constitution—the supreme law of the country. The Puritans thought of their charter as fundamental—it evidenced their will to establish and maintain a "new Society". During the seventeenth century New England was in a constant struggle against attempts from London to infeudate her; the charter was the chief obstacle to the creation of an entailed proprietary caste; it exemplified the settlers' determination to preclude their return to the traditional way of life, and this was the reason for the Stuart attempts to revoke it. However, sociology is fundamental; the charter itself—the written paper, can never be more than a symbol, a guide; social phenomena have little relation to the "integrity" of a governmental grant, and to its judicial interpretation; and the particular content, and the actual location, of such a paper could never have more than incidental meaning.

During the Puritan Absolutism everyone was concentrated on the single-minded pursuit of the religious life. The theory of progress—the identification of the future in this life per se with improvement, was unknown at the time;[a] and man's better life was confined to the after life. The population in general had not then imagined that a voice in the church or a vote in the government is the due of every man; they thought in terms of theology before political economy—of the Will of God, rather than of the social compact and the Bill of Rights; "the sovereignty of God does not wait on a majority vote," and questions of civil rights were hardly even incidental. And there could be no religious toleration in the Bay colony sociology until some factor other than theology became the foundation from which her institutions and values flowed.

And as the emigrants were beginning slowly to settle to their new home they were gratified to find that their new way was proving eminently successful—"the remarkable stability of their society and of their government". Their merger of theology and economy—the principle of the calling, the permissibility of what is not enjoined in Scripture, man's private property estate as a divine sacred trust—was being highly practical. The development of industry—manufactures, merchandising, bank-

382

ing, commerce—introduced the principle of intensive, in addition to extensive, economic production and expansion. The capital way enabled the accumulation of great wealth in small areas, which promoted the town; industry was getting a maximum yield from a minimum area, and the ability to get more from less constantly increased. Capitalism was concentrating on the city, from which the overall economic enterprises were planned, organized and directed. Trade as an *end in itself* had been traditionally identified with the commonalty; the people's ambition and aggressiveness were confined within the mart, which became the field of their keenest competition; there followed a rapid increase in the production of personal property as they concentrated all their time, mind, effort on the processing—producing, repairing, selling, shipping—of things of economic value; and personalty—which is movable, and renders wealth fluid—was moving towards becoming more important than realty. And property in realty—lands, tenements, hereditaments—was also coming within the grasp of commonalty. Clarity concerning the problem of ownership of real estate in colonial New England is predicated upon an understanding of the principles of the fee simple independent title to realty, of reclamation for arable, and of the mortgage. The trader economy introduced the principle of full mastery—of freedom, in ownership of realty: this brought the principle of the mortgage—which enabled ordinary folk to achieve the status of realty owners, to acquire a farm tract and its appurtenances as their own property; and it resulted in the development on a social scale of the commonalty freeholder.

The Puritans were chiefly townsmen, and they had difficulty settling to agriculture; yet farming—for household, market, commerce—became the Bay colony's most important source of wealth. A powerful class of small fee simple independent farmers had taken root in the colony, and they constituted the bulwark of the economic *status quo;* they abhorred the principle of "no land without a lord" or medieval feudalism; and the ungranted areas in the jurisdiction were public property reserved for the people, they were available to any and all who had the capital with which to make them productive, and there was an immediate relation between the granting of land and its seating, and accrual and lapse. And for the colonists as farmers most other concerns were subsidiary. Yet the pioneer economy with its interests in manufacture and commerce had succeeded in establishing itself—the entrep-

383

reneur was beginning to become a social force; and the legislation throughout has the basic features of the capital society.

The Biblical Commonwealth was a dynamic entity. Puritanism was an urban phenomenon, whose strength came from the trader kind of people; its devotees intended to impose the ethos of a town civilization on the entire population, to substitute urban for rural rule; the founders of the Massachusetts Bay colony meant for the trader ways and values to apply to the entire economy, including realty. The wealth of the new society, the increasing number of individual large fortunes, were concentrated on manufactures, commerce, trade, rather than on agriculture alone; personalty was developing towards greater importance than realty, and this led to the eventual extinction of the feudal way. The Reform settlements were expanding as the population was consistently increasing; and the introduction and acceptance of a new social foundation—the capital values, brought human inter-relationships that were becoming more and more involved. The economic cash nexus of capitalism was irresistibly taking the place of the caste blood family relations of feudalism; the supreme value in life was success in the field of economy—the acquisition of wealth; the striving for money was seemingly becoming the only worth-while pursuit; and expansion was bringing growing pains. There followed the exaltation of the business man—he invests capital, creates jobs, pays taxes; he became the symbol of personal success in life, a figure to be emulated; and he was granted franchises, capital loans, lands, monopoly privileges, taxation and militia immunities.

Excessive esteem for the things of this world on the part of all the settlers, who stemmed—some recently, most immediately—from the immemorially pauperized masses, brought an attitude of complacency in the accumulation of wealth. The upward sloping of the pyramid of provincial life, the economic polarization in society—inequality in property possessions, and in social status—created sharp class divisions. There was a stigma attached to poverty; and most men who wanted to be above the common herd had to engage in some lucrative endeavor, and the successful "business man" was looked up to as a hero of the mart. It was thought axiomatic that governmental protection and encouragement of capital interests would, through the "drip-down" method, promote the general good of society—and the consistent increase in colony property did trickle down to the masses, although not proportionately.

384

The population of New England of all classes was energetic, industrious, intelligent—it was in a condition of continuous exertion.

As within the limitations of the welfare of the community there was a tendency to individualism and self-assertiveness. There were chances for the uncommon commoner: there was the probability of a mortgage settlement, and even the possibility of achieving actual ownership of— the private property estate in, a farm tract in the countryside; and there was also the status of entrepreneur—to set up for oneself on the domain as a skilled craftsman; all this was fascinating—it was the opportunity of the ages. Everything in the colony was consistently on the increase, and most all those settled in it had more of the goods of life than when they arrived. Theirs was an expression of the vitality and the ingenuity of men who are conscious that they are shaping their own future—their own fate; the emphasis was on self-reliance and hard work, on innovation and the spirit of cooperation in building something better and bigger than any- thing known before;

> "the standard of the great Puritans, that high ideal of constant purity and personal consecration, had passed into the common everyday living of many people, producing a steady current of social life in New England."

And the Bay colony was a happy blend of collective control and indi- vidual freedom; there were the restraints of religion, and the frontier spirit of self-reliance did on the whole operate in terms of a responsible concern for law and order.

The relations of men to the land are qualitatively different under capitalism from what they are under feudalism; throughout the colonial status agriculture was more important than trade, yet the men of land in a capital community do not have the power and the prestige that they have in an agrarian community. It was inherent in the Puritan social organism for a large class of small property owners to develop; and the conveyance of the individual farm tract introduced a new principle in agriculture— the family farm system. The industrial upsurge introduced efficiency and thrift as primary values, and brought ledger responsibilities necessitating literacy in the use of the alphabet and of numerals. For the first time in history the societal economy came within the basic grasp of common-

385

alty—became a mass phenomenon; and the entire population could—some actually, most potentially—participate in the life of the country, everyone came within the atmosphere of property consciousness and rivalry, and a free-for-all condition was introduced.

During the eighty years to 1700 the history of New England had been full of important—if not, indeed, fundamental—events; the liquidation of the aboriginal menace, attempts at infeudation, the twenty years of the rule of the Parliamentary republic, the monarchal Restoration, the complete Anglicization of the Atlantic seaboard area through the elimination of the Dutch government, the Revolution of 1689, the introduction of religious toleration—indeed, a short period of history to have seen so many changes.

Yet with all of the economic progress life was still harsh, and primitivism was not easily overcome. The poverty and toil of the goody folk made up their basic disciplines; the soil and the climate brought a hard life—and hard labor, which were willingly borne in a stimulating atmosphere. The husbandman of the countryside, the workingman of the town, based their elementary principles of life on strict economy and militant virtues; theirs was the pious, humble, honest living, and they took great pride in working with their hands; women wove, stitched, tended their gardens, cooked and baked—it was hard work but it couldn't have been unbearable; and existence for the family was not marked by comfort or refinement. And the colony was in a constant embattled condition—aboriginals, creditors, interlopers, continental Europeans, infeudation; they were always faced with an adversary, and sometimes with several at once; there was a sense of suffering—of privation in a wilderness; and it was felt that triumph over opposition could be achieved only by the commonwealth of the gathered. This brought a spirit of combativeness—safety preceded peace, and an assemblage gave them a sense of union and of strength.

Man has a subjective attitude towards reality: he is conscious of the ideal, of that which has yet to become real; with the definitive achievement of its fundamental social principles—its institutions and values, the ideal disappears into reality, and it becomes an implicit part of its denizens' being; complete success is oblivion, and it is all the more potent because it is unconscious.

The acceptance by New England of the Toleration Act of 1690 introduced a new principle: the Biblical Commonwealth became history, and was supplanted by the Secular State; the compounded condition of the social institutions of the "new Society" disappeared, as they each achieved a clear identity; and as Puritanism became absorbed into daily life it was erased from the consciousness of its inhabitants.

NOTES

aThere was no political thinking in terms of reactionary, conservative, radical—or respectively tradition bound, present minded, future oriented.

REFERENCES

PROLEGOMENA

1. BIBLE: KJAV—Old Testament Psalms 51;5
2. New Testament Corinthians 1:15;22
3. OT Ezekiel 22;12, 13
4. Henry S. Lucas—Renaissance & Reformation 109
5. Ency Brit ed 1956:vl9;p 127

BOOK ONE—THE BACKGROUND IN ENGLAND

1. H. Maynard Smith—Henry VIII & The Reformation 120
2. J. A. Mackay—The Presbyterian Way Of Life 104
3. Philip Hughes—The Reformation In England 3;146
4. James A. Williamson—The Tudor Age pVII
5. Wm Haller—Liberty & Reformation In The Puritan Revolution 47
6. Hughes 1;282
7. Ibid 2;11fte
8. Haller 47
9. Hughes 3;296fte
10. John Thorn—A History Of England 318
11. M. M. Knappen—Tudor Puritanism 253
12. Ibid 317
13. Hughes 2;120fte
14. Ibid 1;93
15. Ibid 1;322fte
16. Mackay 62
17. OT Deuteronomy 15;11
18. John H. Bratt— The Rise & Development Of Calvinism 29
19. Knappen 469
20. Hughes 3;374
21. Ibid 2;90

22. Knappen 363
23. Bratt 21
24. OT Kings 2:15,16
25. NT Colossians 2;8
26. Knappen 47fte
27. H. Henry Meeter—Basic Ideas Of Calvinism 126fte
28. Perry Miller—The NE Mind, 17th Century 77
29. NT Acts 7;55
30. John G. Palfrey History Of New England 2;88
31. Moncure Conway—Barons Of The Potomac & Rappahannock p3
32. Hughes 1;260
33. Oxford History Of England 9;144
34. Allen French—Charles 1 & The Puritan Upheaval 228
35. OT Psalms 18;43

BOOK TWO: CHAPTER ONE—LAUNCHING

1. T. J. Wertenbaker—The Golden Age Of Colonial Culture p5
2. Herbert L. Osgood—American Colonies In The 17th Century 1;12
3. Palfrey 3;35
4 T J. Wertenbaker The Puritan Oligarchy pVIII
5. OT Exodus 5;4
6. Mackay 12
7. Osgood 17th Cent 1;145
8. Wertenbaker—The Puritan Oligarchy 74
9. Wm B. Weeden—Economic & Social History Of NE 1620-1789 1;165
10. Osgood 17th Cent 1;30
11. George F. Dow—Every Day Life In The Massachusetts Bay Colony 12
12. OT Psalms 104;20
13. Ibid 91;5
14. Thorstein Veblen—The Theory Of The Leisure Class 136, 7

CHAPTER TWO—FOUNDING

1. A. B. Hart—Commonwealth History Of Massachusetts 1;477
2. A. B. Hart—American History As Told By Contemporaries 1;284
3. Osgood—17th Cent 3;15
4. Ency Brit ed1956:15;263
5. Hart—CHMass 1;470
6. OT Psalms 111;10
7. Thomas C. Hall—The Religious Background Of American Culture p. 174
8. Wm Bradford—Of Plymouth Plantation; 1620-47 p172
9. Cyclone Covey—Roger Williams 71

389

10. OT Psalms 51;5
11. NT Corinthians 1:15;22
12. OT Exodus 20;3
13. OT Psalms 135;5
14. OT Jeremiah 46;10
15. NT Acts 7;55
16. Osgood—17th Cent 1;209
17. Larzer Ziff—Puritanism In America 69, 70
18. Hart-CHMass 1;176
19. Ibid 1;178
20. C. Covey—Roger Williams 114
21. Osgood—17th Cent 1;220
22. Palfrey 2;475
23. Ibid 1;472
24. OT Jeremiah 31;33
25. Osgood—17th Cent 1;185
26. CHMass 1;116

CHAPTER THREE—ESTABLISHMENT

1. NT Matthew 20;11
2. Weeden 1;400
3. Ibid 1;241
4. Hart— CHMass1;477
7. Palfrey 2;56
8. Hart-CHMass 1;38
9. Osgood—17th Cent 1;168
10. Ibid 1;311
11. Palfrey 1;376
12. C. Covey—Roger Williams 97,8
13. Palfrey 1;375
14. Ibid 1;383
15. Ibid 2;256
16. Ibid 1;442
17. Osgood—17th Cent 1;163
18. Ibid 1;164,5
19. OT Ezra 8;24-34 & Kings 2:22;4
20. Weeden 1;149
21. OT Ecclesiastes 5;19
22. OT Proverbs 22;29

23. OT Nehemiah 5;10
24. OT Ezekiel 22;12,13
25. OT Kings 1:8;63

CHAPTER FOUR—THE ABORIGINALS

1. Palfrey 1;32
2. C. Covey—Roger Williams 244
3. Ibid 199
4. Ibid 204
5. Douglas E. Leach—Flintlock & Tomahawk 243
6. Hart-CHMass 1;455

CHAPTER FIVE—WITCHCRAFT

1. Palfrey 4;287
2. Ibid 4;70fte
3. Weeden 1;150
4. W. S. Nevins—Witchcraft In Salem 1692 pVIII

CHAPTER SIX—RELATIONS WITH LONDON

1. Osgood—17th Cent 1;173
2. Hart-CHMass 1;230
3. Ibid 1;105
4. C. Covey—Roger Williams 102
5. Ibid 102
6. Osgood—17th Cent 1;497
7. Palfrey 2;579fte
8. Ibid 2;581
9. Hart-CHMass 1;557
10. Palfrey 3;358
11. Ibid 3;529
12. A. B. Hart—American History As Told By Contemporaries 2;136
13. Palfrey 2;608fte
14. Ibid 3;348
15. Ibid 3;344
16. Osgood—17th Cent 3;408,9
17. Osgood—17th Cent 3;408
18. Palfrey 3;552
19. Wm MacDonald—American Documentary Source Book p88

INDEX

aboriginal 16, 33, 340, 345
African 172
Anglican 82, 90-92, 104, 114,
 115, 122, 135, 145, 146, 156,
 248, 249
anti-Christ 4, 80
Aquinas 37, 38
Aristarchus 16, 244
aristocracy 9, 13, 28, 29, 34, 37,
 46, 48, 80, 141, 144, 150, 179,
 304, 315
Aristotle 5, 13, 23, 25, 30, 31, 122
art 8, 29, 34, 37, 159
Augustine 21, 133
Assembly 305
Athanasian Creed 17

Bradford 181, 190, 201, 223, 250,
 270, 355

Caesar 5, 21, 38, 88, 247, 255
Cambridge University 253
Catholicism 90, 92
Church of England 79, 93, 129,
 158, 159, 181
classics 23, 27, 29, 33-37, 50
craftsman 44
culture 15, 25, 28, 29, 33-37, 50,
 57

Deism 125

Descartes 4
divine right 47

Elizabeth I 55, 57, 86, 89, 90, 92,
 93, 116, 117, 146, 148, 163,
 188
Elizabethan era 67, 91, 106, 114,
 117, 129, 131, 141, 162, 174,
 183, 196
emperor 21
empiricism 24, 33, 34, 38
Episcopacy 43, 54, 55, 58, 84-87,
 89, 90, 98, 115, 125, 126, 130,
 141, 142, 154, 266, 371
Establishment 110, 117, 118, 122,
 151
Europe 15, 16, 19, 21, 28, 33

federal 143, 155, 176, 177
federalism 147
fee simple independent title 48
feud 44
feudalism 8-10, 22, 28, 29, 31, 32,
 43-49, 52, 56, 58, 59, 69,
 71-73, 76, 106, 140, 143, 144,
 147, 151, 155, 157, 158, 160,
 179, 180, 184, 185, 187, 189,
 216, 218, 233, 245, 290, 308,
 314-316, 329, 352, 360,
 365-367, 369, 370, 372-375,
 377, 381, 383-385

393

franchise 45, 305, 311, 384

Greece 9, 16, 27, 33, 304
Goethe 4, 66

heathen 25
Hebraism 15, 17, 19, 26, 27, 32,
    34, 35, 84-86, 92, 94, 96, 110,
    121-123, 125, 158, 242, 247,
    253, 254, 258, 267, 271, 272,
    291, 317
heliocentric 16, 37
Hellas 15, 23, 35
Hellenes 13, 28, 37
Hellenism 23, 27, 32, 34, 48, 50,
    85, 91, 92, 122-125, 158
Henry VIII 57, 79, 86, 90-93, 147
    233, 248
hierarchy 9, 19, 20, 46, 48, 83, 85,
    123, 146, 228, 245, 250, 305,
    309, 314, 316, 339
horse 45
House of Lords 233
Huguenots 43, 55
humanism 23, 27, 29, 34-
    36
humanitarianism 30
humanities 26, 28
Hundred 305
Hutchinson 263, 265, 267, 269,
    280

Indian 172, 212, 296, 334, 335,
    338, 342-344, 347, 348, 350,
    356, 365, 374
industrialism 9
infeudate 48, 141, 352, 364,
    366-369, 371-374, 382

Israel 253, 264, 270, 272
Jews 15, 38, 39, 131, 260, 274
Judaea 9, 15, 16, 241
Judaism 37, 95, 109, 318

labor 7, 8, 13, 47
Latin 20, 27-29, 34, 50, 97, 98,
    173, 175, 292, 301, 378
Latins 43, 165
lord 44, 46, 49

Macaulay 3
manor 44-46, 56, 58
Marian 114, 164
Mary 90, 115
Monarchy 21, 28, 47
monasteries 57
monasticism 22, 185
"Mother Plymouth" 249

native 348
naturalism 23, 35
nature 36
nobility 142, 157
non-Caucasians 262, 334
Nonconformist 133, 137, 139,
    153, 158, 159, 178, 247-252,
    283, 361

Occident 35, 180, 317
Occidental 15, 16, 38, 178
oligarchy 309, 310
other-worldliness 52

pagan 51, 276
paganism 16, 36, 122
Papacy 21, 36, 89, 99
Papists 377

patricians 31, 32, 45, 47, 50, 51,
142, 145, 275
philosophy 6, 15, 24, 26, 27, 33,
35, 36, 38
Pilgrims 191, 202, 248-250, 252,
259, 267, 270, 325, 353
Plato 26, 31
Plymouth 191, 248, 250-252, 355
Pope 20, 104
Presbyterian 43, 125, 127,
129-131, 141-143, 153, 154,
158-159, 178, 216, 233, 247,
266
pre-technology 7, 13
Primitive 36, 172, 209, 211, 242,
336, 337, 339, 349, 356, 359,
364, 386
progress 16
Protestantism 102, 105, 120, 128,
154, 253

Quaker 266

rationalism 6, 11, 23-25, 27,
33-38, 45
reason 6, 26, 29
Reform 98, 100, 107, 110, 114,
116, 122, 124, 125-127, 136,
218, 224, 234, 252, 254, 257,
259, 269, 273, 278, 279, 281,
283, 286, 302, 312-314, 357,
360, 362, 376, 384
Reformation 62, 78-80, 83, 84,
87, 91, 93, 94, 99, 103, 106,
109, 111, 113, 115, 117-119,
121, 123, 125, 131, 135,
137-139, 143, 156, 178, 179,
182, 185, 188, 245, 248, 252,
253, 272, 275, 313, 317, 371
Reformers 96, 97, 101, 104, 200,
219, 233, 246, 251, 277, 287,
319, 367, 372
Renaissance 15, 33, 36-38, 50,
77, 85, 86, 92, 120-125, 158
republic 28
Roman Catholic Church 17,
19-23, 33, 37, 38, 54, 58, 77,
81, 96-100, 113-118, 131, 145,
247, 249
Romanism 43, 125
Roman See 80
Rome 9, 12, 15, 20, 21, 27, 35,
57, 83, 85, 87, 91, 122, 248

savage 341
science 4, 7, 16, 33-39, 56,
59
Scientism 16
serfdom 45
Shakespeare 5, 45, 98
Sinai 272

technology 7, 13, 16
third estate 46, 54
Thomism 37, 38
tradition 22, 27, 28, 45, 68, 94,
96, 97, 116, 125, 141, 209,
318, 319
tribalism 10, 16
Tudor 54, 55, 67, 83, 88, 90, 91,
93, 99, 101, 114, 117, 119,
125, 128-131, 142, 147, 150,
156, 187, 188, 196, 197, 245,
248, 259

Universities 33, 114

Vatican 19, 21

West 15, 19
Williams 181, 251, 266, 268, 269,
  341, 342, 361
witchcraft 23
Winthrop 150, 151, 180-182, 192,
196, 202, 261, 271, 273, 307,
  355, 365, 369, 381
Wycliffe 43, 54, 55, 77, 78, 92,
  93, 106, 125, 128, 129, 131,
  132, 135, 136, 138, 181, 245,
  248, 250, 251, 259, 355, 361